NAOKI URASAWA'S

20th CENTURY BOYS

**Naoki Urasawa's
20th Century Boys
Volume 19**

VIZ Signature Edition

STORY AND ART BY NAOKI URASAWA

20 SEIKI SHONEN 19 by Naoki URASAWA/Studio Nuts
© 2005 Naoki URASAWA/Studio Nuts
With the cooperation of Takashi NAGASAKI
All rights reserved. Original Japanese
edition published in 2005 by Shogakukan Inc., Tokyo.

English Adaptation/Akemi Wegmüller
Touch-up Art & Lettering/Freeman Wong
Cover & Interior Design/Sam Elzway
Editor/Andy Nakatani

Printed in the U.S.A.

Published by VIZ Media, LLC
P.O. Box 77010
San Francisco, CA 94107

10 9 8 7 6 5 4 3 2 1
First printing, February 2011

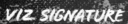

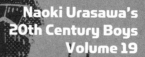

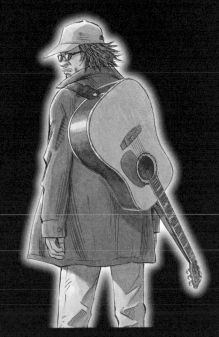

NAOKI URASAWA'S
20th CENTURY BOYS

VOL 19
THE MAN WHO CAME BACK

Story & Art by
NAOKI URASAWA

With the cooperation of
Takashi NAGASAKI

PROFILES

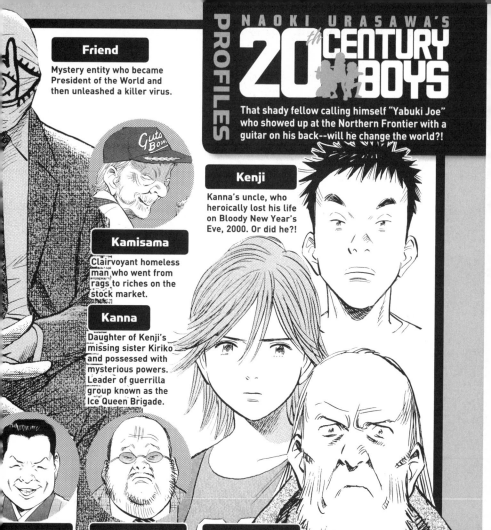

NAOKI URASAWA'S 20th CENTURY BOYS

That shady fellow calling himself "Yabuki Joe" who showed up at the Northern Frontier with a guitar on his back--will he change the world?!

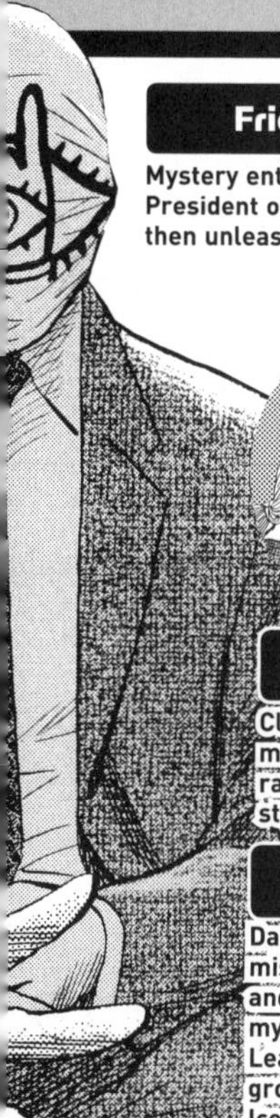

Friend

Mystery entity who became President of the World and then unleashed a killer virus.

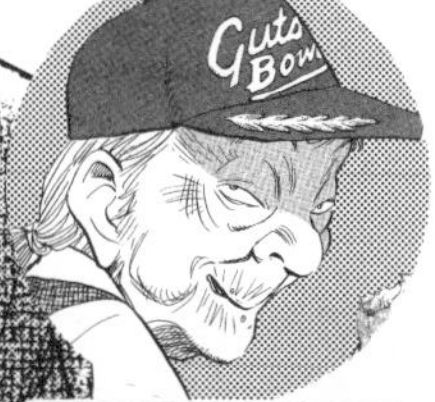

Kamisama

Clairvoyant homeless man who went from rags to riches on the stock market.

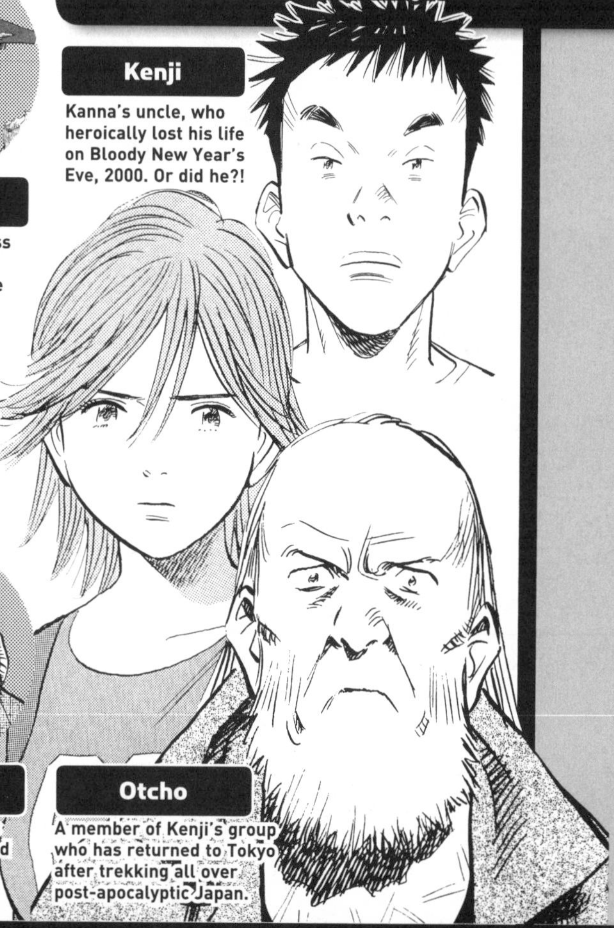

Kenji

Kanna's uncle, who heroically lost his life on Bloody New Year's Eve, 2000. Or did he?!

Kanna

Daughter of Kenji's missing sister Kiriko and possessed with mysterious powers. Leader of guerrilla group known as the Ice Queen Brigade.

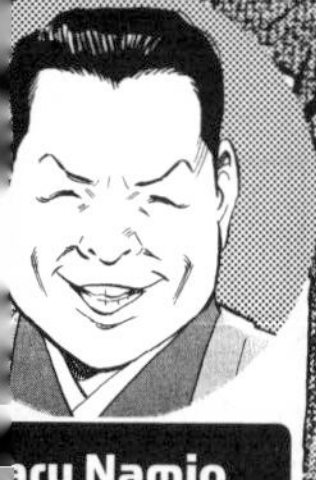

aru Namio

ally revered
who sang the
Hello Expo Song."
ning for Kenji.

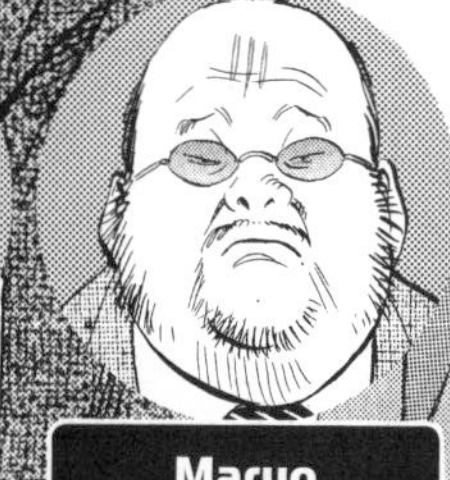

Maruo

A member of Kenji's group from childhood and Haru Namio's manager.

Otcho

A member of Kenji's group who has returned to Tokyo after trekking all over post-apocalyptic Japan.

ne Friend then became leader of the world, but is ssassinated in 2015 by Yamane, a member of the riends organization. But incredibly, the Friend omes back to life at the Expo opening ceremony, st in time to shield the Pope from an assassin's ullet. Deified by the world for this miracle, the riend then orders the dispersal of a killer virus round the world, resulting in the destruction of e world as we know it...

And now, three years later, the Friend has become President of the World, ruling over a Japan in terror. Meanwhile at the far northern frontier of the country, a man with a guitar shows up and gets through the border crossing while singing a song. He is headed for Tokyo, where freedom fighter Kanna hears a shocking story from the Friend's closest advisor, Manjome...!!

I CENTURY BOYS

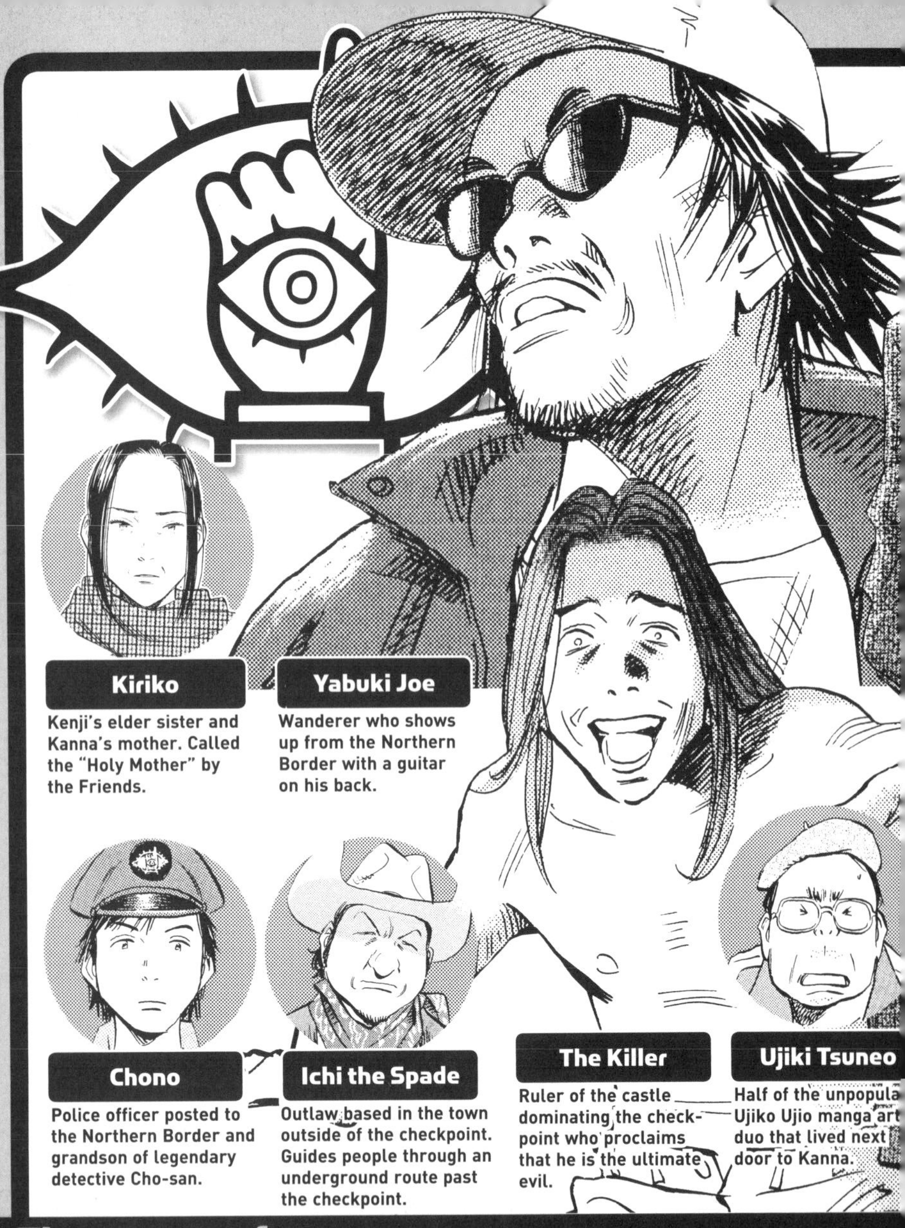

Kiriko

Kenji's elder sister and Kanna's mother. Called the "Holy Mother" by the Friends.

Yabuki Joe

Wanderer who shows up from the Northern Border with a guitar on his back.

Chono

Police officer posted to the Northern Border and grandson of legendary detective Cho-san.

Ichi the Spade

Outlaw based in the town outside of the checkpoint. Guides people through an underground route past the checkpoint.

The Killer

Ruler of the castle dominating the checkpoint who proclaims that he is the ultimate evil.

Ujiki Tsuneo

Half of the unpopula Ujiko Ujio manga art duo that lived next door to Kanna.

The story so far...

In the early 1970s, Kenji and his friends were elementary schoolers who dreamed of the exciting future that awaited them in the 21st century. In their secret headquarters, out in an empty lot, they made up a ridiculous scenario about a League of Evil, whose plan to destroy the world would be thwarted by a group of heroes. They wrote this story in *The Book of Prophecy*.

Later in 1997, the adult Kenji is raising his missin sister's baby Kanna and is shocked when he realizes that a series of ominous incidents is following *The Book of Prophecy*, and that a charismatic leade known only as the Friend seems to be behind it all. On the last night of the 20th century, later known as "Bloody New Year's Eve," the Friend acts the par of the hero who saved the world and Kenji, who los his life trying to stop him, was branded a terrorist.

A SUMMARY OF 2

CONTENTS
VOL 19
THE MAN WHO CAME BACK

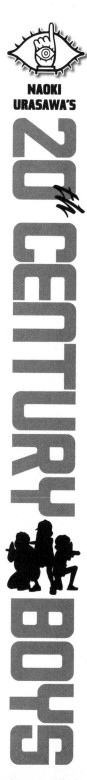

NAOKI URASAWA'S

20 CENTURY BOYS

Chapter 1 Final Prey

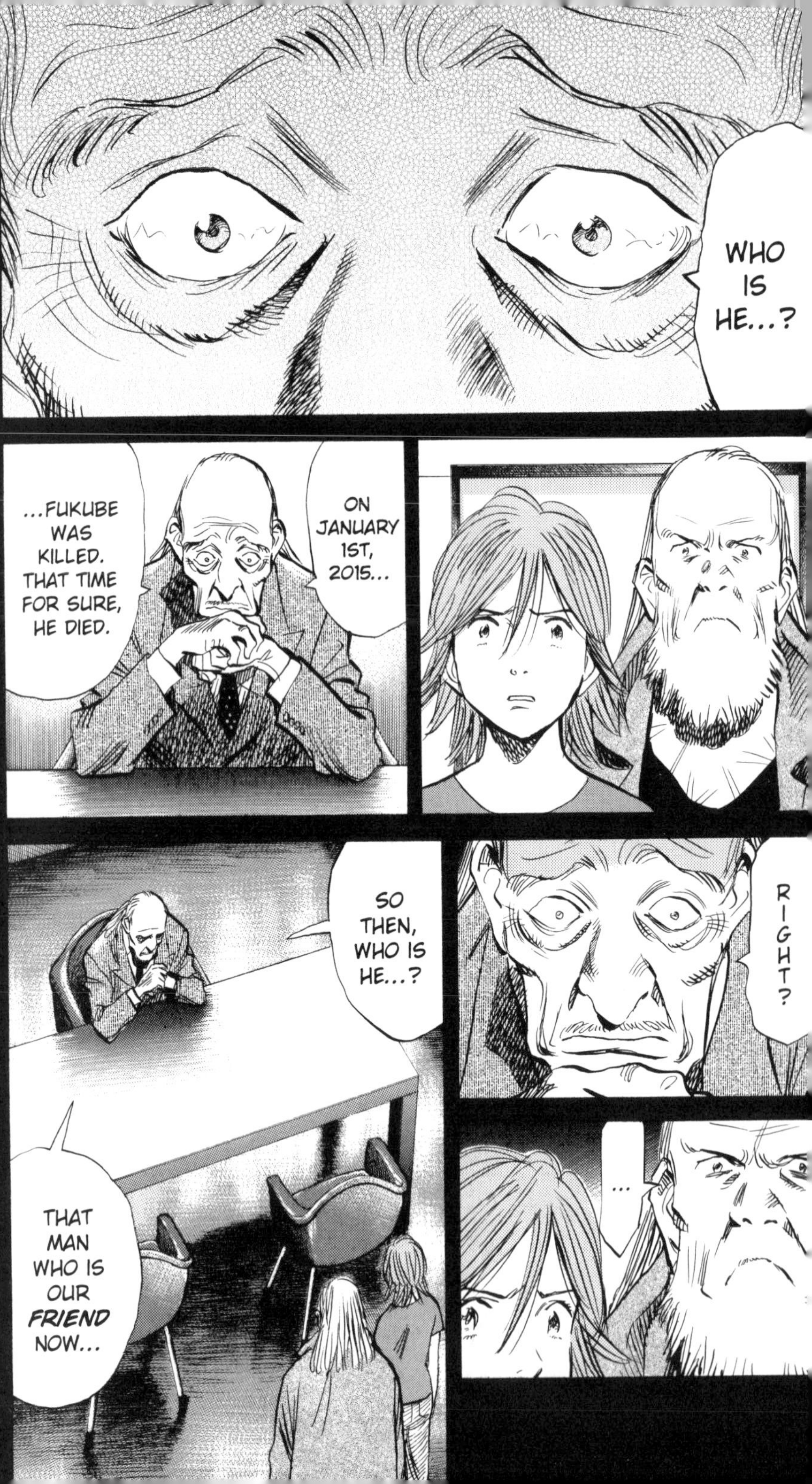
WHO IS HE...?
ON JANUARY 1ST, 2015...
...FUKUBE WAS KILLED. THAT TIME FOR SURE, HE DIED.
RIGHT?
...
SO THEN, WHO IS HE...?
THAT MAN WHO IS OUR *FRIEND* NOW...

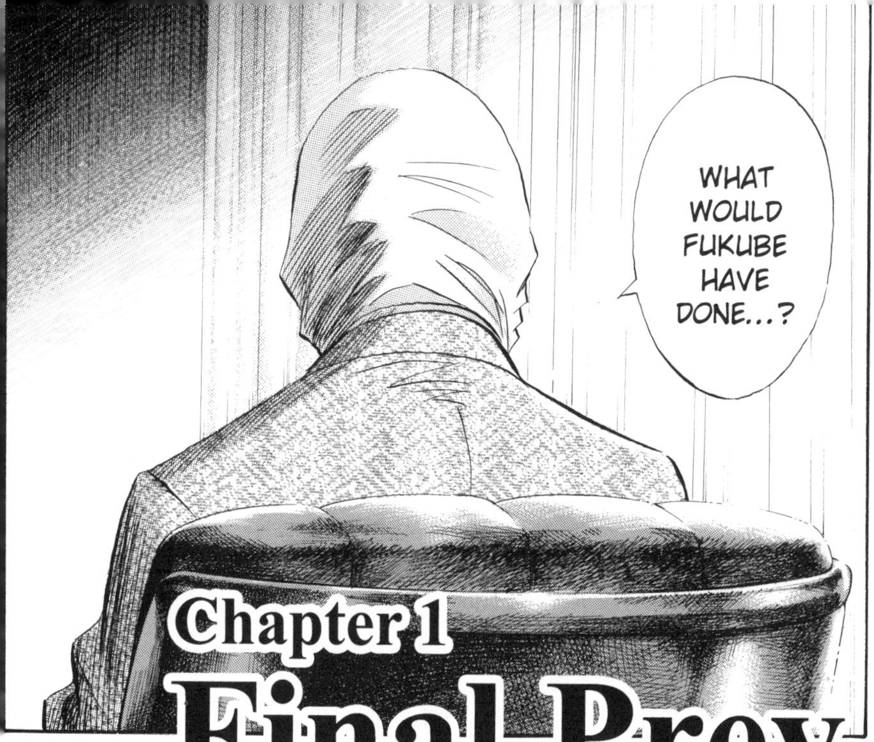
WHAT WOULD FUKUBE HAVE DONE...?

Chapter 1
Final Prey

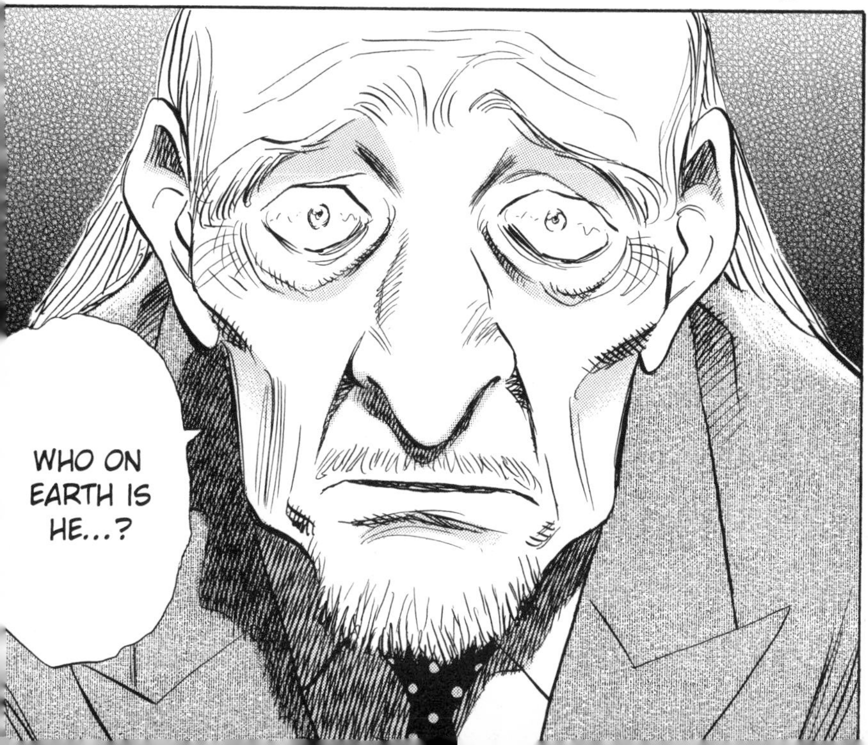
WHO ON EARTH IS HE...?

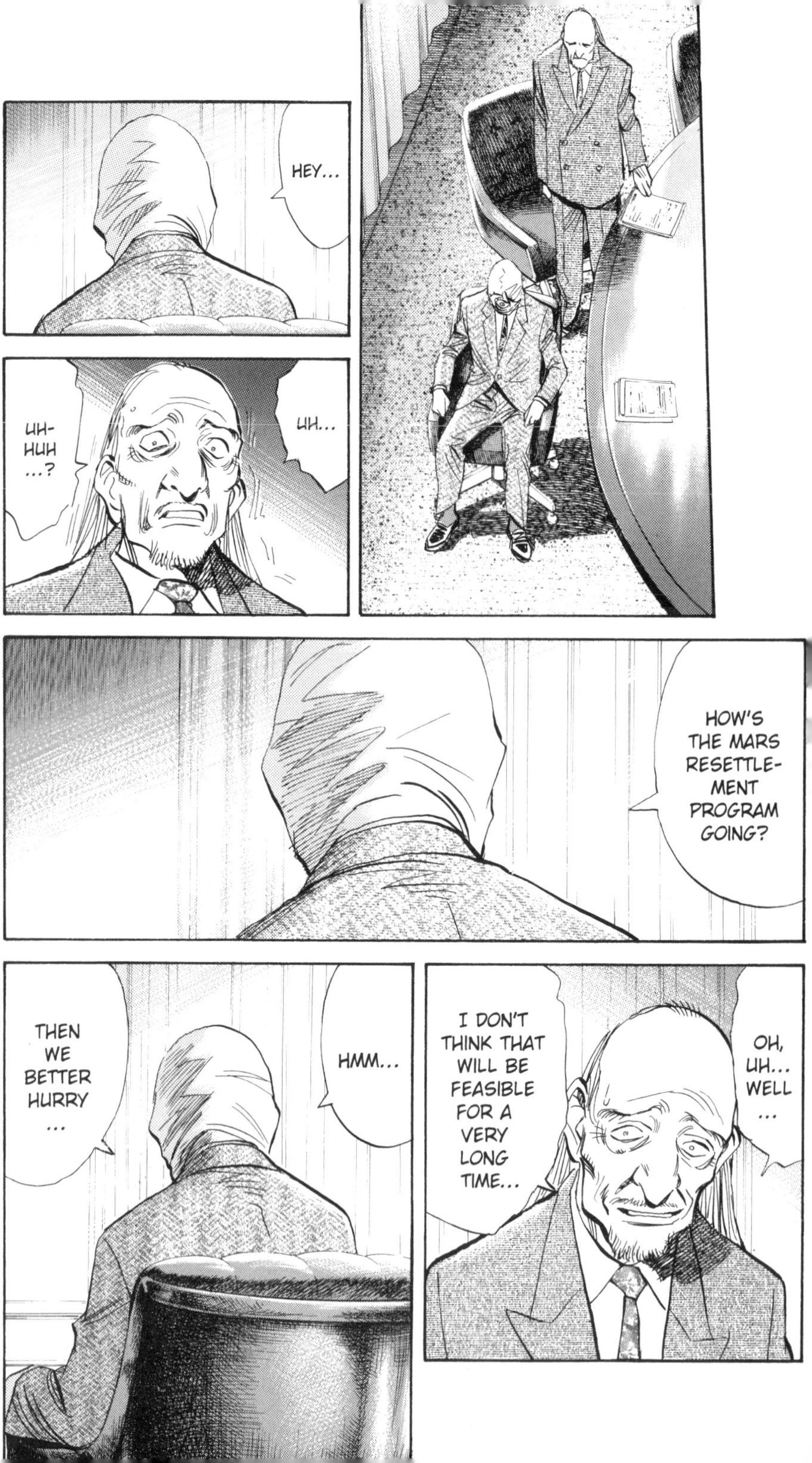
HEY...
UH...
UH-HUH...?
HOW'S THE MARS RESETTLEMENT PROGRAM GOING?
OH, UH... WELL...
I DON'T THINK THAT WILL BE FEASIBLE FOR A VERY LONG TIME...
HMM...
THEN WE BETTER HURRY...

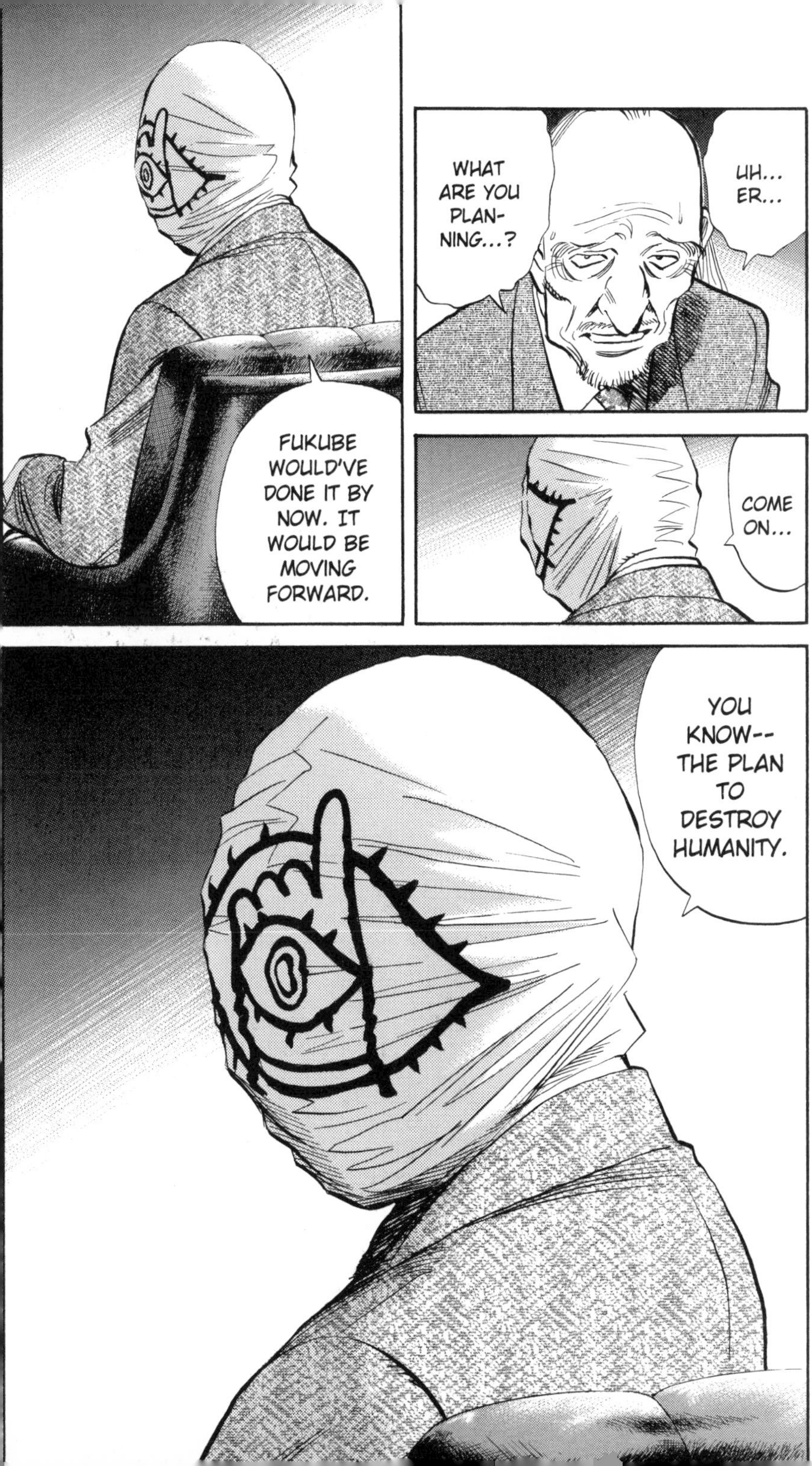
UH... ER...
WHAT ARE YOU PLAN-NING...?
COME ON...
FUKUBE WOULD'VE DONE IT BY NOW. IT WOULD BE MOVING FORWARD.
YOU KNOW-- THE PLAN TO DESTROY HUMANITY.

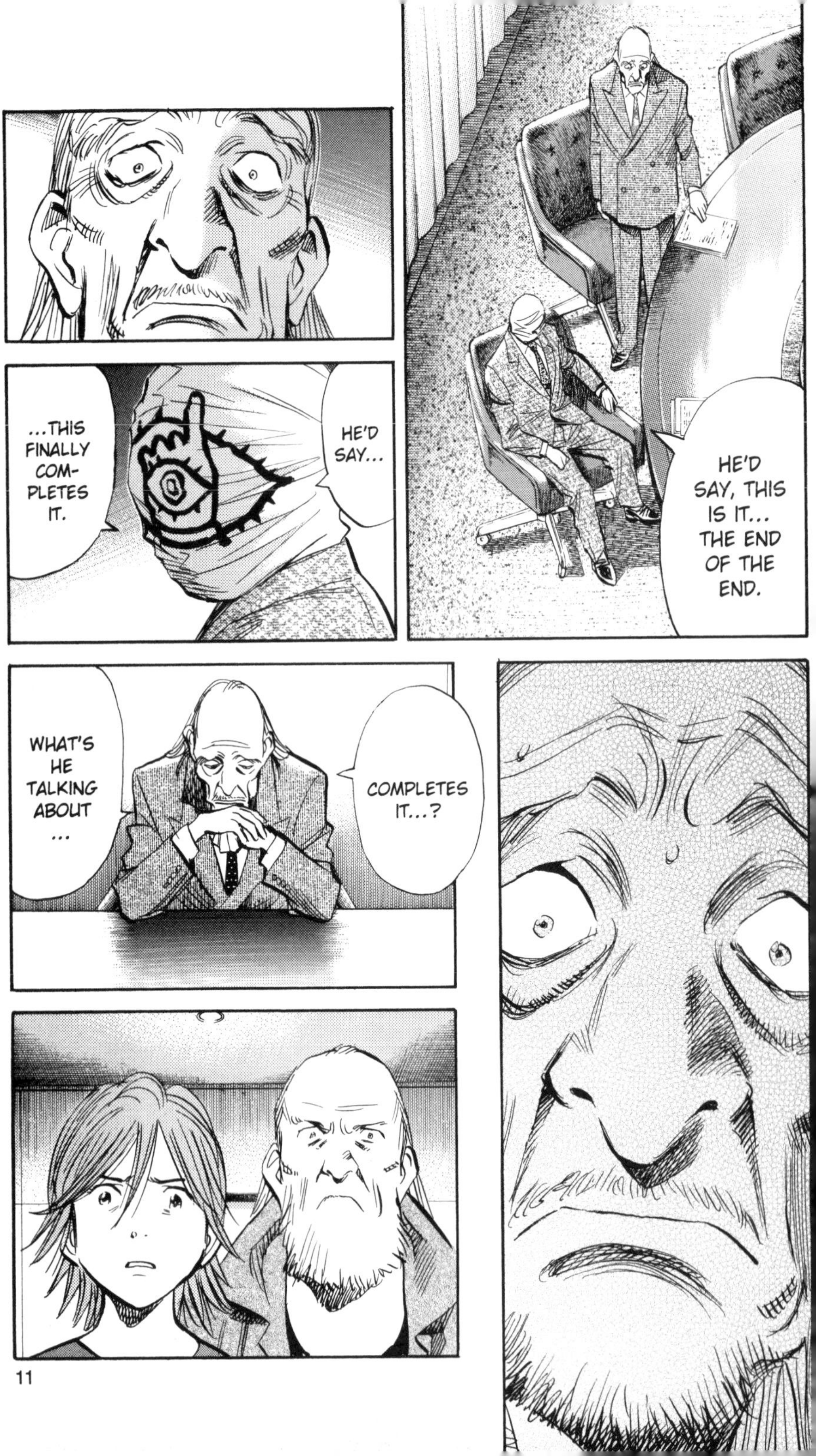
HE'D SAY, THIS IS IT... THE END OF THE END.
HE'D SAY...
...THIS FINALLY COM-PLETES IT.
COMPLETES IT...?
WHAT'S HE TALKING ABOUT ...

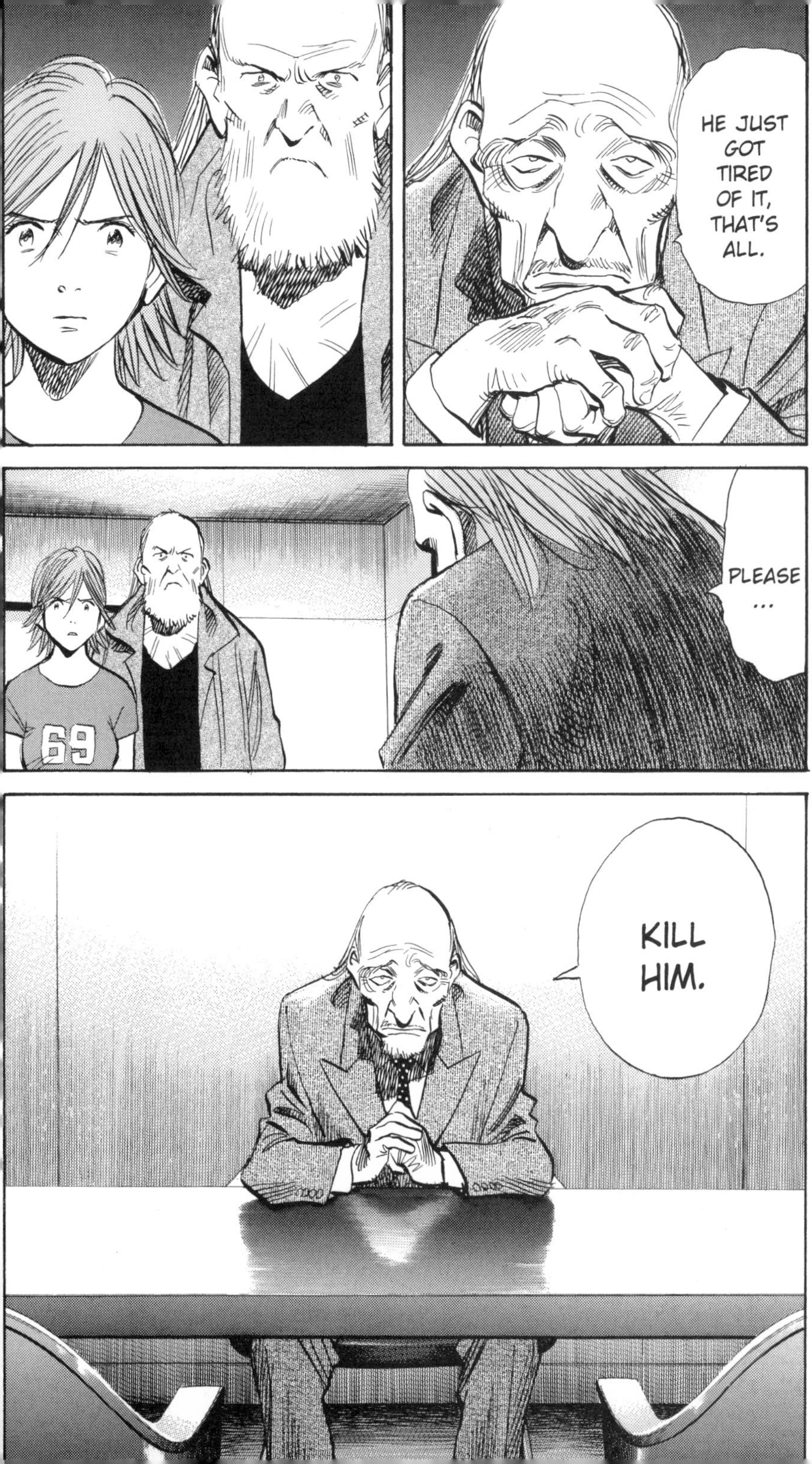
HE JUST GOT TIRED OF IT, THAT'S ALL.
PLEASE ...
69
KILL HIM.

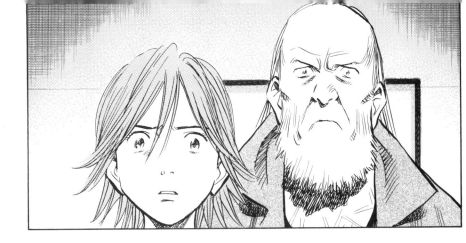

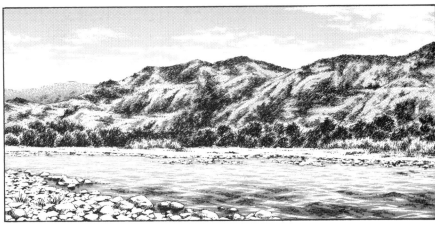

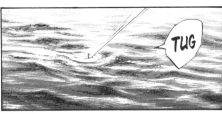

TUG

HEY! HEY...

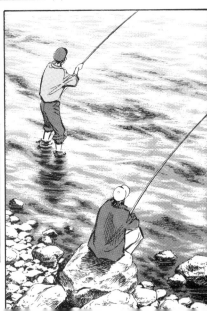

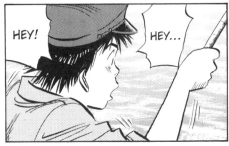

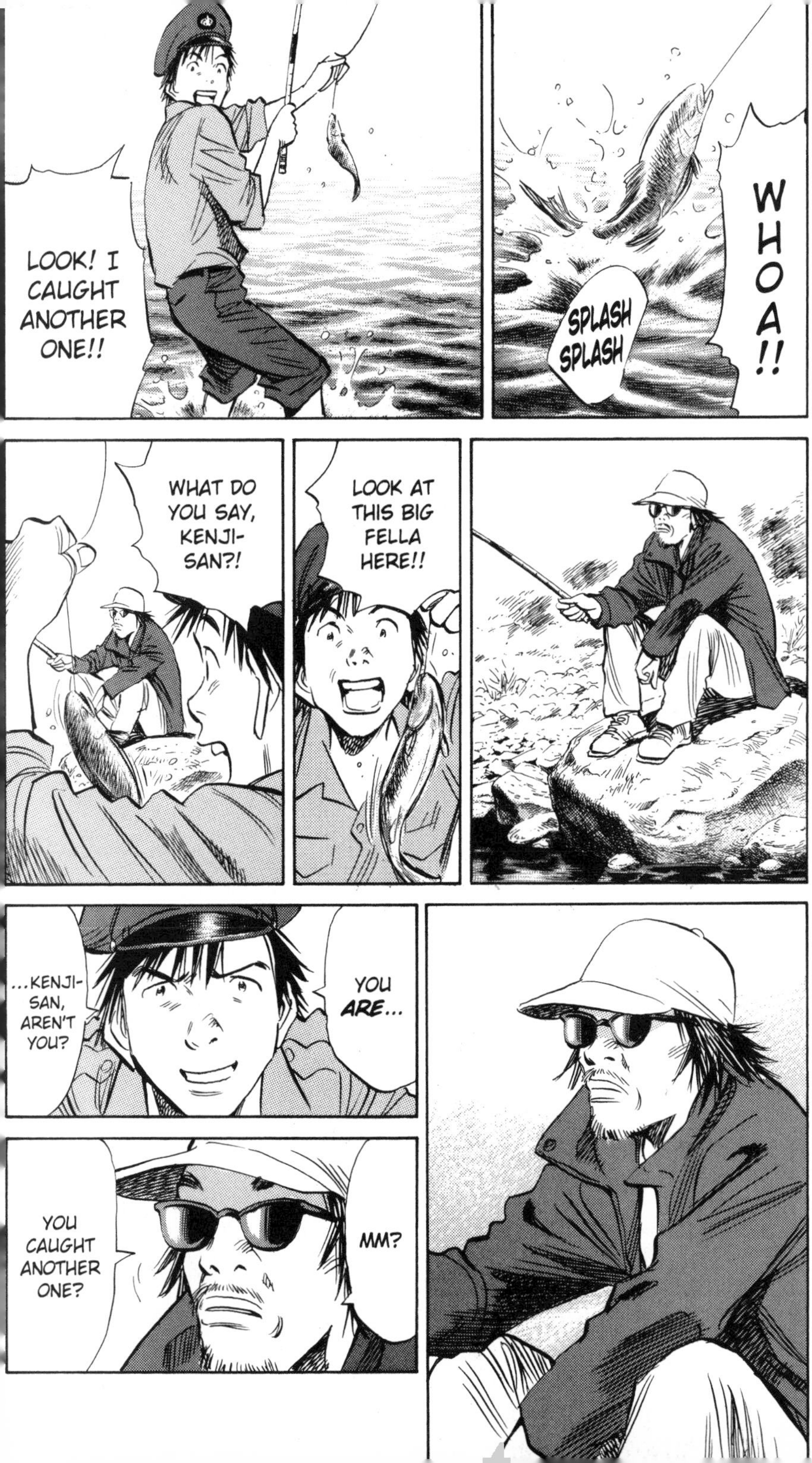
WHOA!!
SPLASH SPLASH
LOOK! I CAUGHT ANOTHER ONE!!
LOOK AT THIS BIG FELLA HERE!!
WHAT DO YOU SAY, KENJI-SAN?!
YOU ARE...
...KENJI-SAN, AREN'T YOU?
MM?
YOU CAUGHT ANOTHER ONE?

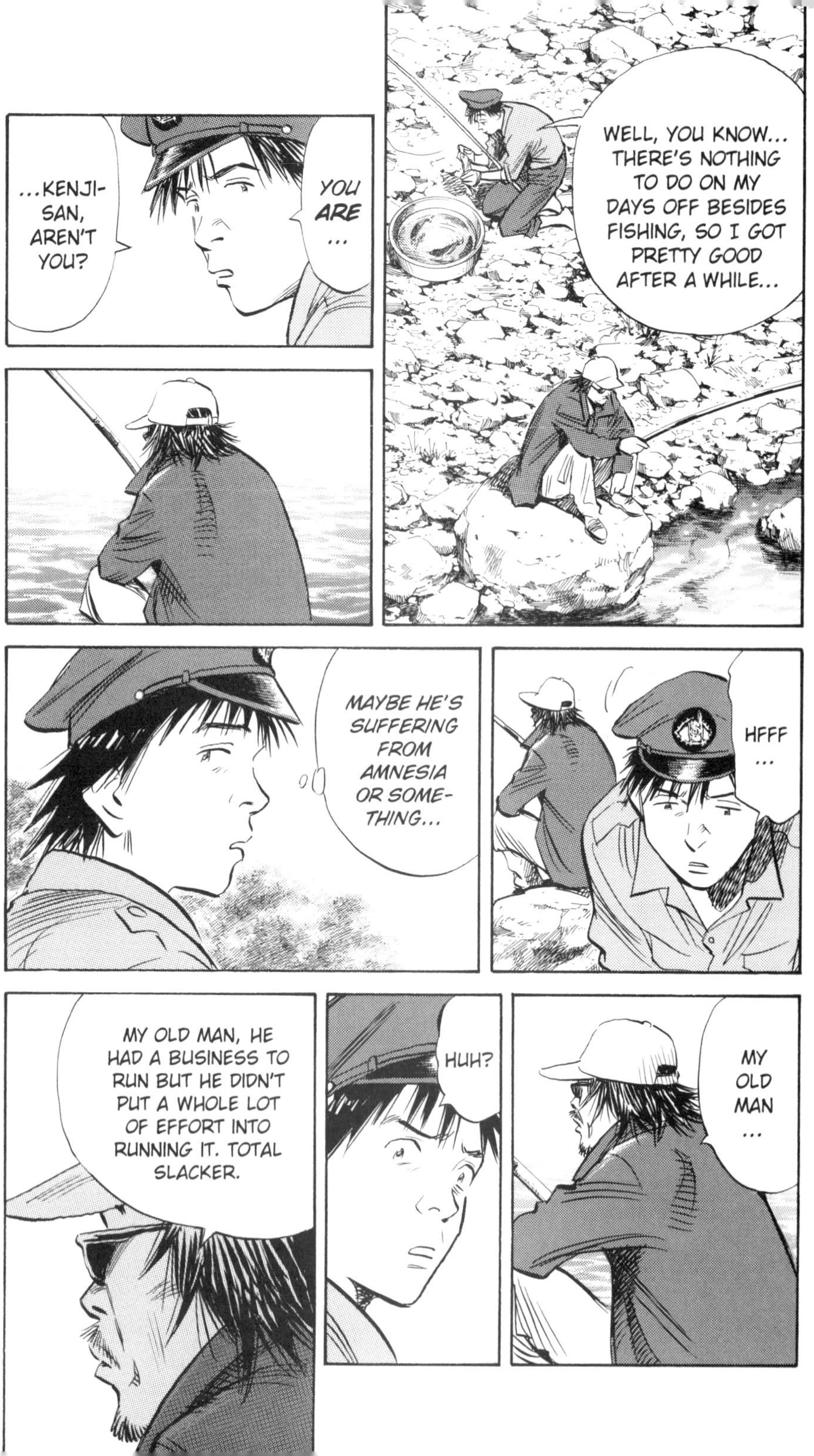
WELL, YOU KNOW... THERE'S NOTHING TO DO ON MY DAYS OFF BESIDES FISHING, SO I GOT PRETTY GOOD AFTER A WHILE...
YOU *ARE* ...
...KENJI-SAN, AREN'T YOU?
HFFF ...
MAYBE HE'S SUFFERING FROM AMNESIA OR SOME-THING...
MY OLD MAN ...
HUH?
MY OLD MAN, HE HAD A BUSINESS TO RUN BUT HE DIDN'T PUT A WHOLE LOT OF EFFORT INTO RUNNING IT. TOTAL SLACKER.

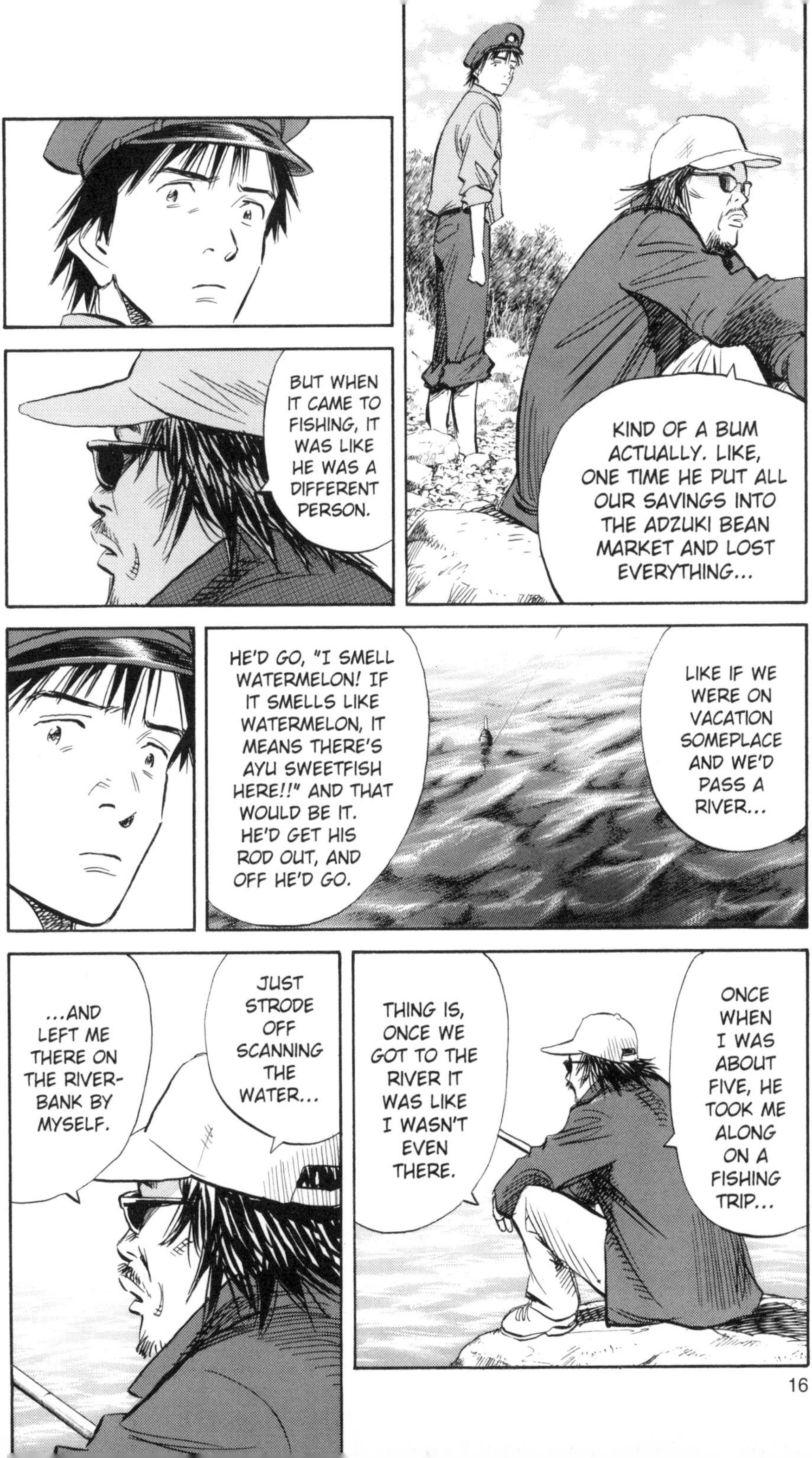
KIND OF A BUM ACTUALLY. LIKE, ONE TIME HE PUT ALL OUR SAVINGS INTO THE ADZUKI BEAN MARKET AND LOST EVERYTHING...
BUT WHEN IT CAME TO FISHING, IT WAS LIKE HE WAS A DIFFERENT PERSON.
LIKE IF WE WERE ON VACATION SOMEPLACE AND WE'D PASS A RIVER...
HE'D GO, "I SMELL WATERMELON! IF IT SMELLS LIKE WATERMELON, IT MEANS THERE'S AYU SWEETFISH HERE!!" AND THAT WOULD BE IT. HE'D GET HIS ROD OUT, AND OFF HE'D GO.
ONCE WHEN I WAS ABOUT FIVE, HE TOOK ME ALONG ON A FISHING TRIP...
THING IS, ONCE WE GOT TO THE RIVER IT WAS LIKE I WASN'T EVEN THERE.
JUST STRODE OFF SCANNING THE WATER...
...AND LEFT ME THERE ON THE RIVER-BANK BY MYSELF.

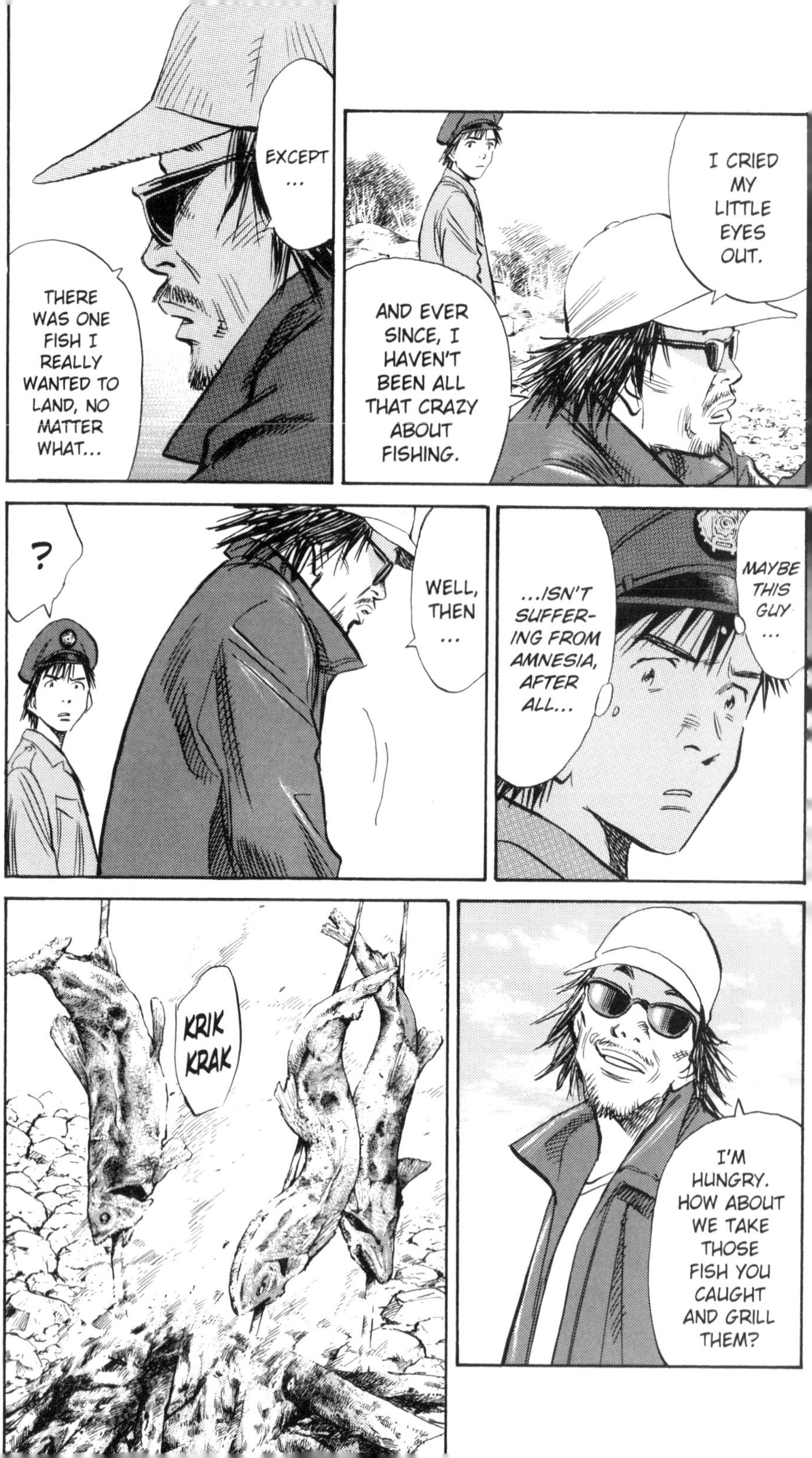
I CRIED MY LITTLE EYES OUT.
AND EVER SINCE, I HAVEN'T BEEN ALL THAT CRAZY ABOUT FISHING.
EXCEPT...
THERE WAS ONE FISH I REALLY WANTED TO LAND, NO MATTER WHAT...
MAYBE THIS GUY...
...ISN'T SUFFERING FROM AMNESIA, AFTER ALL...
WELL, THEN...
?
I'M HUNGRY. HOW ABOUT WE TAKE THOSE FISH YOU CAUGHT AND GRILL THEM?
KRIK KRAK

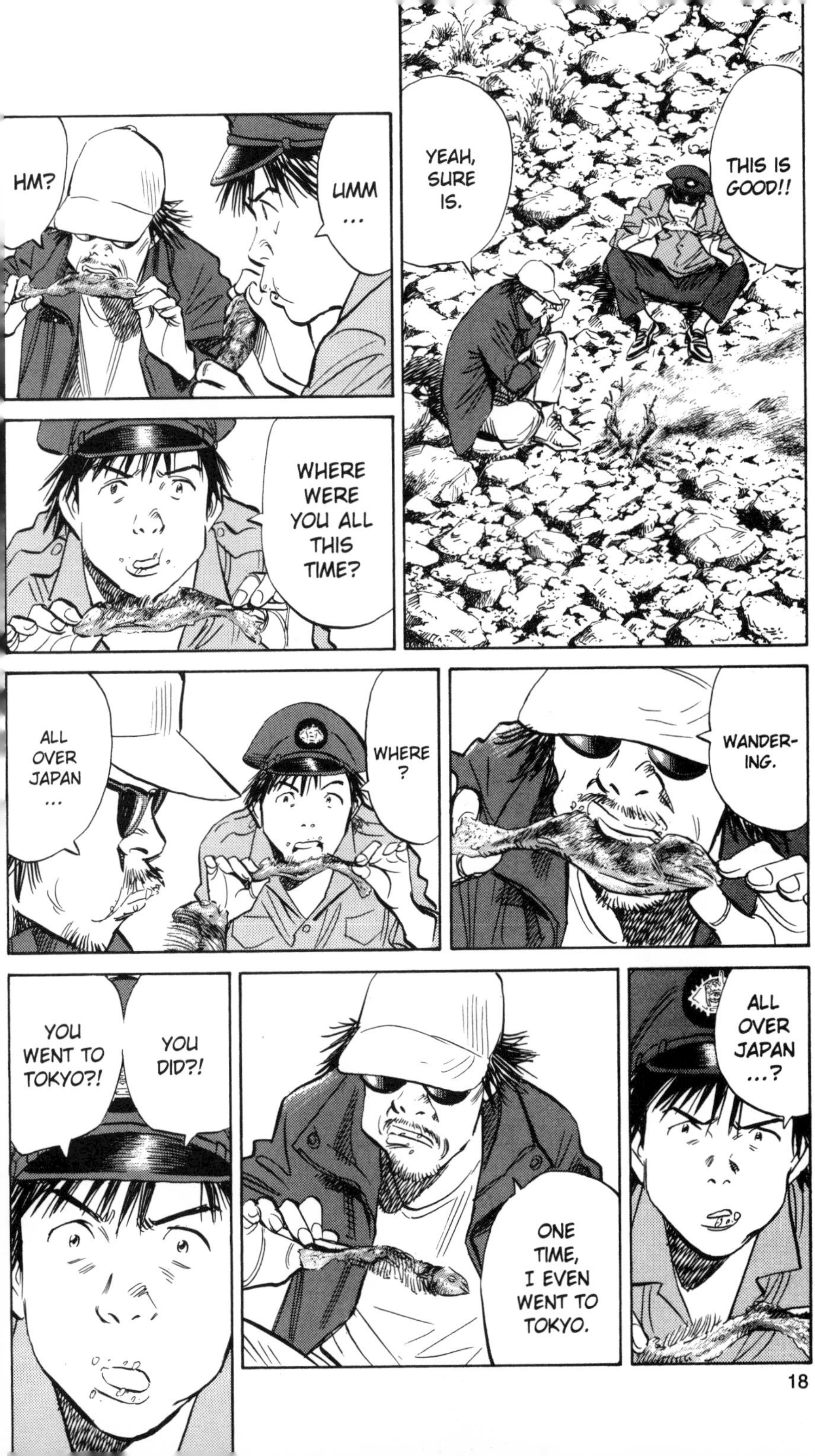
THIS IS GOOD!!
YEAH, SURE IS.
UMM ...
HM?
WHERE WERE YOU ALL THIS TIME?
WANDERING.
WHERE?
ALL OVER JAPAN ...
ALL OVER JAPAN ...?
ONE TIME, I EVEN WENT TO TOKYO.
YOU DID?!
YOU WENT TO TOKYO?!

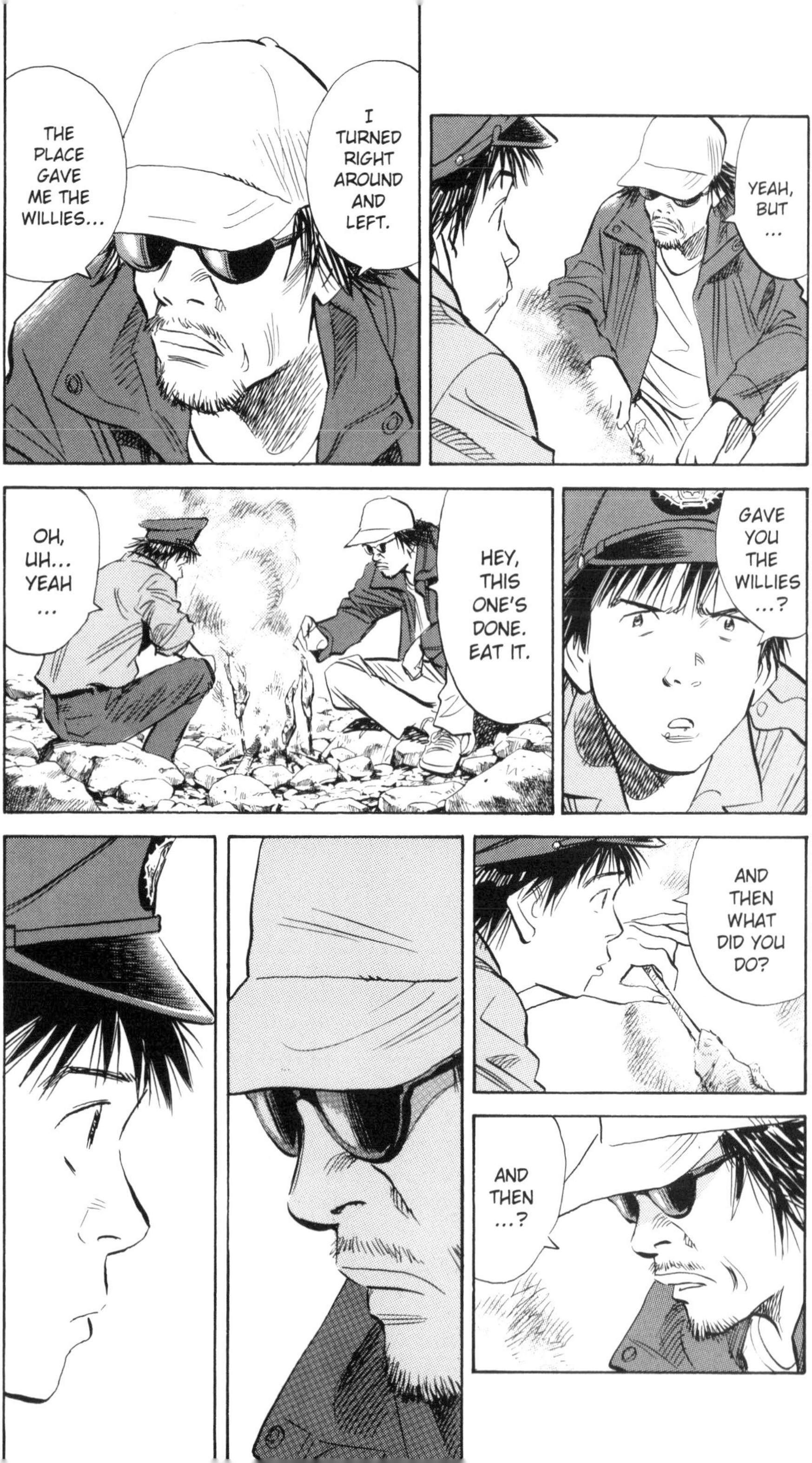
YEAH, BUT ...
I TURNED RIGHT AROUND AND LEFT.
THE PLACE GAVE ME THE WILLIES...
GAVE YOU THE WILLIES ...?
HEY, THIS ONE'S DONE. EAT IT.
OH, UH... YEAH ...
AND THEN WHAT DID YOU DO?
AND THEN ...?

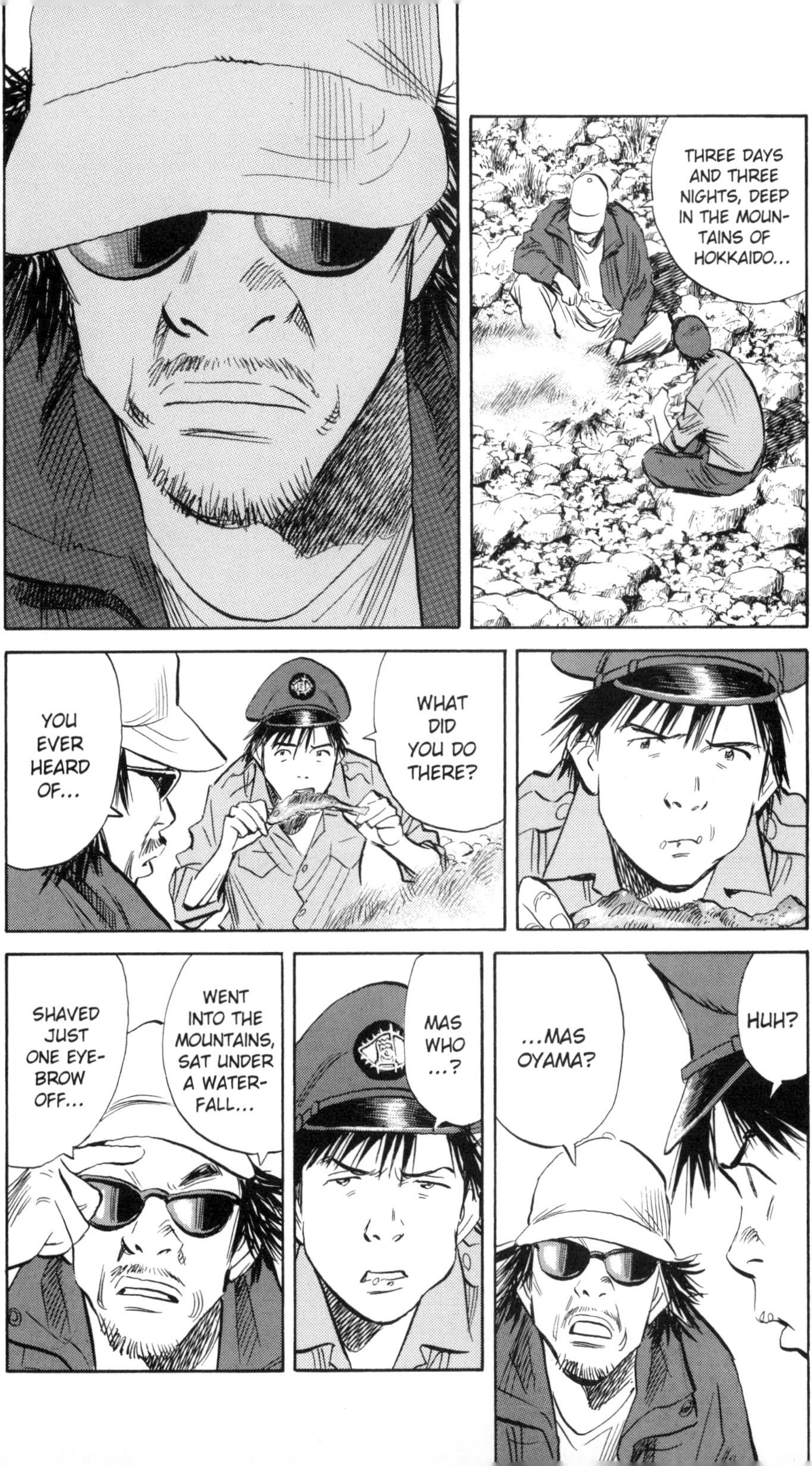
THREE DAYS AND THREE NIGHTS, DEEP IN THE MOUN-TAINS OF HOKKAIDO...
WHAT DID YOU DO THERE?
YOU EVER HEARD OF...
HUH?
...MAS OYAMA?
MAS WHO ...?
WENT INTO THE MOUNTAINS, SAT UNDER A WATER-FALL...
SHAVED JUST ONE EYE-BROW OFF...

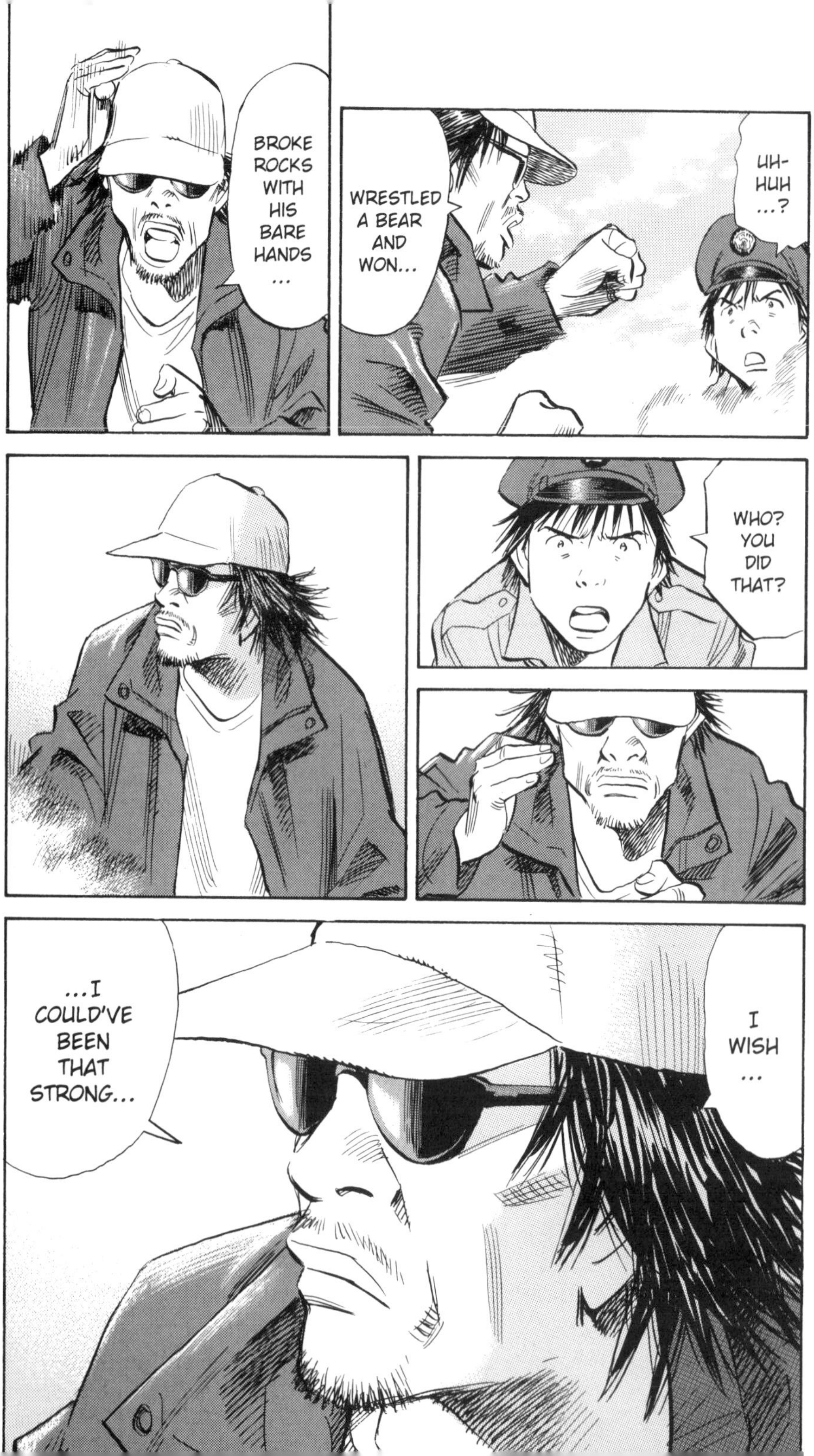
UH-HUH ...?
WRESTLED A BEAR AND WON...
BROKE ROCKS WITH HIS BARE HANDS ...
WHO? YOU DID THAT?
I WISH ...
...I COULD'VE BEEN THAT STRONG...

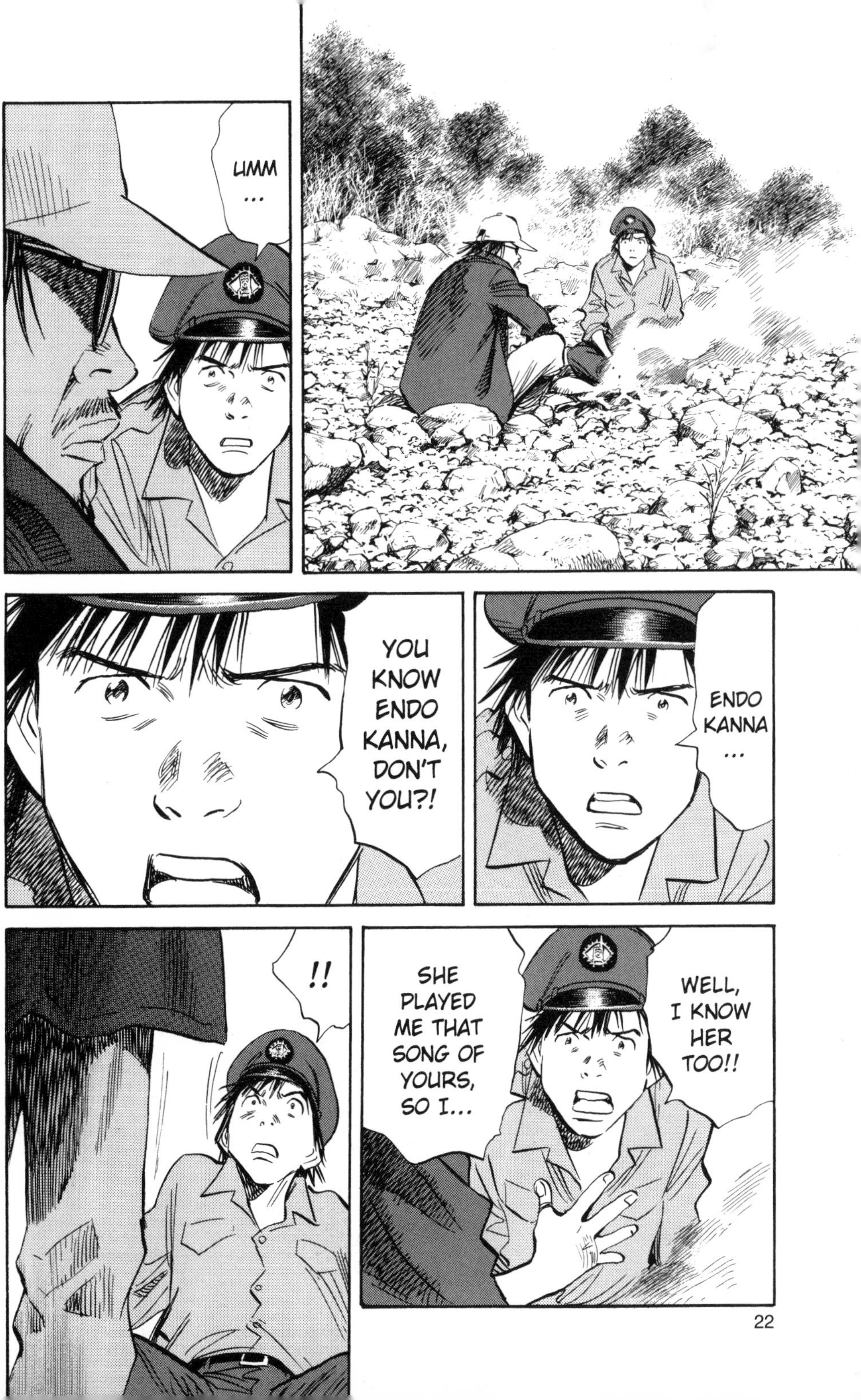
UMM ...
ENDO KANNA ...
YOU KNOW ENDO KANNA, DON'T YOU?!
WELL, I KNOW HER TOO!!
SHE PLAYED ME THAT SONG OF YOURS, SO I...
!!

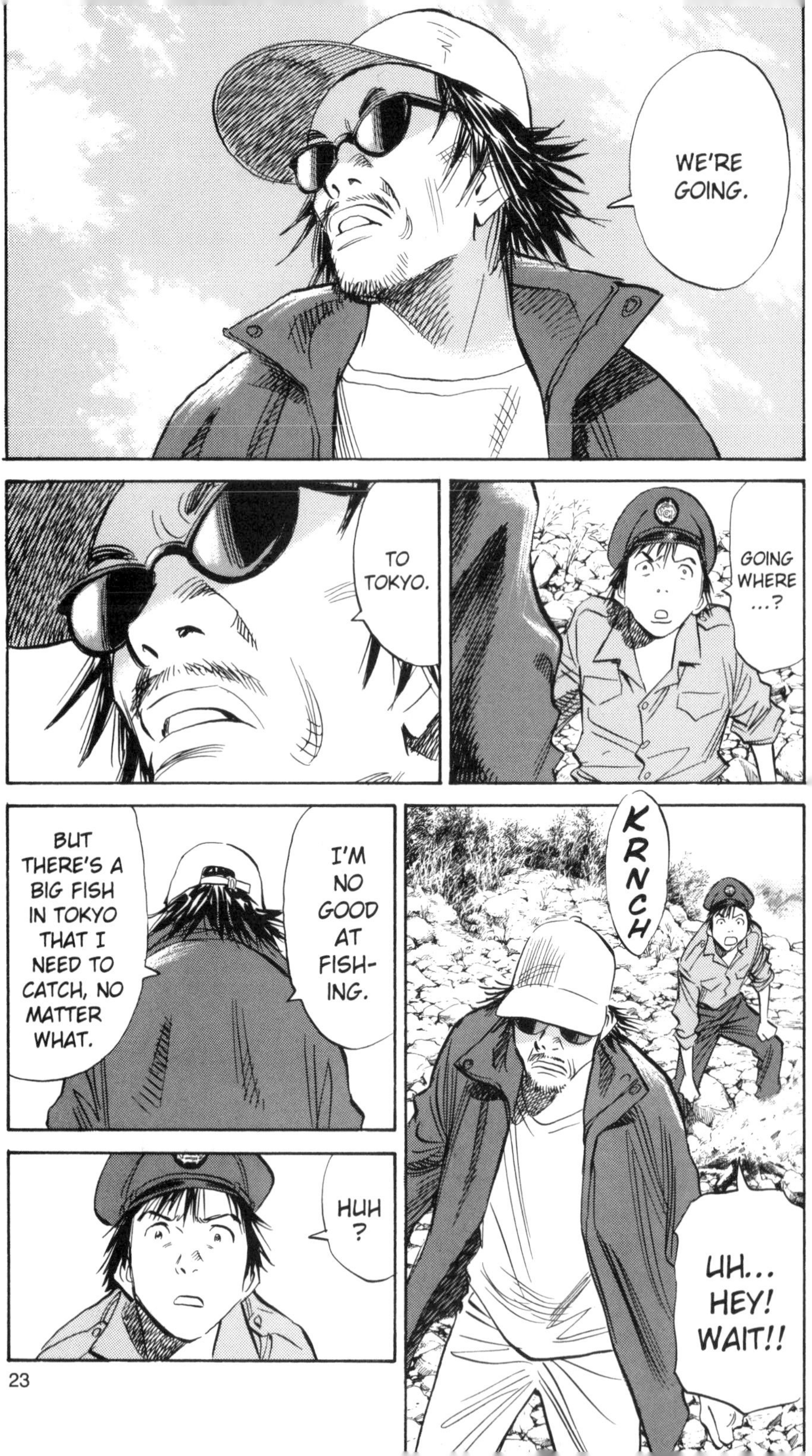
WE'RE GOING.
GOING WHERE ...?
TO TOKYO.
KRNCH
UH... HEY! WAIT!!
I'M NO GOOD AT FISH-ING.
BUT THERE'S A BIG FISH IN TOKYO THAT I NEED TO CATCH, NO MATTER WHAT.
HUH ?

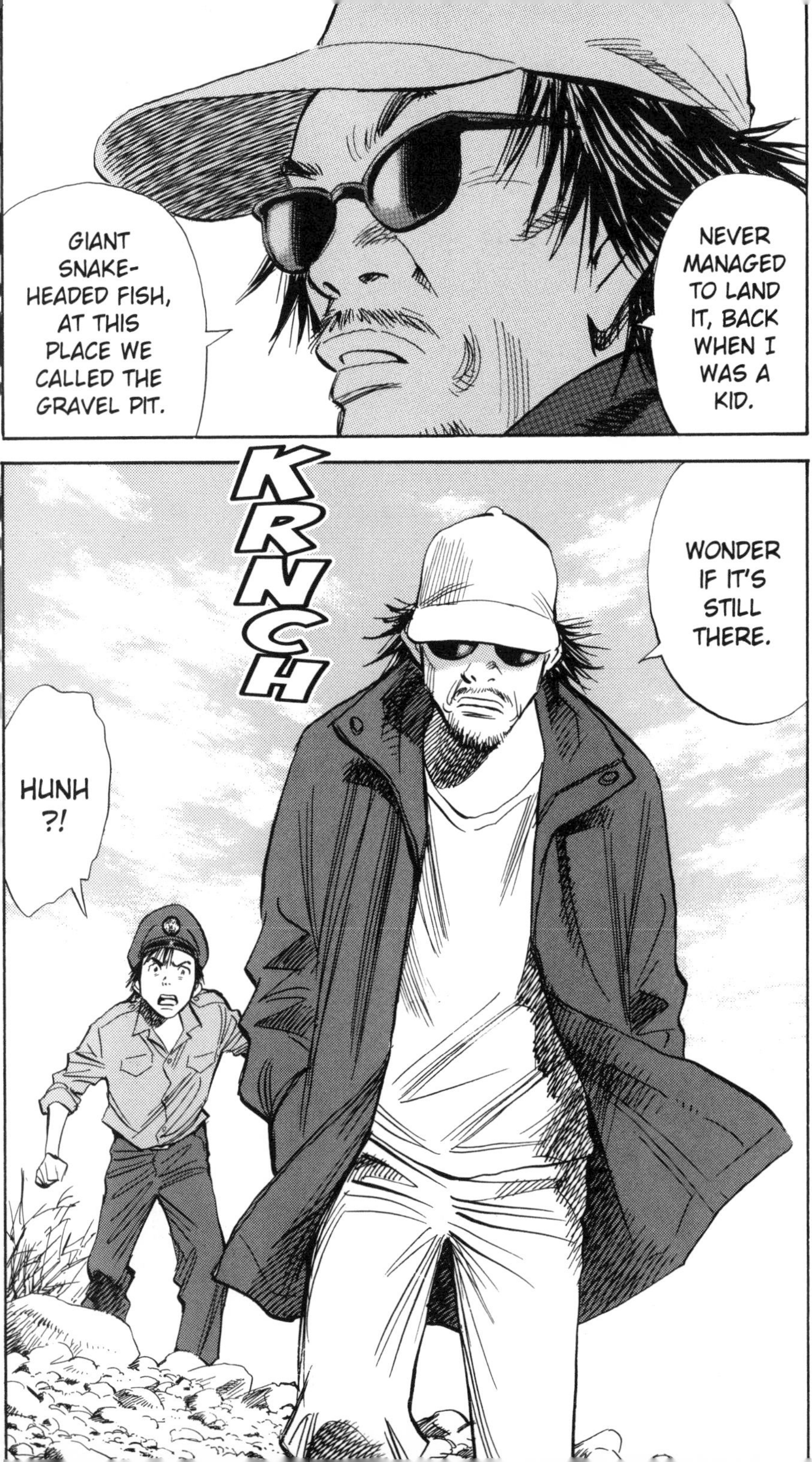
NEVER MANAGED TO LAND IT, BACK WHEN I WAS A KID.
GIANT SNAKE-HEADED FISH, AT THIS PLACE WE CALLED THE GRAVEL PIT.
WONDER IF IT'S STILL THERE.
KRNCH
HUNH ?!

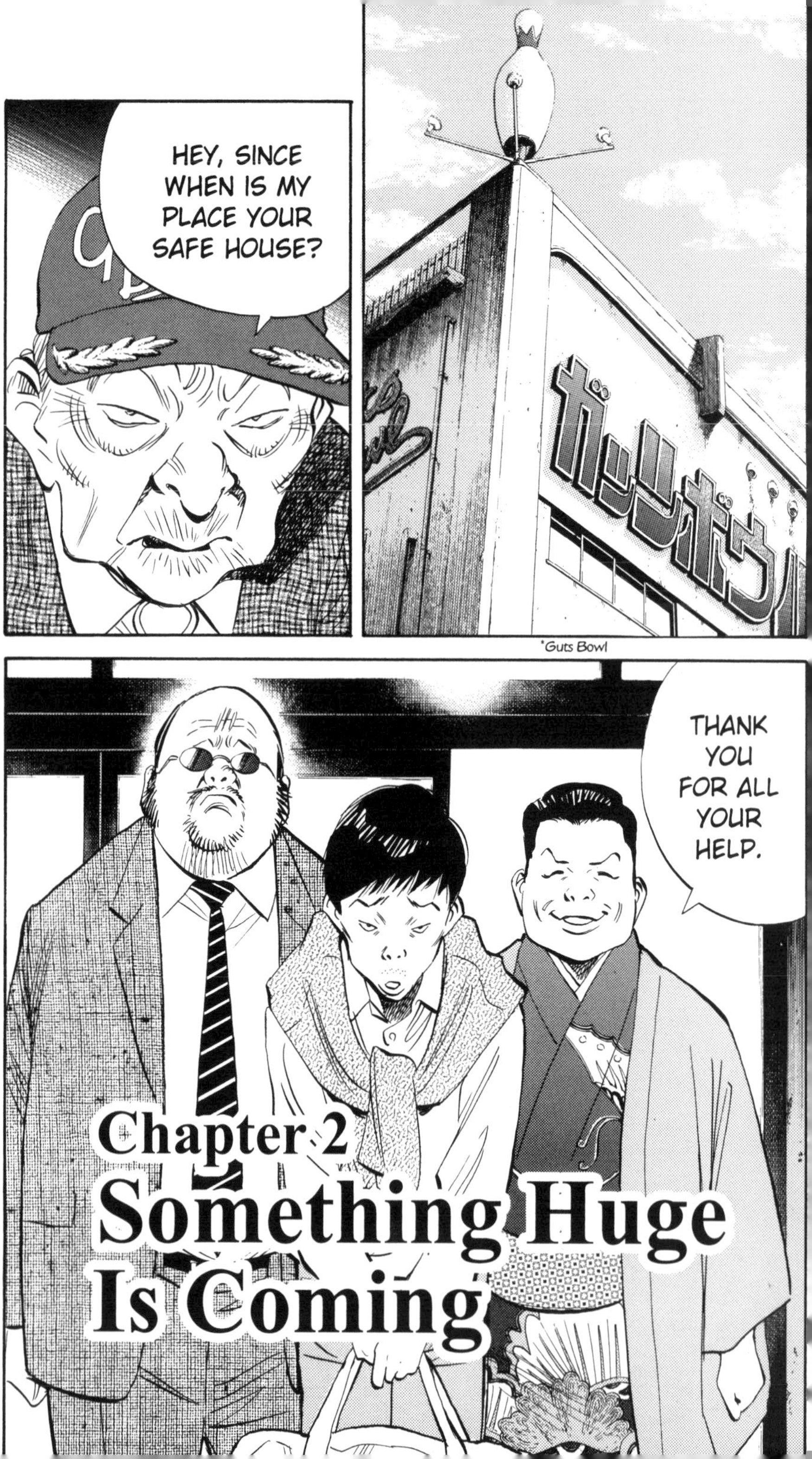
*Guts Bowl
HEY, SINCE WHEN IS MY PLACE YOUR SAFE HOUSE?
THANK YOU FOR ALL YOUR HELP.
Chapter 2
Something Huge Is Coming

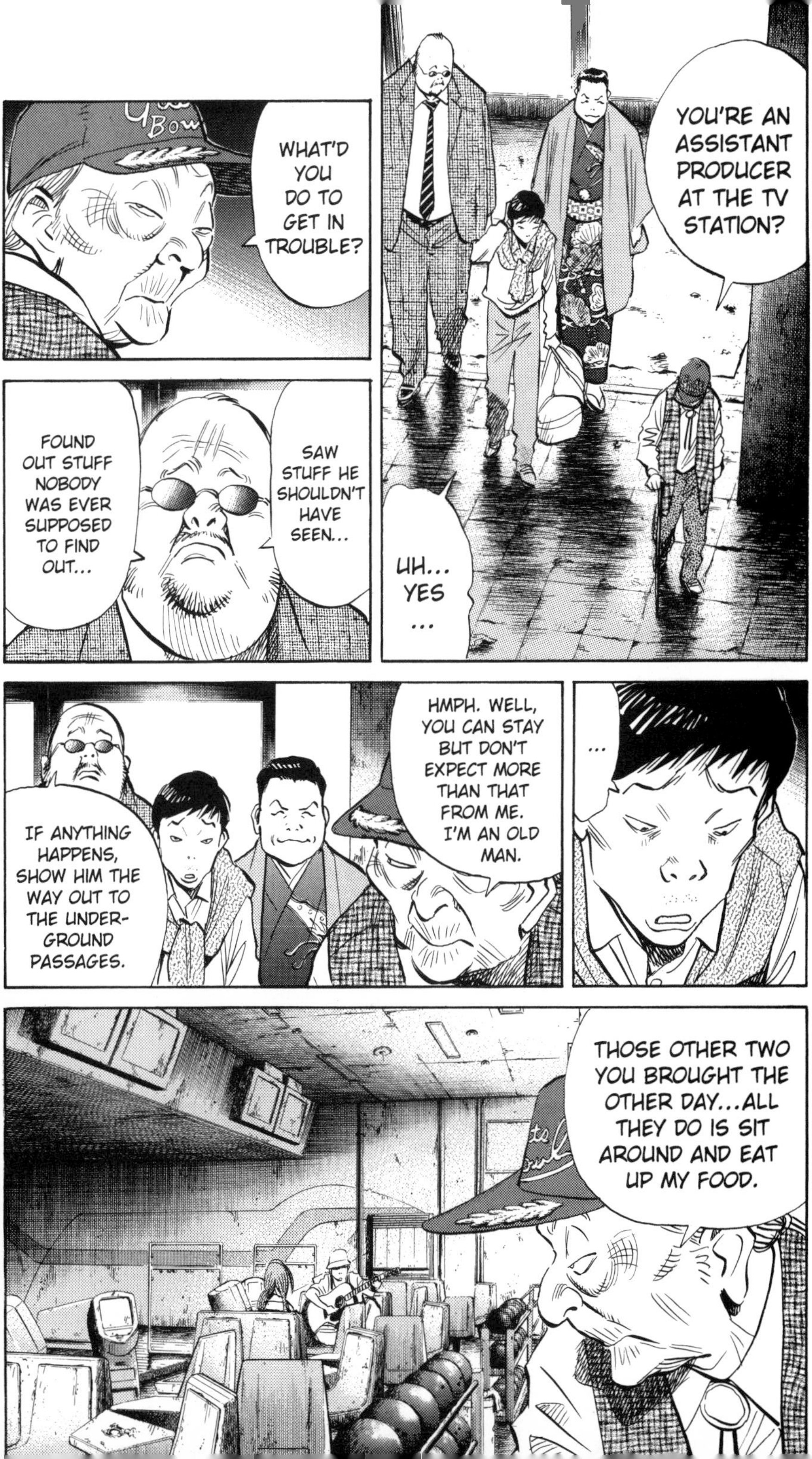
YOU'RE AN ASSISTANT PRODUCER AT THE TV STATION?
UH... YES ...
WHAT'D YOU DO TO GET IN TROUBLE?
SAW STUFF HE SHOULDN'T HAVE SEEN...
FOUND OUT STUFF NOBODY WAS EVER SUPPOSED TO FIND OUT...
...
HMPH. WELL, YOU CAN STAY BUT DON'T EXPECT MORE THAN THAT FROM ME. I'M AN OLD MAN.
IF ANYTHING HAPPENS, SHOW HIM THE WAY OUT TO THE UNDER-GROUND PASSAGES.
THOSE OTHER TWO YOU BROUGHT THE OTHER DAY...ALL THEY DO IS SIT AROUND AND EAT UP MY FOOD.

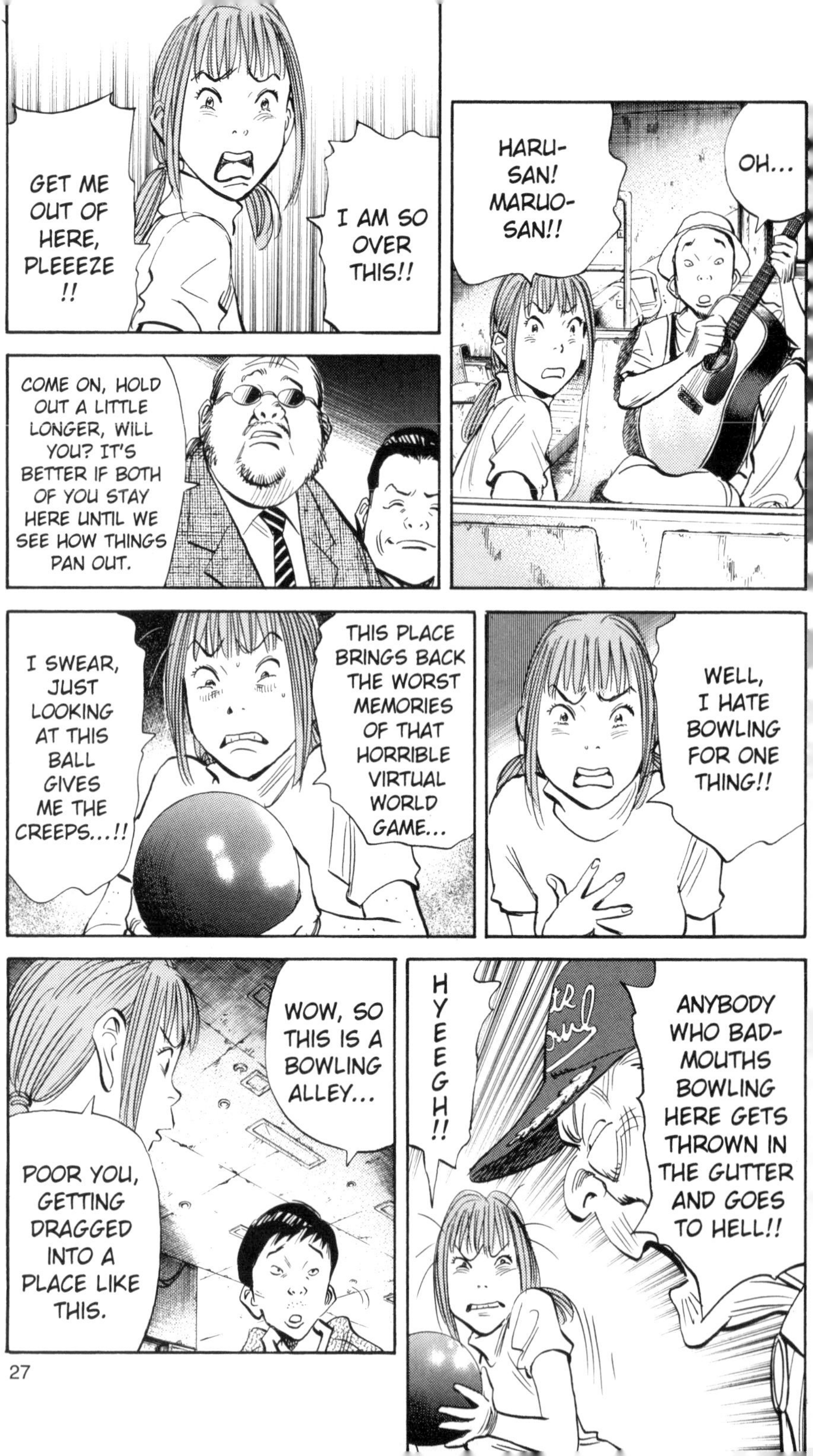
HARU-SAN! MARUO-SAN!!
OH...
GET ME OUT OF HERE, PLEEEZE!!
I AM SO OVER THIS!!
COME ON, HOLD OUT A LITTLE LONGER, WILL YOU? IT'S BETTER IF BOTH OF YOU STAY HERE UNTIL WE SEE HOW THINGS PAN OUT.
WELL, I HATE BOWLING FOR ONE THING!!
THIS PLACE BRINGS BACK THE WORST MEMORIES OF THAT HORRIBLE VIRTUAL WORLD GAME...
I SWEAR, JUST LOOKING AT THIS BALL GIVES ME THE CREEPS...!!
ANYBODY WHO BAD-MOUTHS BOWLING HERE GETS THROWN IN THE GUTTER AND GOES TO HELL!!
HYEEGH!!
WOW, SO THIS IS A BOWLING ALLEY...
POOR YOU, GETTING DRAGGED INTO A PLACE LIKE THIS.

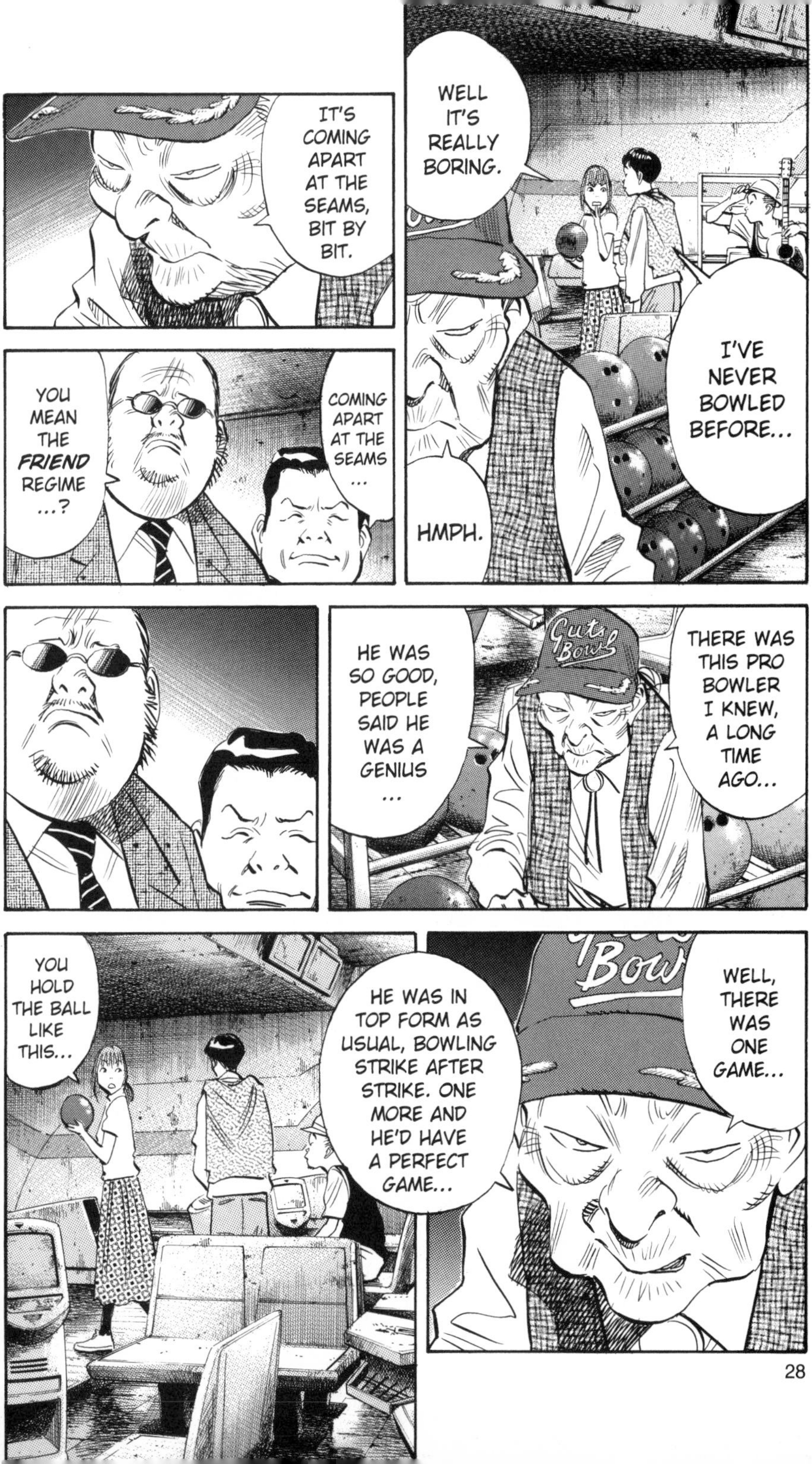
WELL IT'S REALLY BORING.
I'VE NEVER BOWLED BEFORE...
HMPH.
IT'S COMING APART AT THE SEAMS, BIT BY BIT.
COMING APART AT THE SEAMS...
YOU MEAN THE *FRIEND* REGIME...?
THERE WAS THIS PRO BOWLER I KNEW, A LONG TIME AGO...
HE WAS SO GOOD, PEOPLE SAID HE WAS A GENIUS...
Guts Bowl
WELL, THERE WAS ONE GAME...
HE WAS IN TOP FORM AS USUAL, BOWLING STRIKE AFTER STRIKE. ONE MORE AND HE'D HAVE A PERFECT GAME...
YOU HOLD THE BALL LIKE THIS...

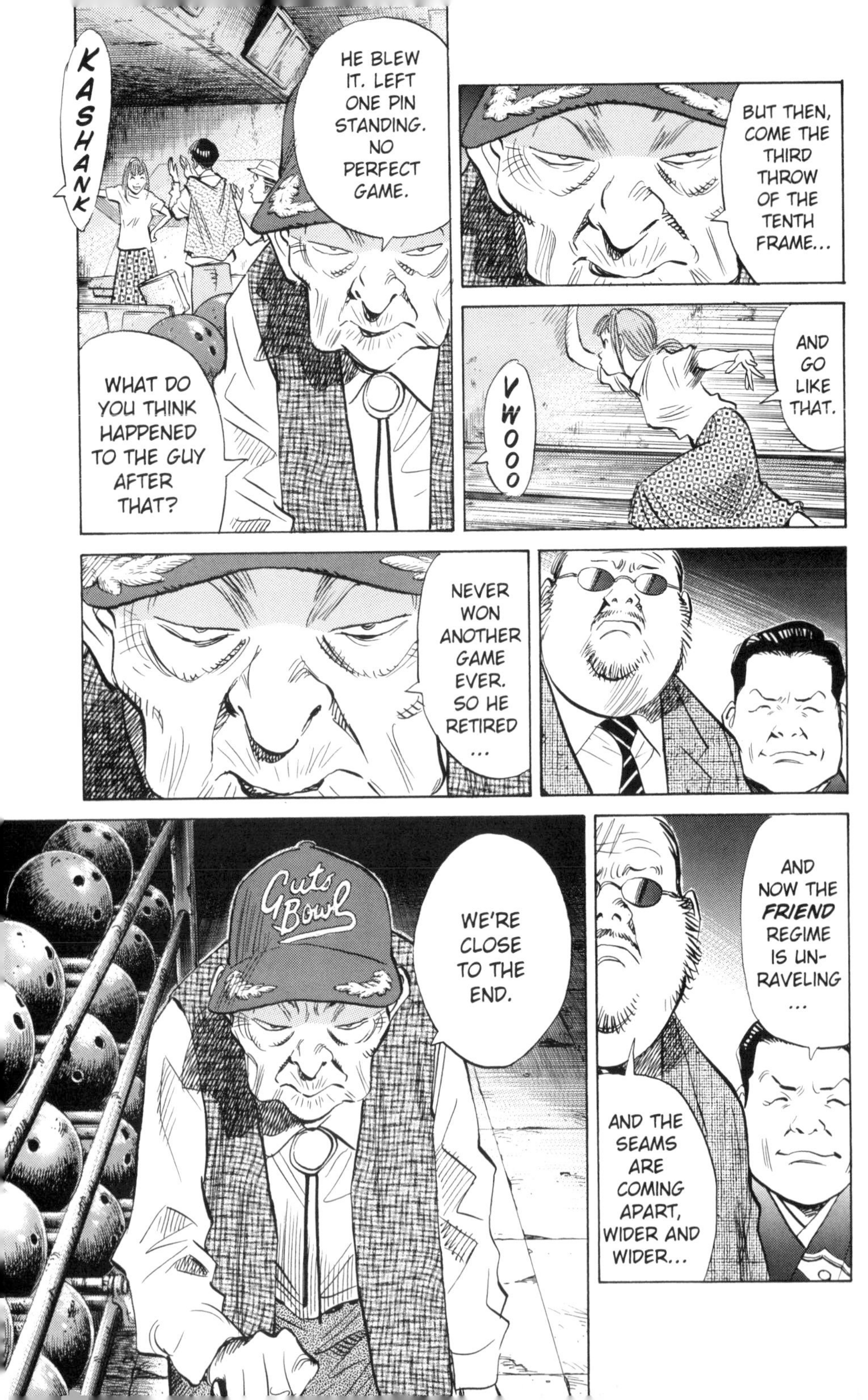
BUT THEN, COME THE THIRD THROW OF THE TENTH FRAME...
AND GO LIKE THAT.
VWOOO
HE BLEW IT. LEFT ONE PIN STANDING. NO PERFECT GAME.
KASHANK
WHAT DO YOU THINK HAPPENED TO THE GUY AFTER THAT?
NEVER WON ANOTHER GAME EVER. SO HE RETIRED ...
AND NOW THE FRIEND REGIME IS UNRAVELING ...
AND THE SEAMS ARE COMING APART, WIDER AND WIDER...
Guts Bowl
WE'RE CLOSE TO THE END.

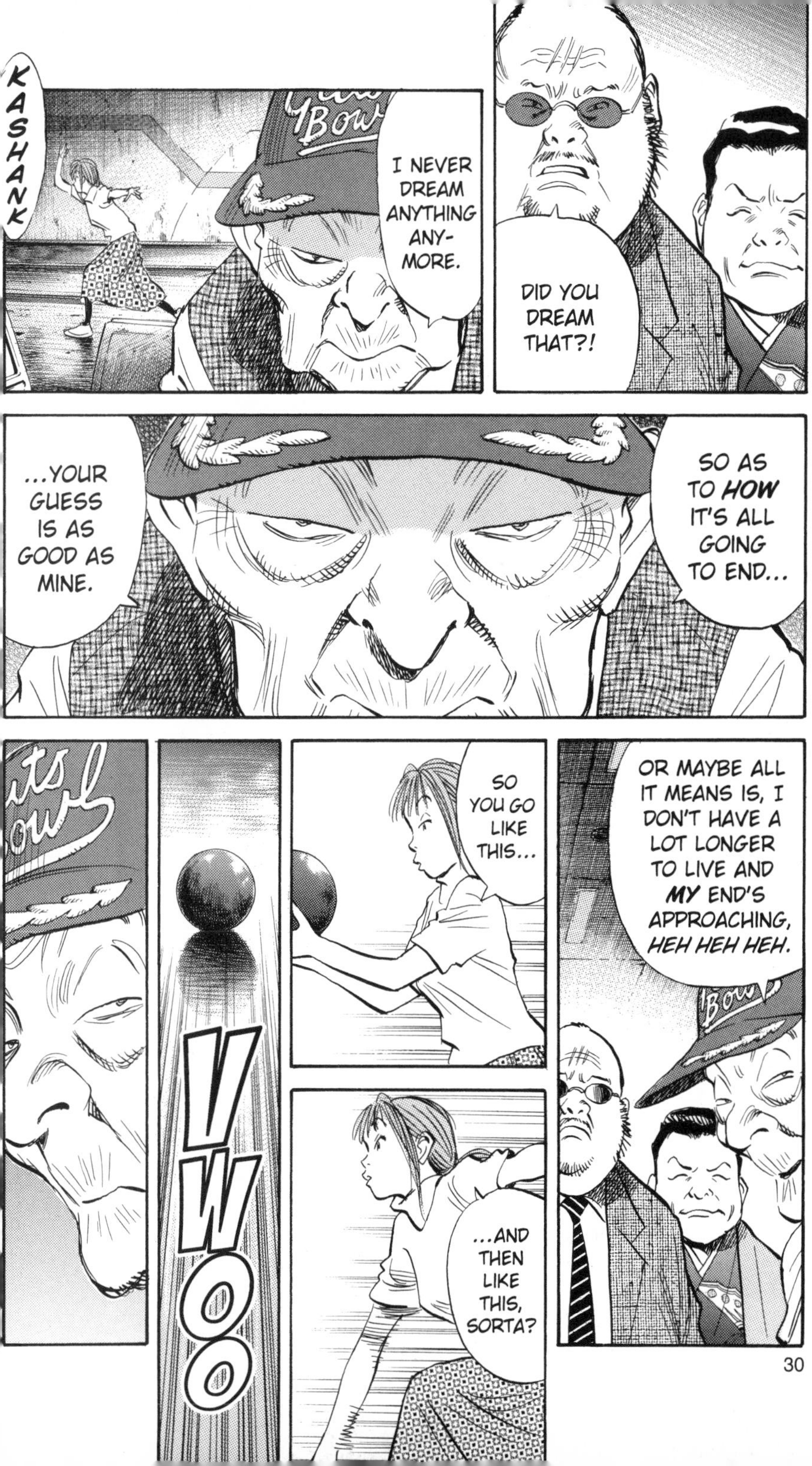
DID YOU DREAM THAT?!
KASHANK
I NEVER DREAM ANYTHING ANY-MORE.
SO AS TO ***HOW*** IT'S ALL GOING TO END...
...YOUR GUESS IS AS GOOD AS MINE.
OR MAYBE ALL IT MEANS IS, I DON'T HAVE A LOT LONGER TO LIVE AND ***MY*** END'S APPROACHING, ***HEH HEH HEH.***
SO YOU GO LIKE THIS...
...AND THEN LIKE THIS, SORTA?
VWOOO

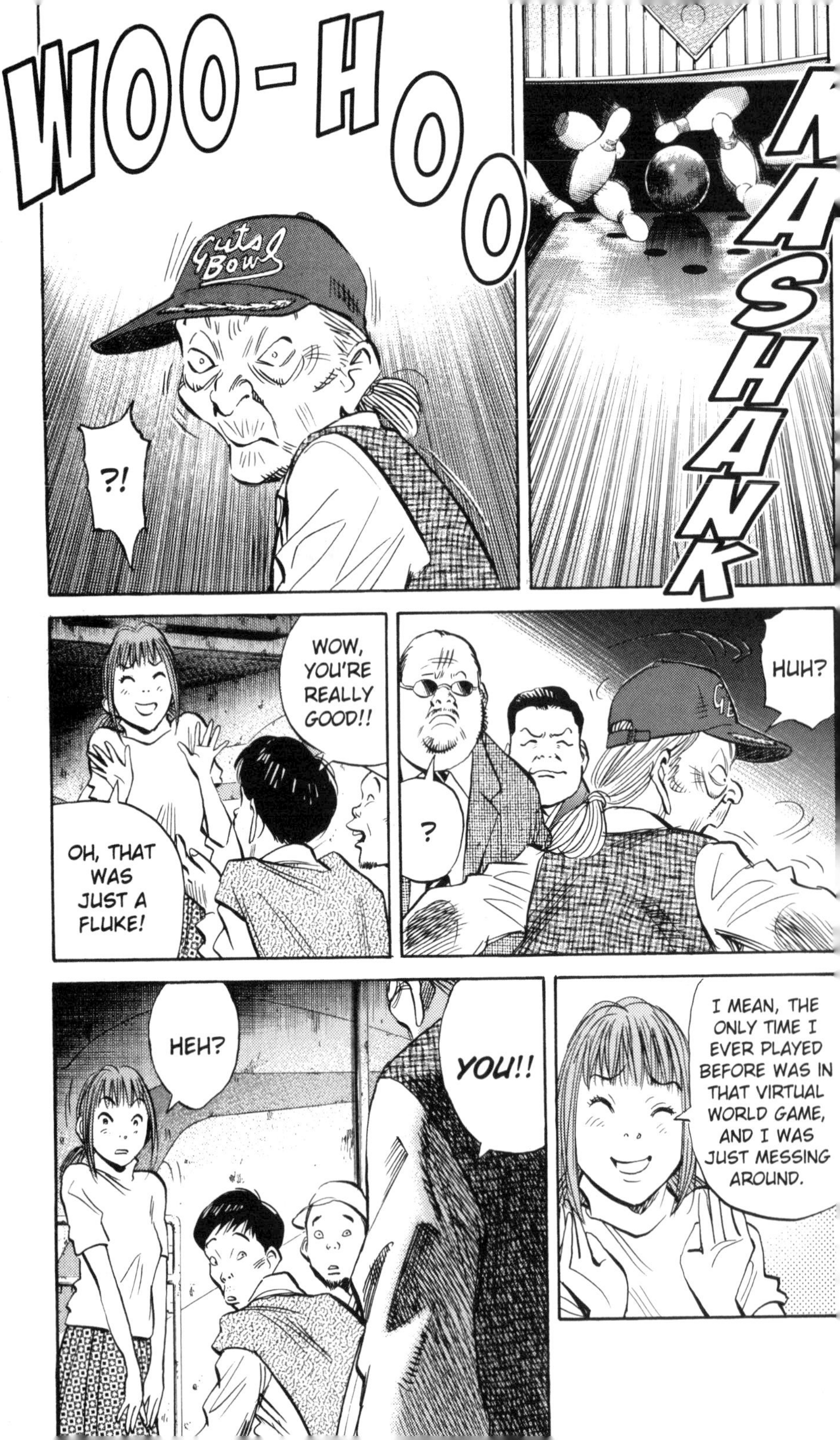
KASHANK
WOO-HOOO
?!
HUH?
?
WOW, YOU'RE REALLY GOOD!!
OH, THAT WAS JUST A FLUKE!
I MEAN, THE ONLY TIME I EVER PLAYED BEFORE WAS IN THAT VIRTUAL WORLD GAME, AND I WAS JUST MESSING AROUND.
YOU!!
HEH?

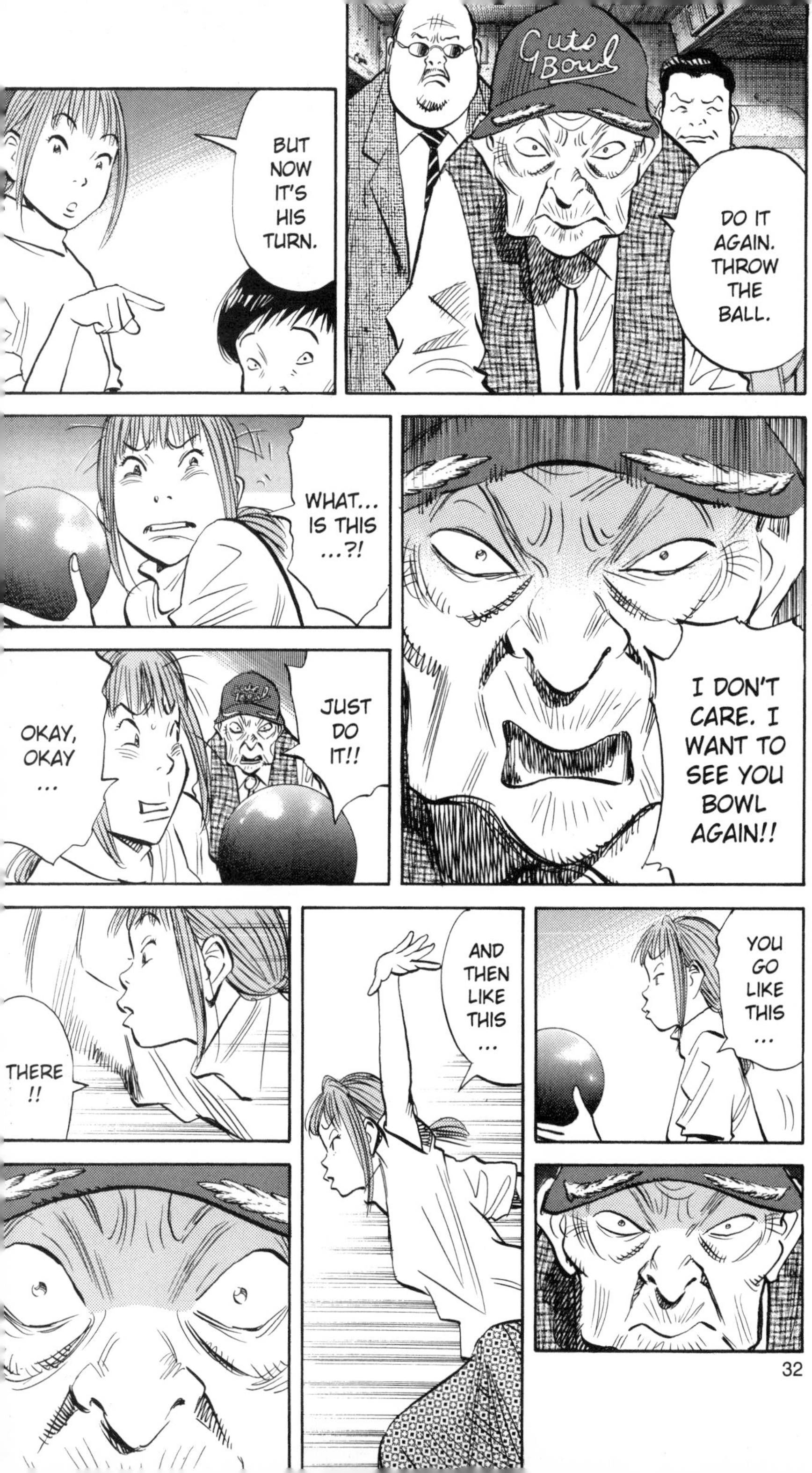
Cute Bowl
DO IT AGAIN. THROW THE BALL.
BUT NOW IT'S HIS TURN.
I DON'T CARE. I WANT TO SEE YOU BOWL AGAIN!!
WHAT... IS THIS ...?!
JUST DO IT!!
OKAY, OKAY ...
YOU GO LIKE THIS ...
AND THEN LIKE THIS ...
THERE !!

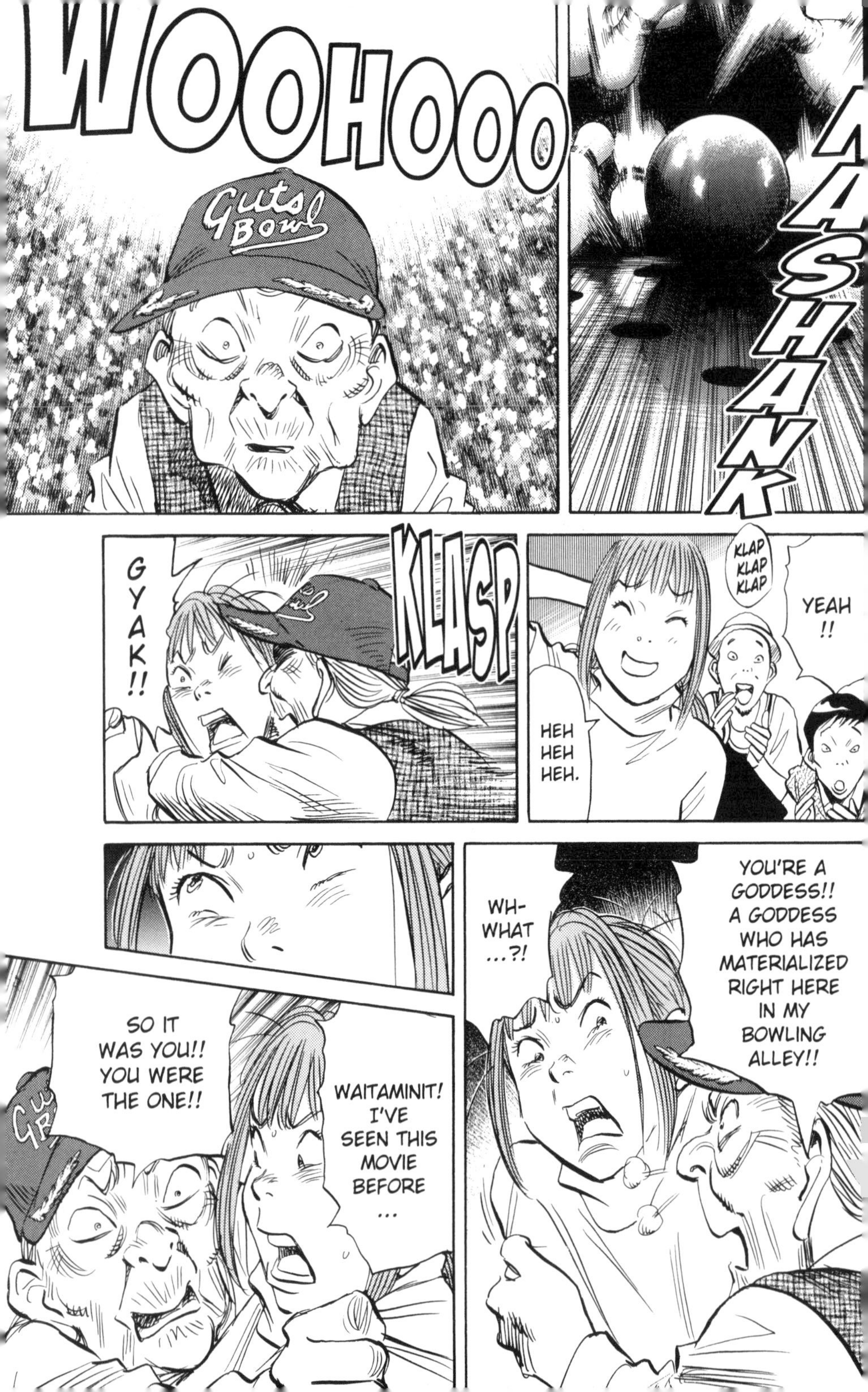
KASHANK
WOOHOOO
KLAP KLAP KLAP
YEAH!!
HEH HEH HEH.
KLASP
GYAK!!
YOU'RE A GODDESS!! A GODDESS WHO HAS MATERIALIZED RIGHT HERE IN MY BOWLING ALLEY!!
WH-WHAT ...?!
WAITAMINIT! I'VE SEEN THIS MOVIE BEFORE ...
SO IT WAS YOU!! YOU WERE THE ONE!!

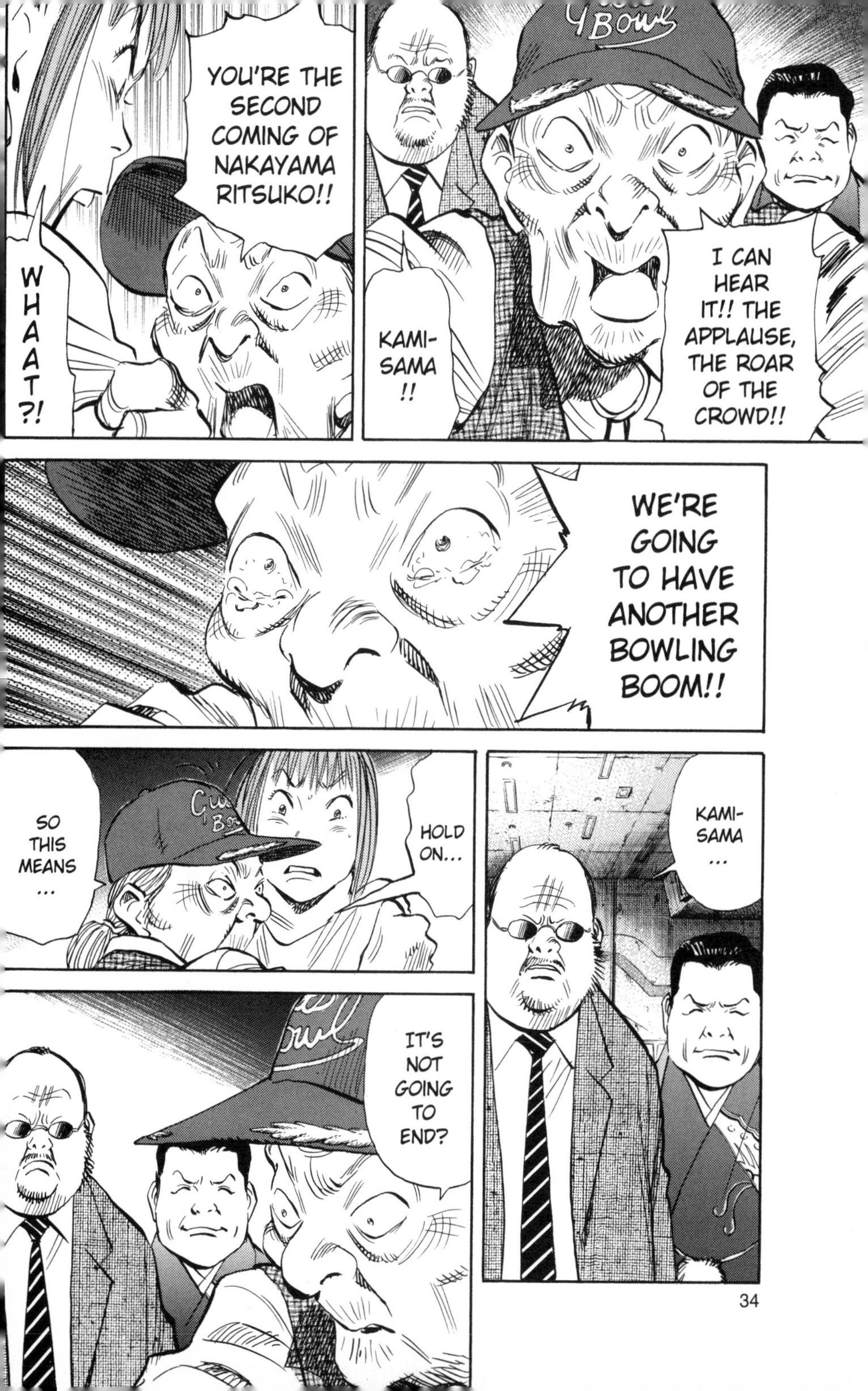
I CAN HEAR IT!! THE APPLAUSE, THE ROAR OF THE CROWD!!
KAMI-SAMA!!
YOU'RE THE SECOND COMING OF NAKAYAMA RITSUKO!!
WHAAAT?!
WE'RE GOING TO HAVE ANOTHER BOWLING BOOM!!
KAMI-SAMA...
HOLD ON...
SO THIS MEANS...
IT'S NOT GOING TO END?

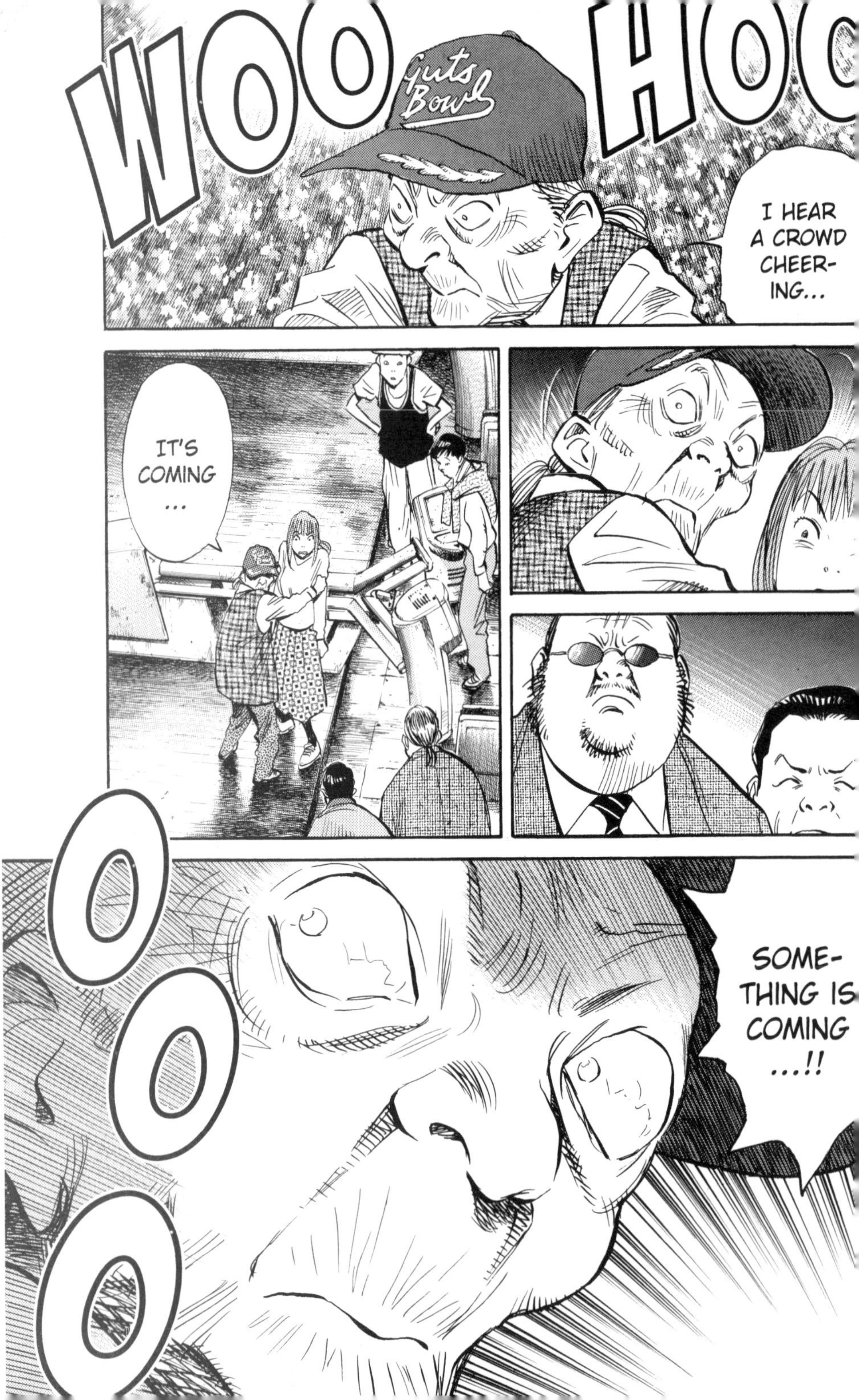

WOO HOO
Guts Bowl
I HEAR A CROWD CHEERING...
IT'S COMING...
OOO
SOMETHING IS COMING...!!

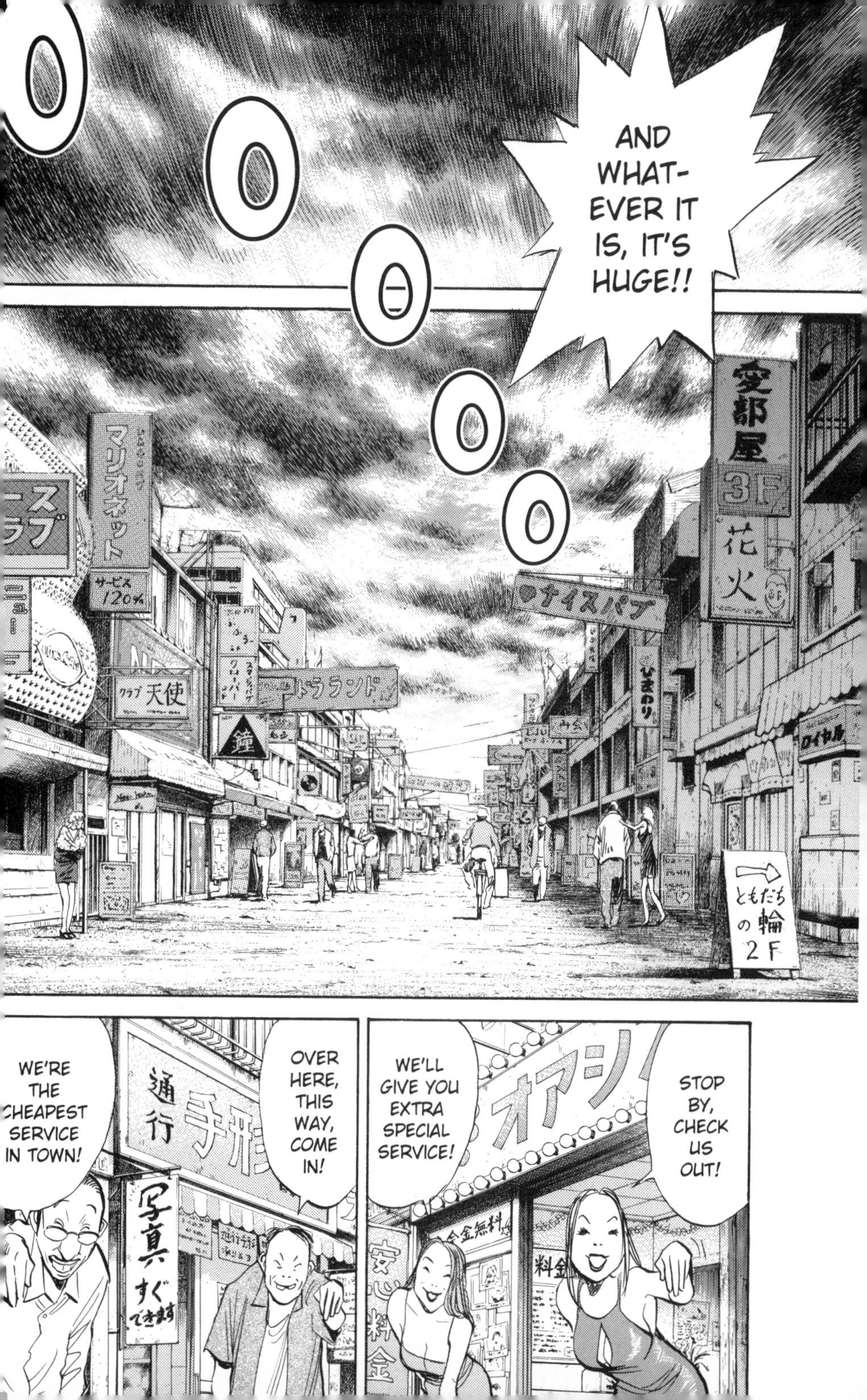
AND WHAT-EVER IT IS, IT'S HUGE!!
STOP BY, CHECK US OUT!
WE'LL GIVE YOU EXTRA SPECIAL SERVICE!
OVER HERE, THIS WAY, COME IN!
WE'RE THE CHEAPEST SERVICE IN TOWN!

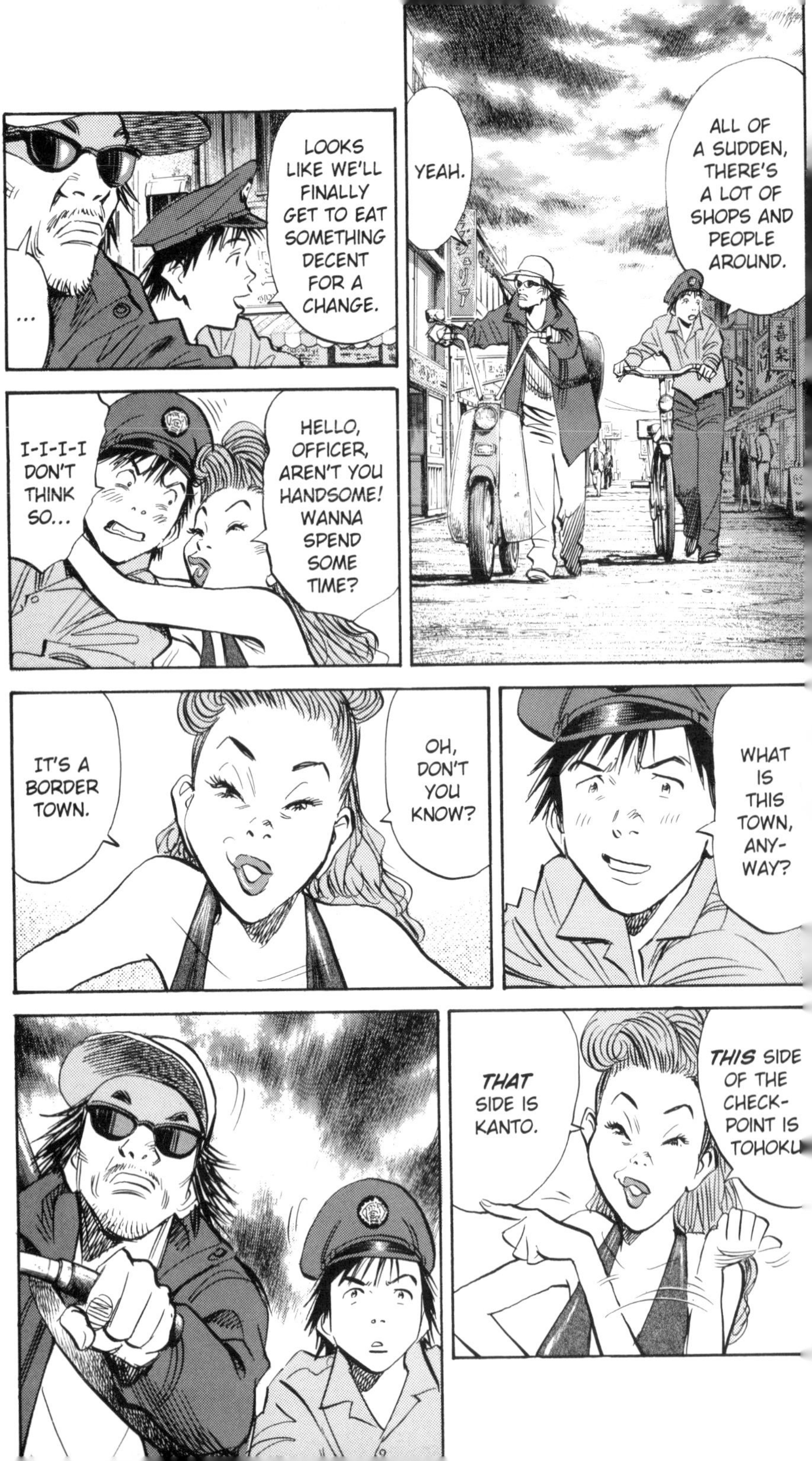
ALL OF A SUDDEN, THERE'S A LOT OF SHOPS AND PEOPLE AROUND.
YEAH.
LOOKS LIKE WE'LL FINALLY GET TO EAT SOMETHING DECENT FOR A CHANGE.
...
HELLO, OFFICER, AREN'T YOU HANDSOME! WANNA SPEND SOME TIME?
I-I-I-I DON'T THINK SO...
WHAT IS THIS TOWN, ANYWAY?
OH, DON'T YOU KNOW?
IT'S A BORDER TOWN.
THIS SIDE OF THE CHECKPOINT IS TOHOKU
THAT SIDE IS KANTO.

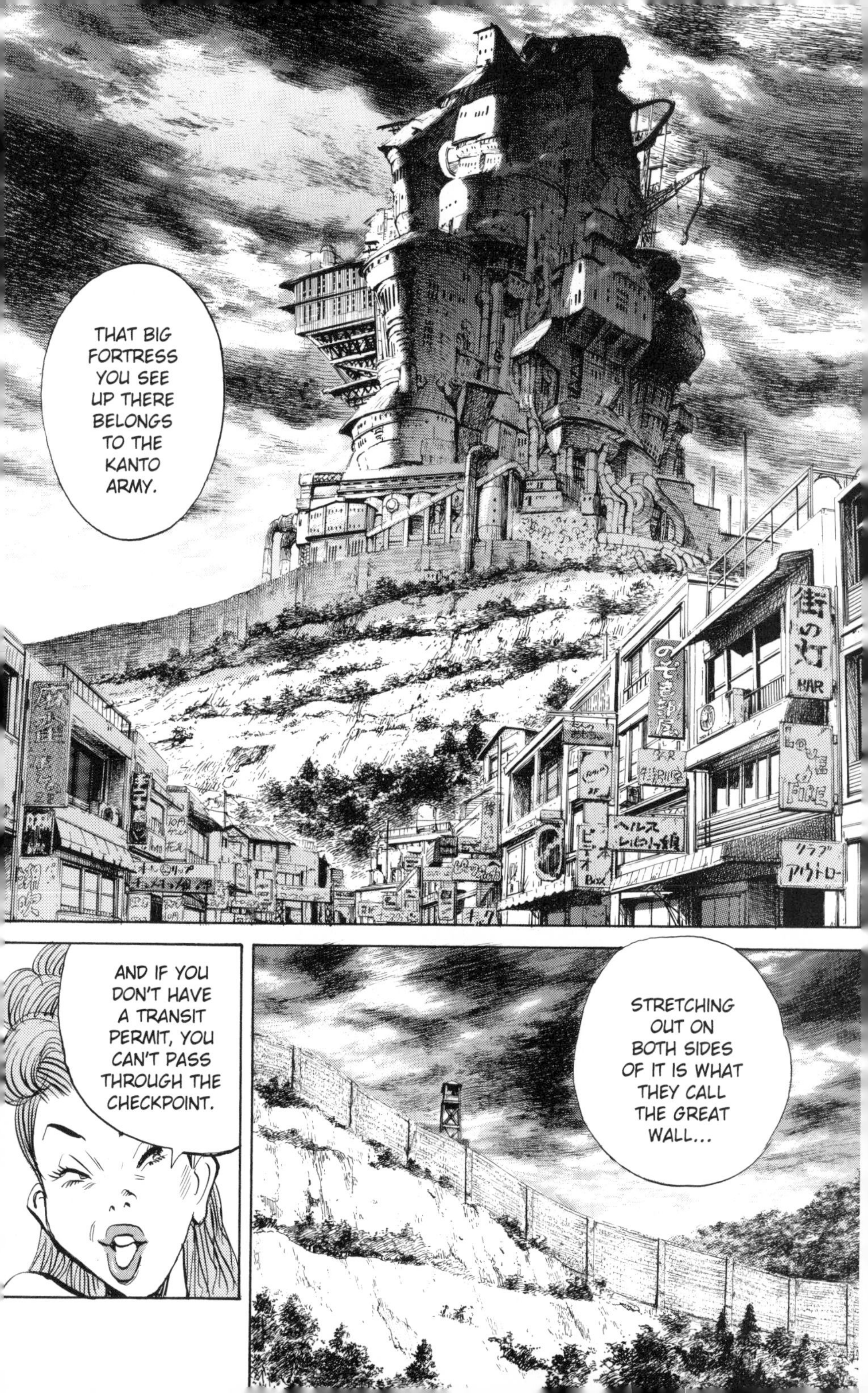
THAT BIG FORTRESS YOU SEE UP THERE BELONGS TO THE KANTO ARMY.
STRETCHING OUT ON BOTH SIDES OF IT IS WHAT THEY CALL THE GREAT WALL...
AND IF YOU DON'T HAVE A TRANSIT PERMIT, YOU CAN'T PASS THROUGH THE CHECKPOINT.

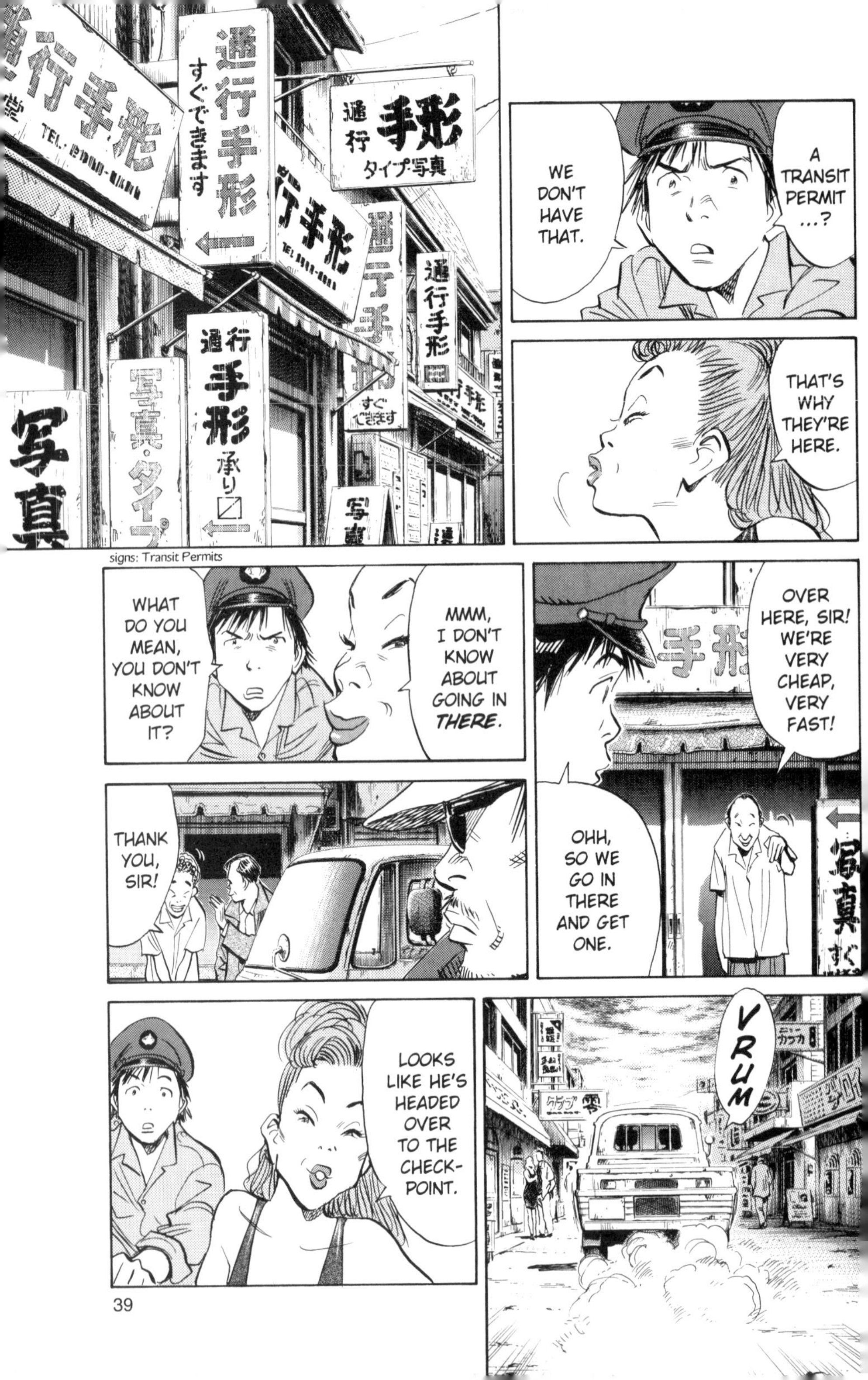
A TRANSIT PERMIT ...?
WE DON'T HAVE THAT.
THAT'S WHY THEY'RE HERE.
通行手形
すぐできます
通行手形 タイプ・写真
写真
OVER HERE, SIR! WE'RE VERY CHEAP, VERY FAST!
OHH, SO WE GO IN THERE AND GET ONE.
MMM, I DON'T KNOW ABOUT GOING IN *THERE*.
WHAT DO YOU MEAN, YOU DON'T KNOW ABOUT IT?
THANK YOU, SIR!
VRUM
LOOKS LIKE HE'S HEADED OVER TO THE CHECK-POINT.
signs: Transit Permits

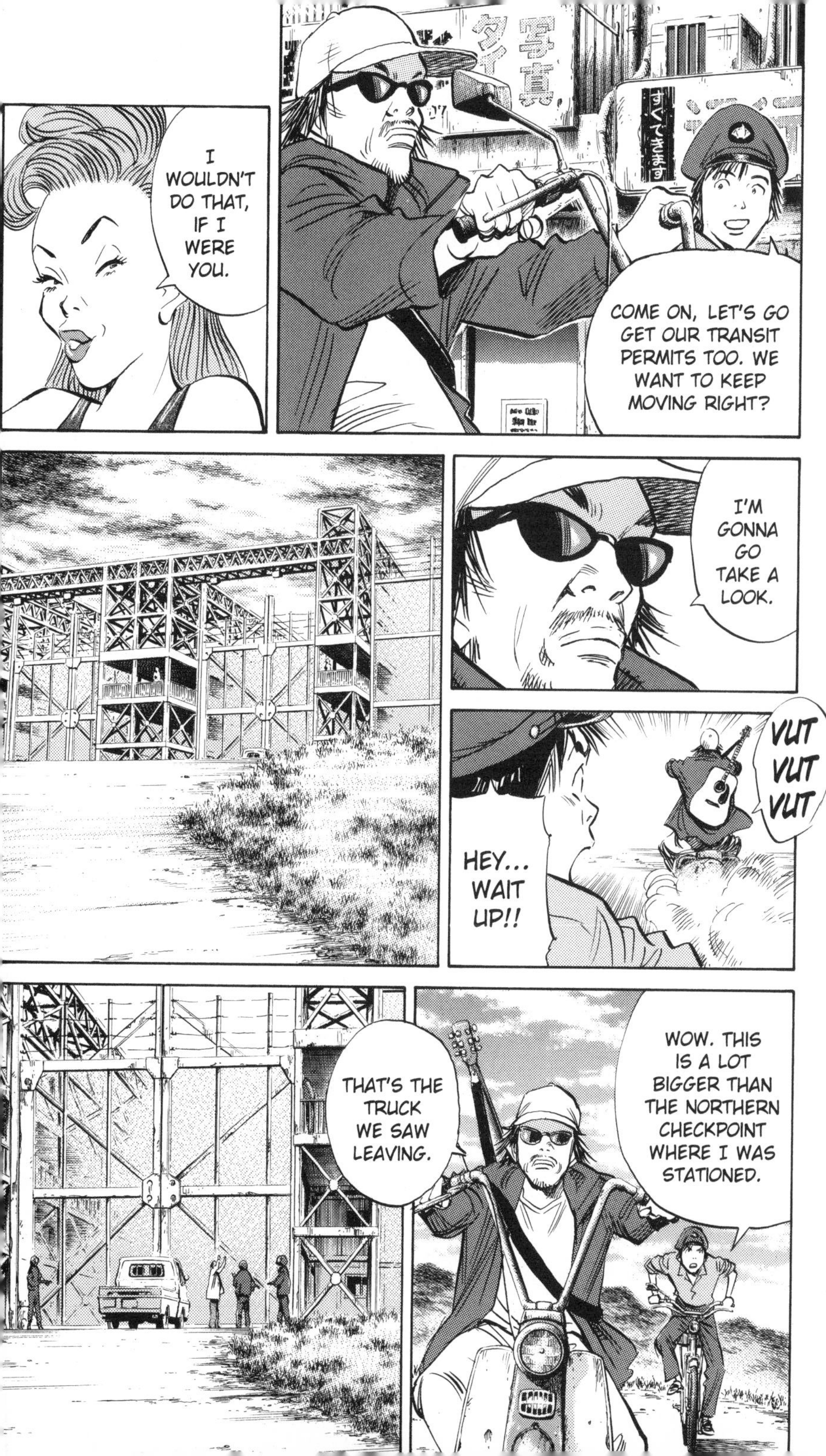
写真
すぐできます
COME ON, LET'S GO GET OUR TRANSIT PERMITS TOO. WE WANT TO KEEP MOVING RIGHT?
I WOULDN'T DO THAT, IF I WERE YOU.
I'M GONNA GO TAKE A LOOK.
VUT VUT VUT
HEY... WAIT UP!!
WOW. THIS IS A LOT BIGGER THAN THE NORTHERN CHECKPOINT WHERE I WAS STATIONED.
THAT'S THE TRUCK WE SAW LEAVING.

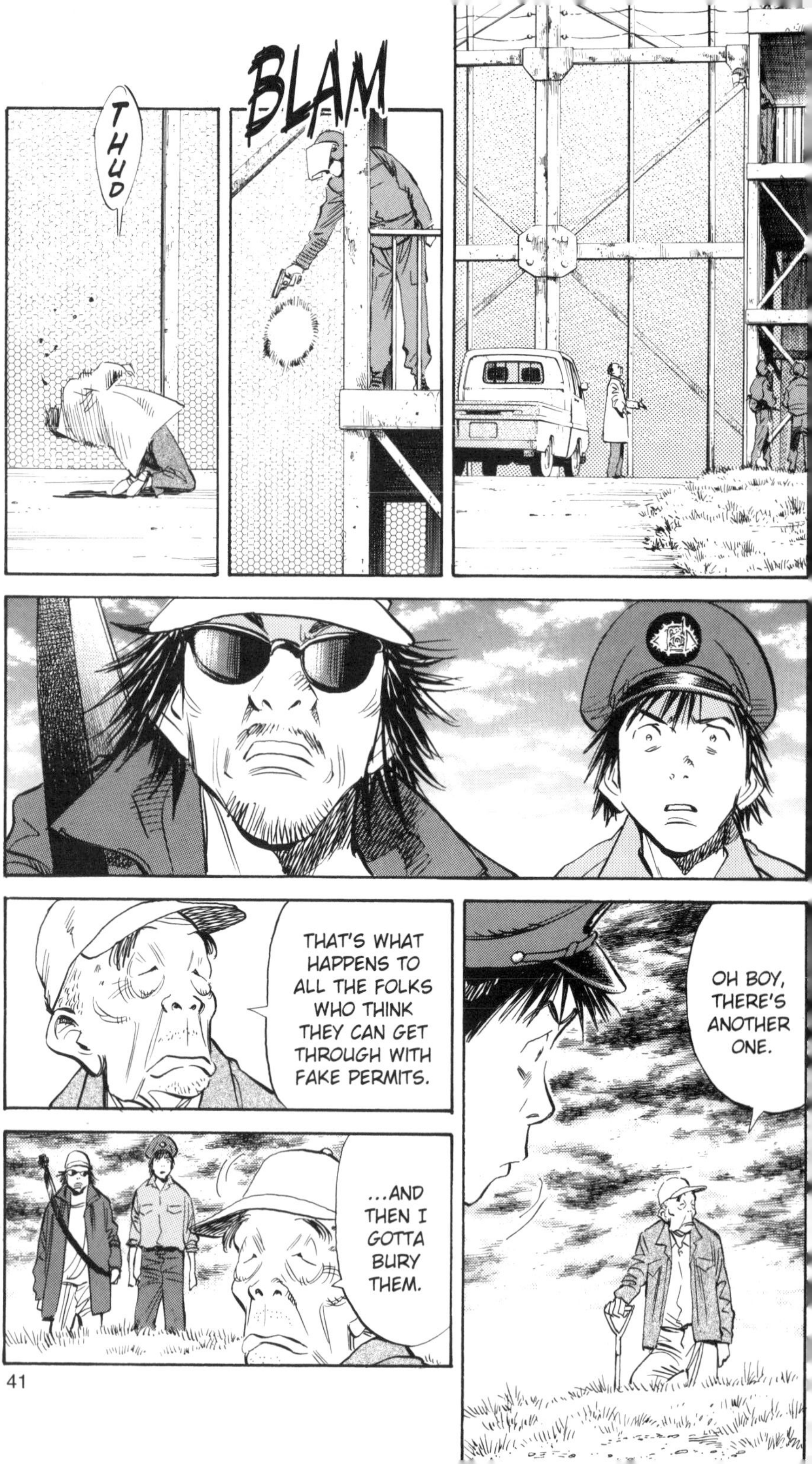
BLAM
THUD
OH BOY, THERE'S ANOTHER ONE.
THAT'S WHAT HAPPENS TO ALL THE FOLKS WHO THINK THEY CAN GET THROUGH WITH FAKE PERMITS.
...AND THEN I GOTTA BURY THEM.

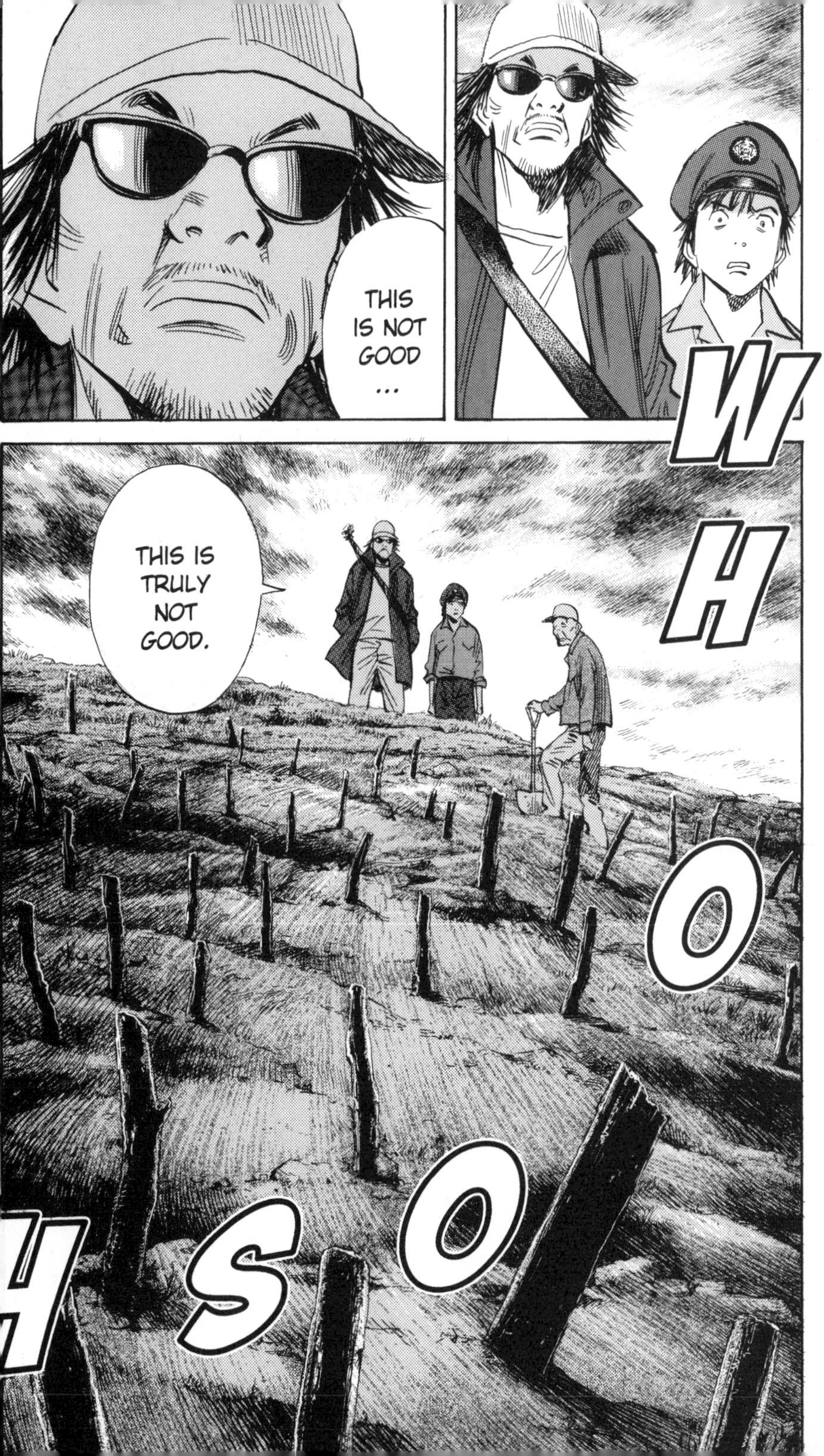
THIS IS NOT GOOD ...
THIS IS TRULY NOT GOOD.
WHOOSH

Chapter 3 Ichi the Spade

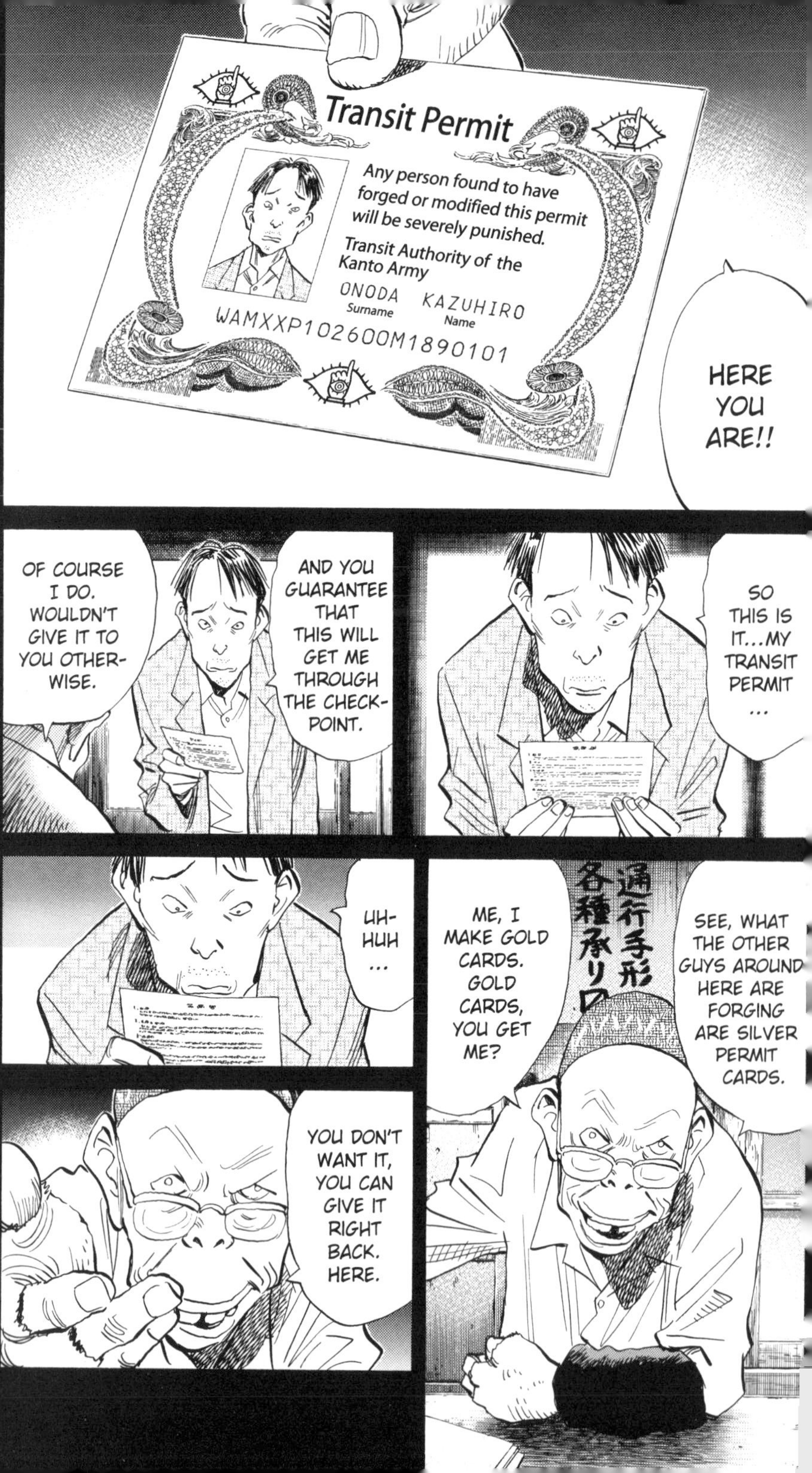
Transit Permit
Any person found to have forged or modified this permit will be severely punished.
Transit Authority of the Kanto Army
ONODA KAZUHIRO
Surname Name
WAMXXP102600M1890101
HERE YOU ARE!!
SO THIS IS IT...MY TRANSIT PERMIT ...
AND YOU GUARANTEE THAT THIS WILL GET ME THROUGH THE CHECK-POINT.
OF COURSE I DO. WOULDN'T GIVE IT TO YOU OTHER-WISE.
SEE, WHAT THE OTHER GUYS AROUND HERE ARE FORGING ARE SILVER PERMIT CARDS.
通行手形 各種承り口
ME, I MAKE GOLD CARDS. GOLD CARDS, YOU GET ME?
UH-HUH ...
YOU DON'T WANT IT, YOU CAN GIVE IT RIGHT BACK. HERE.

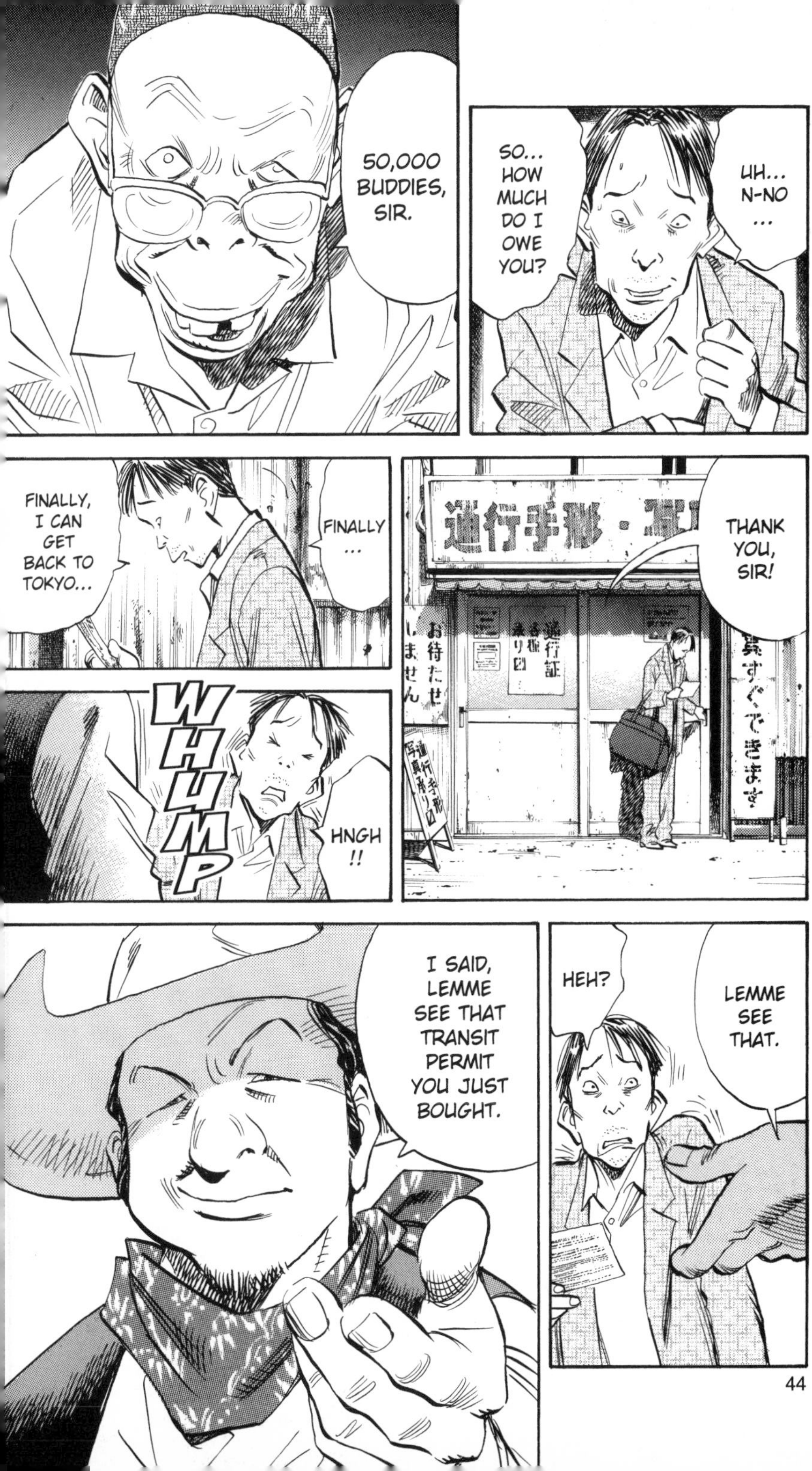
UH... N-NO ...
SO... HOW MUCH DO I OWE YOU?
50,000 BUDDIES, SIR.
THANK YOU, SIR!
FINALLY ...
FINALLY, I CAN GET BACK TO TOKYO...
WHUMP
HNGH !!
LEMME SEE THAT.
HEH?
I SAID, LEMME SEE THAT TRANSIT PERMIT YOU JUST BOUGHT.

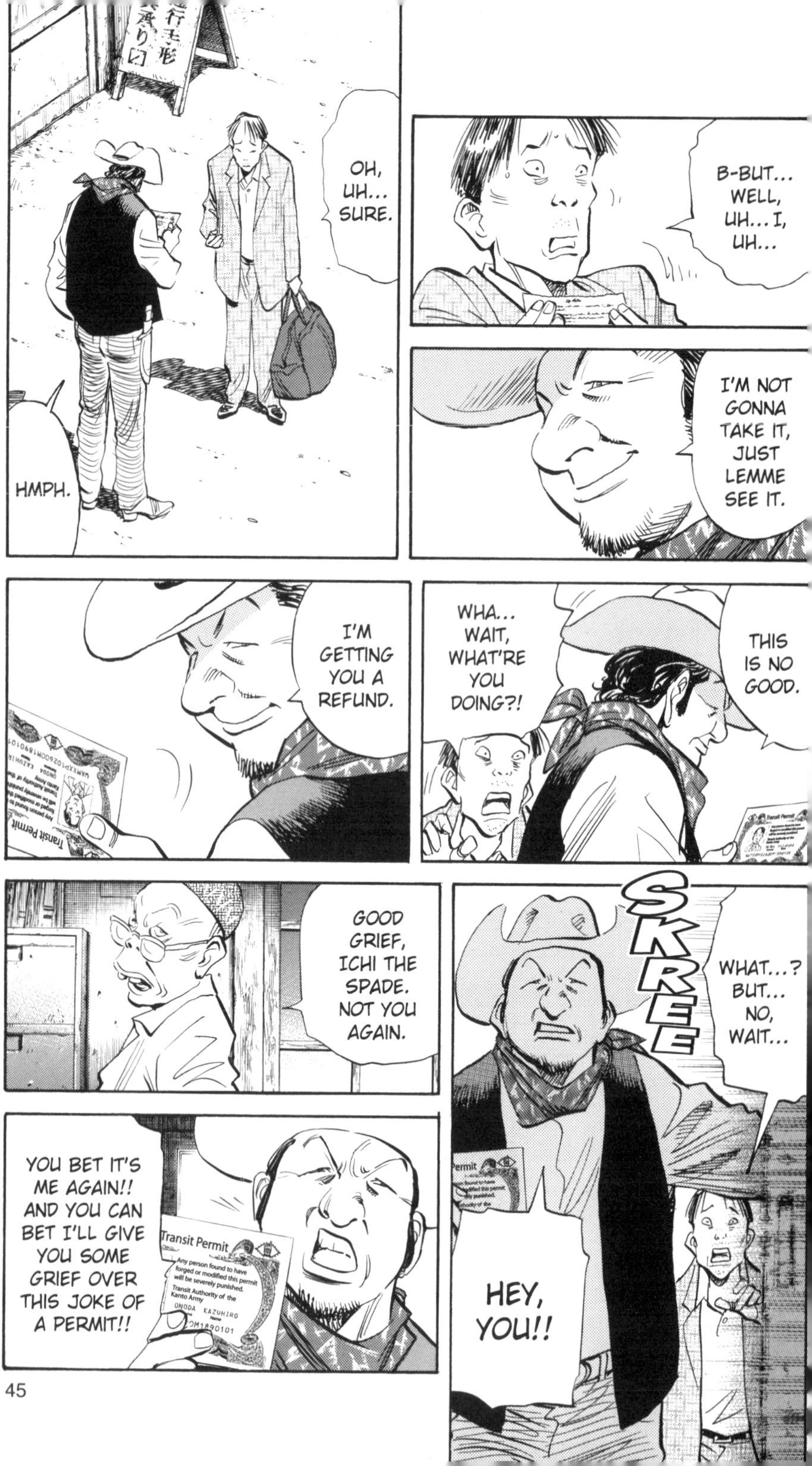
B-BUT... WELL, UH... I, UH...
I'M NOT GONNA TAKE IT, JUST LEMME SEE IT.
OH, UH... SURE.
HMPH.
THIS IS NO GOOD.
WHA... WAIT, WHAT'RE YOU DOING?!
I'M GETTING YOU A REFUND.
SKREE
WHAT...? BUT... NO, WAIT...
HEY, YOU!!
GOOD GRIEF, ICHI THE SPADE. NOT YOU AGAIN.
YOU BET IT'S ME AGAIN!! AND YOU CAN BET I'LL GIVE YOU SOME GRIEF OVER THIS JOKE OF A PERMIT!!
Transit Permit
Any person found to have forged or modified this permit will be severely punished.
Transit Authority of the Kanto Army
ONODA KAZUHIRO

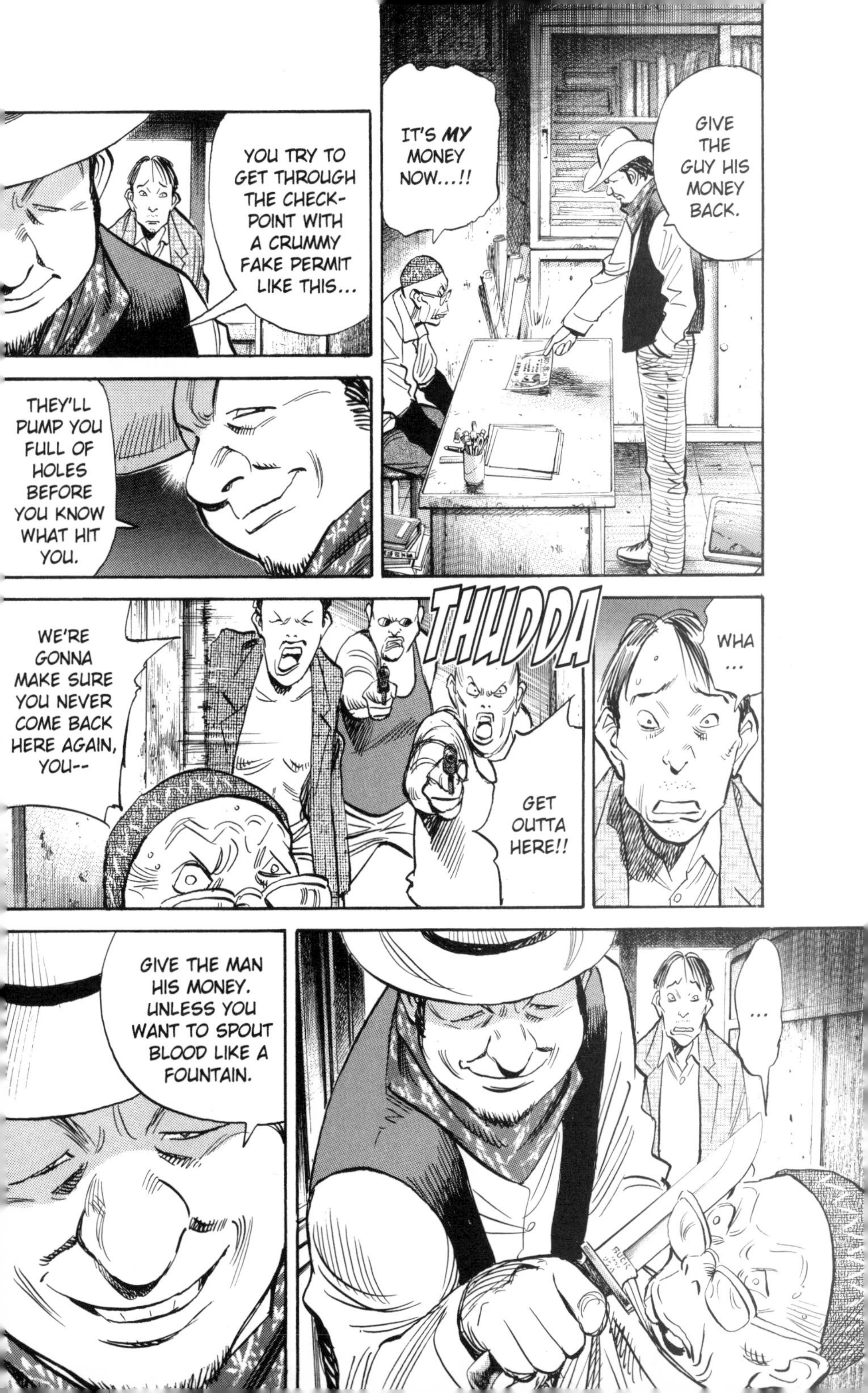
GIVE THE GUY HIS MONEY BACK.
IT'S **MY** MONEY NOW...!!
YOU TRY TO GET THROUGH THE CHECK-POINT WITH A CRUMMY FAKE PERMIT LIKE THIS...
THEY'LL PUMP YOU FULL OF HOLES BEFORE YOU KNOW WHAT HIT YOU.
WHA ...
THUDDA
WE'RE GONNA MAKE SURE YOU NEVER COME BACK HERE AGAIN, YOU--
GET OUTTA HERE!!
...
GIVE THE MAN HIS MONEY. UNLESS YOU WANT TO SPOUT BLOOD LIKE A FOUNTAIN.

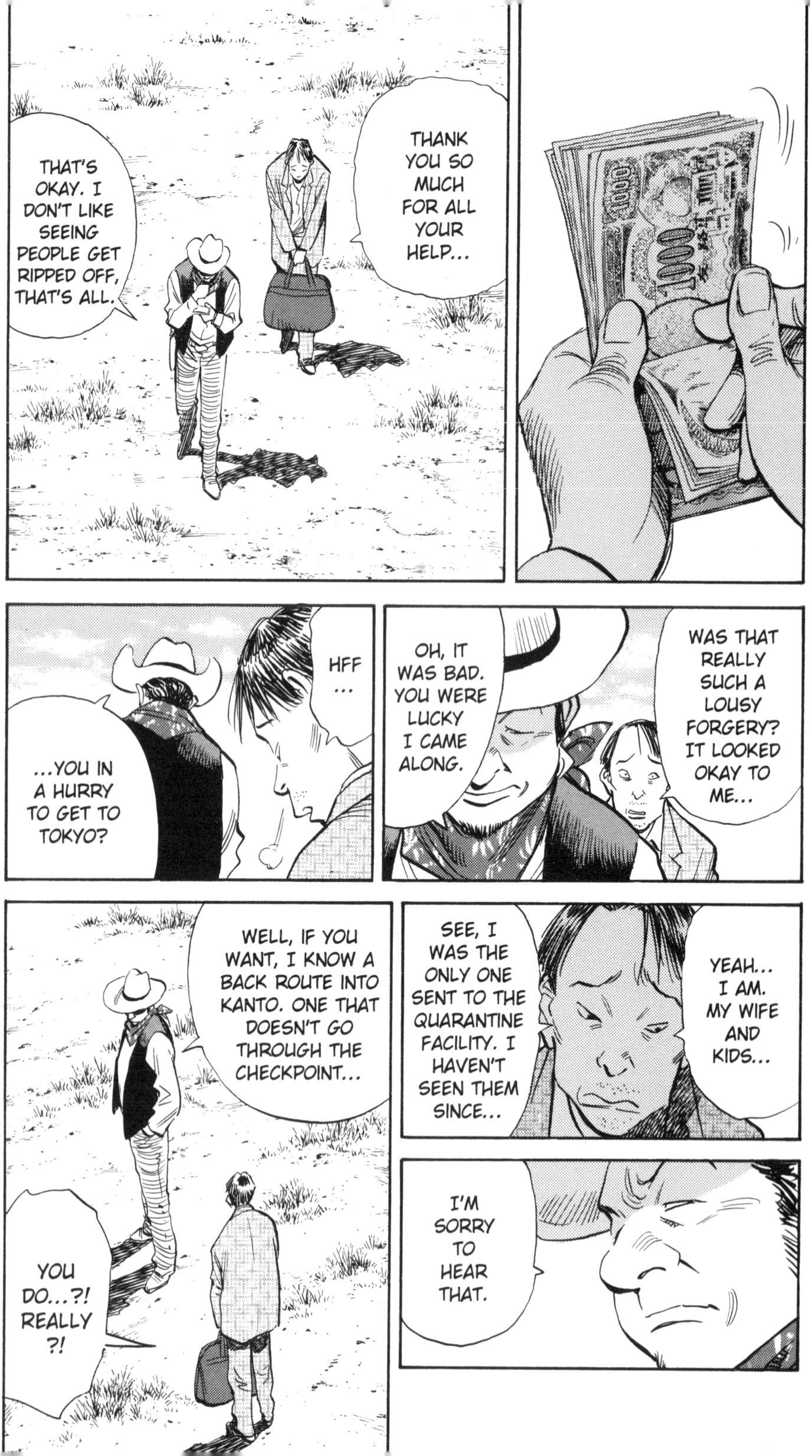
THANK YOU SO MUCH FOR ALL YOUR HELP...
THAT'S OKAY. I DON'T LIKE SEEING PEOPLE GET RIPPED OFF, THAT'S ALL.
WAS THAT REALLY SUCH A LOUSY FORGERY? IT LOOKED OKAY TO ME...
OH, IT WAS BAD. YOU WERE LUCKY I CAME ALONG.
HFF...
...YOU IN A HURRY TO GET TO TOKYO?
YEAH... I AM. MY WIFE AND KIDS...
SEE, I WAS THE ONLY ONE SENT TO THE QUARANTINE FACILITY. I HAVEN'T SEEN THEM SINCE...
I'M SORRY TO HEAR THAT.
WELL, IF YOU WANT, I KNOW A BACK ROUTE INTO KANTO. ONE THAT DOESN'T GO THROUGH THE CHECKPOINT...
YOU DO...?! REALLY?!

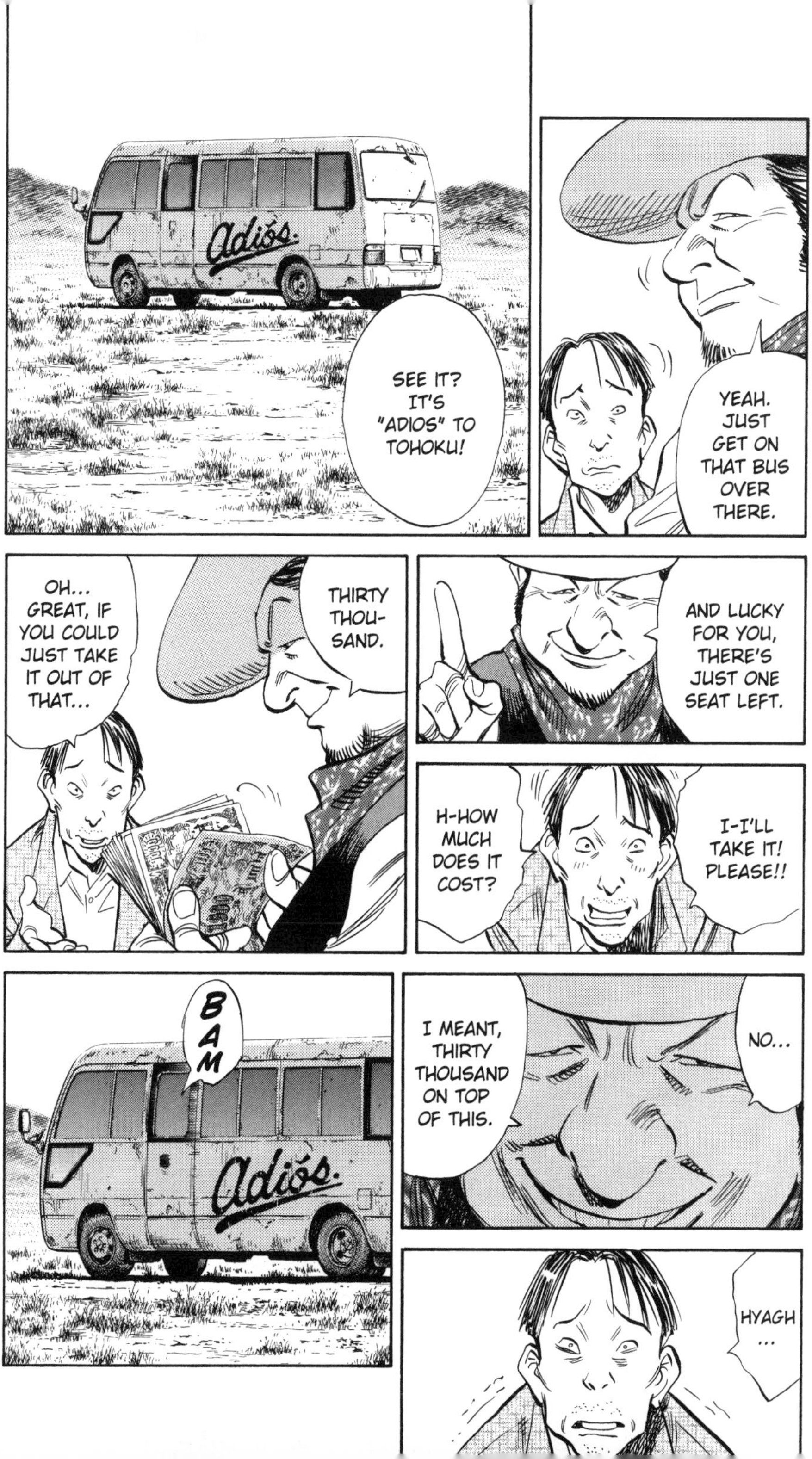
YEAH. JUST GET ON THAT BUS OVER THERE.
adiós.
SEE IT? IT'S "ADIOS" TO TOHOKU!
AND LUCKY FOR YOU, THERE'S JUST ONE SEAT LEFT.
I-I'LL TAKE IT! PLEASE!!
H-HOW MUCH DOES IT COST?
THIRTY THOU-SAND.
OH... GREAT, IF YOU COULD JUST TAKE IT OUT OF THAT...
NO...
I MEANT, THIRTY THOUSAND ON TOP OF THIS.
HYAGH ...
BAM
adiós.

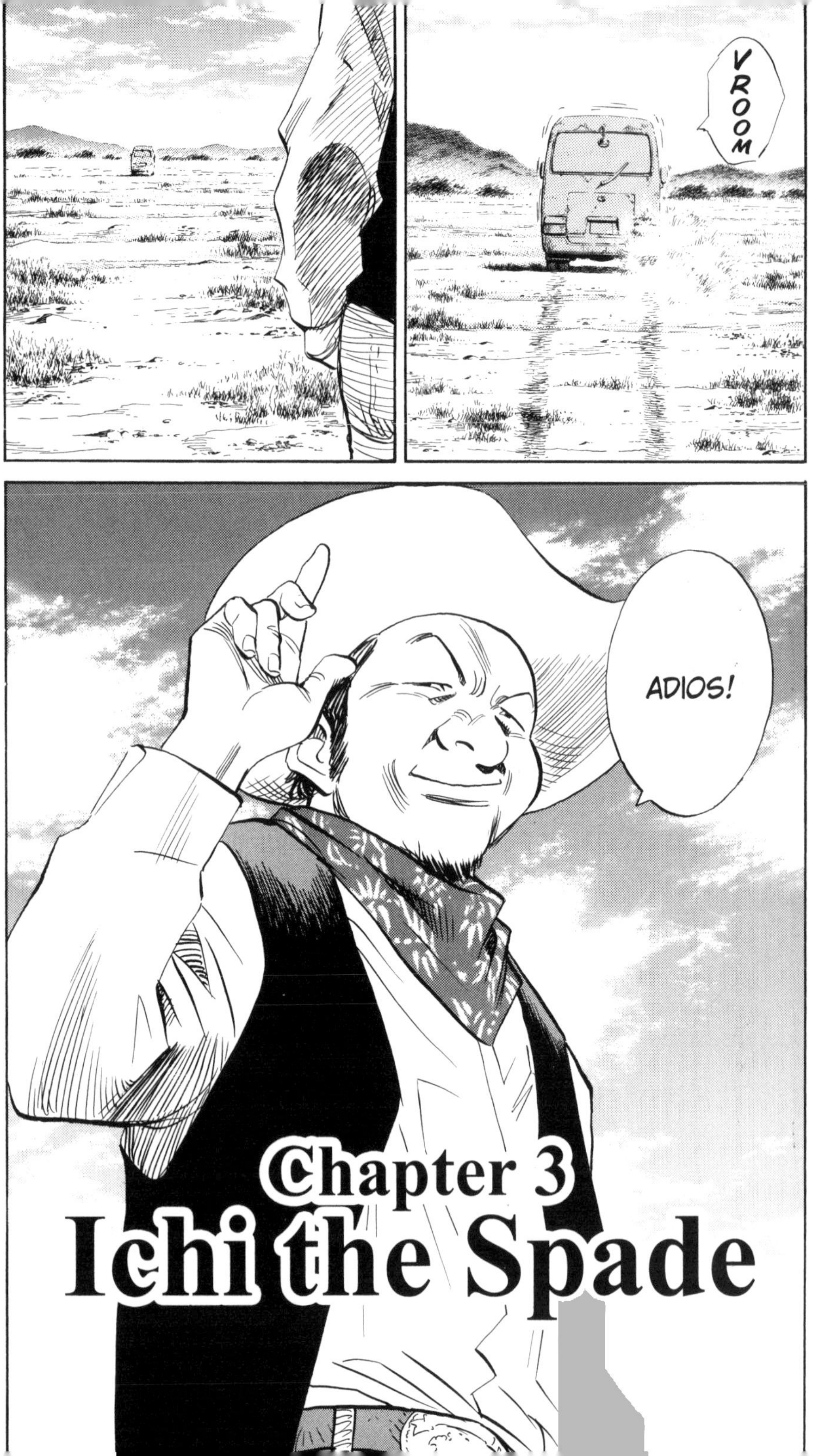
VROOM
ADIOS!
Chapter 3
Ichi the Spade

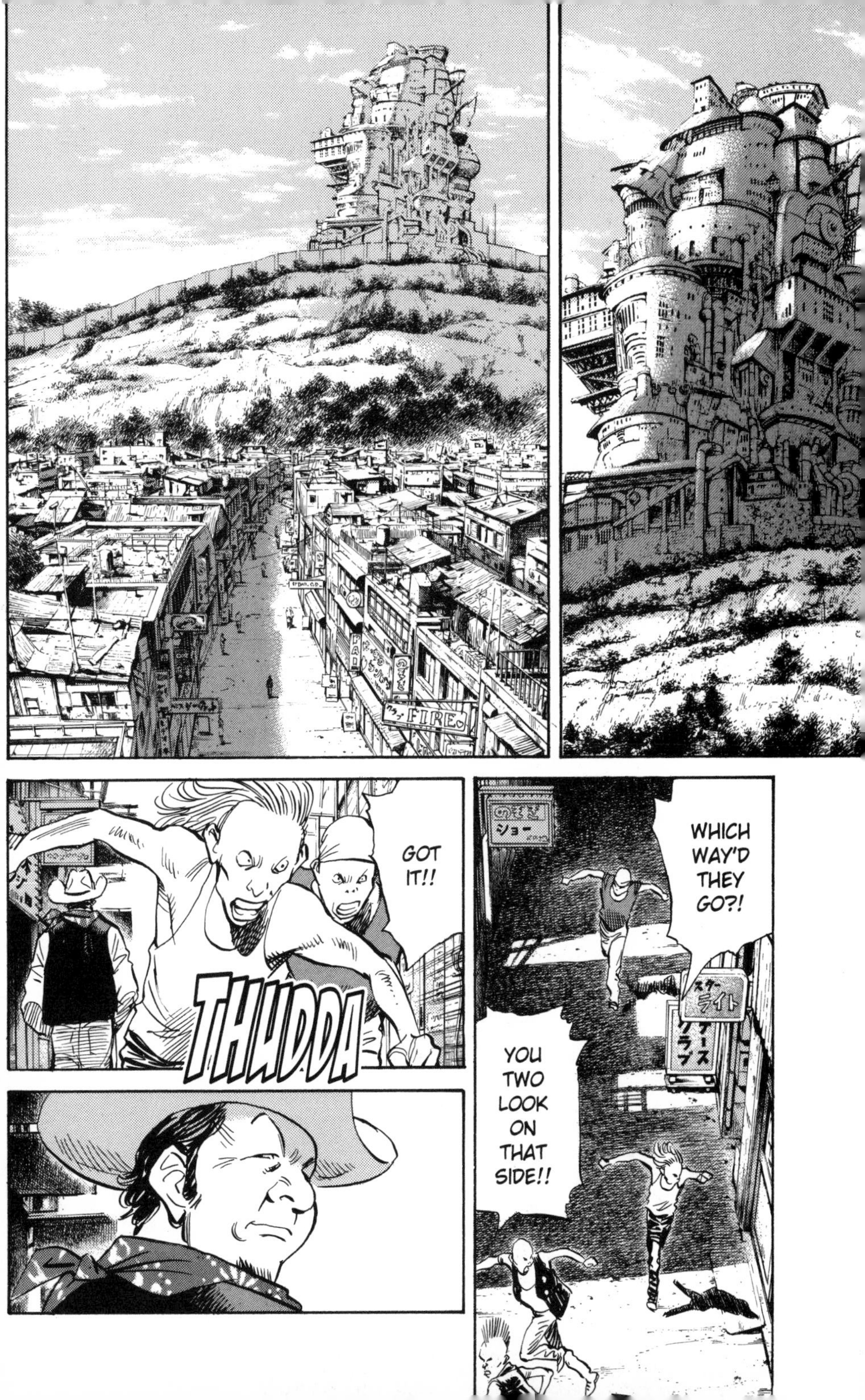
FIRE
WHICH WAY'D THEY GO?!
YOU TWO LOOK ON THAT SIDE!!
GOT IT!!
THUDDA

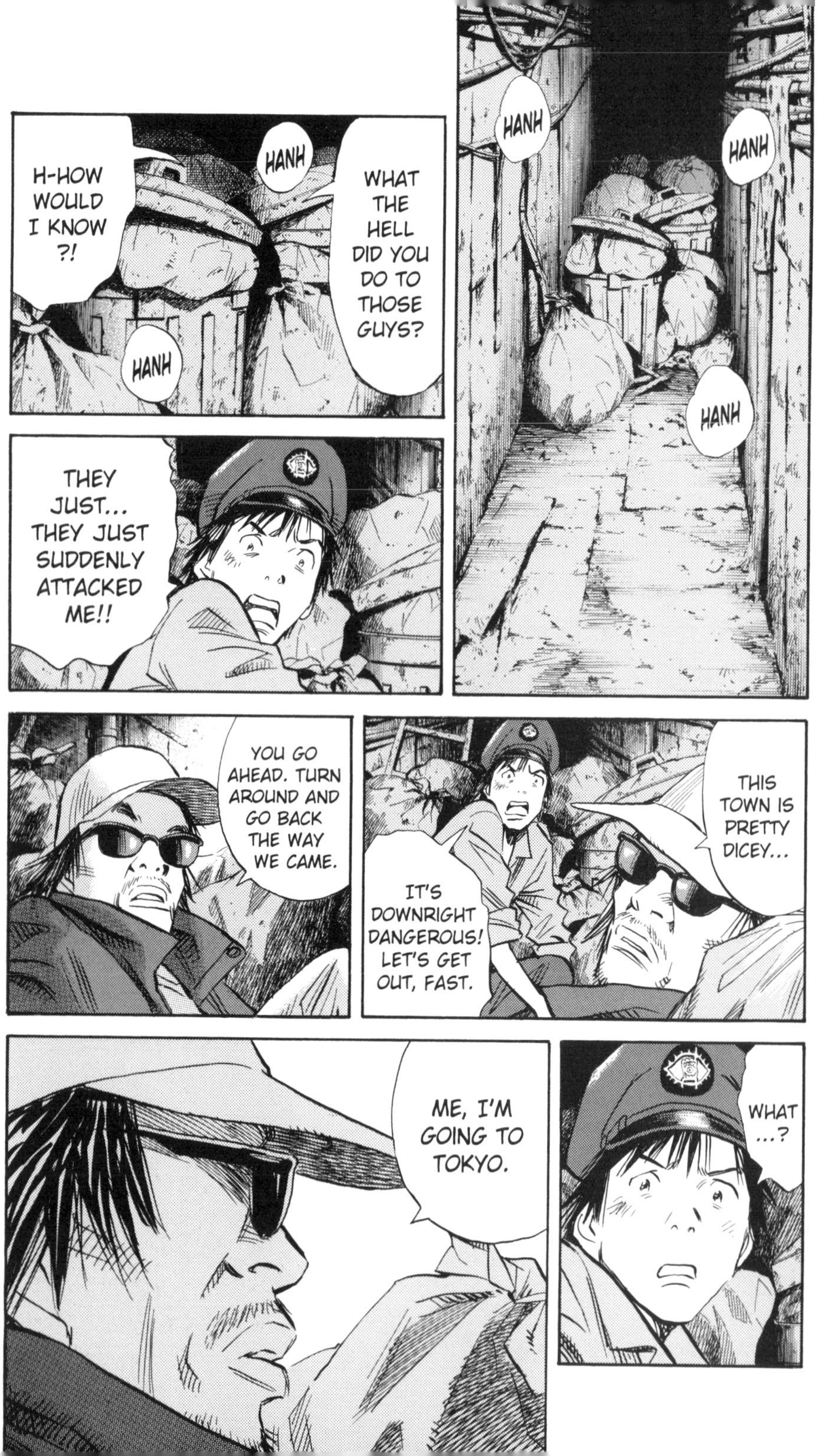
HANH
HANH
HANH
WHAT THE HELL DID YOU DO TO THOSE GUYS?
HANH
H-HOW WOULD I KNOW ?!
HANH
THEY JUST... THEY JUST SUDDENLY ATTACKED ME!!
THIS TOWN IS PRETTY DICEY...
IT'S DOWNRIGHT DANGEROUS! LET'S GET OUT, FAST.
YOU GO AHEAD. TURN AROUND AND GO BACK THE WAY WE CAME.
WHAT ...?
ME, I'M GOING TO TOKYO.

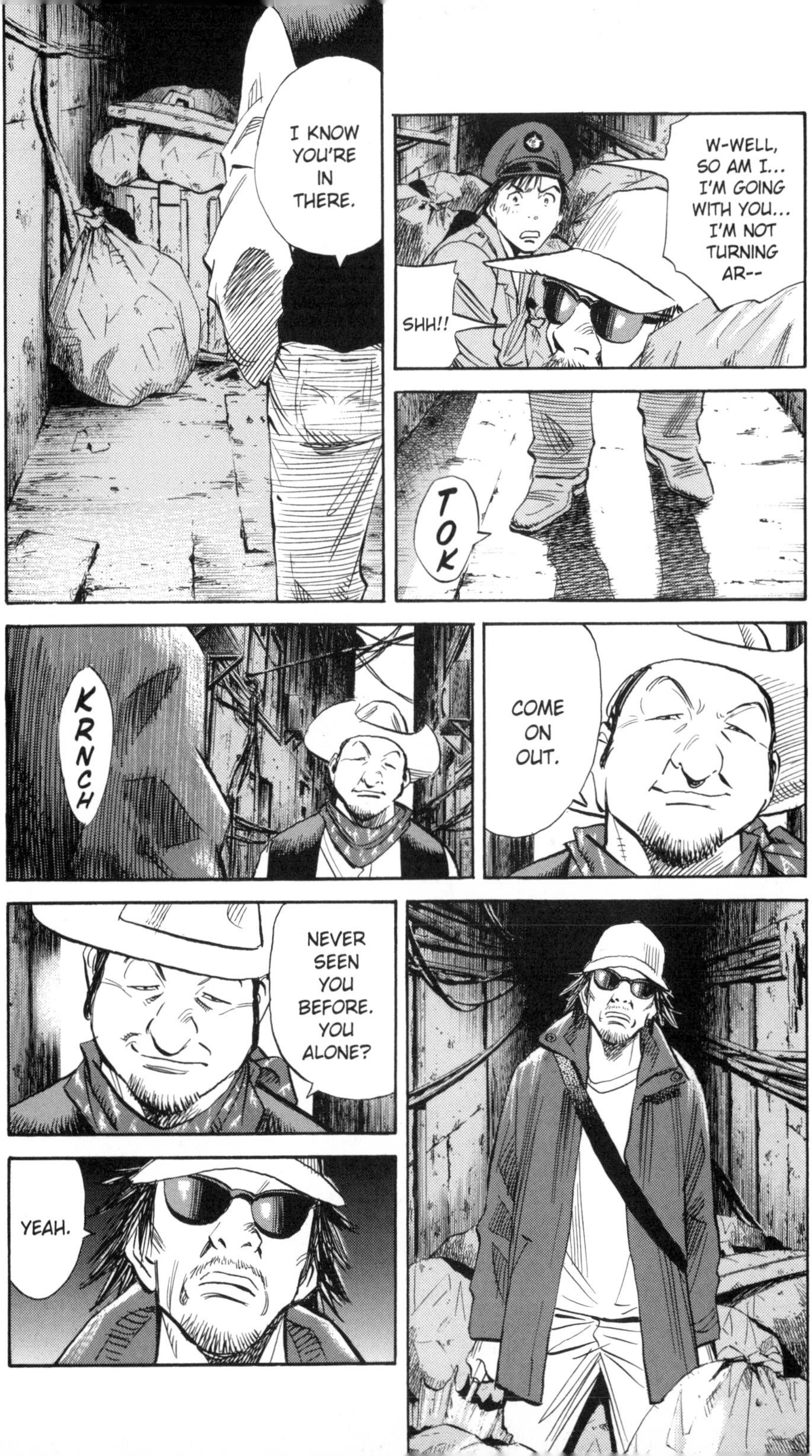
W-WELL, SO AM I... I'M GOING WITH YOU... I'M NOT TURNING AR--
SHH!!
TOK
I KNOW YOU'RE IN THERE.
COME ON OUT.
KRNCH
NEVER SEEN YOU BEFORE. YOU ALONE?
YEAH.

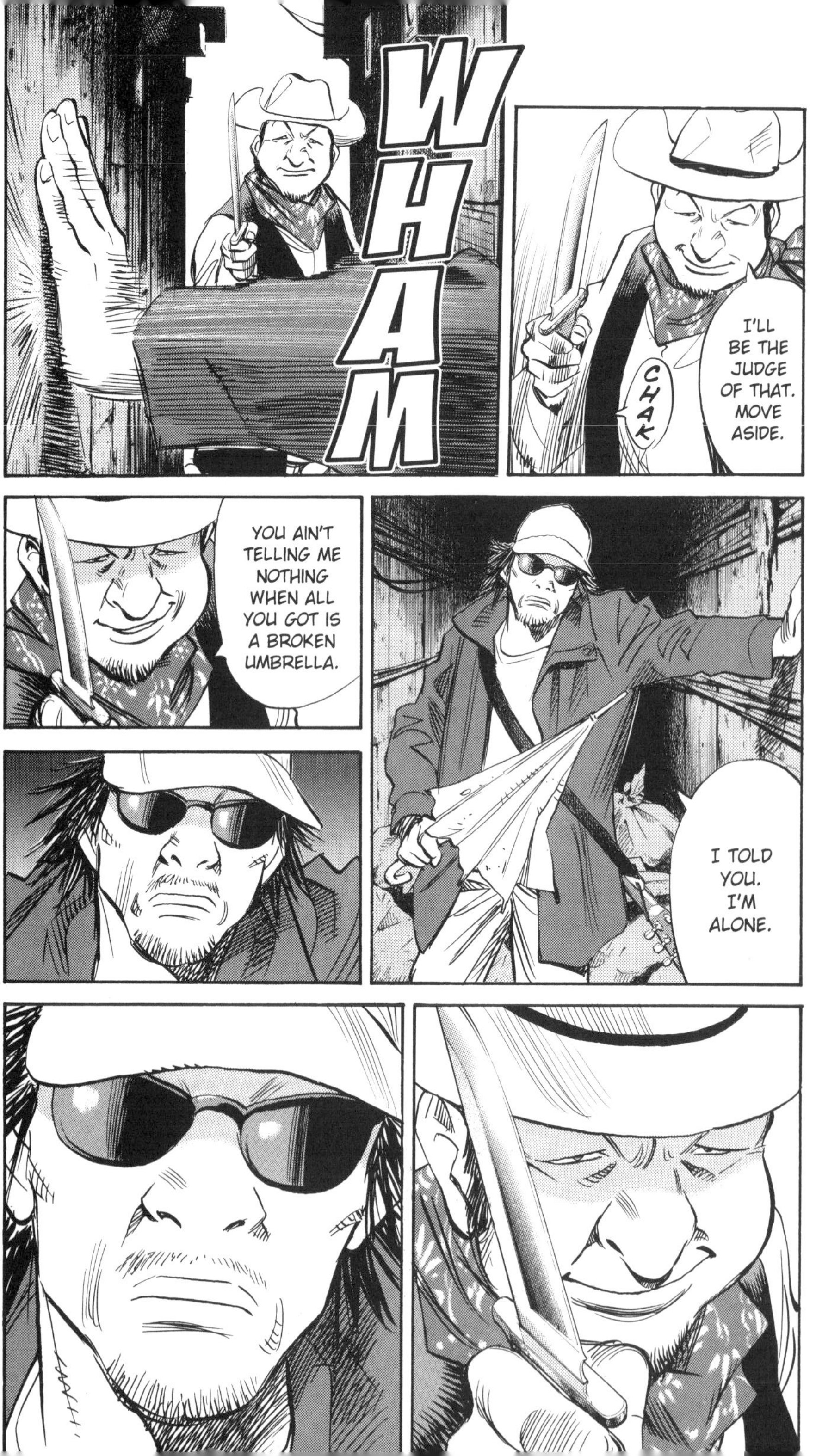
I'LL BE THE JUDGE OF THAT. MOVE ASIDE.
CHAK
WHAM
I TOLD YOU. I'M ALONE.
YOU AIN'T TELLING ME NOTHING WHEN ALL YOU GOT IS A BROKEN UMBRELLA.

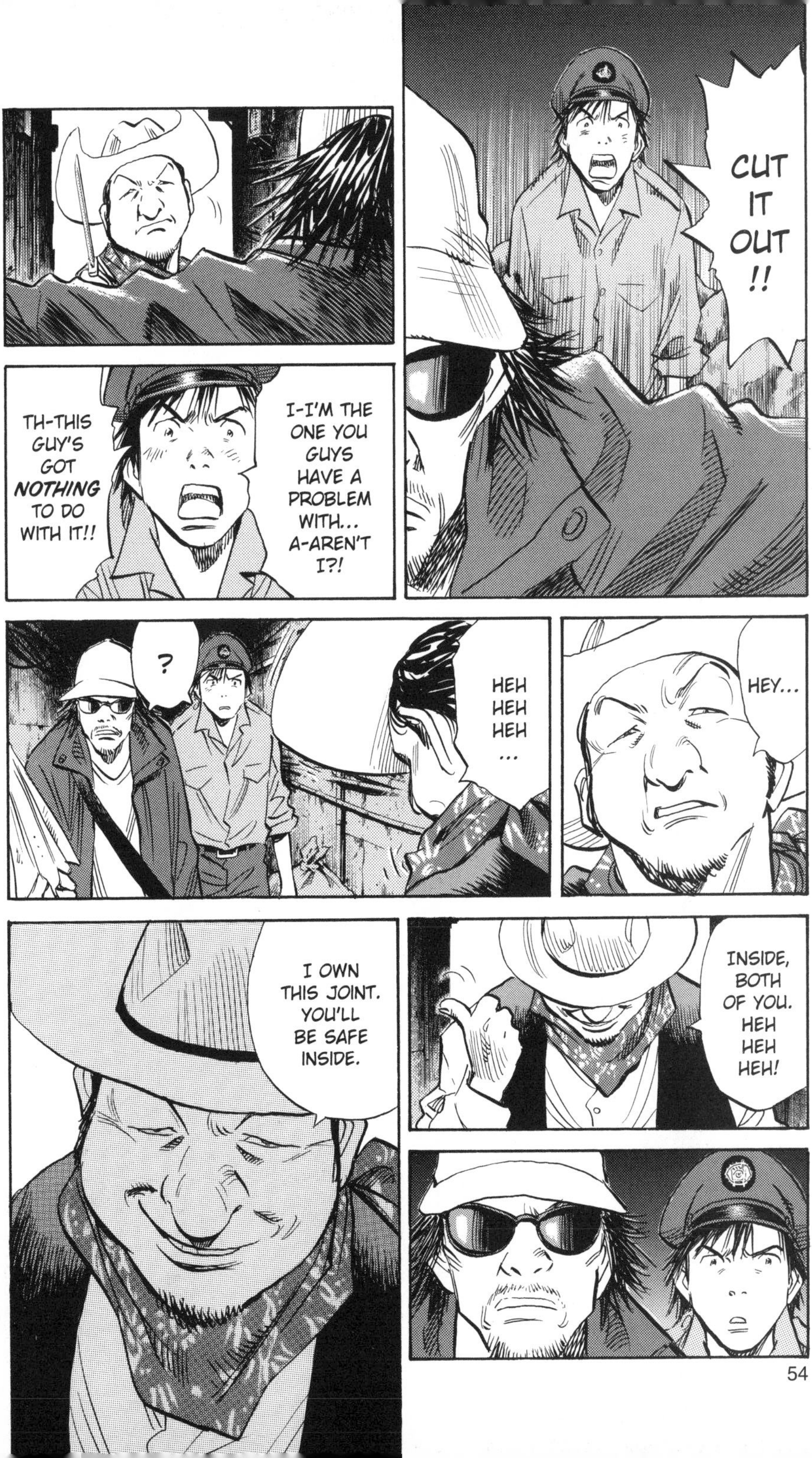
CUT IT OUT!!
I-I'M THE ONE YOU GUYS HAVE A PROBLEM WITH... A-AREN'T I?!
TH-THIS GUY'S GOT NOTHING TO DO WITH IT!!
HEY...
HEH HEH HEH...
?
INSIDE, BOTH OF YOU. HEH HEH HEH!
I OWN THIS JOINT. YOU'LL BE SAFE INSIDE.

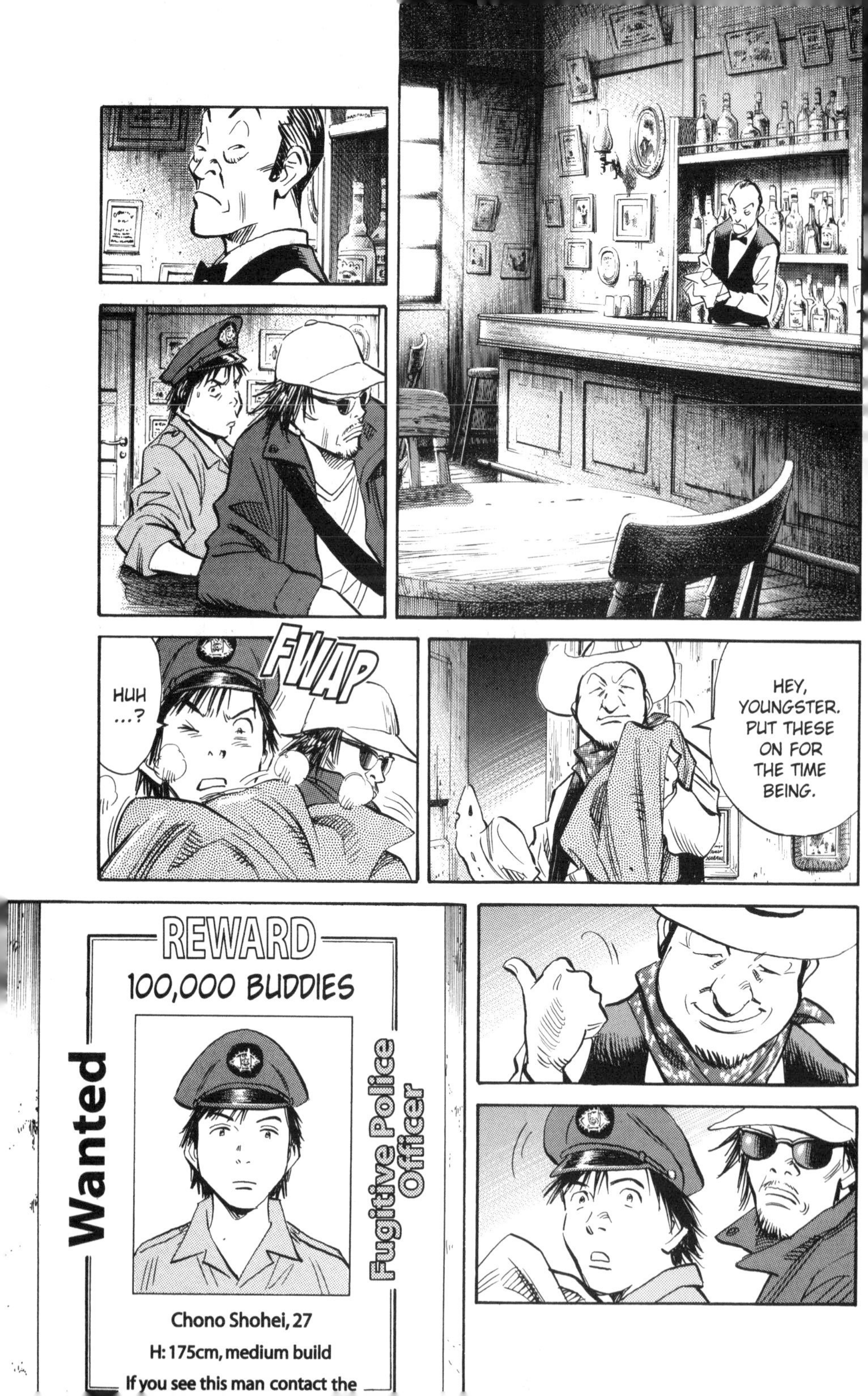
HEY, YOUNGSTER. PUT THESE ON FOR THE TIME BEING.
FWAP
HUH ...?
REWARD
100,000 BUDDIES
Wanted
Fugitive Police Officer
Chono Shohei, 27
H: 175cm, medium build
If you see this man contact the

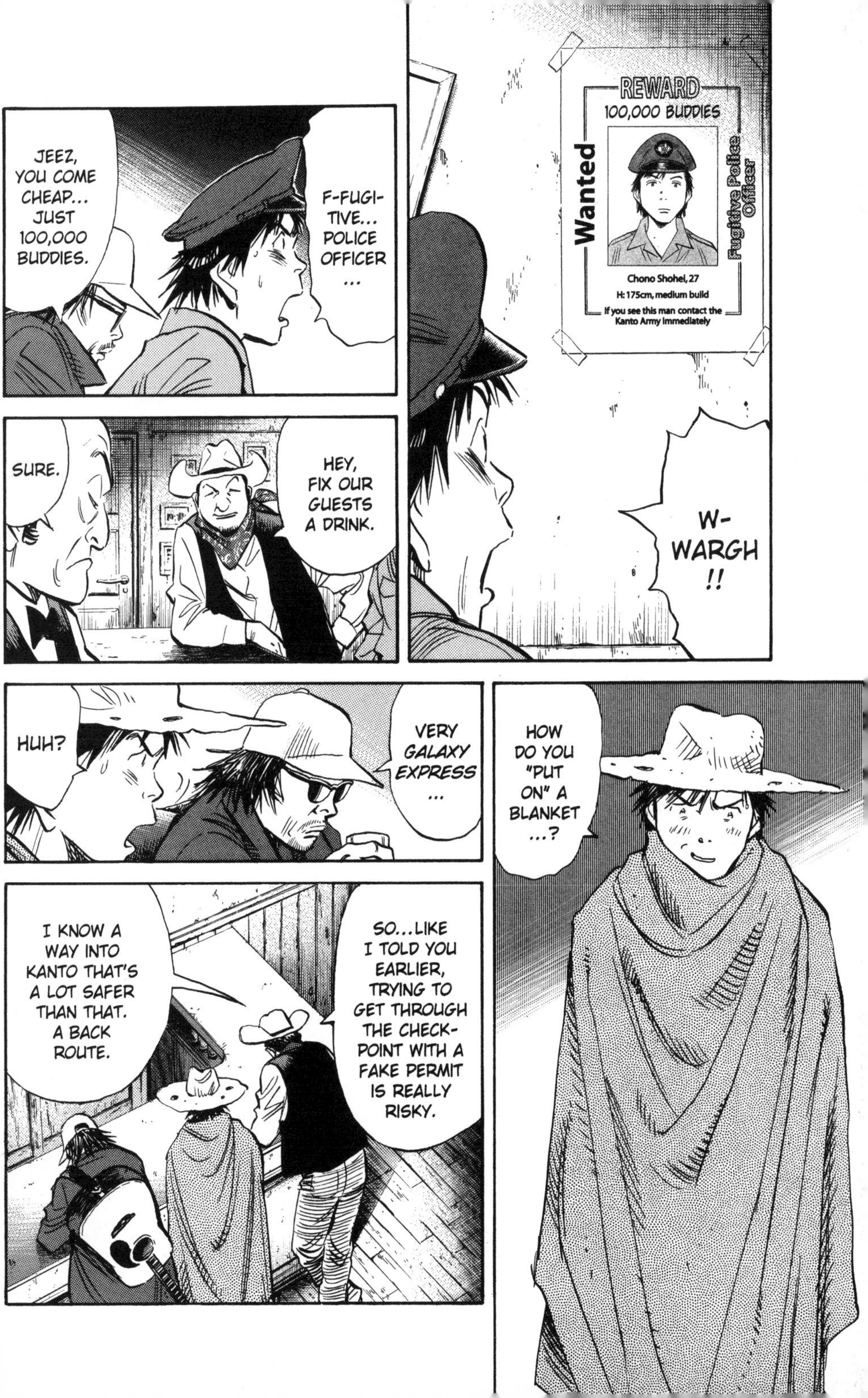
REWARD
100,000 BUDDIES
Wanted
Fugitive Police Officer
Chono Shohei, 27
H: 175cm, medium build
If you see this man contact the Kanto Army immediately
W-WARGH!!
F-FUGITIVE... POLICE OFFICER...
JEEZ, YOU COME CHEAP... JUST 100,000 BUDDIES.
HEY, FIX OUR GUESTS A DRINK.
SURE.
HOW DO YOU "PUT ON" A BLANKET...?
VERY GALAXY EXPRESS...
HUH?
SO...LIKE I TOLD YOU EARLIER, TRYING TO GET THROUGH THE CHECKPOINT WITH A FAKE PERMIT IS REALLY RISKY.
I KNOW A WAY INTO KANTO THAT'S A LOT SAFER THAN THAT. A BACK ROUTE.

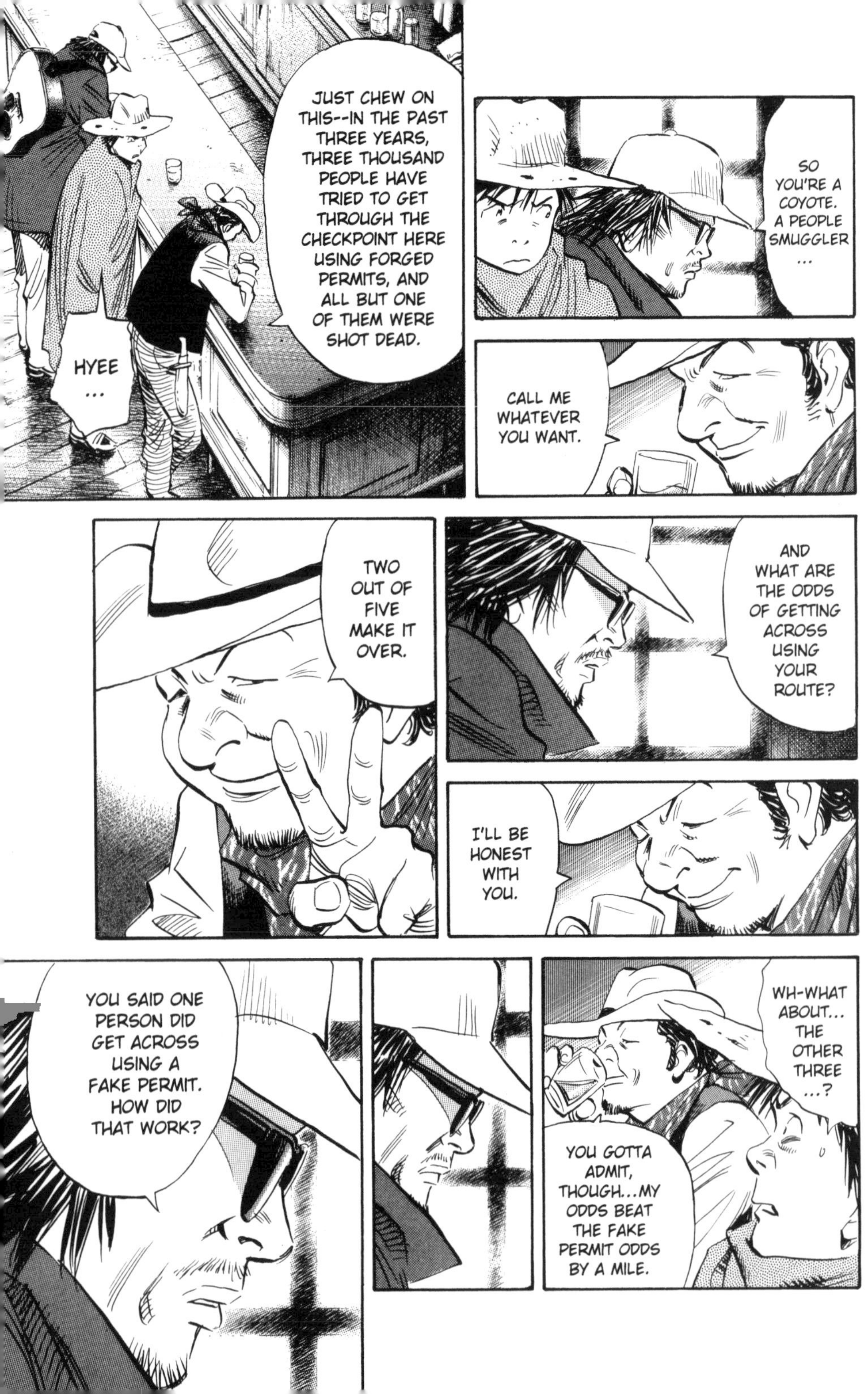
SO YOU'RE A COYOTE. A PEOPLE SMUGGLER ...
CALL ME WHATEVER YOU WANT.
JUST CHEW ON THIS--IN THE PAST THREE YEARS, THREE THOUSAND PEOPLE HAVE TRIED TO GET THROUGH THE CHECKPOINT HERE USING FORGED PERMITS, AND ALL BUT ONE OF THEM WERE SHOT DEAD.
HYEE ...
AND WHAT ARE THE ODDS OF GETTING ACROSS USING YOUR ROUTE?
I'LL BE HONEST WITH YOU.
TWO OUT OF FIVE MAKE IT OVER.
WH-WHAT ABOUT... THE OTHER THREE ...?
YOU GOTTA ADMIT, THOUGH...MY ODDS BEAT THE FAKE PERMIT ODDS BY A MILE.
YOU SAID ONE PERSON DID GET ACROSS USING A FAKE PERMIT. HOW DID THAT WORK?

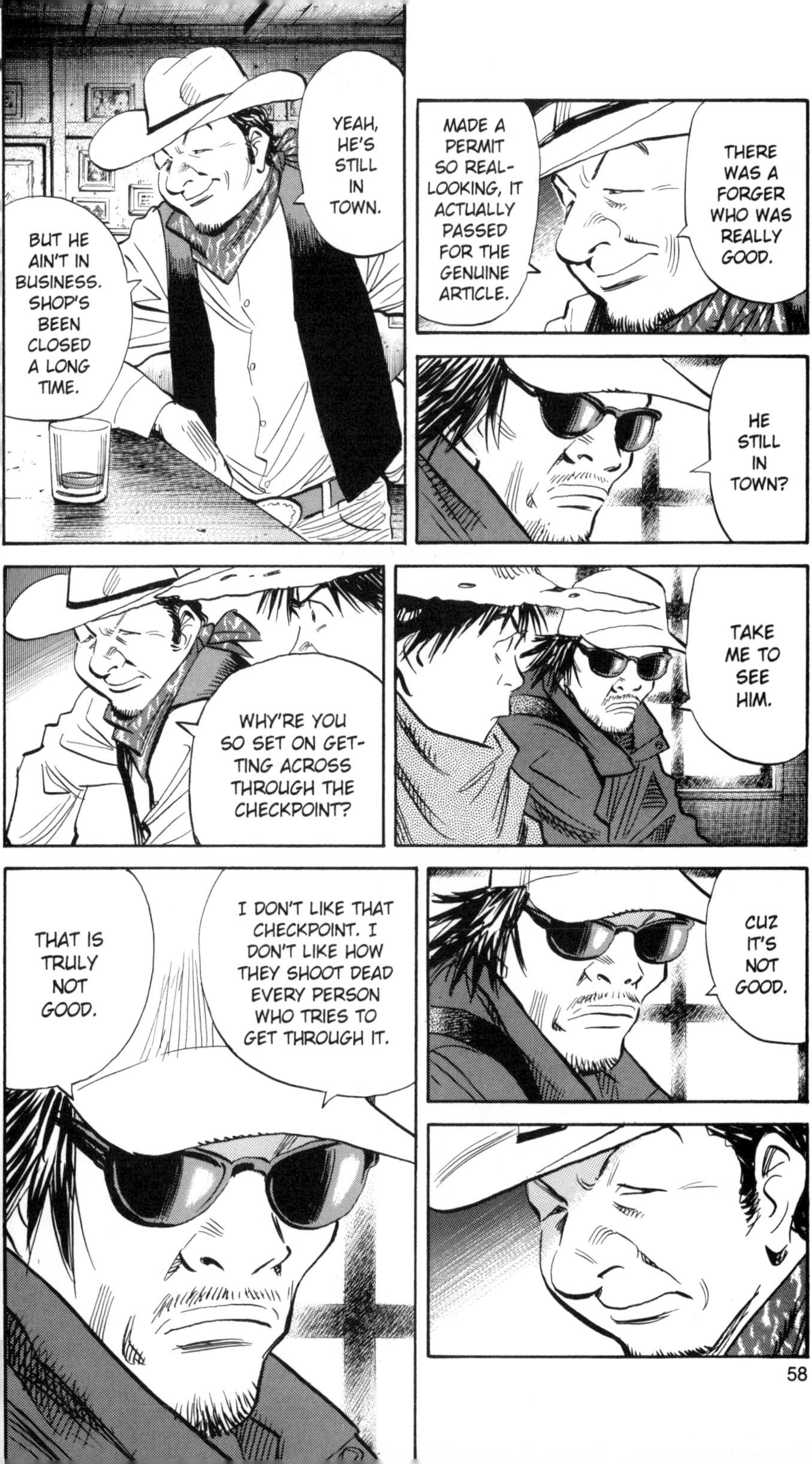
THERE WAS A FORGER WHO WAS REALLY GOOD.
MADE A PERMIT SO REAL-LOOKING, IT ACTUALLY PASSED FOR THE GENUINE ARTICLE.
HE STILL IN TOWN?
YEAH, HE'S STILL IN TOWN.
BUT HE AIN'T IN BUSINESS. SHOP'S BEEN CLOSED A LONG TIME.
TAKE ME TO SEE HIM.
WHY'RE YOU SO SET ON GETTING ACROSS THROUGH THE CHECKPOINT?
CUZ IT'S NOT GOOD.
I DON'T LIKE THAT CHECKPOINT. I DON'T LIKE HOW THEY SHOOT DEAD EVERY PERSON WHO TRIES TO GET THROUGH IT.
THAT IS TRULY NOT GOOD.

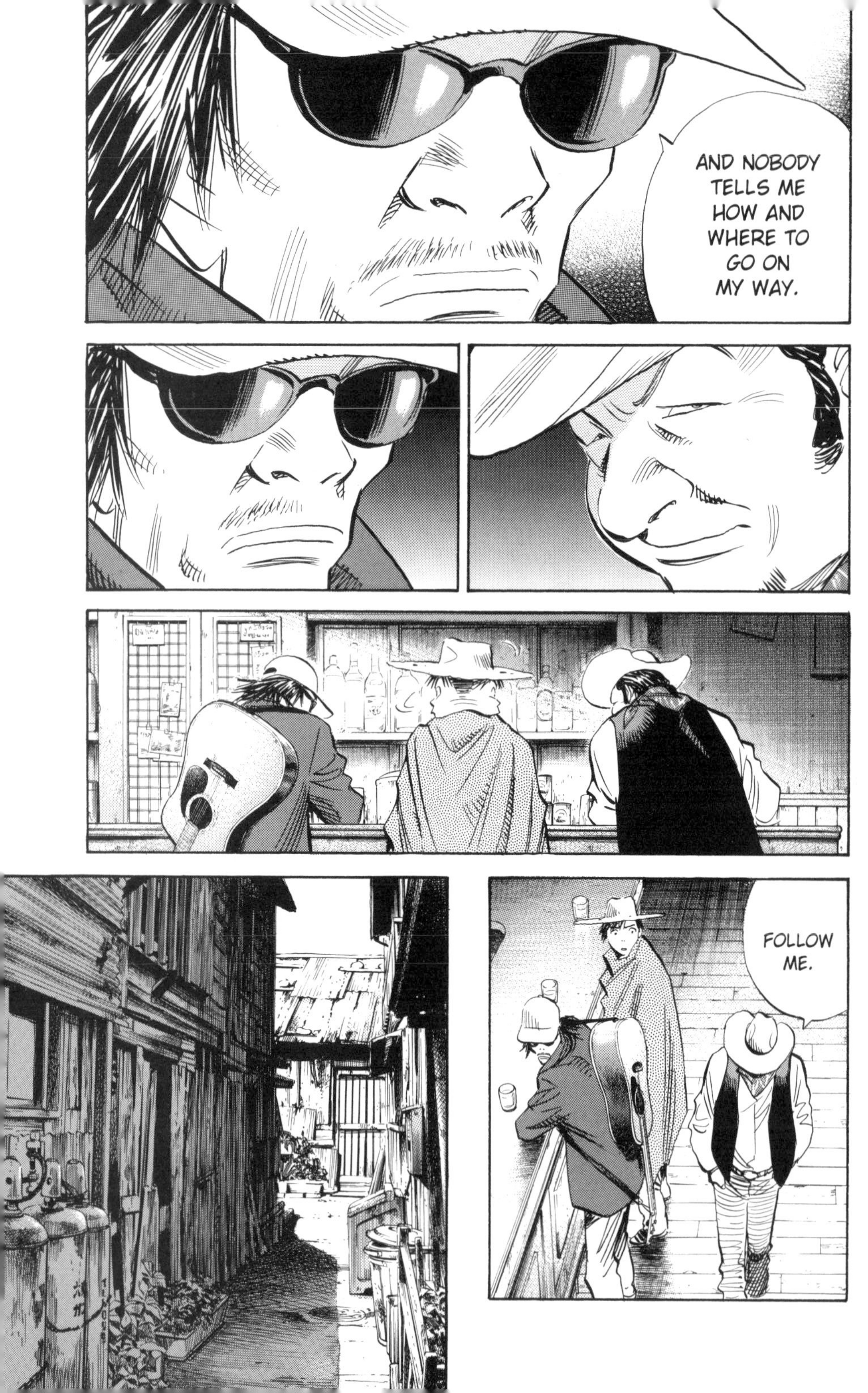
AND NOBODY TELLS ME HOW AND WHERE TO GO ON MY WAY.
FOLLOW ME.

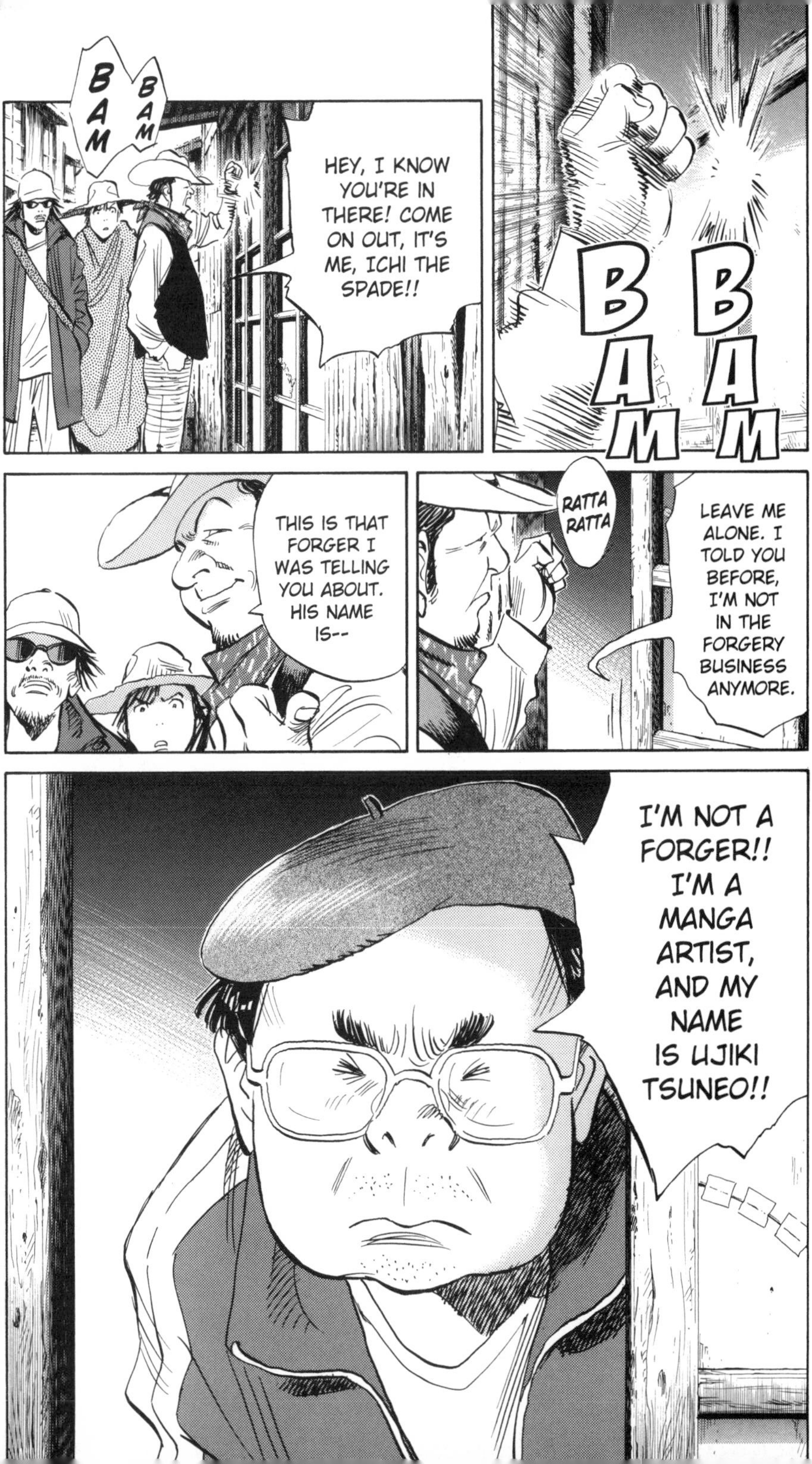
BAM BAM
BAM BAM
HEY, I KNOW YOU'RE IN THERE! COME ON OUT, IT'S ME, ICHI THE SPADE!!
RATTA RATTA
LEAVE ME ALONE. I TOLD YOU BEFORE, I'M NOT IN THE FORGERY BUSINESS ANYMORE.
THIS IS THAT FORGER I WAS TELLING YOU ABOUT. HIS NAME IS--
I'M NOT A FORGER!! I'M A MANGA ARTIST, AND MY NAME IS UJIKI TSUNEO!!

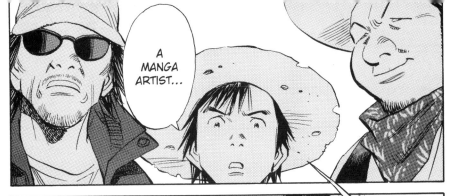

A MANGA ARTIST...

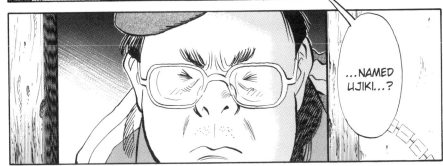

...NAMED UJIKI...?

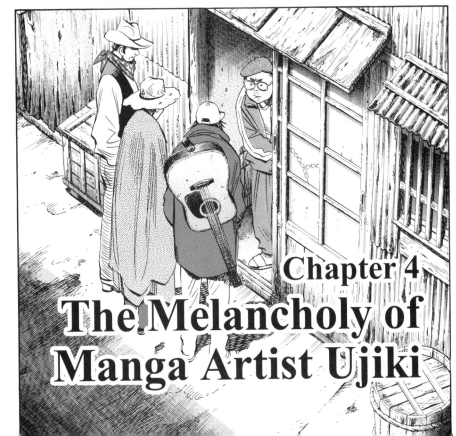

Chapter 4
The Melancholy of
Manga Artist Ujiki

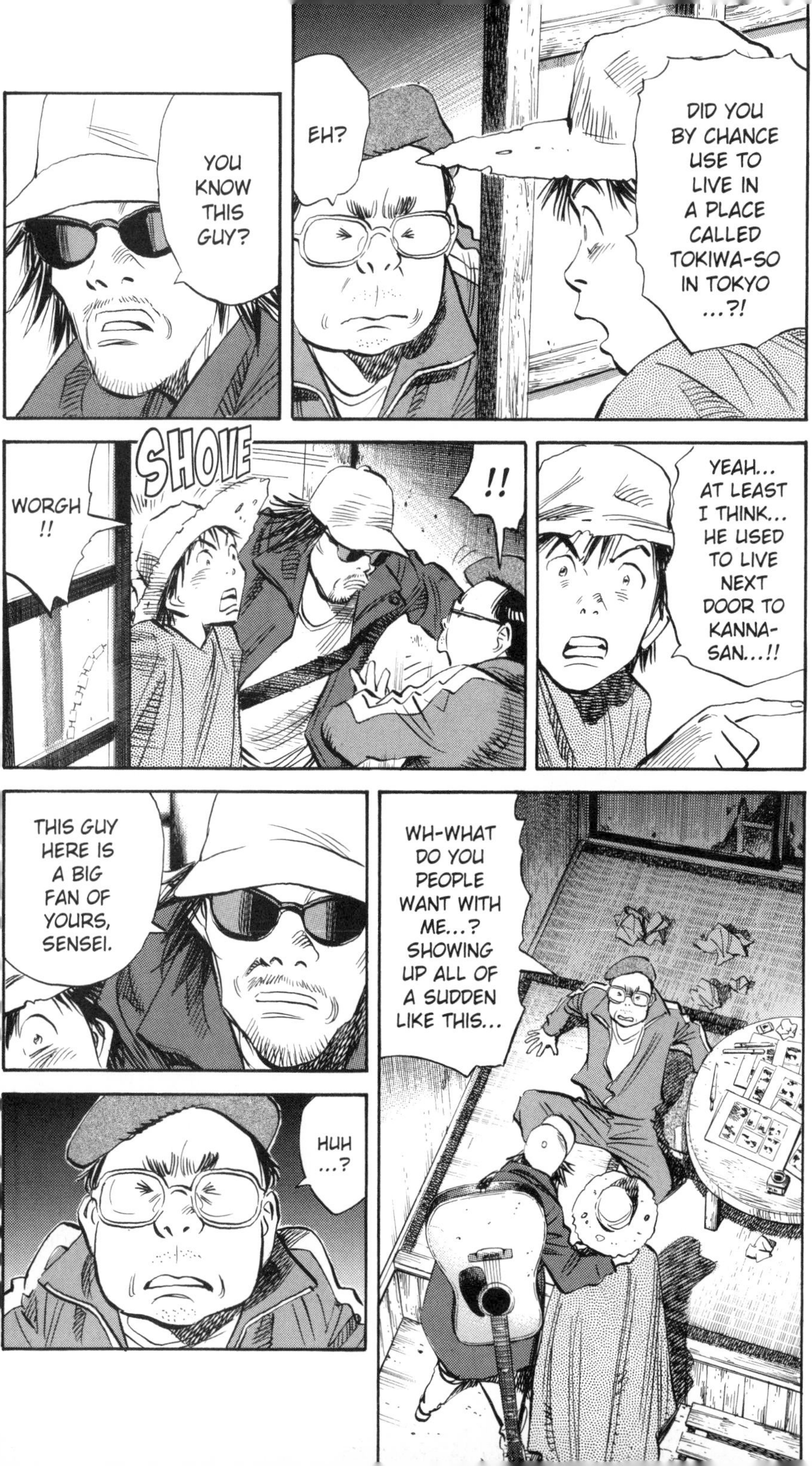
DID YOU BY CHANCE USE TO LIVE IN A PLACE CALLED TOKIWA-SO IN TOKYO ...?!
EH?
YOU KNOW THIS GUY?
YEAH... AT LEAST I THINK... HE USED TO LIVE NEXT DOOR TO KANNA-SAN...!!
!!
SHOVE
WORGH !!
WH-WHAT DO YOU PEOPLE WANT WITH ME...? SHOWING UP ALL OF A SUDDEN LIKE THIS...
THIS GUY HERE IS A BIG FAN OF YOURS, SENSEI.
HUH ...?

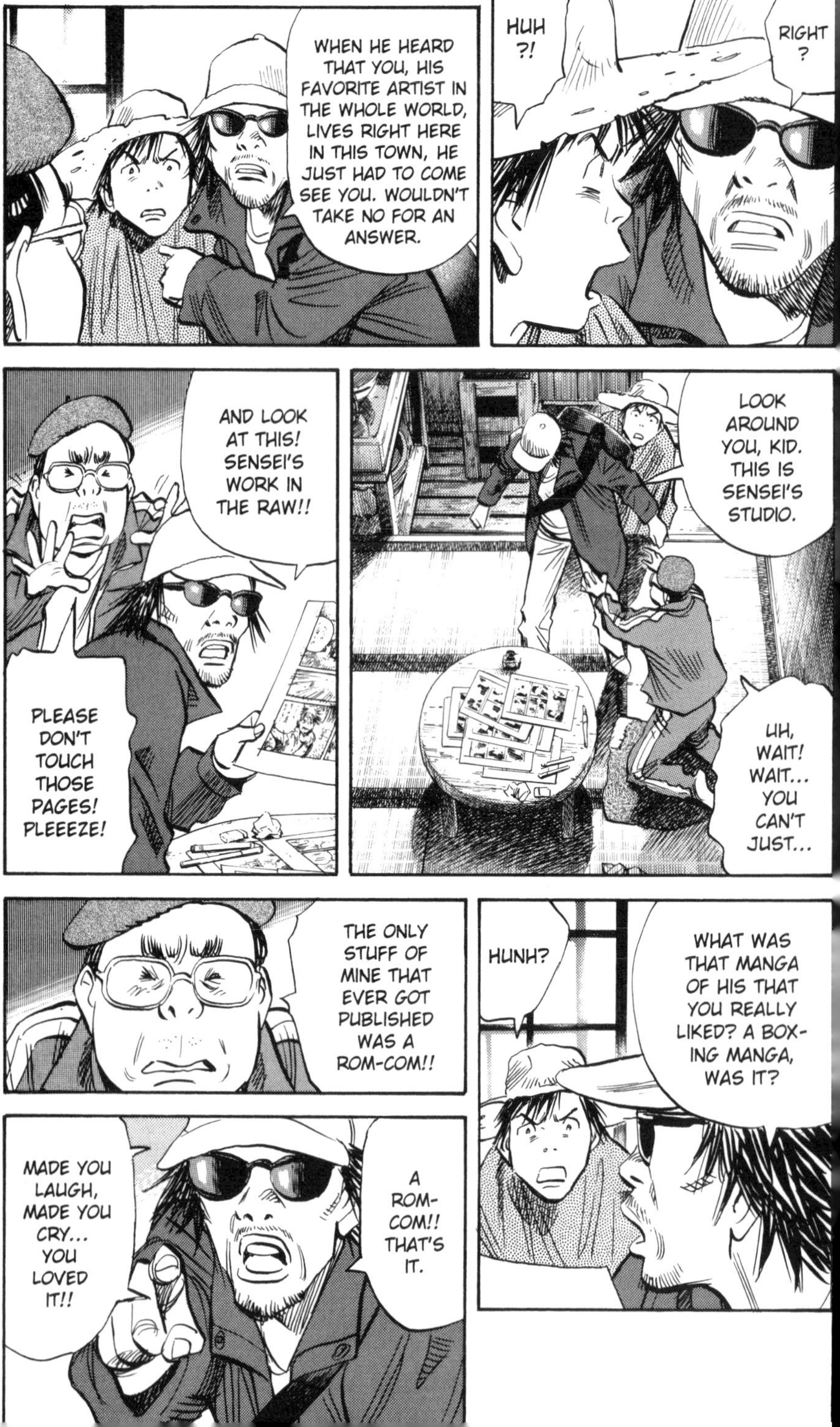
RIGHT ?
HUH ?!
WHEN HE HEARD THAT YOU, HIS FAVORITE ARTIST IN THE WHOLE WORLD, LIVES RIGHT HERE IN THIS TOWN, HE JUST HAD TO COME SEE YOU. WOULDN'T TAKE NO FOR AN ANSWER.
LOOK AROUND YOU, KID. THIS IS SENSEI'S STUDIO.
UH, WAIT! WAIT... YOU CAN'T JUST...
AND LOOK AT THIS! SENSEI'S WORK IN THE RAW!!
PLEASE DON'T TOUCH THOSE PAGES! PLEEEZE!
WHAT WAS THAT MANGA OF HIS THAT YOU REALLY LIKED? A BOX-ING MANGA, WAS IT?
HUNH?
THE ONLY STUFF OF MINE THAT EVER GOT PUBLISHED WAS A ROM-COM!!
A ROM-COM!! THAT'S IT.
MADE YOU LAUGH, MADE YOU CRY... YOU LOVED IT!!

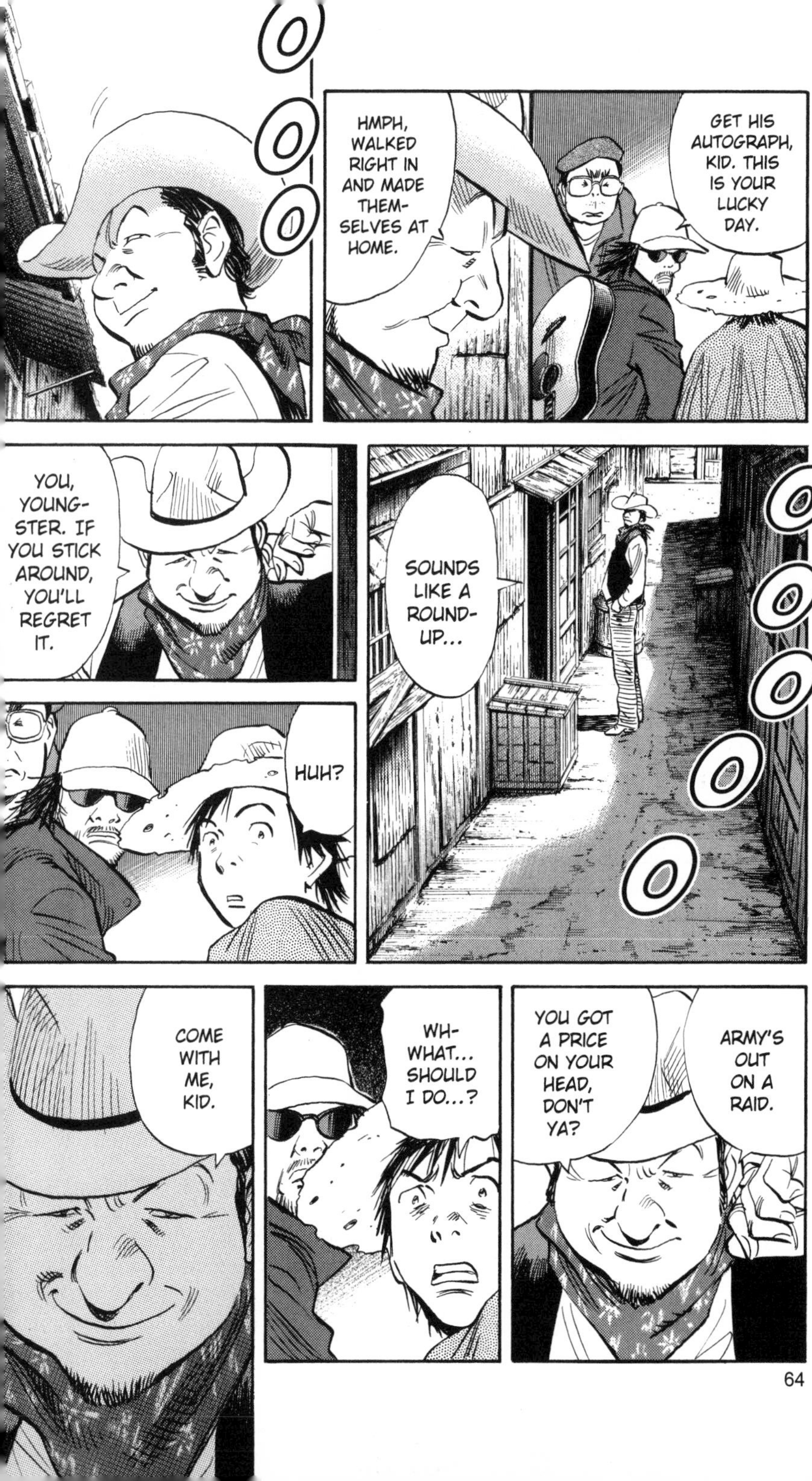
GET HIS AUTOGRAPH, KID. THIS IS YOUR LUCKY DAY.
HMPH, WALKED RIGHT IN AND MADE THEMSELVES AT HOME.
SOUNDS LIKE A ROUND-UP...
YOU, YOUNGSTER. IF YOU STICK AROUND, YOU'LL REGRET IT.
HUH?
ARMY'S OUT ON A RAID.
YOU GOT A PRICE ON YOUR HEAD, DON'T YA?
WH-WHAT... SHOULD I DO...?
COME WITH ME, KID.

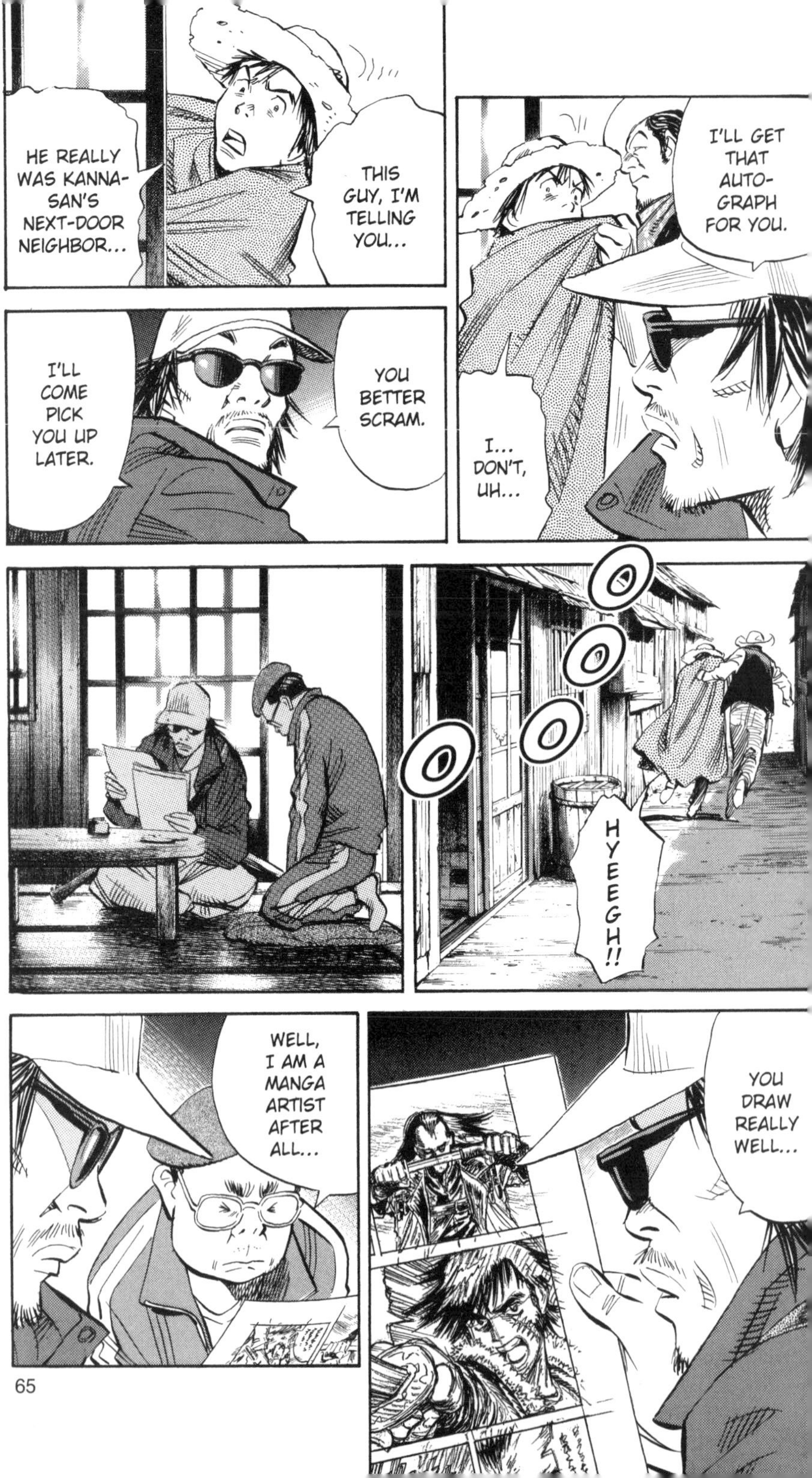
I'LL GET THAT AUTO-GRAPH FOR YOU.
I... DON'T, UH...
THIS GUY, I'M TELLING YOU...
HE REALLY WAS KANNA-SAN'S NEXT-DOOR NEIGHBOR...
YOU BETTER SCRAM.
I'LL COME PICK YOU UP LATER.
HYEEEGH!!
YOU DRAW REALLY WELL...
WELL, I AM A MANGA ARTIST AFTER ALL...

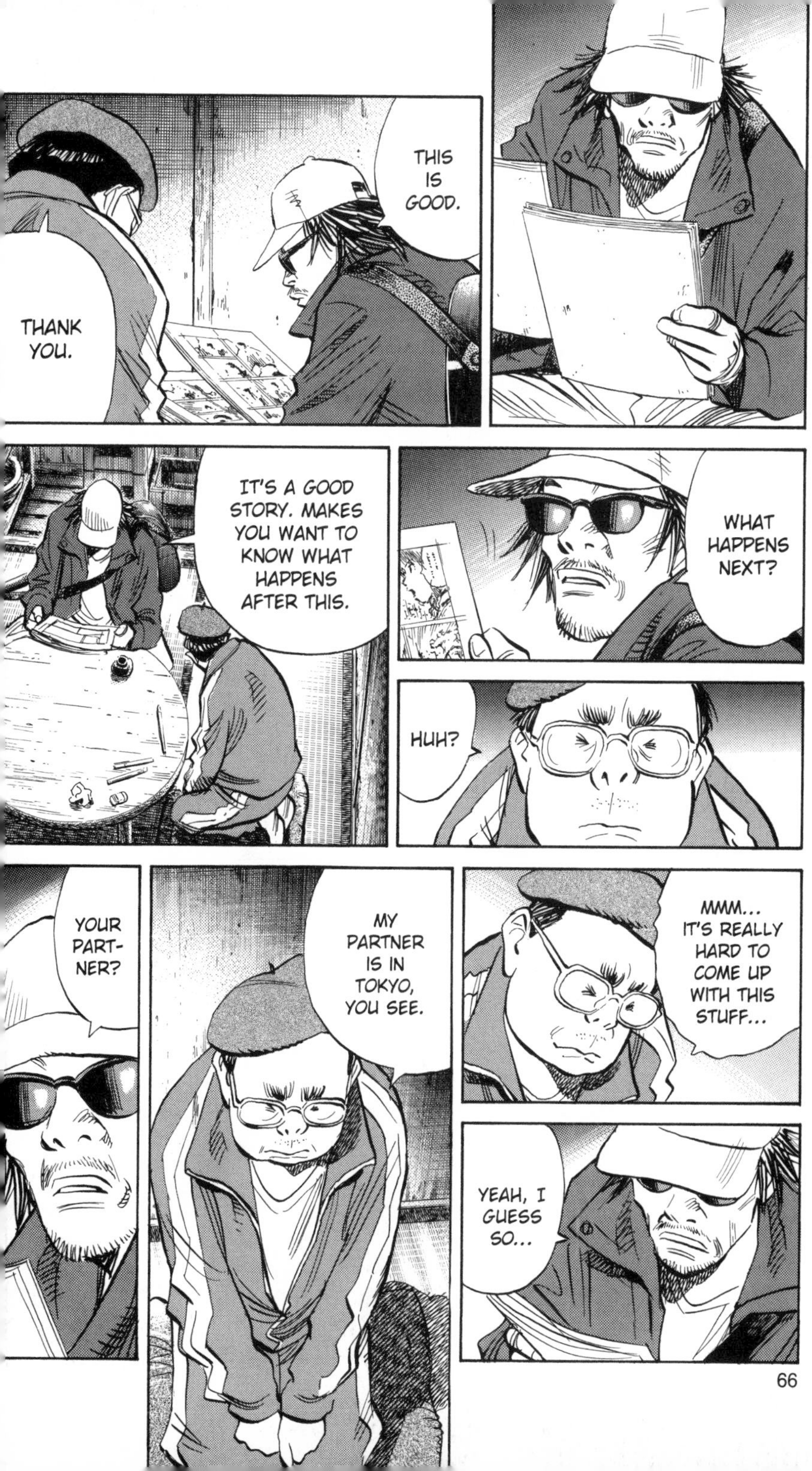
THIS IS GOOD.
THANK YOU.
WHAT HAPPENS NEXT?
HUH?
IT'S A GOOD STORY. MAKES YOU WANT TO KNOW WHAT HAPPENS AFTER THIS.
MMM... IT'S REALLY HARD TO COME UP WITH THIS STUFF...
YEAH, I GUESS SO...
MY PARTNER IS IN TOKYO, YOU SEE.
YOUR PART-NER?

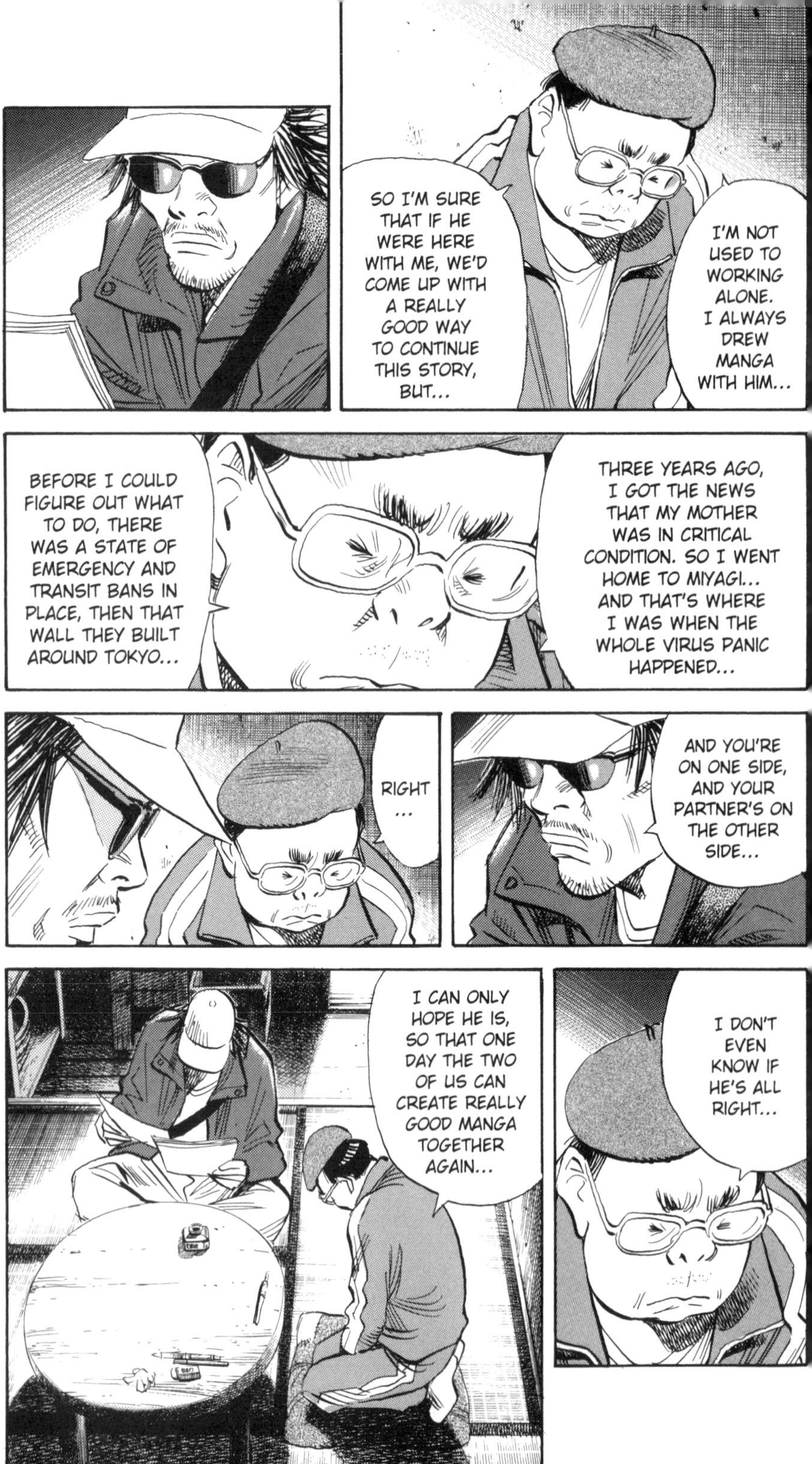

I'M NOT USED TO WORKING ALONE. I ALWAYS DREW MANGA WITH HIM...
SO I'M SURE THAT IF HE WERE HERE WITH ME, WE'D COME UP WITH A REALLY GOOD WAY TO CONTINUE THIS STORY, BUT...
THREE YEARS AGO, I GOT THE NEWS THAT MY MOTHER WAS IN CRITICAL CONDITION. SO I WENT HOME TO MIYAGI... AND THAT'S WHERE I WAS WHEN THE WHOLE VIRUS PANIC HAPPENED...
BEFORE I COULD FIGURE OUT WHAT TO DO, THERE WAS A STATE OF EMERGENCY AND TRANSIT BANS IN PLACE, THEN THAT WALL THEY BUILT AROUND TOKYO...
AND YOU'RE ON ONE SIDE, AND YOUR PARTNER'S ON THE OTHER SIDE...
RIGHT ...
I DON'T EVEN KNOW IF HE'S ALL RIGHT...
I CAN ONLY HOPE HE IS, SO THAT ONE DAY THE TWO OF US CAN CREATE REALLY GOOD MANGA TOGETHER AGAIN...

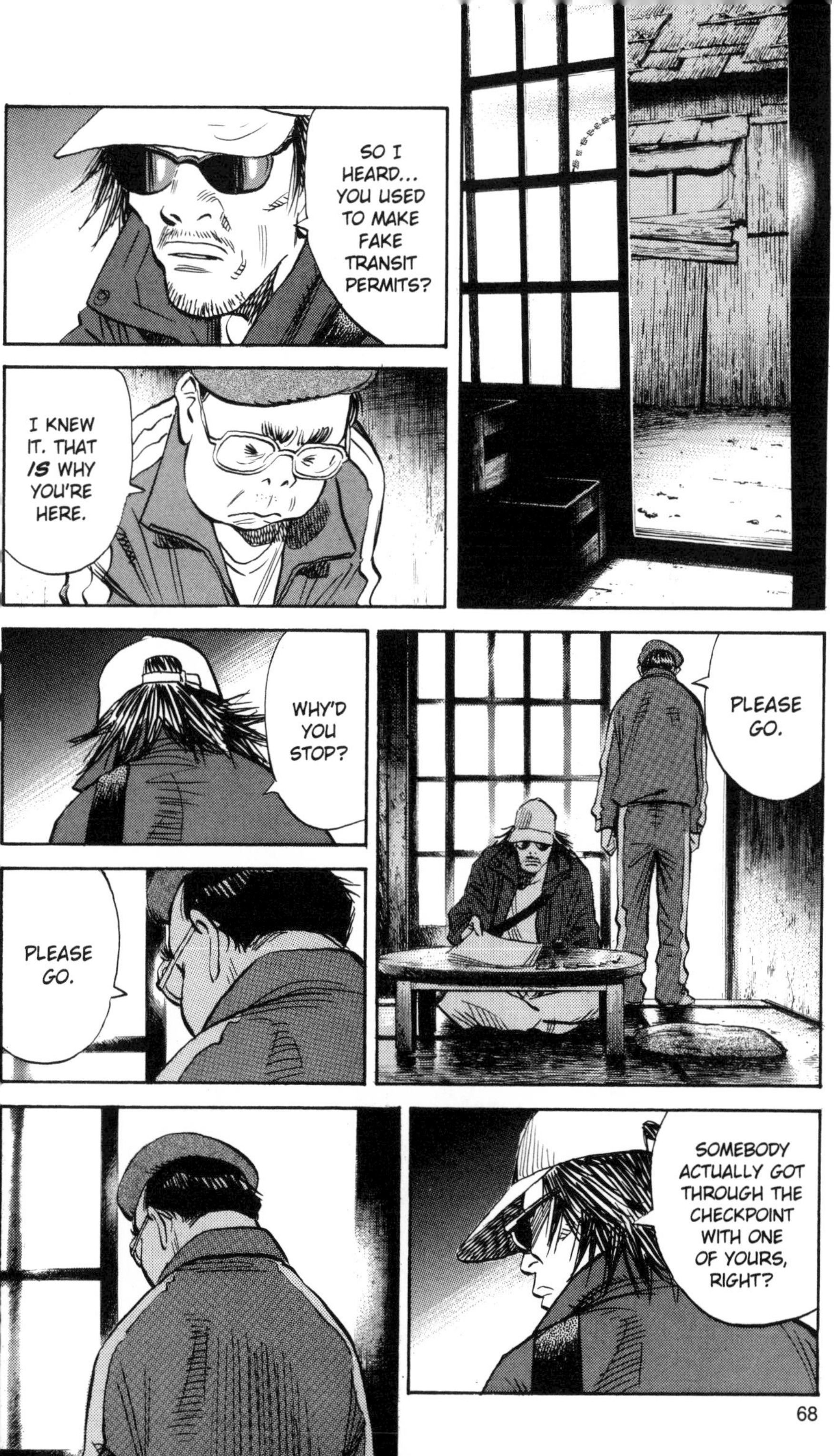
SO I HEARD... YOU USED TO MAKE FAKE TRANSIT PERMITS?
I KNEW IT. THAT *IS* WHY YOU'RE HERE.
PLEASE GO.
WHY'D YOU STOP?
PLEASE GO.
SOMEBODY ACTUALLY GOT THROUGH THE CHECKPOINT WITH ONE OF YOURS, RIGHT?

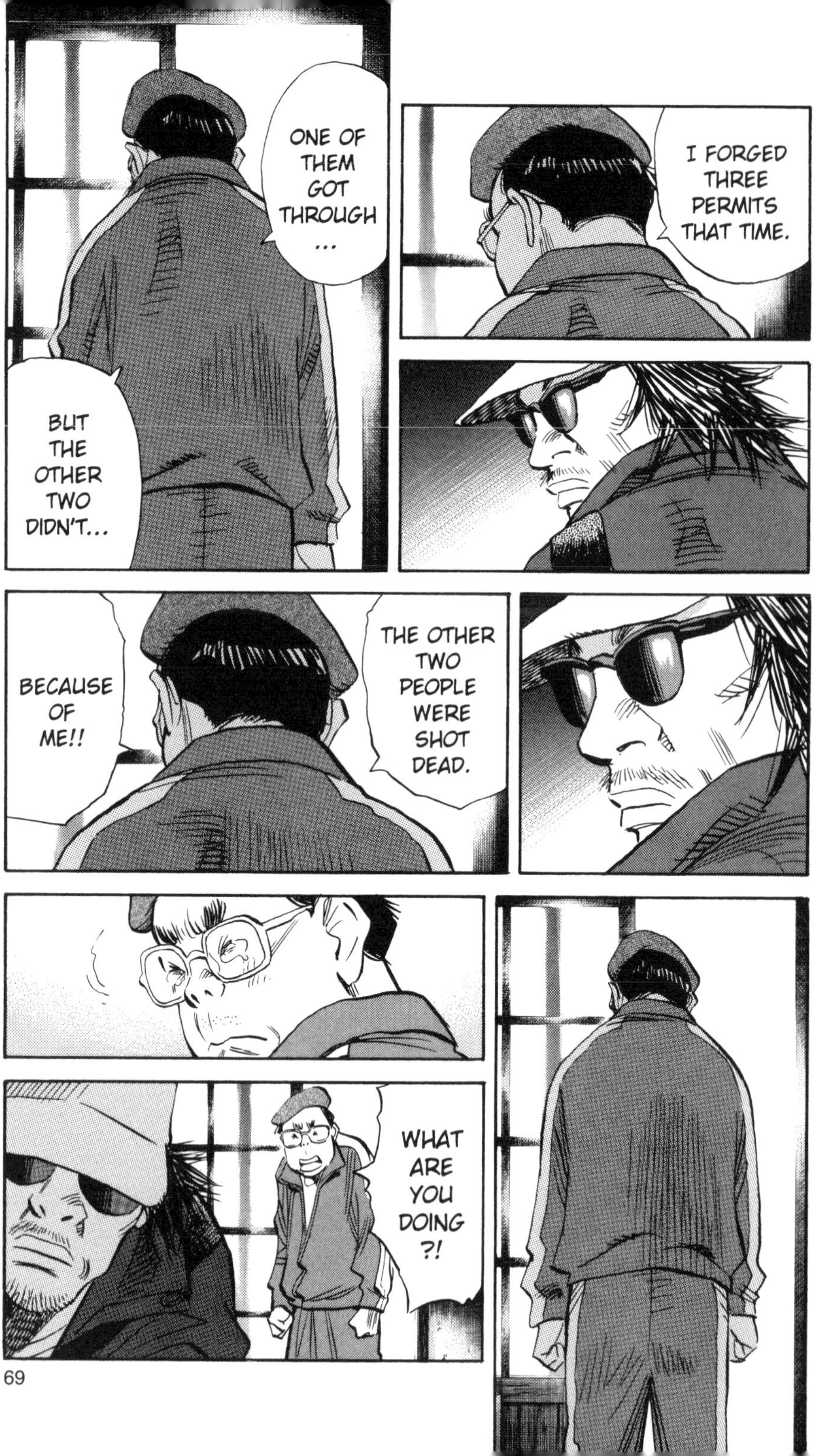
I FORGED THREE PERMITS THAT TIME.
ONE OF THEM GOT THROUGH...
BUT THE OTHER TWO DIDN'T...
THE OTHER TWO PEOPLE WERE SHOT DEAD.
BECAUSE OF ME!!
WHAT ARE YOU DOING?!

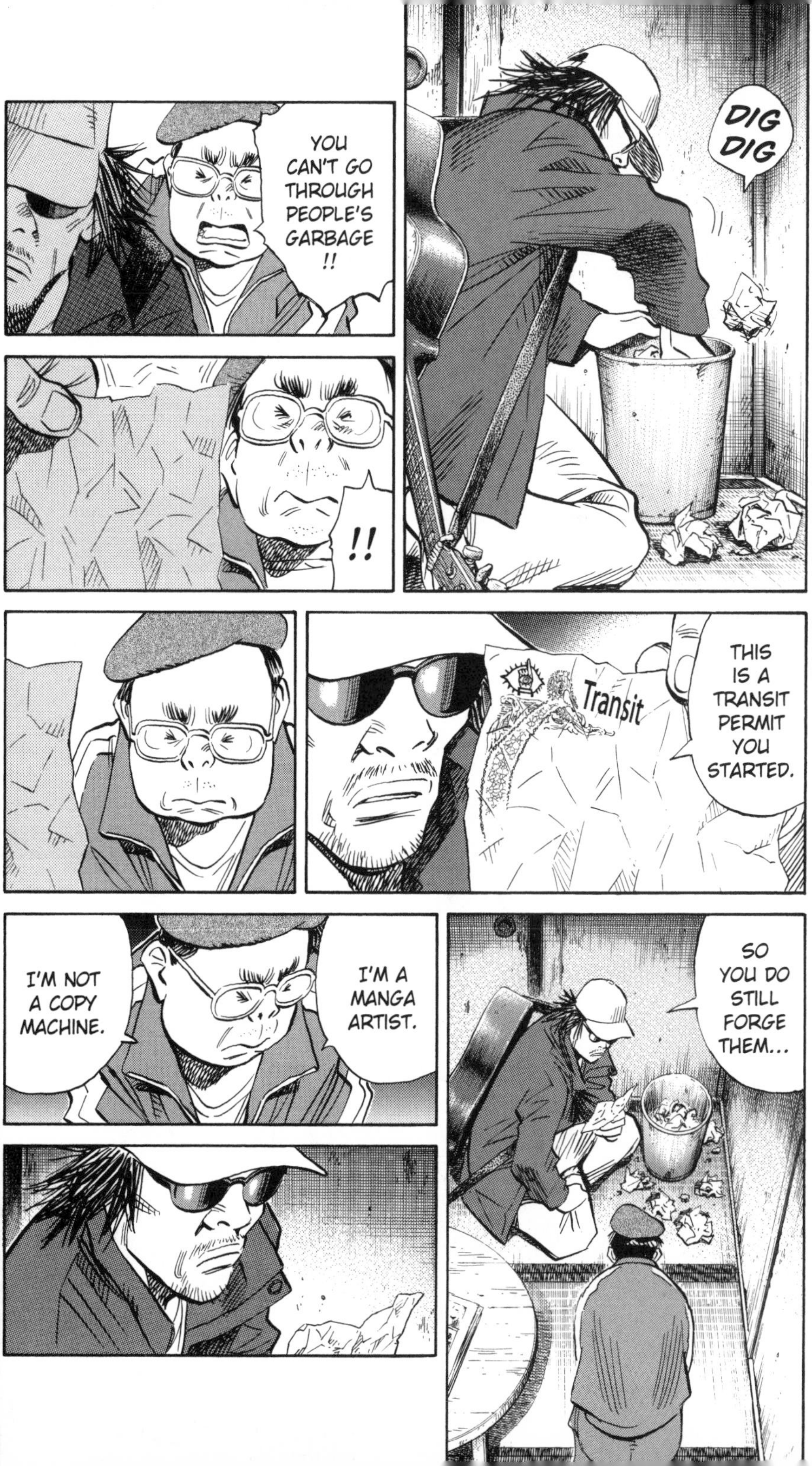
DIG DIG
YOU CAN'T GO THROUGH PEOPLE'S GARBAGE!!
!!
THIS IS A TRANSIT PERMIT YOU STARTED.
Transit
SO YOU DO STILL FORGE THEM...
I'M A MANGA ARTIST.
I'M NOT A COPY MACHINE.

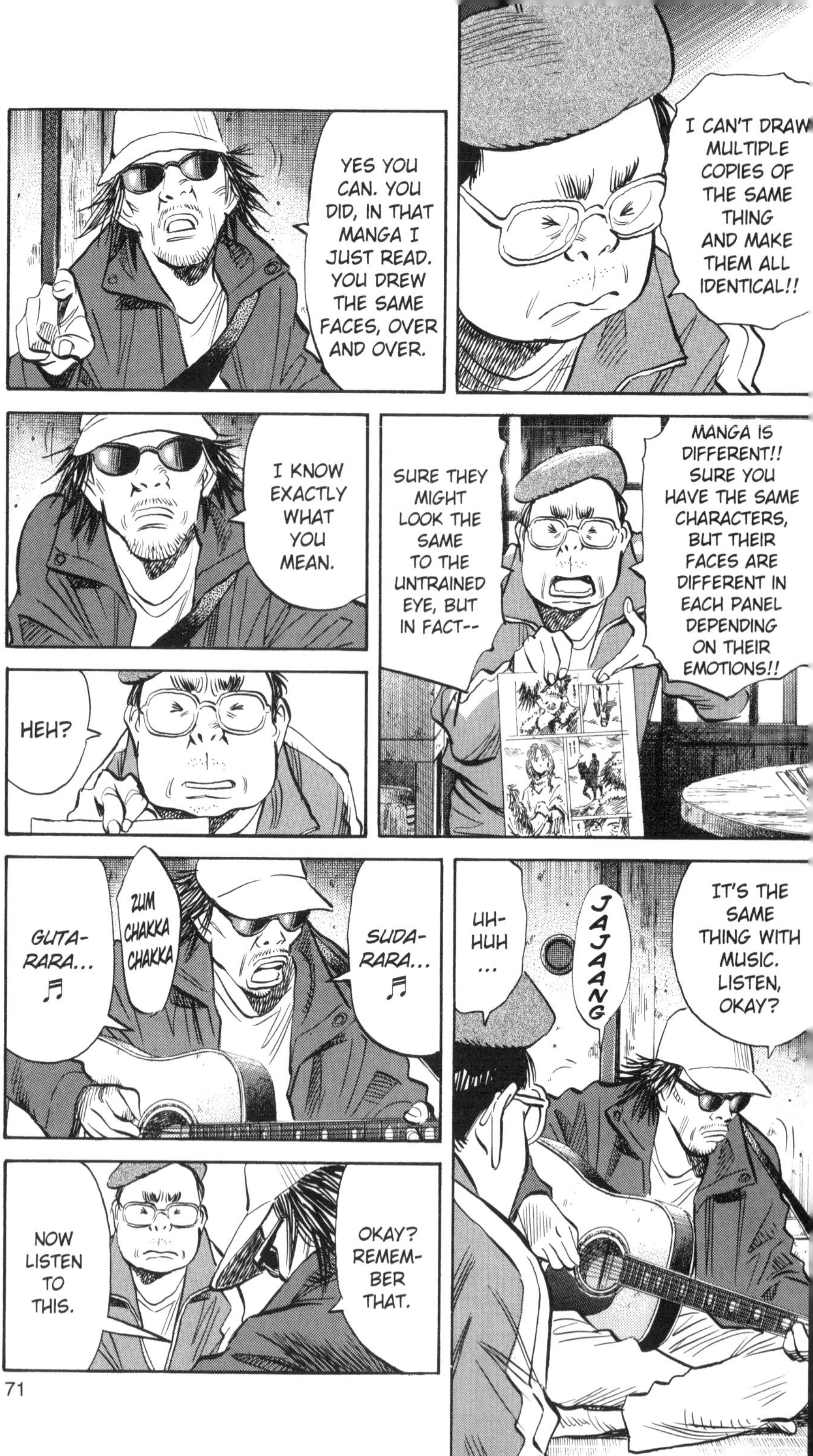
I CAN'T DRAW MULTIPLE COPIES OF THE SAME THING AND MAKE THEM ALL IDENTICAL!!
YES YOU CAN. YOU DID, IN THAT MANGA I JUST READ. YOU DREW THE SAME FACES, OVER AND OVER.
MANGA IS DIFFERENT!! SURE YOU HAVE THE SAME CHARACTERS, BUT THEIR FACES ARE DIFFERENT IN EACH PANEL DEPENDING ON THEIR EMOTIONS!!
SURE THEY MIGHT LOOK THE SAME TO THE UNTRAINED EYE, BUT IN FACT--
I KNOW EXACTLY WHAT YOU MEAN.
HEH?
IT'S THE SAME THING WITH MUSIC. LISTEN, OKAY?
JAJAANG
UH-HUH...
SUDA-RARA... ♫
ZUM CHAKKA CHAKKA
GUTA-RARA... ♫
OKAY? REMEMBER THAT.
NOW LISTEN TO THIS.

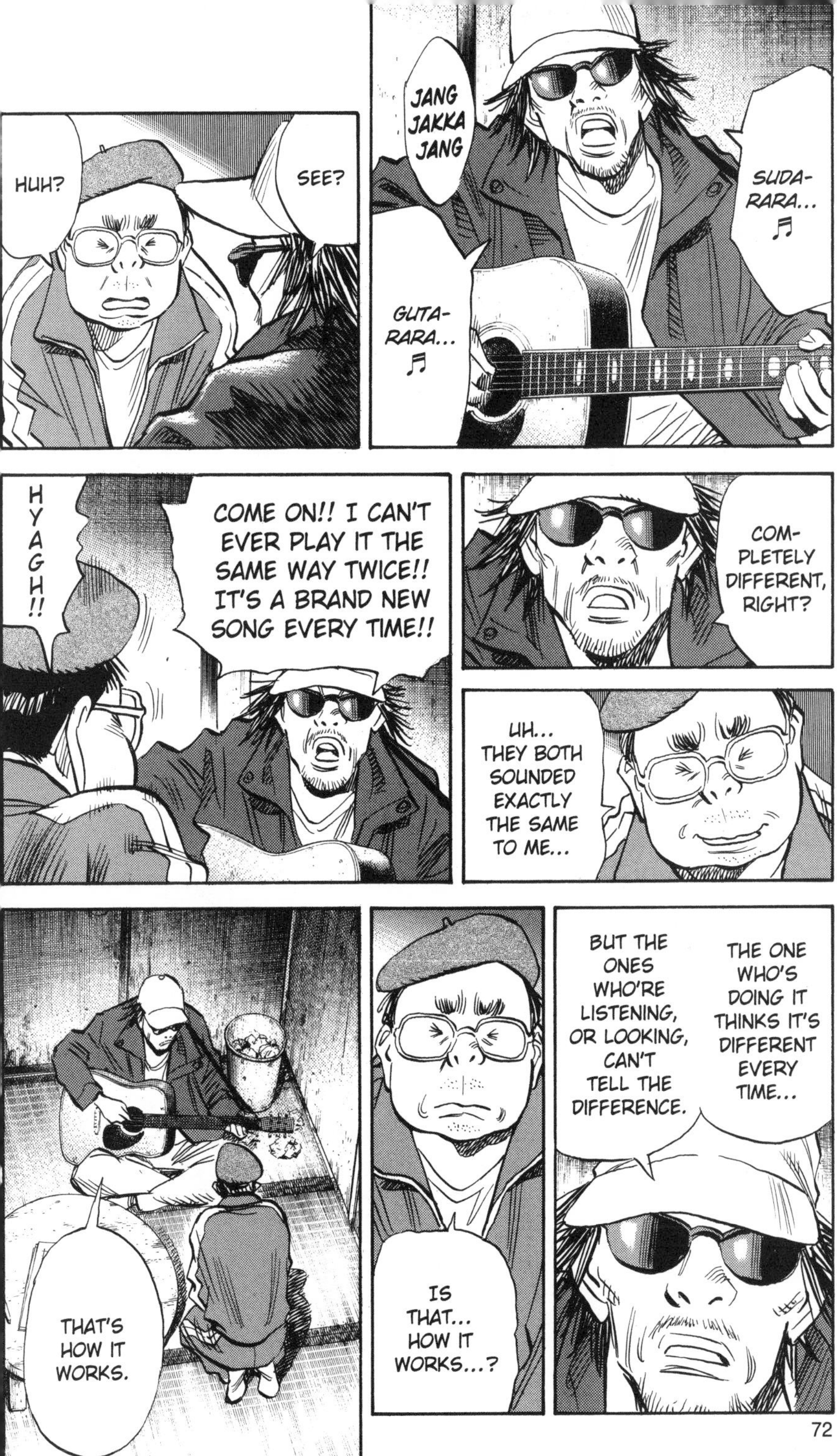
JANG JAKKA JANG
SUDA-RARA... ♬
GUTA-RARA... ♬
SEE?
HUH?
COM-PLETELY DIFFERENT, RIGHT?
UH... THEY BOTH SOUNDED EXACTLY THE SAME TO ME...
COME ON!! I CAN'T EVER PLAY IT THE SAME WAY TWICE!! IT'S A BRAND NEW SONG EVERY TIME!!
HYAGH!!
THE ONE WHO'S DOING IT THINKS IT'S DIFFERENT EVERY TIME...
BUT THE ONES WHO'RE LISTENING, OR LOOKING, CAN'T TELL THE DIFFERENCE.
IS THAT... HOW IT WORKS...?
THAT'S HOW IT WORKS.

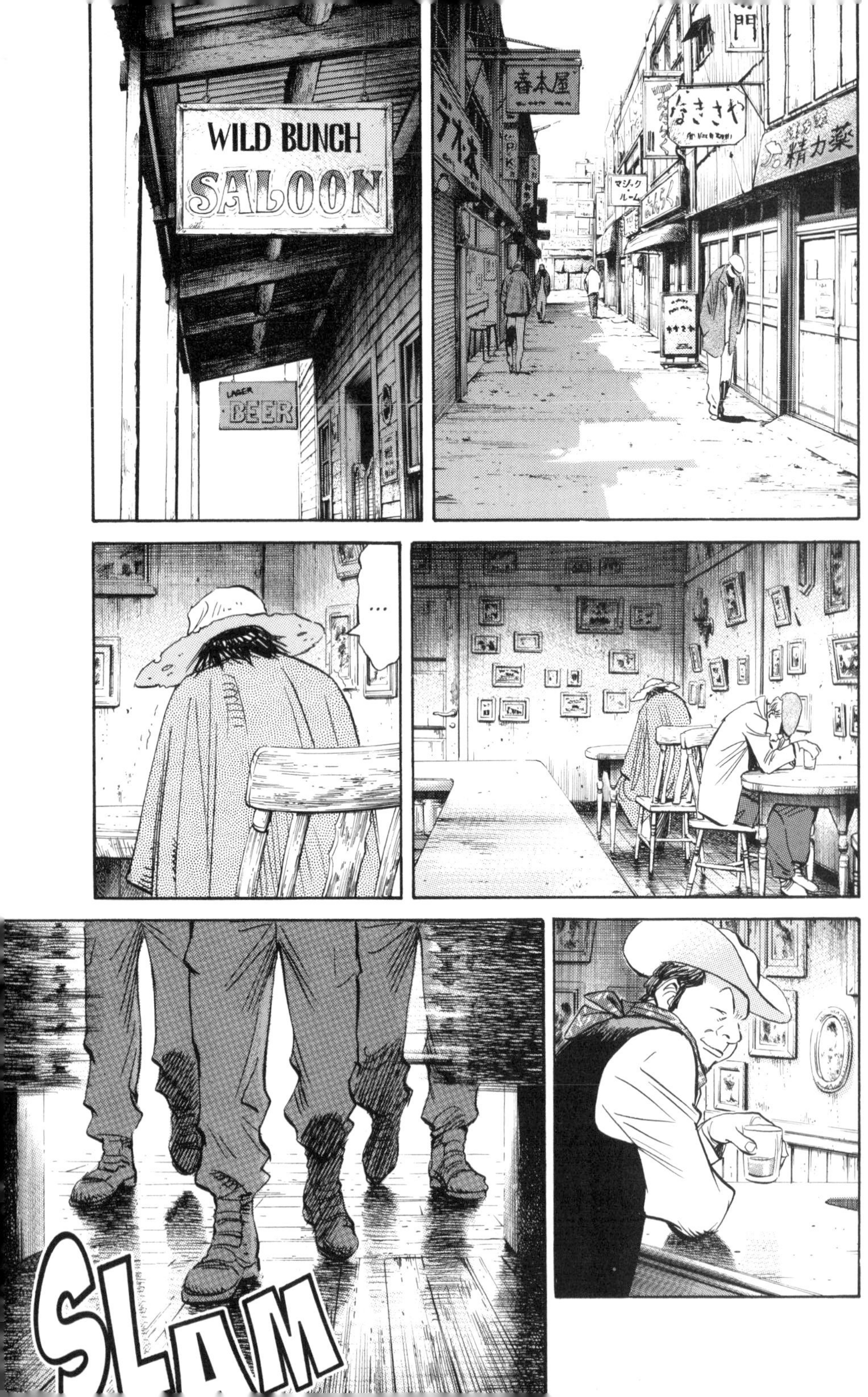
春木屋
精力薬
WILD BUNCH
SALOON
LAGER
BEER
...
SLAM

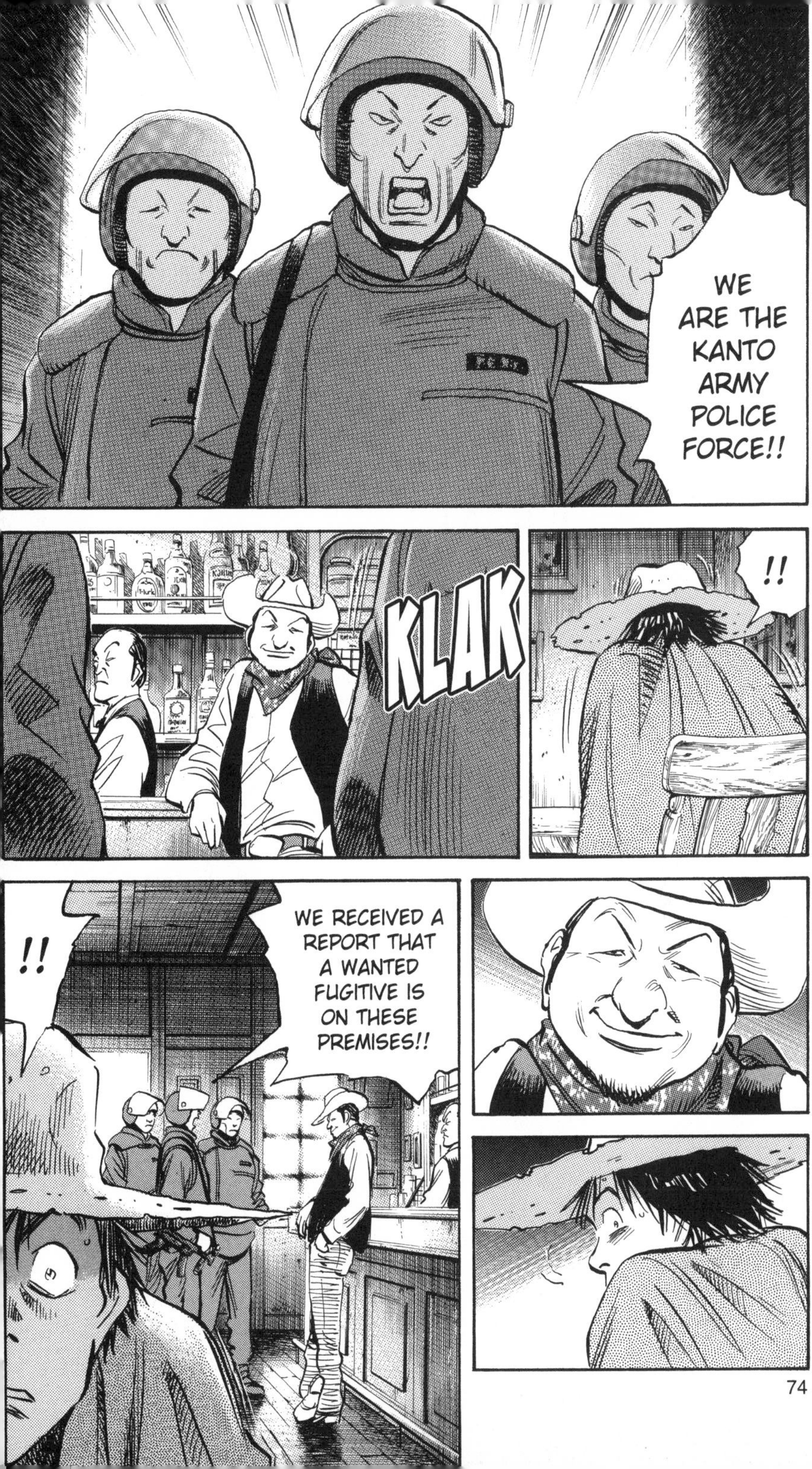
WE ARE THE KANTO ARMY POLICE FORCE!!
!!
KLAK
WE RECEIVED A REPORT THAT A WANTED FUGITIVE IS ON THESE PREMISES!!
!!

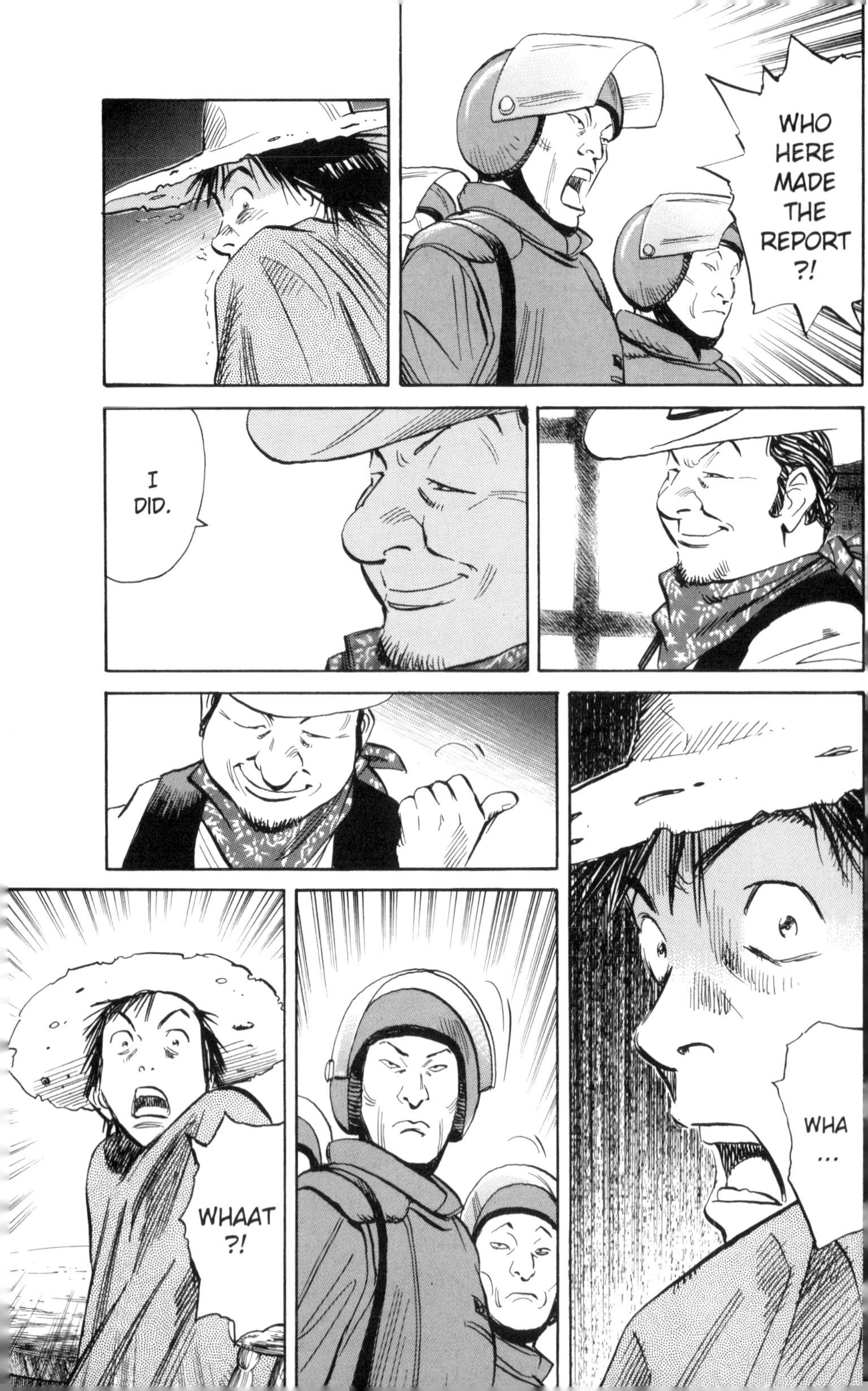
WHO HERE MADE THE REPORT ?!
I DID.
WHA ...
WHAAT ?!

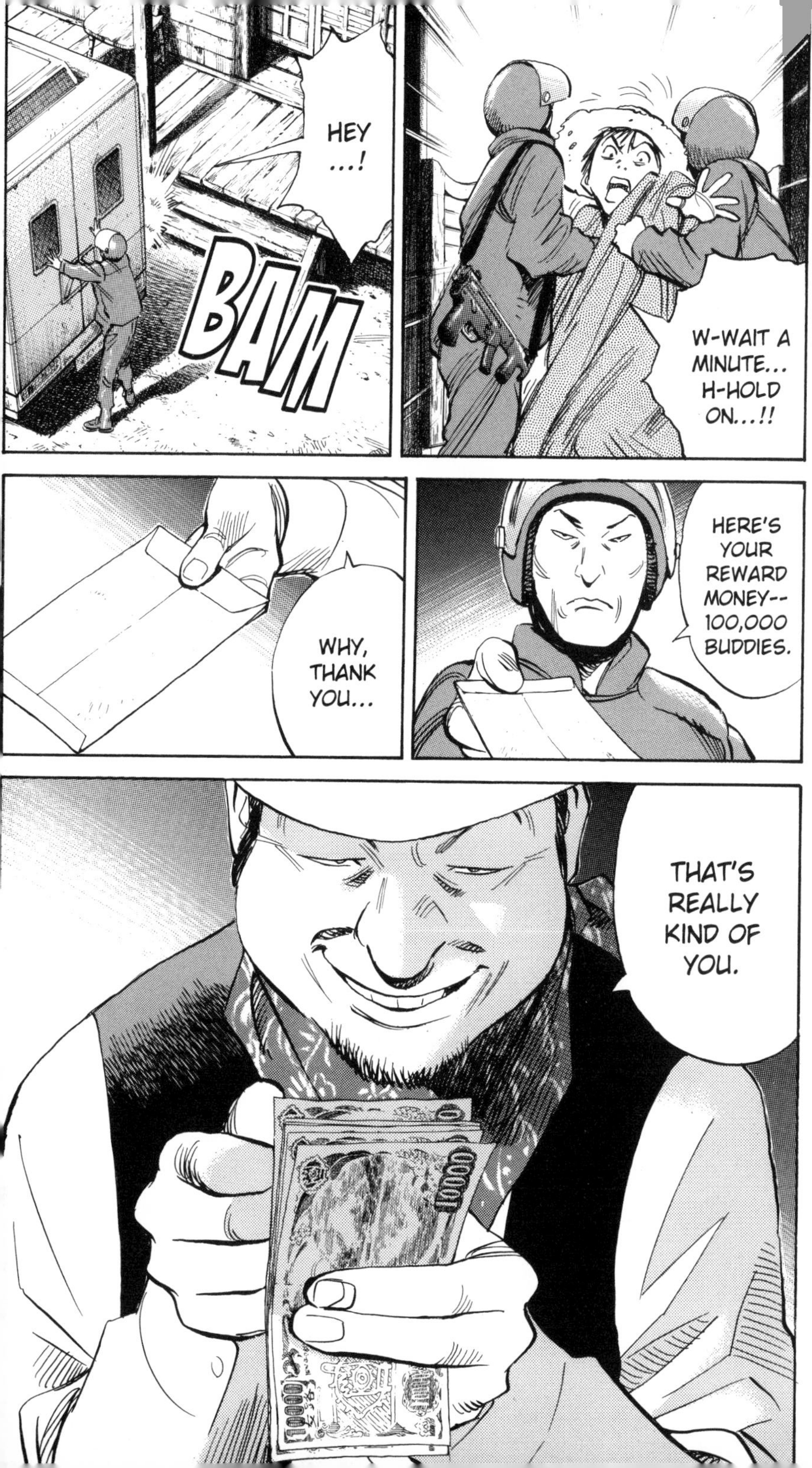
W-WAIT A MINUTE... H-HOLD ON...!!
HEY ...!
BAM
HERE'S YOUR REWARD MONEY-- 100,000 BUDDIES.
WHY, THANK YOU...
THAT'S REALLY KIND OF YOU.

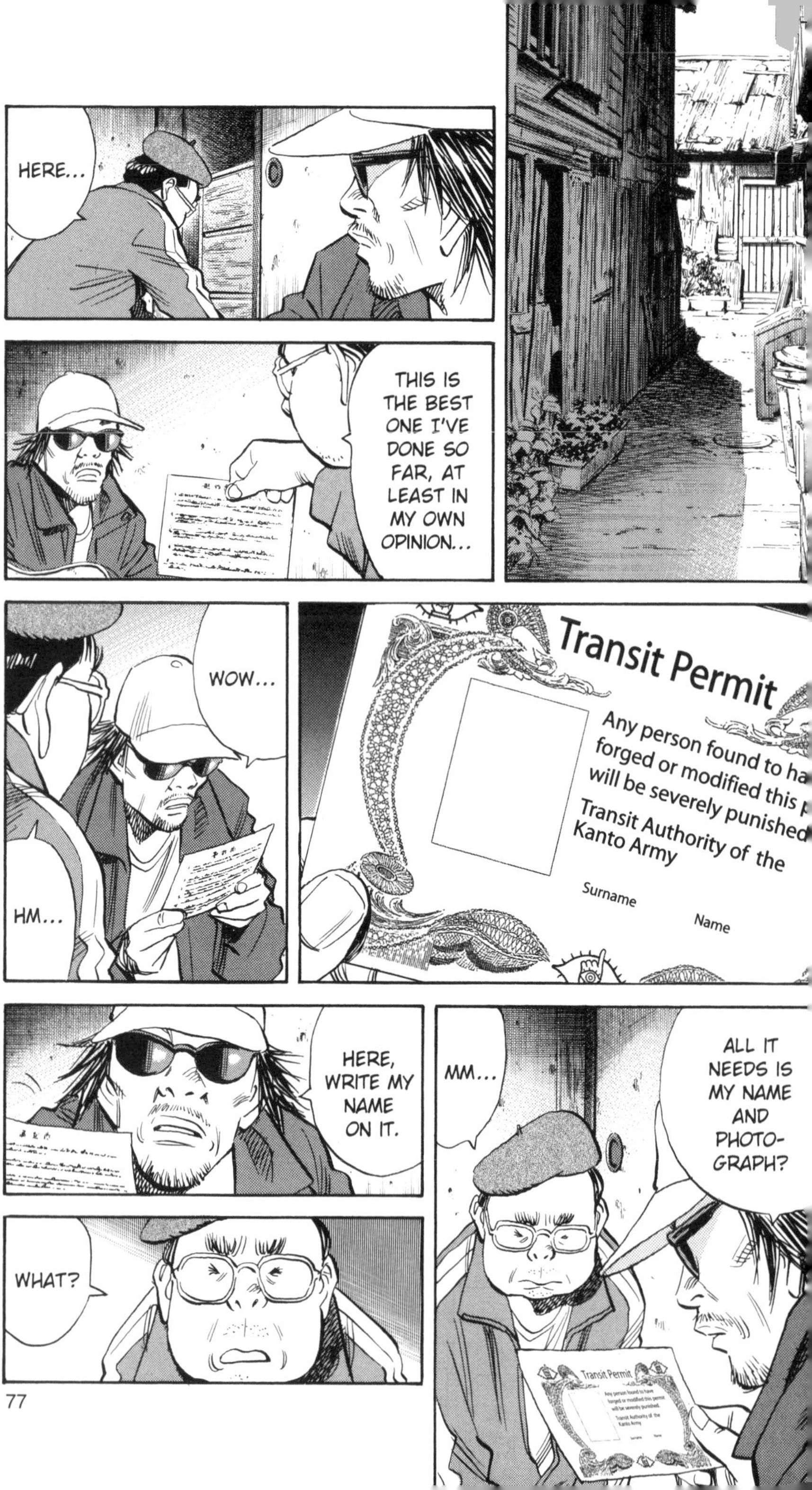
HERE...
THIS IS THE BEST ONE I'VE DONE SO FAR, AT LEAST IN MY OWN OPINION...
Transit Permit
Any person found to ha
forged or modified this
will be severely punished
Transit Authority of the
Kanto Army
Surname
Name
WOW...
HM...
ALL IT NEEDS IS MY NAME AND PHOTOGRAPH?
MM...
HERE, WRITE MY NAME ON IT.
WHAT?

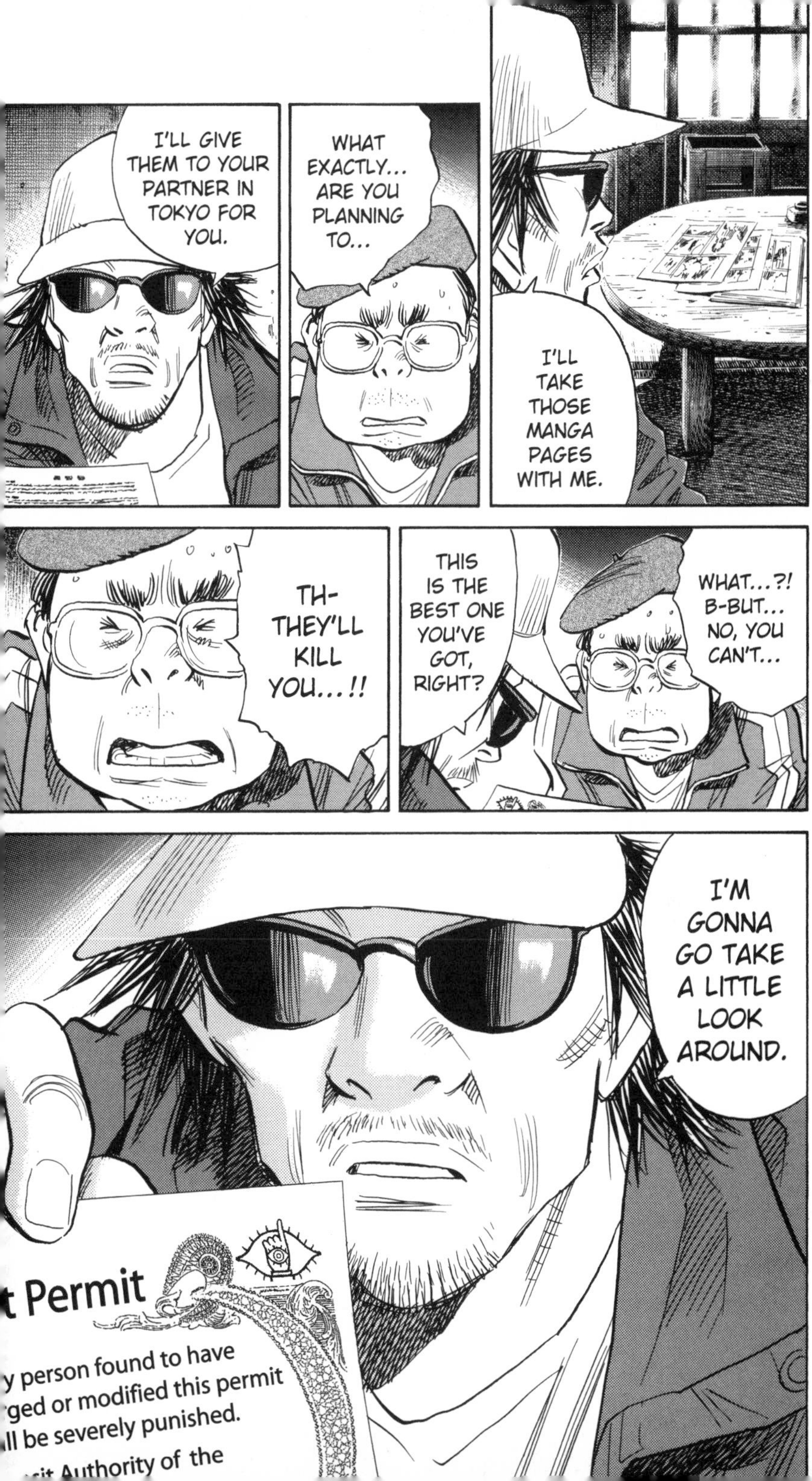
I'LL TAKE THOSE MANGA PAGES WITH ME.
WHAT EXACTLY... ARE YOU PLANNING TO...
I'LL GIVE THEM TO YOUR PARTNER IN TOKYO FOR YOU.
WHAT...?! B-BUT... NO, YOU CAN'T...
THIS IS THE BEST ONE YOU'VE GOT, RIGHT?
TH- THEY'LL KILL YOU...!!
I'M GONNA GO TAKE A LITTLE LOOK AROUND.
t Permit
y person found to have
ged or modified this permit
ll be severely punished.
Authority of the

Chapter 5 The One Who Got Through

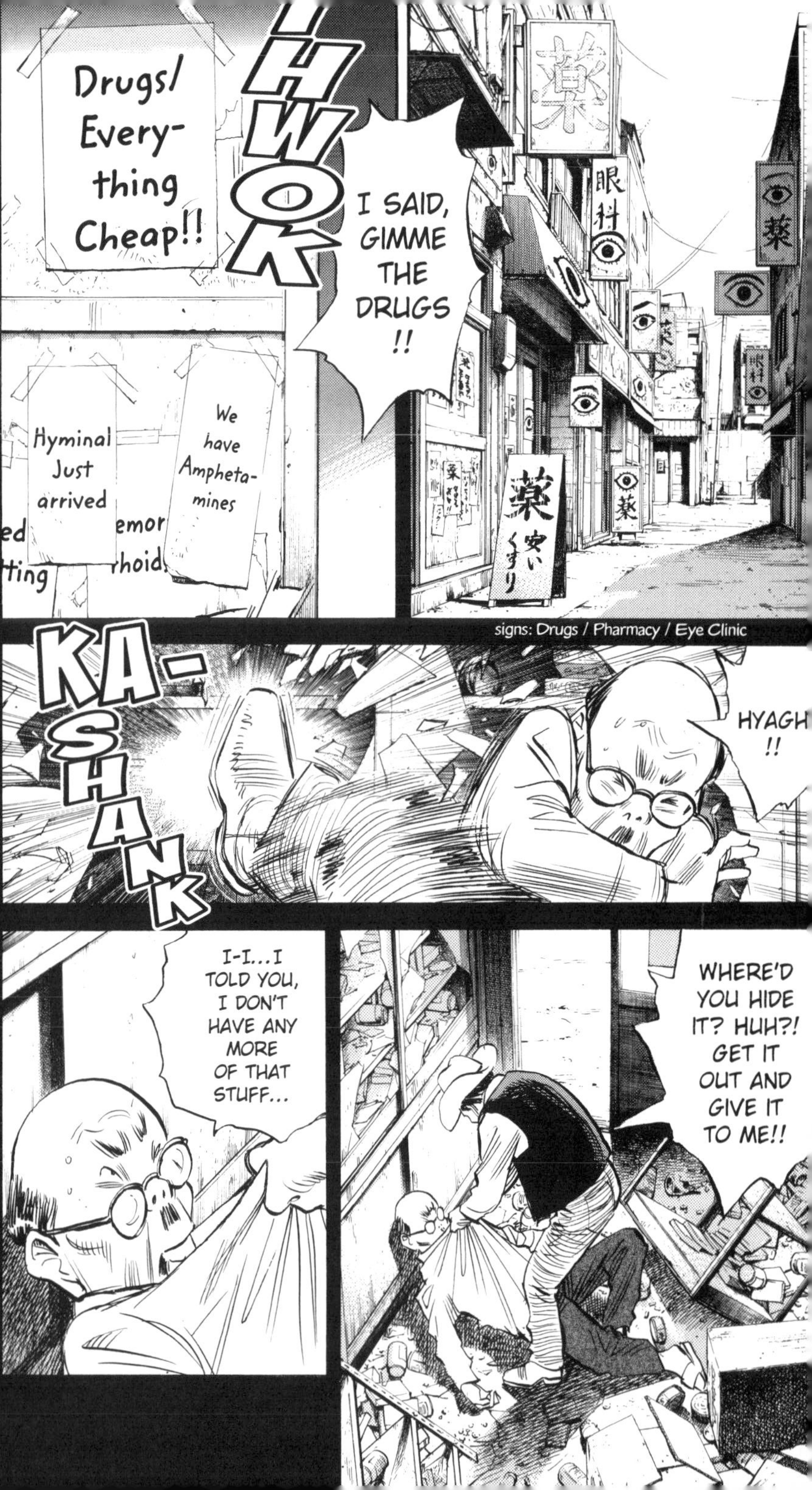
薬
眼科
薬
薬 安いくすり
I SAID, GIMME THE DRUGS!!
THWOK
Drugs/ Every-thing Cheap!!
We have Ampheta-mines
Hyminal Just arrived
signs: Drugs / Pharmacy / Eye Clinic
HYAGH!!
KA-SHANK
WHERE'D YOU HIDE IT? HUH?! GET IT OUT AND GIVE IT TO ME!!
I-I...I TOLD YOU, I DON'T HAVE ANY MORE OF THAT STUFF...

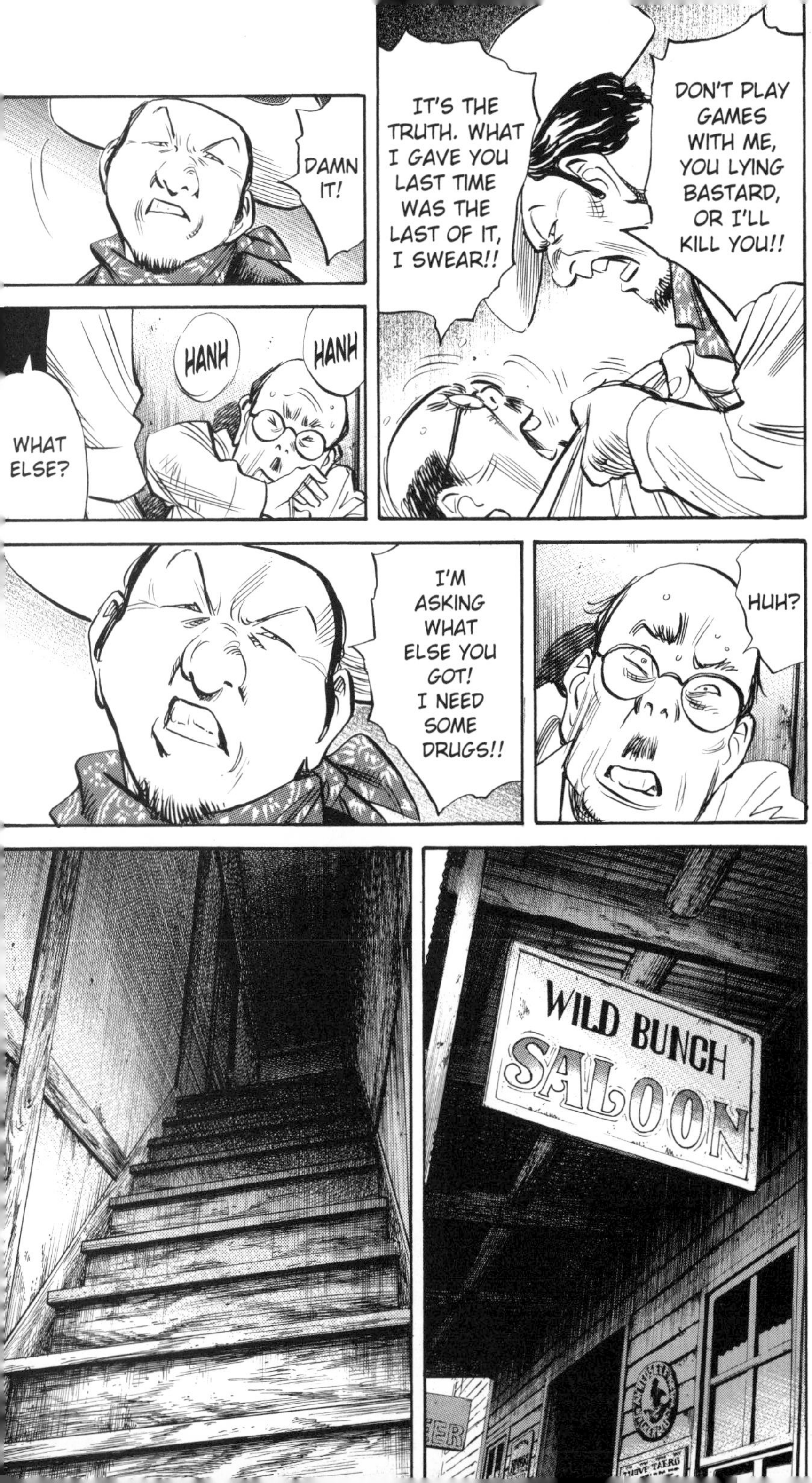
DON'T PLAY GAMES WITH ME, YOU LYING BASTARD, OR I'LL KILL YOU!!
IT'S THE TRUTH. WHAT I GAVE YOU LAST TIME WAS THE LAST OF IT, I SWEAR!!
DAMN IT!
HANH
HANH
WHAT ELSE?
HUH?
I'M ASKING WHAT ELSE YOU GOT! I NEED SOME DRUGS!!
WILD BUNCH SALOON

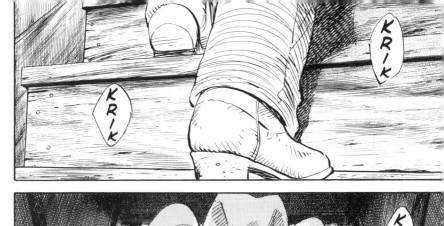

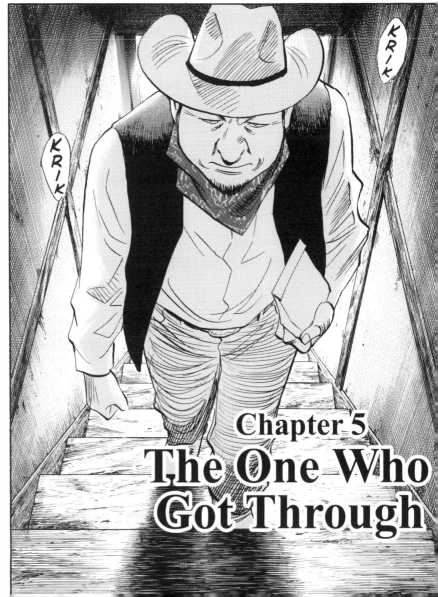

Chapter 5
The One Who Got Through

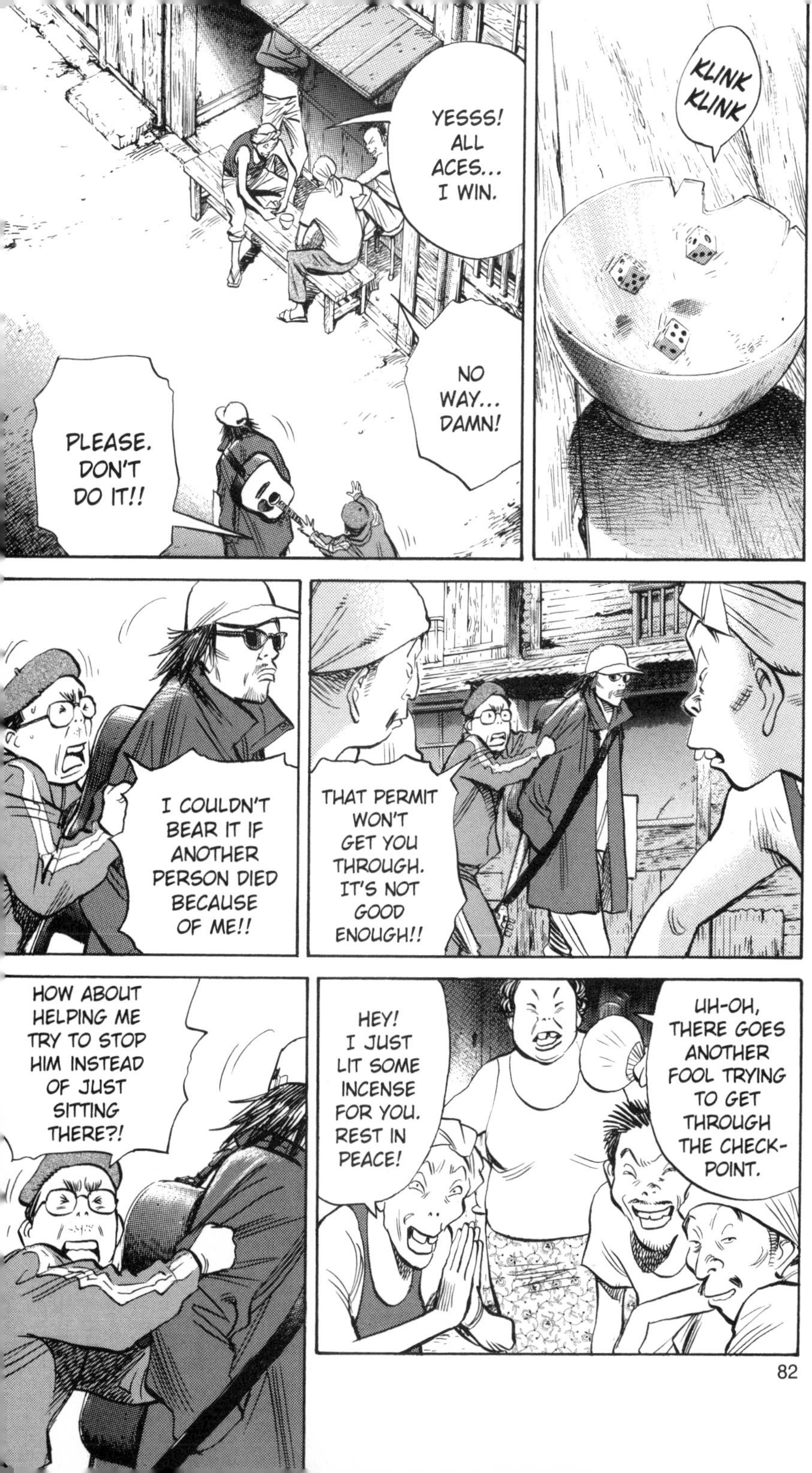
KLINK KLINK
YESSS! ALL ACES... I WIN.
NO WAY... DAMN!
PLEASE. DON'T DO IT!!
THAT PERMIT WON'T GET YOU THROUGH. IT'S NOT GOOD ENOUGH!!
I COULDN'T BEAR IT IF ANOTHER PERSON DIED BECAUSE OF ME!!
UH-OH, THERE GOES ANOTHER FOOL TRYING TO GET THROUGH THE CHECK-POINT.
HEY! I JUST LIT SOME INCENSE FOR YOU. REST IN PEACE!
HOW ABOUT HELPING ME TRY TO STOP HIM INSTEAD OF JUST SITTING THERE?!

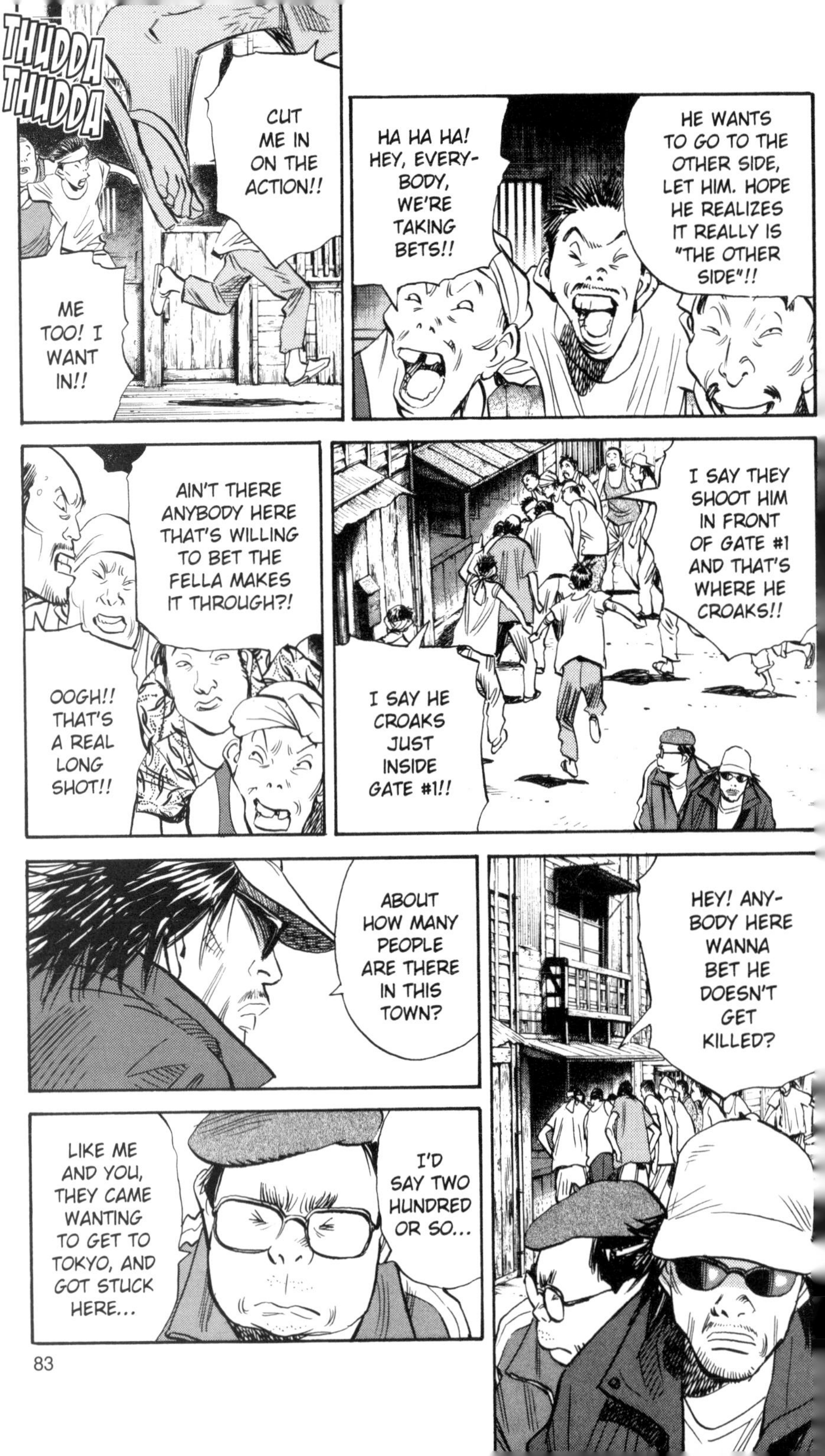
HE WANTS TO GO TO THE OTHER SIDE, LET HIM. HOPE HE REALIZES IT REALLY IS "THE OTHER SIDE"!!
HA HA HA! HEY, EVERY-BODY, WE'RE TAKING BETS!!
THUDDA THUDDA
CUT ME IN ON THE ACTION!!
ME TOO! I WANT IN!!
I SAY THEY SHOOT HIM IN FRONT OF GATE #1 AND THAT'S WHERE HE CROAKS!!
I SAY HE CROAKS JUST INSIDE GATE #1!!
AIN'T THERE ANYBODY HERE THAT'S WILLING TO BET THE FELLA MAKES IT THROUGH?!
OOGH!! THAT'S A REAL LONG SHOT!!
HEY! ANY-BODY HERE WANNA BET HE DOESN'T GET KILLED?
ABOUT HOW MANY PEOPLE ARE THERE IN THIS TOWN?
I'D SAY TWO HUNDRED OR SO...
LIKE ME AND YOU, THEY CAME WANTING TO GET TO TOKYO, AND GOT STUCK HERE...

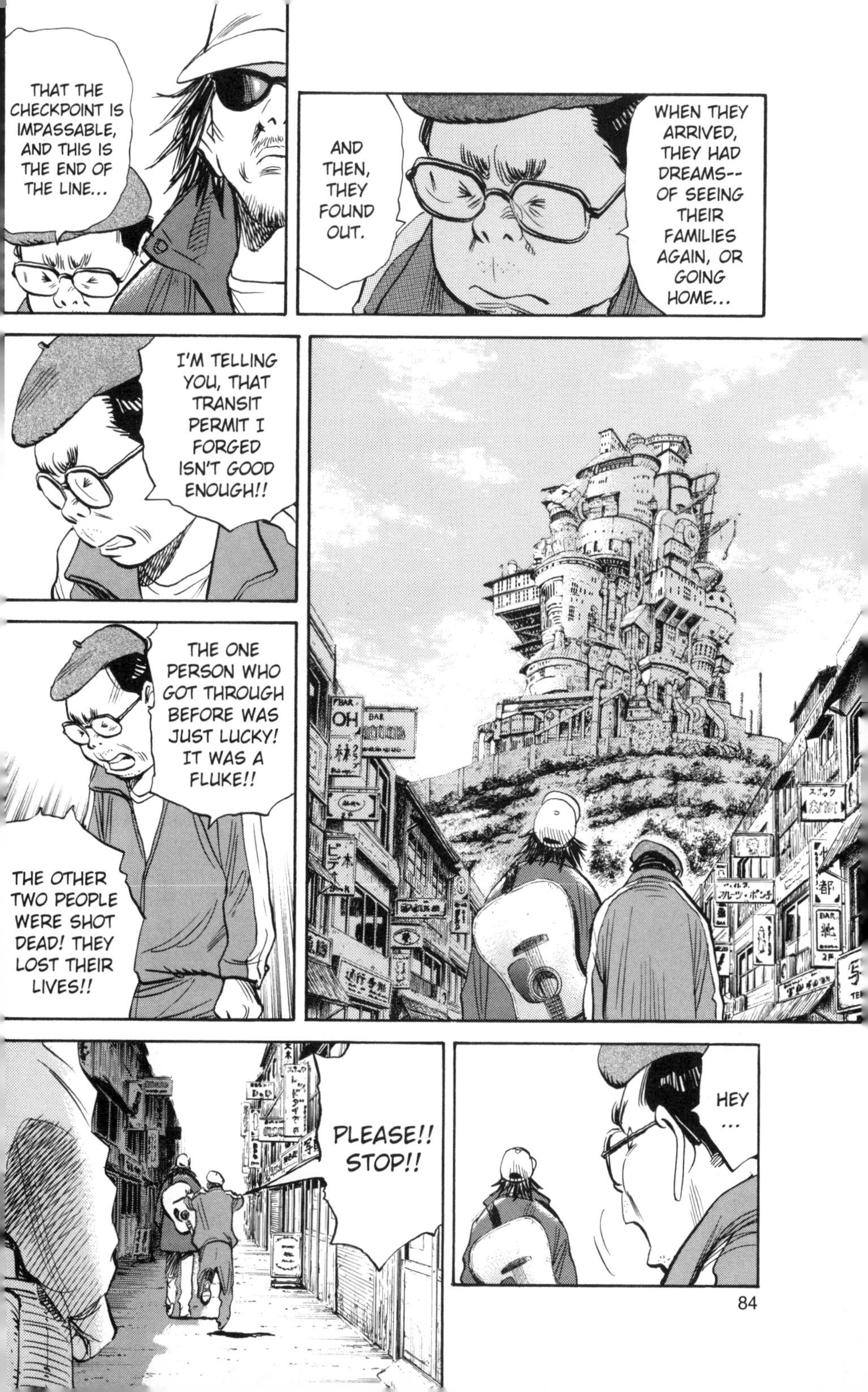
WHEN THEY ARRIVED, THEY HAD DREAMS-- OF SEEING THEIR FAMILIES AGAIN, OR GOING HOME...
AND THEN, THEY FOUND OUT.
THAT THE CHECKPOINT IS IMPASSABLE, AND THIS IS THE END OF THE LINE...
I'M TELLING YOU, THAT TRANSIT PERMIT I FORGED ISN'T GOOD ENOUGH!!
THE ONE PERSON WHO GOT THROUGH BEFORE WAS JUST LUCKY! IT WAS A FLUKE!!
THE OTHER TWO PEOPLE WERE SHOT DEAD! THEY LOST THEIR LIVES!!
HEY ...
PLEASE!! STOP!!

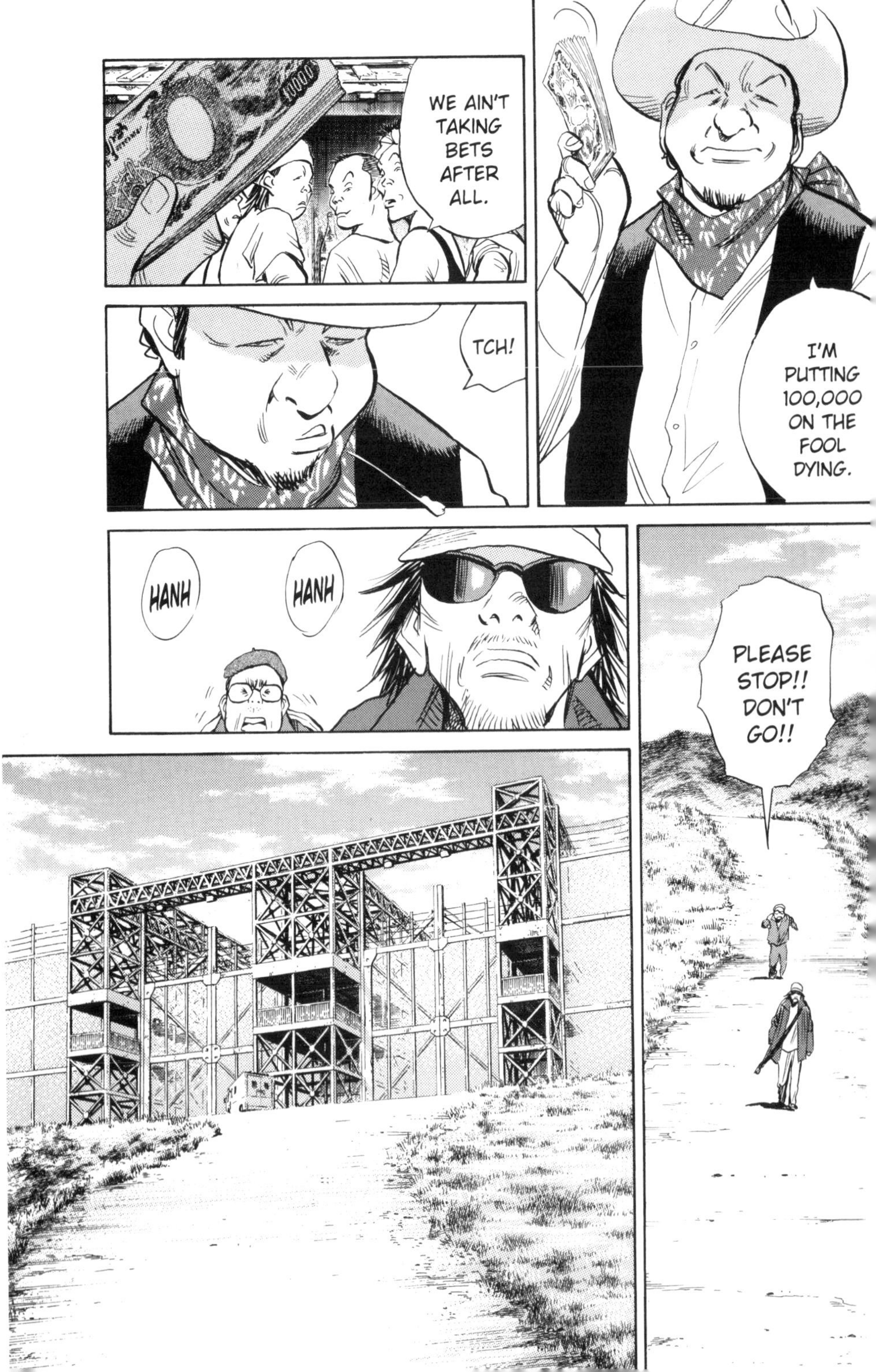
I'M PUTTING 100,000 ON THE FOOL DYING.
WE AIN'T TAKING BETS AFTER ALL.
TCH!
PLEASE STOP!! DON'T GO!!
HANH
HANH

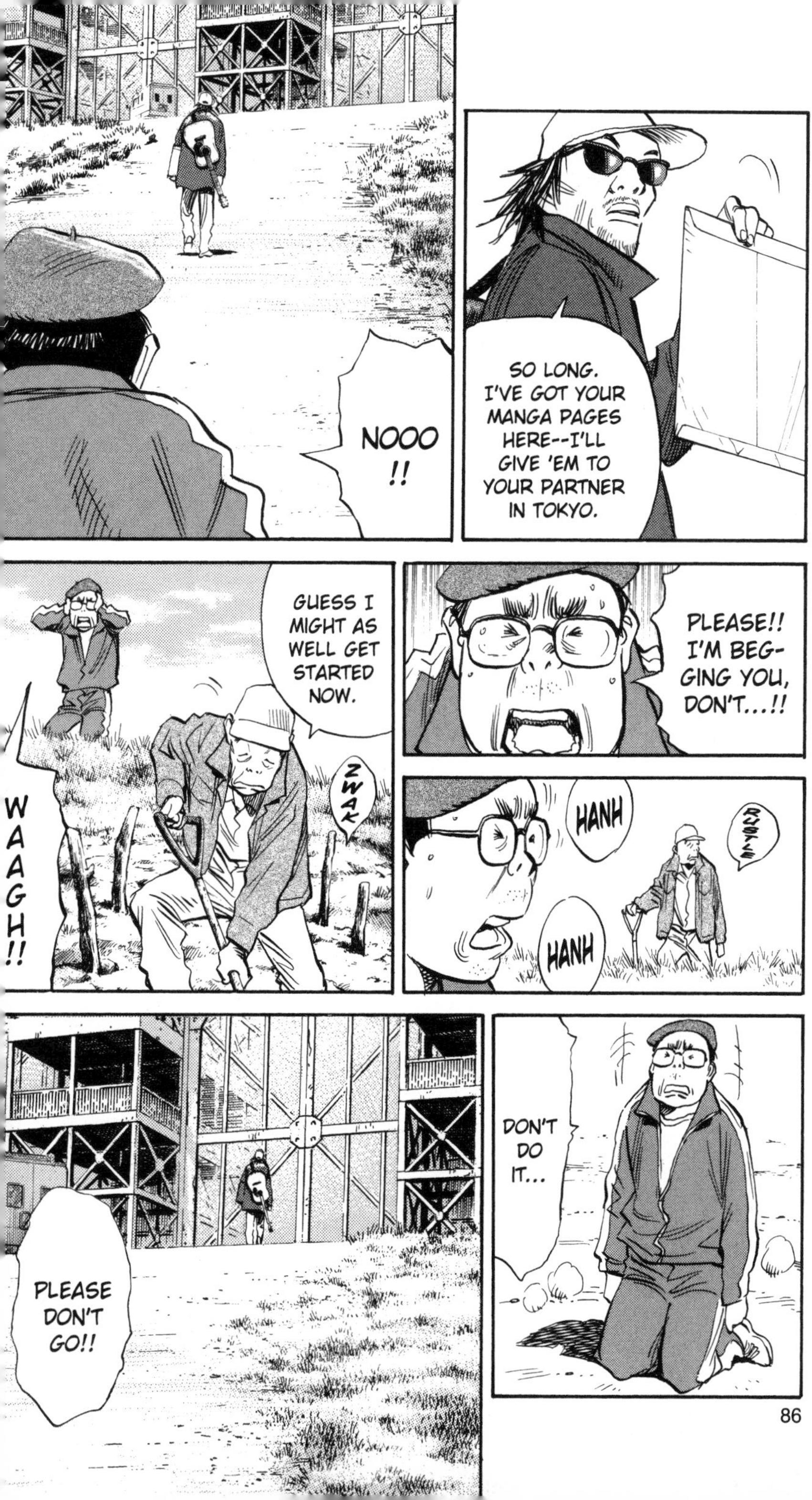
SO LONG. I'VE GOT YOUR MANGA PAGES HERE--I'LL GIVE 'EM TO YOUR PARTNER IN TOKYO.
NOOO !!
PLEASE!! I'M BEG-GING YOU, DON'T...!!
RUSTLE
HANH
HANH
GUESS I MIGHT AS WELL GET STARTED NOW.
ZWAK
WAAAGH!!
DON'T DO IT...
PLEASE DON'T GO!!

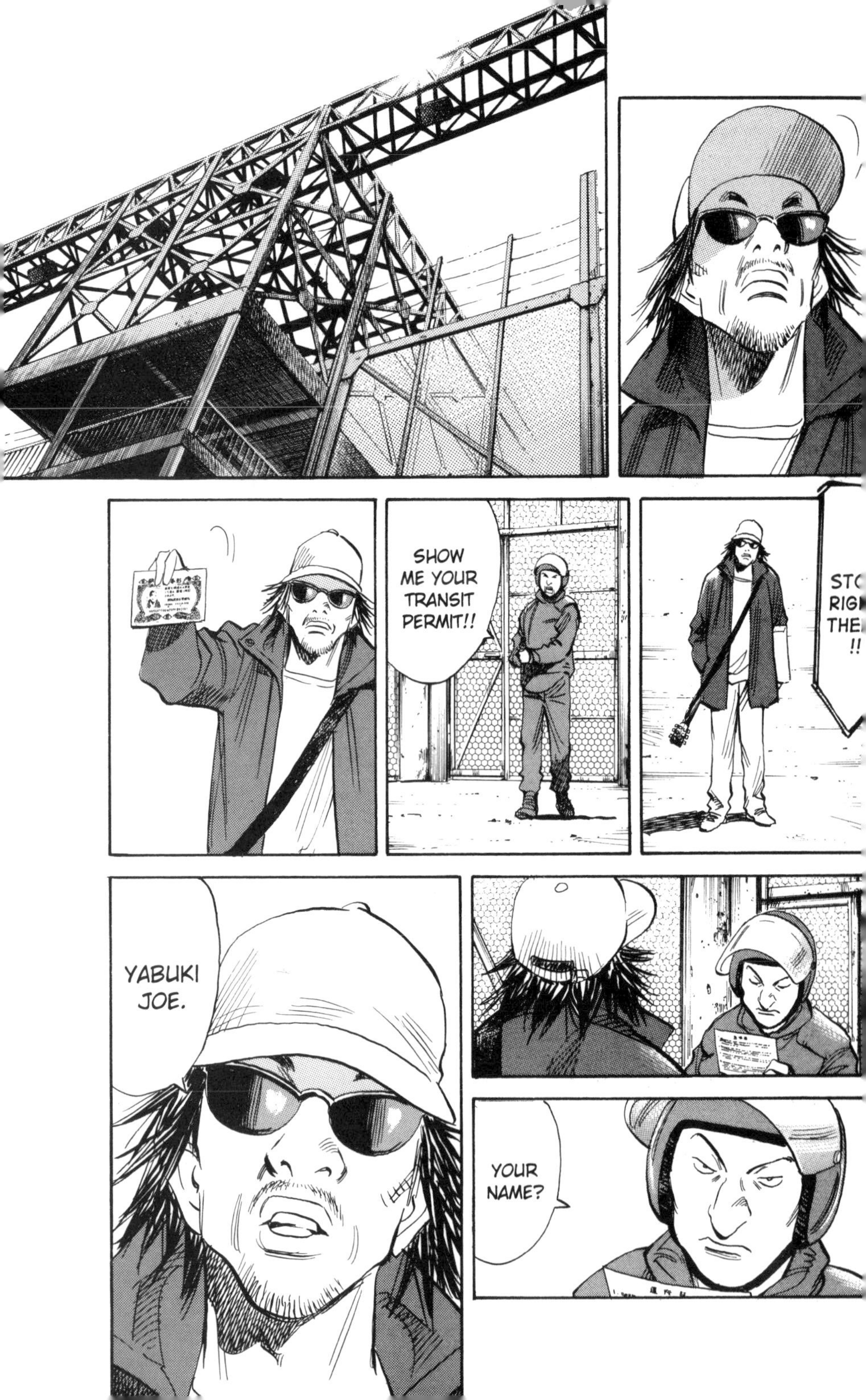
SHOW ME YOUR TRANSIT PERMIT!!
YOUR NAME?
YABUKI JOE.

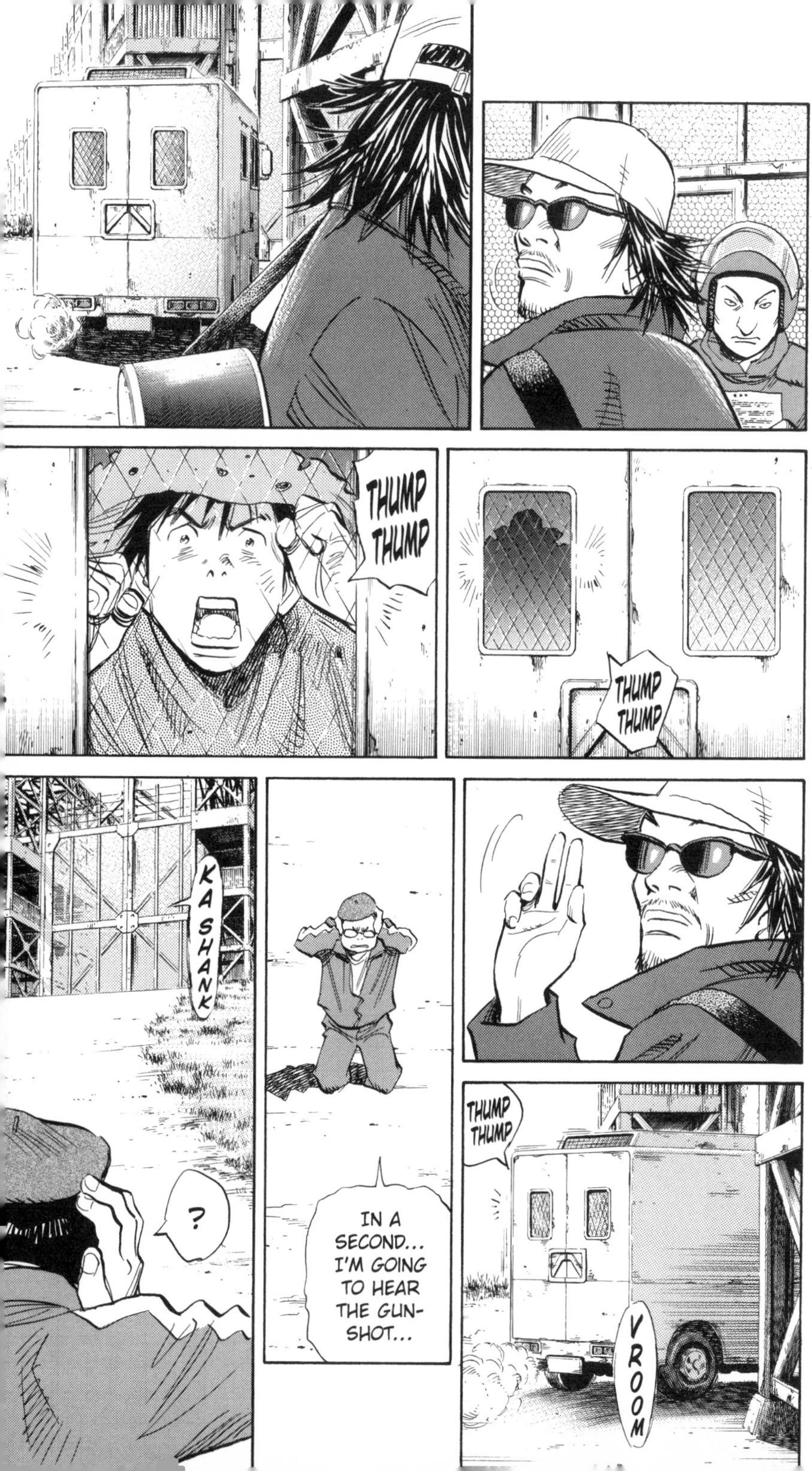
THUMP THUMP
THUMP THUMP
THUMP THUMP
VROOM
IN A SECOND... I'M GOING TO HEAR THE GUN-SHOT...
KASHANK
?

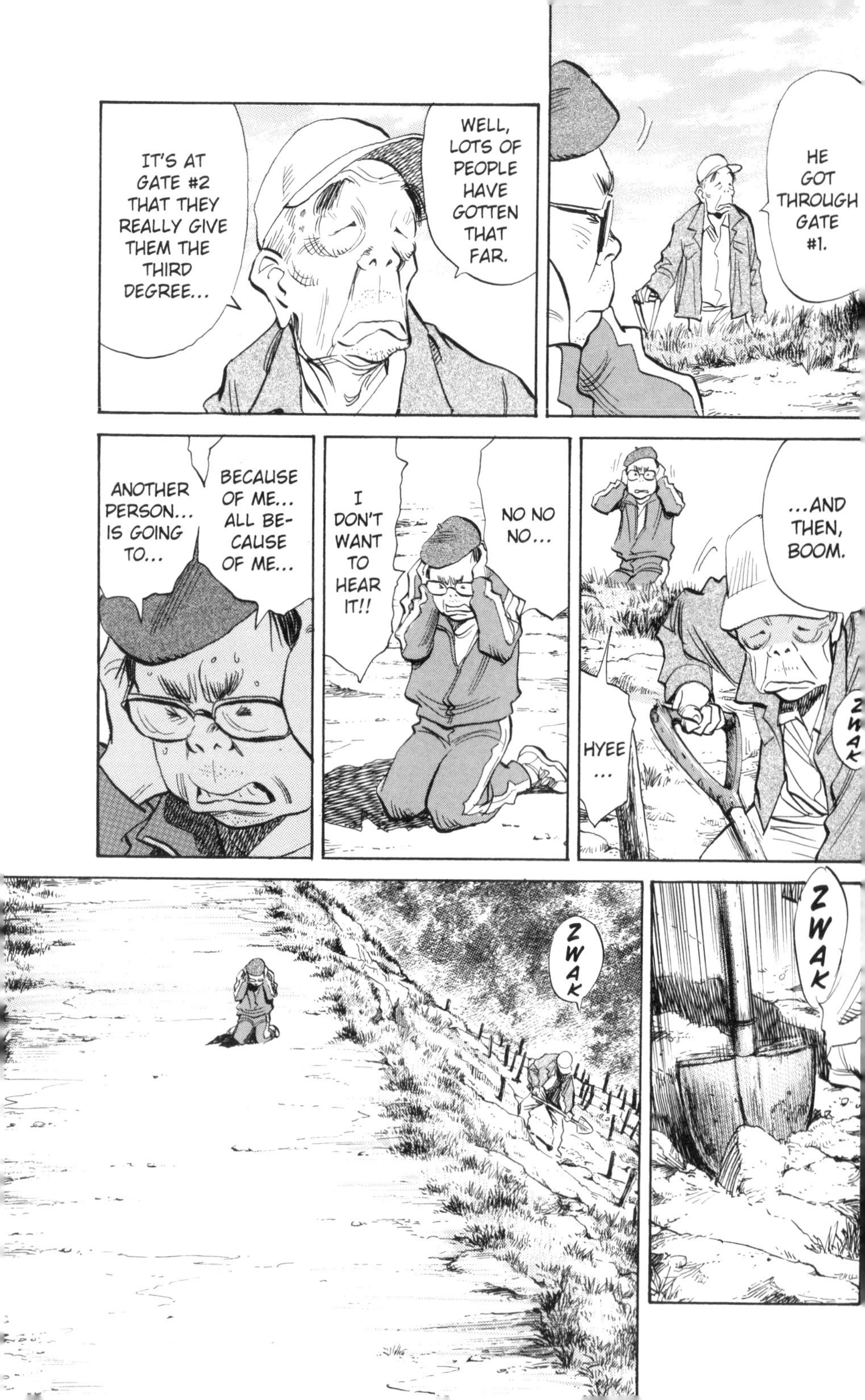
HE GOT THROUGH GATE #1.
WELL, LOTS OF PEOPLE HAVE GOTTEN THAT FAR.
IT'S AT GATE #2 THAT THEY REALLY GIVE THEM THE THIRD DEGREE...
...AND THEN, BOOM.
ZWAK
HYEE...
NO NO NO...
I DON'T WANT TO HEAR IT!!
BECAUSE OF ME... ALL BE-CAUSE OF ME...
ANOTHER PERSON... IS GOING TO...
ZWAK
ZWAK

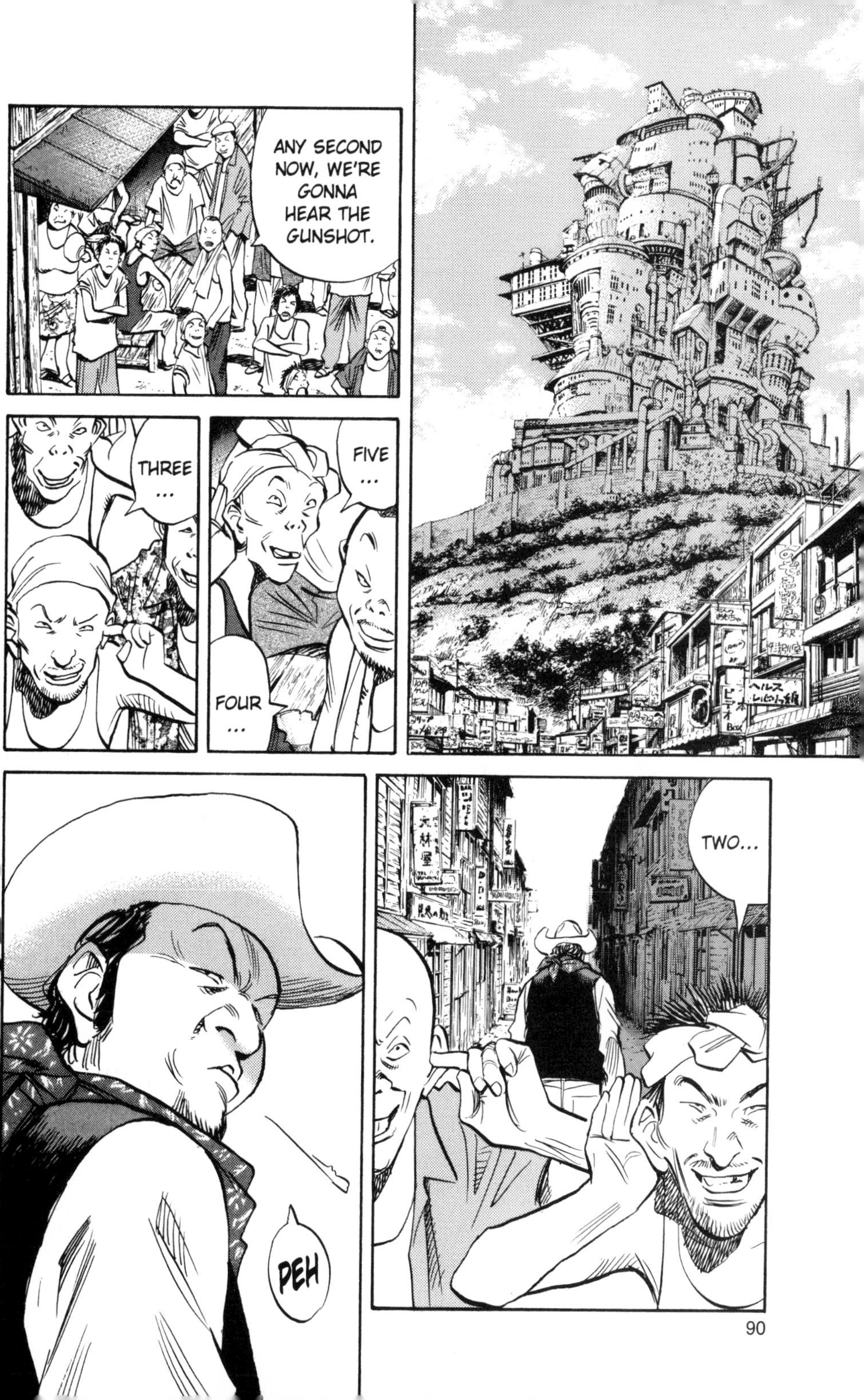
ANY SECOND NOW, WE'RE GONNA HEAR THE GUNSHOT.
FIVE ...
FOUR ...
THREE ...
TWO...
PEH

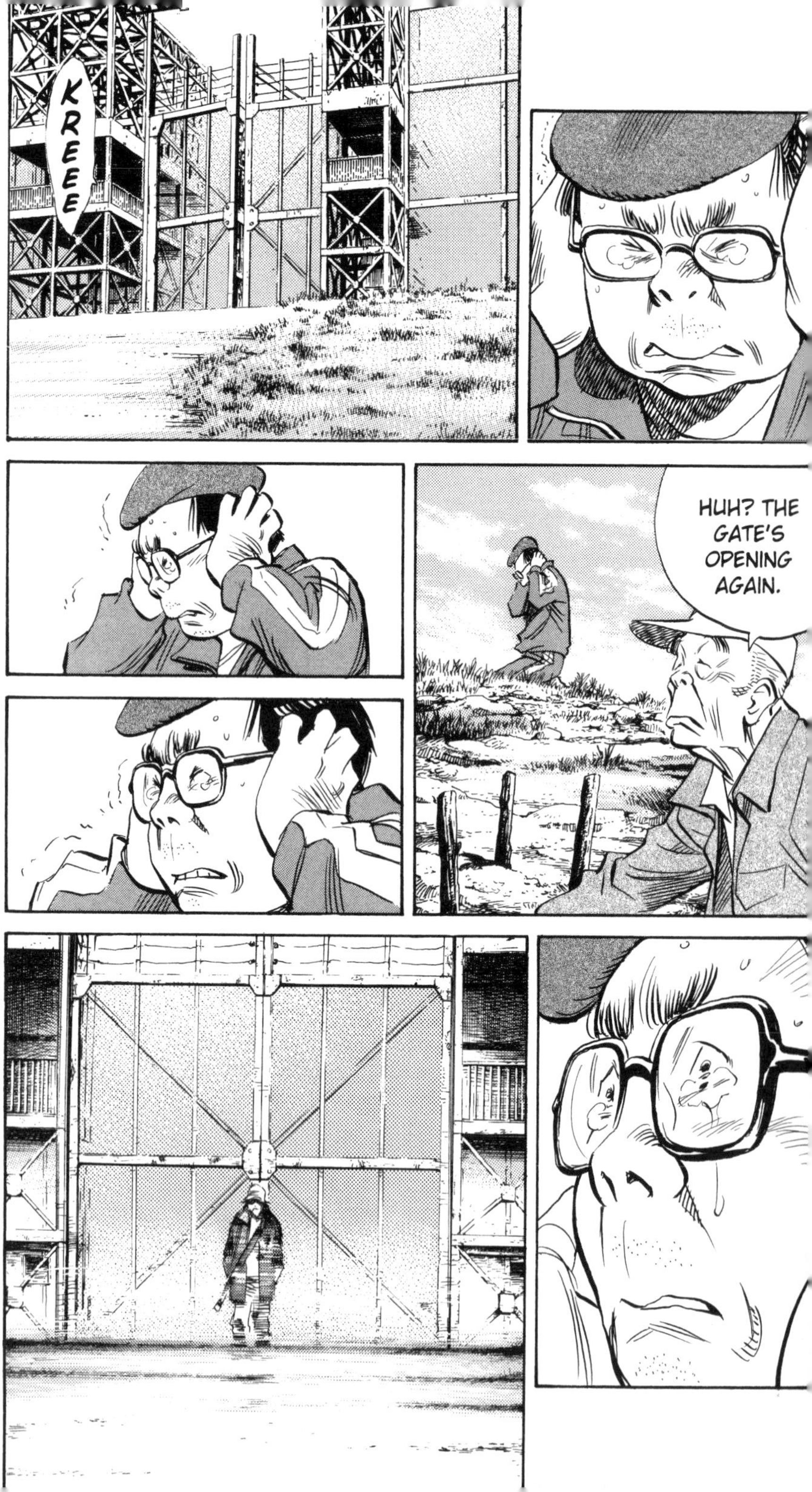
KREEE
HUH? THE GATE'S OPENING AGAIN.

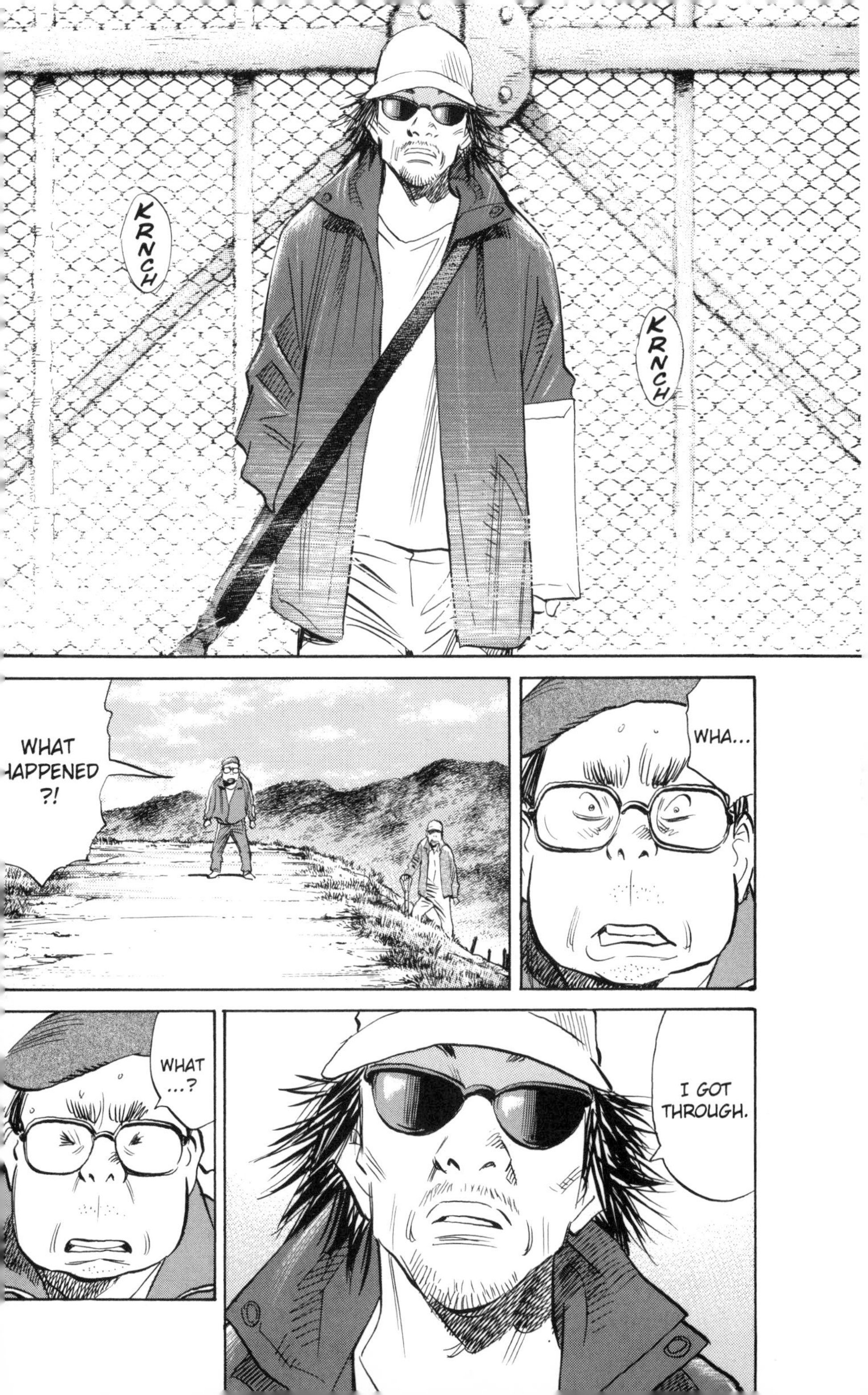
KRNCH
KRNCH
WHA...
WHAT HAPPENED ?!
I GOT THROUGH.
WHAT ...?

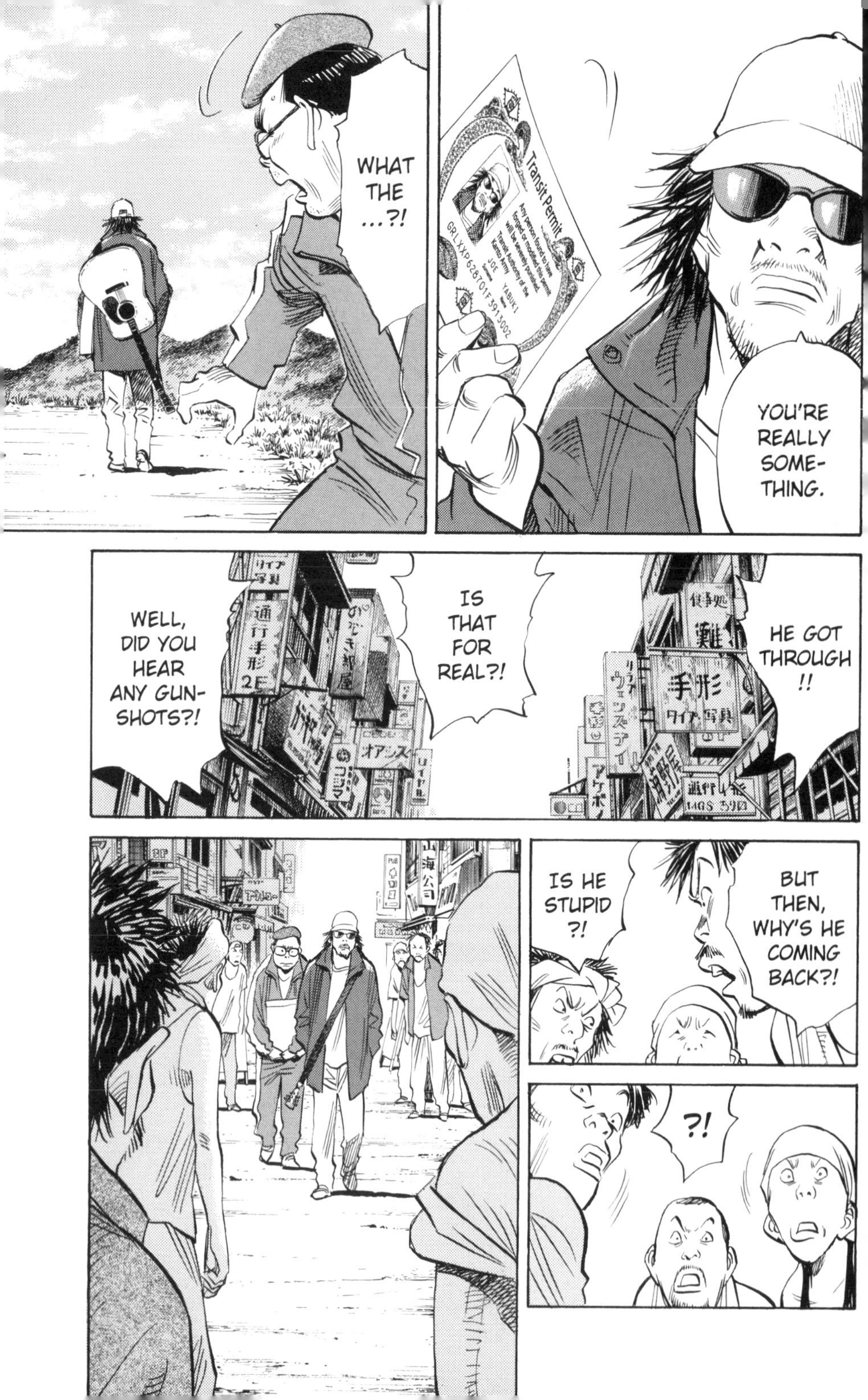
Transit Permit
JOE YABUKI
GRLXXP628701F3913002
YOU'RE REALLY SOME-THING.
WHAT THE ...?!
HE GOT THROUGH !!
IS THAT FOR REAL?!
WELL, DID YOU HEAR ANY GUN-SHOTS?!
BUT THEN, WHY'S HE COMING BACK?!
IS HE STUPID ?!
?!

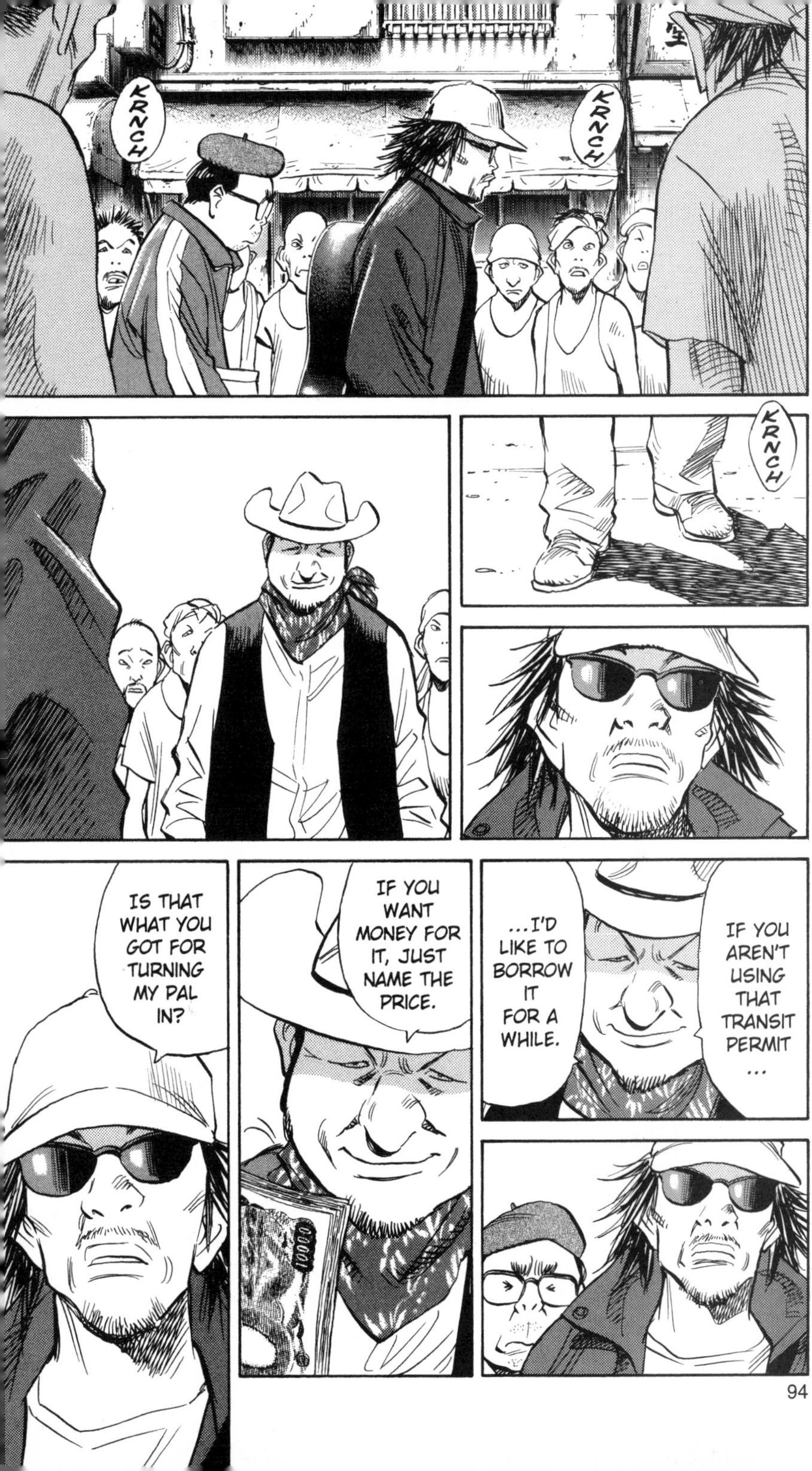
KRNCH
KRNCH
KRNCH
IF YOU AREN'T USING THAT TRANSIT PERMIT...
...I'D LIKE TO BORROW IT FOR A WHILE.
IF YOU WANT MONEY FOR IT, JUST NAME THE PRICE.
IS THAT WHAT YOU GOT FOR TURNING MY PAL IN?

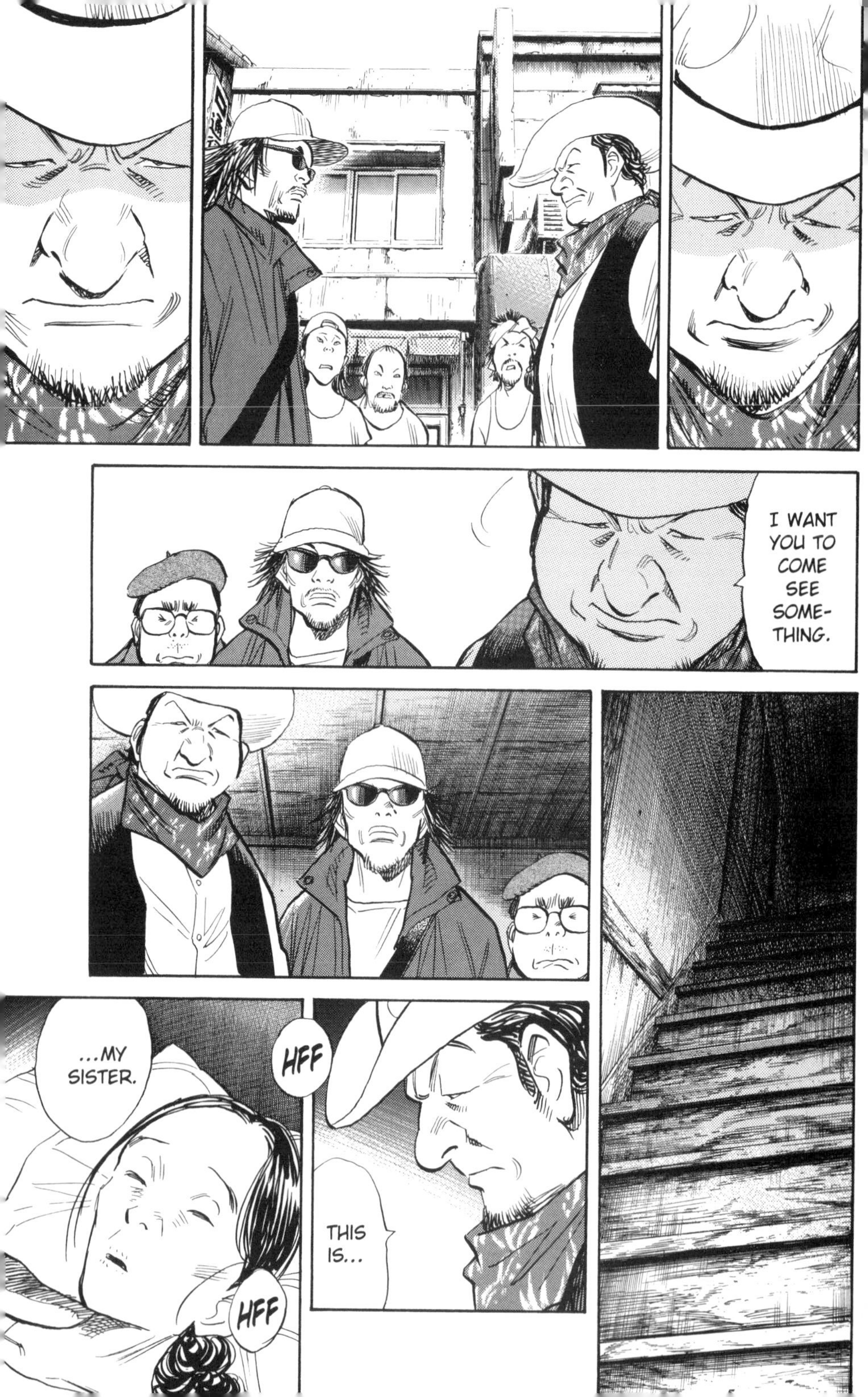
I WANT YOU TO COME SEE SOME-THING.
HFF
THIS IS...
...MY SISTER.
HFF

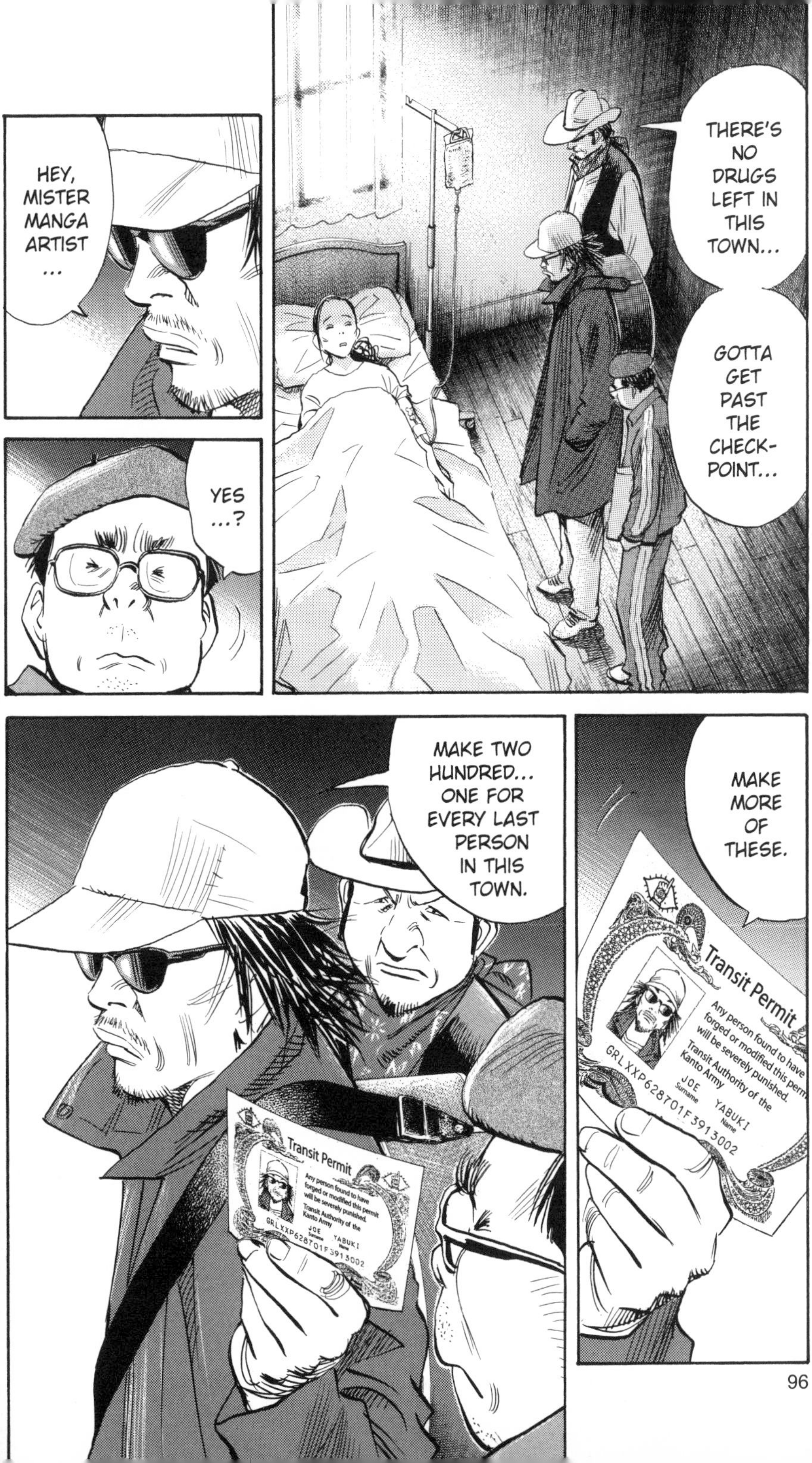
THERE'S NO DRUGS LEFT IN THIS TOWN...
GOTTA GET PAST THE CHECK-POINT...
HEY, MISTER MANGA ARTIST ...
YES ...?
MAKE MORE OF THESE.
Transit Permit
Any person found to have forged or modified this permit will be severely punished.
Transit Authority of the Kanto Army
JOE
Surname
YABUKI
Name
GRLXXP628701F3913002
MAKE TWO HUNDRED... ONE FOR EVERY LAST PERSON IN THIS TOWN.

Chapter 6 The Great Escape

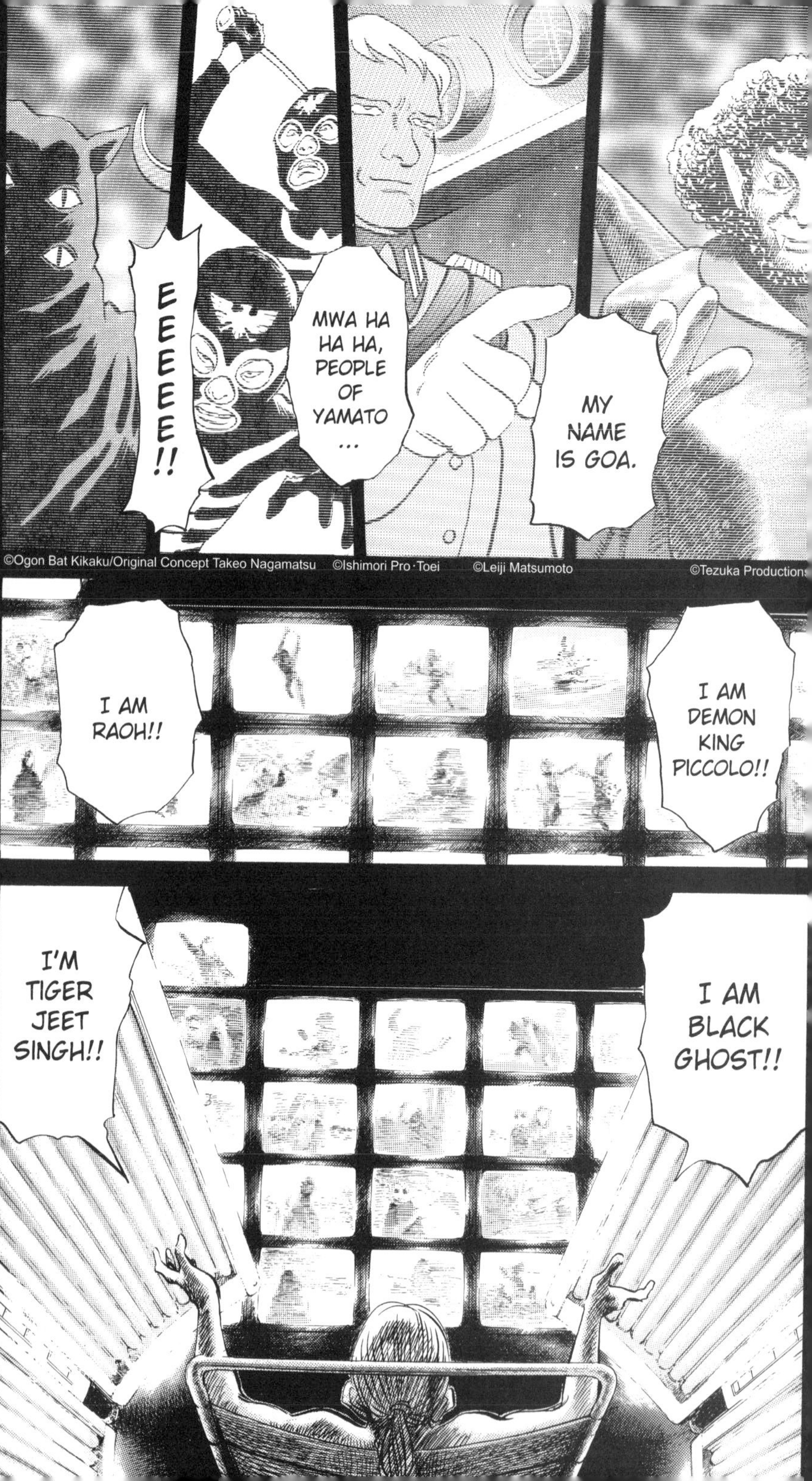

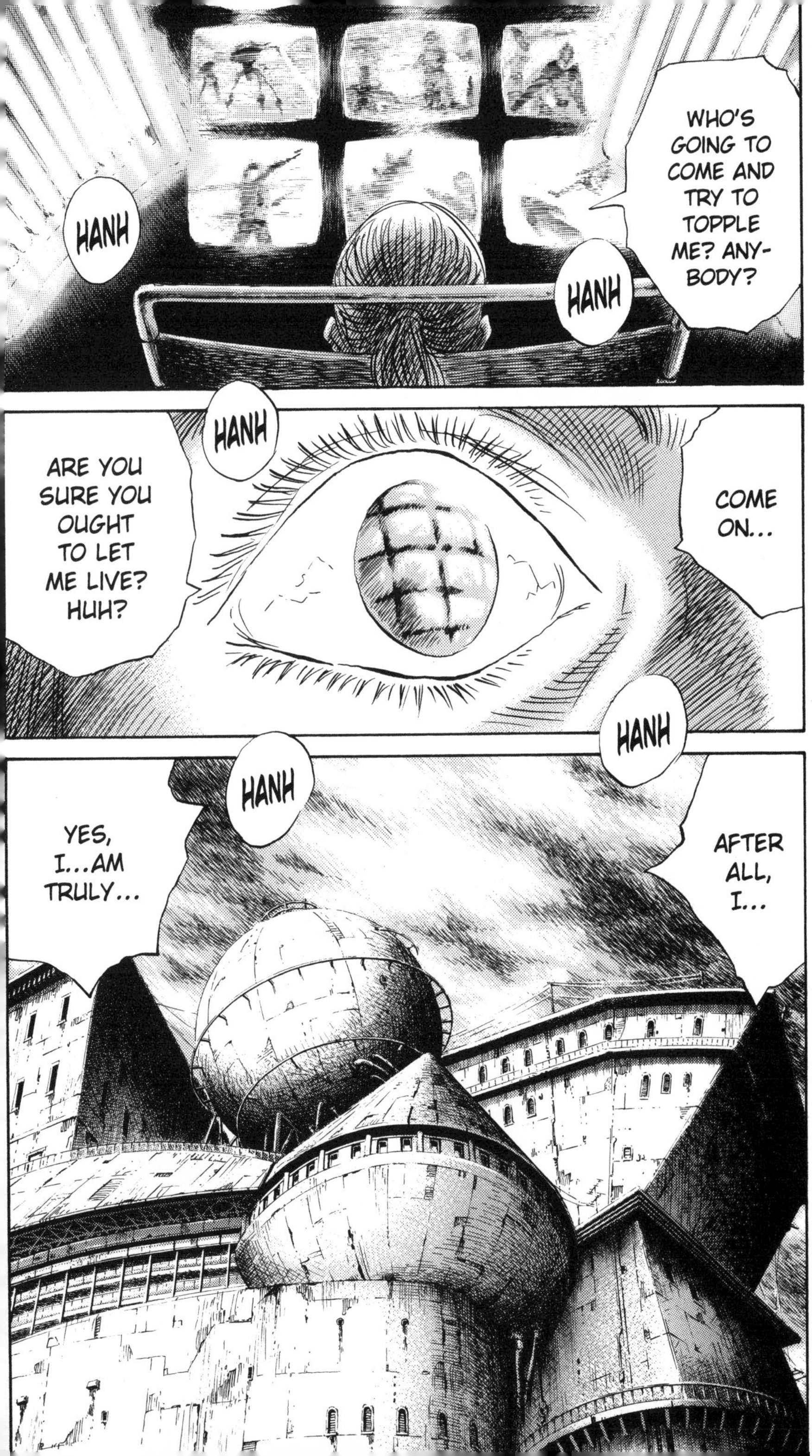
WHO'S GOING TO COME AND TRY TO TOPPLE ME? ANY-BODY?
HANH
HANH
COME ON...
HANH
ARE YOU SURE YOU OUGHT TO LET ME LIVE? HUH?
HANH
HANH
AFTER ALL, I...
YES, I...AM TRULY...

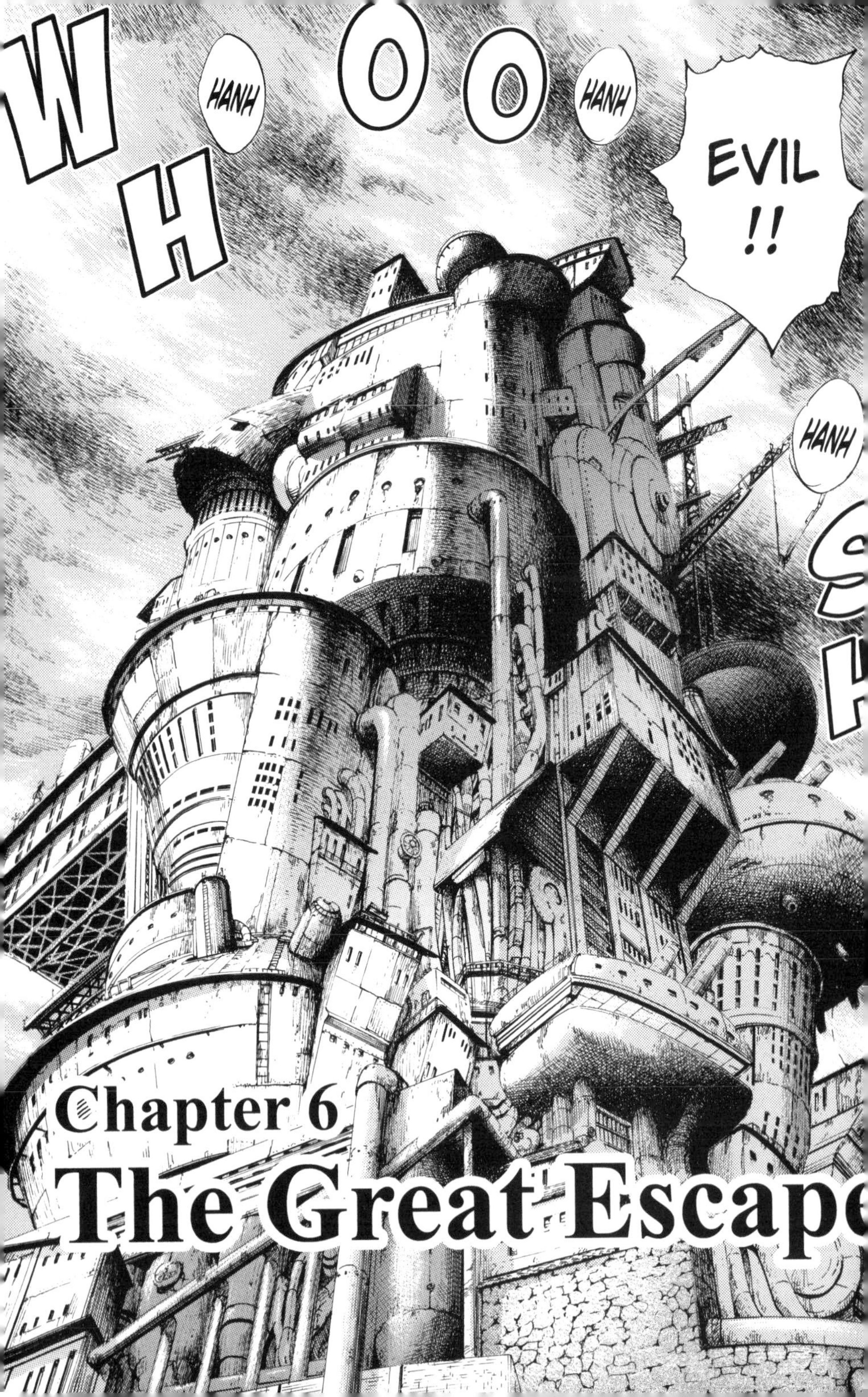
EVIL !!
HANH
HANH
HANH
WHOOSH

Chapter 6
The Great Escape

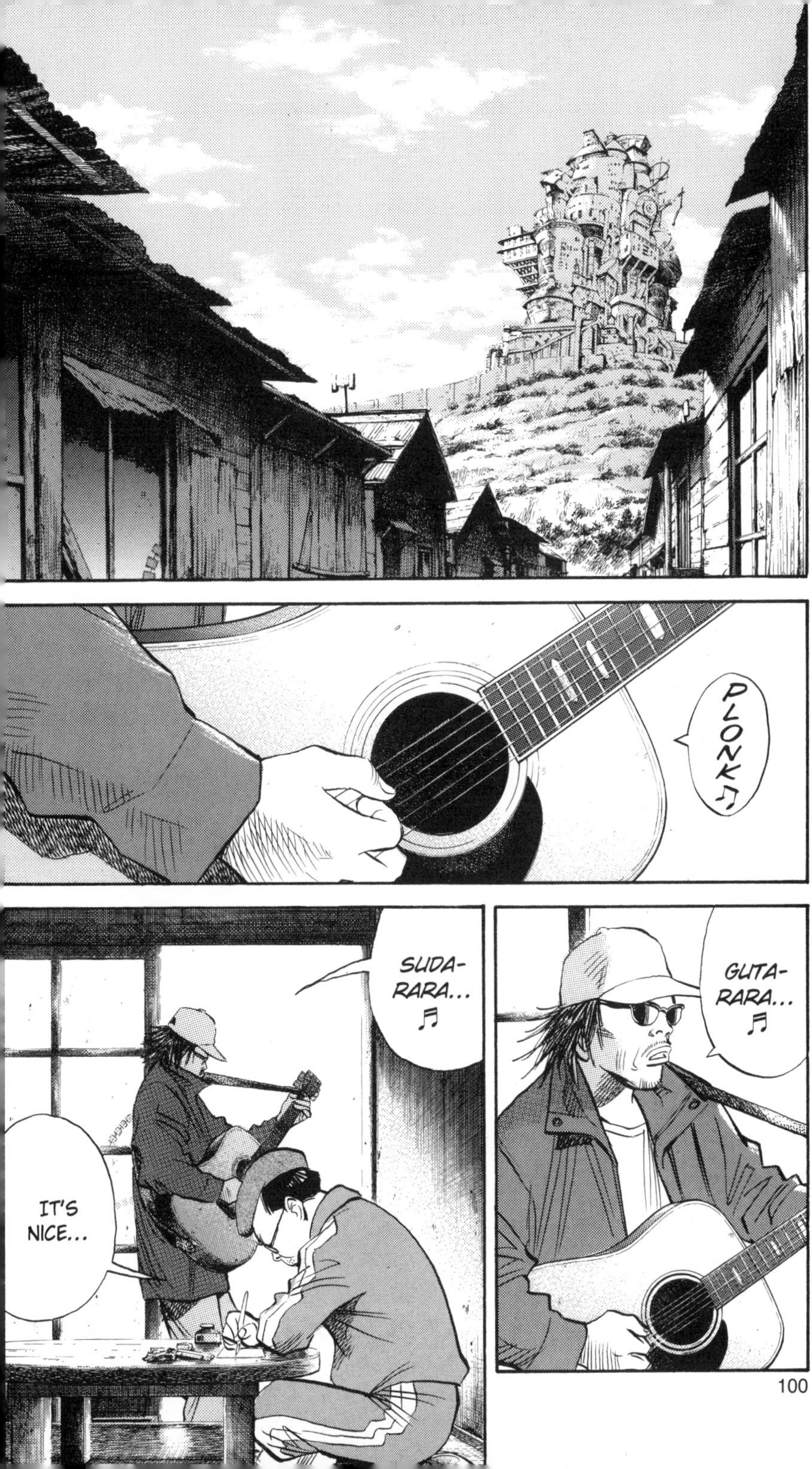

PLONK♫
GUTA-RARA... ♬
SUDA-RARA... ♬
IT'S NICE...

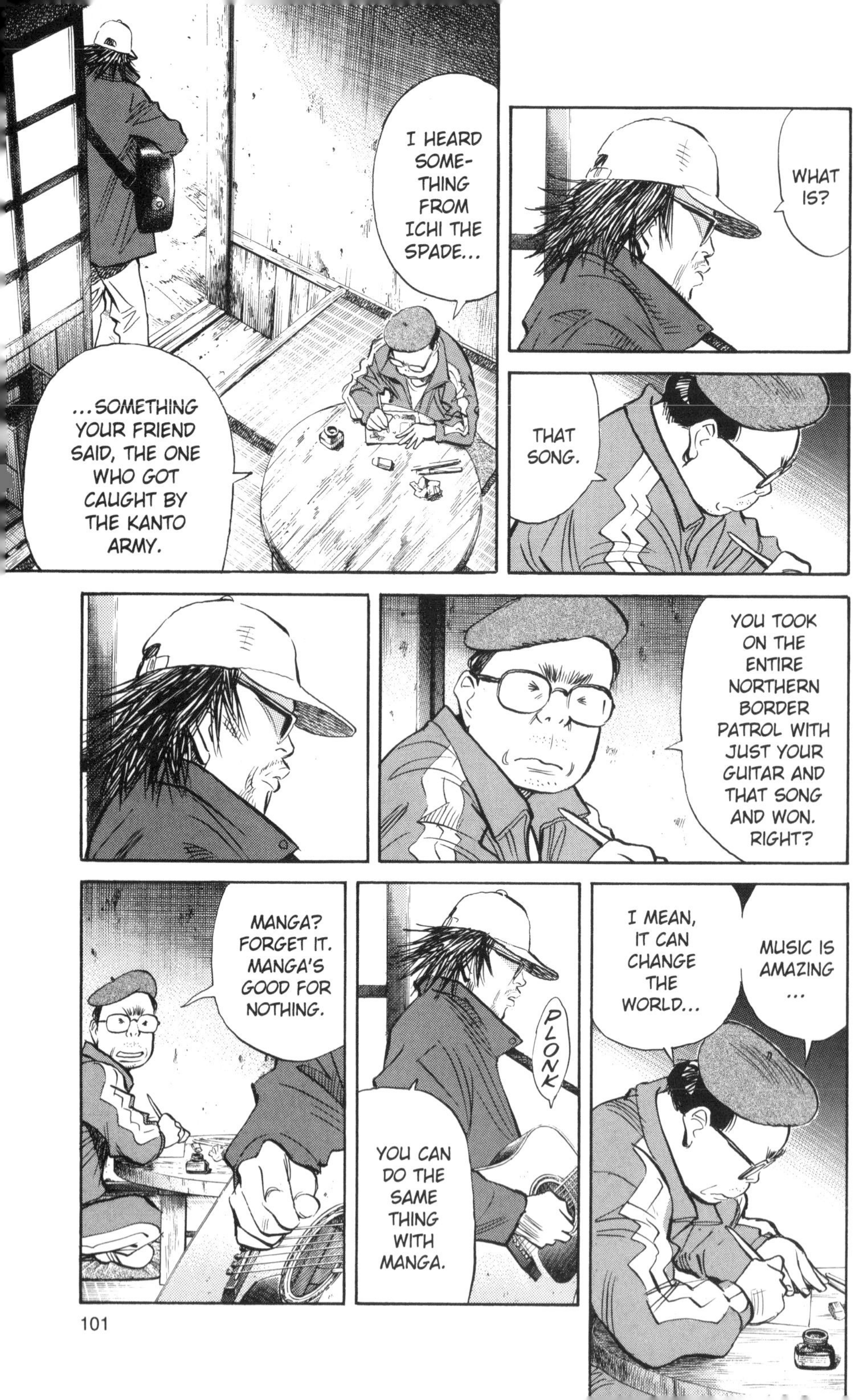

I HEARD SOMETHING FROM ICHI THE SPADE...
...SOMETHING YOUR FRIEND SAID, THE ONE WHO GOT CAUGHT BY THE KANTO ARMY.
WHAT IS?
THAT SONG.
YOU TOOK ON THE ENTIRE NORTHERN BORDER PATROL WITH JUST YOUR GUITAR AND THAT SONG AND WON. RIGHT?
MUSIC IS AMAZING ...
I MEAN, IT CAN CHANGE THE WORLD...
PLONK
YOU CAN DO THE SAME THING WITH MANGA.
MANGA? FORGET IT. MANGA'S GOOD FOR NOTHING.

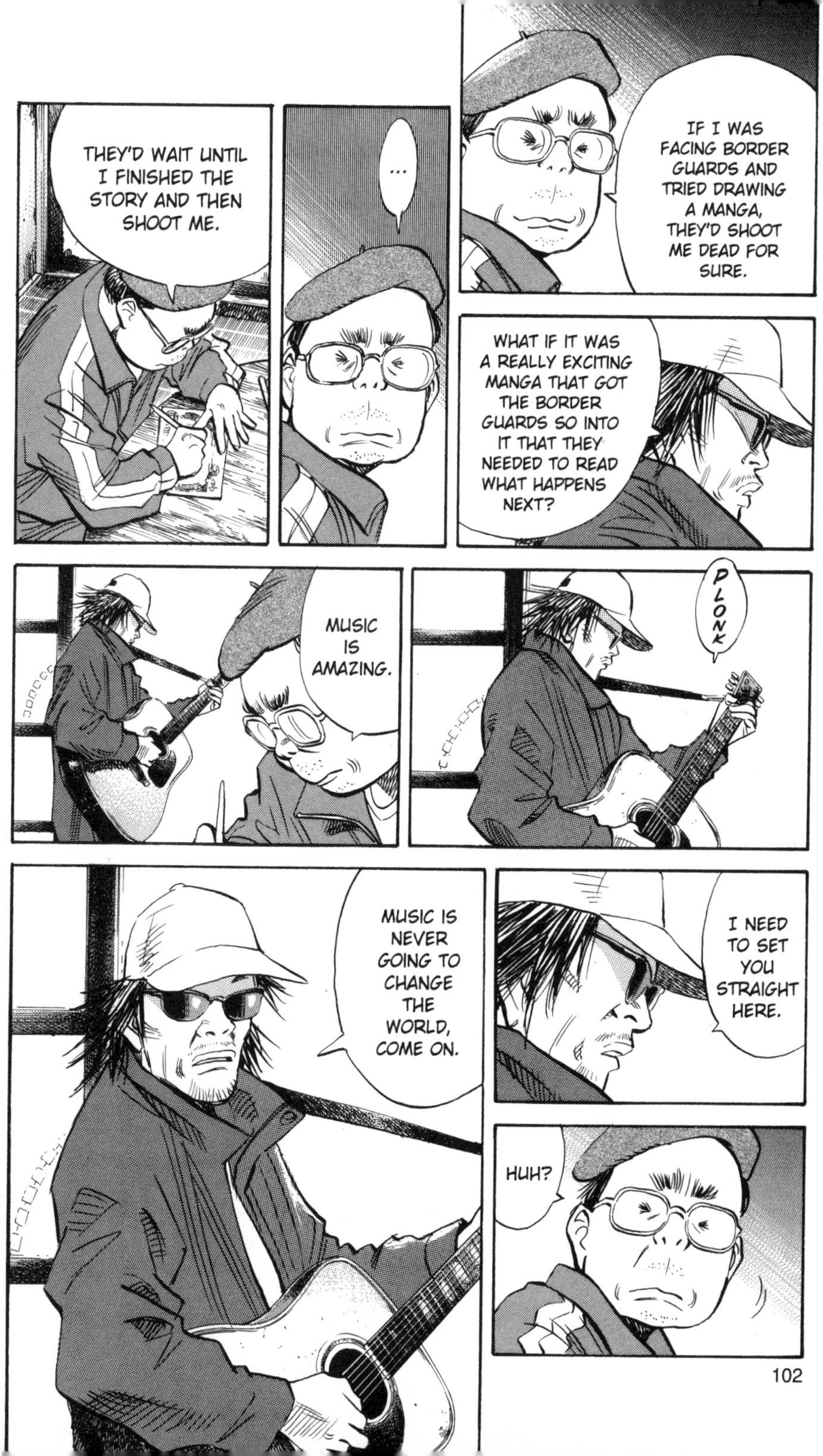
IF I WAS FACING BORDER GUARDS AND TRIED DRAWING A MANGA, THEY'D SHOOT ME DEAD FOR SURE.
WHAT IF IT WAS A REALLY EXCITING MANGA THAT GOT THE BORDER GUARDS SO INTO IT THAT THEY NEEDED TO READ WHAT HAPPENS NEXT?
...
THEY'D WAIT UNTIL I FINISHED THE STORY AND THEN SHOOT ME.
PLONK
MUSIC IS AMAZING.
I NEED TO SET YOU STRAIGHT HERE.
HUH?
MUSIC IS NEVER GOING TO CHANGE THE WORLD, COME ON.

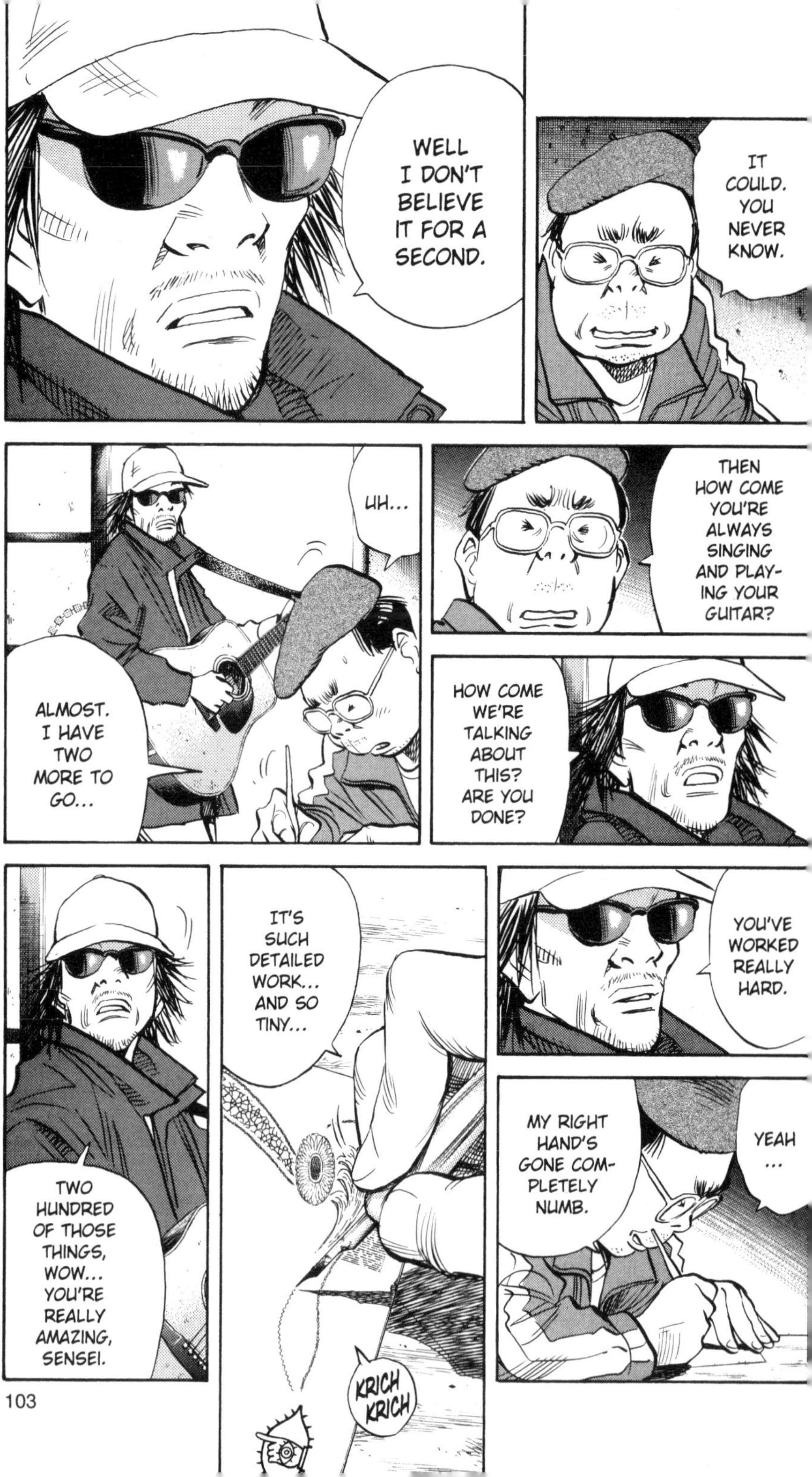
IT COULD. YOU NEVER KNOW.
WELL I DON'T BELIEVE IT FOR A SECOND.
THEN HOW COME YOU'RE ALWAYS SINGING AND PLAY-ING YOUR GUITAR?
HOW COME WE'RE TALKING ABOUT THIS? ARE YOU DONE?
UH...
ALMOST. I HAVE TWO MORE TO GO...
YOU'VE WORKED REALLY HARD.
YEAH...
MY RIGHT HAND'S GONE COM-PLETELY NUMB.
IT'S SUCH DETAILED WORK... AND SO TINY...
KRICH KRICH
TWO HUNDRED OF THOSE THINGS, WOW... YOU'RE REALLY AMAZING, SENSEI.

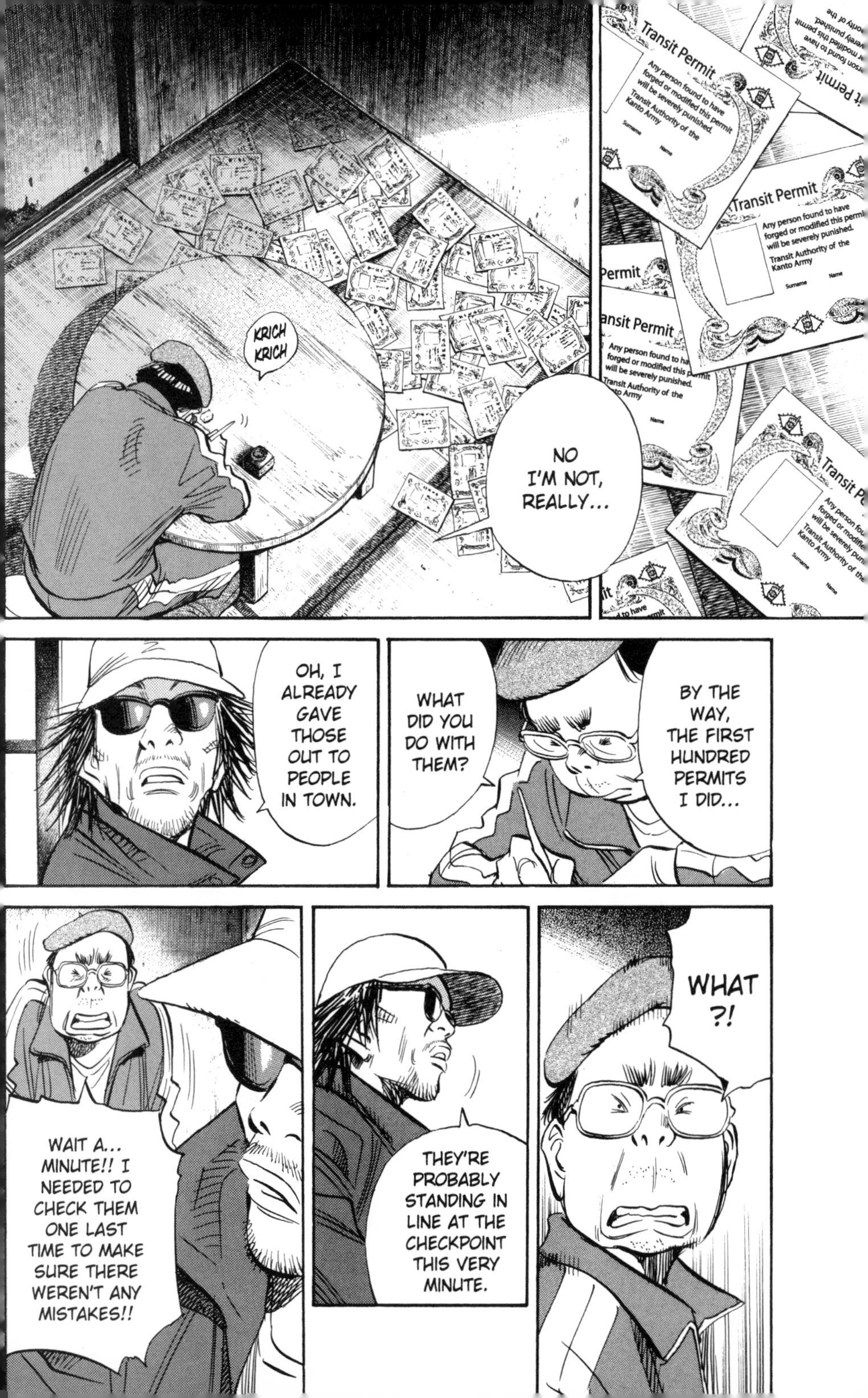
Transit Permit
Any person found to have forged or modified this permit will be severely punished.
Transit Authority of the Kanto Army
Surname
Name
NO I'M NOT, REALLY...
KRICH KRICH
BY THE WAY, THE FIRST HUNDRED PERMITS I DID...
WHAT DID YOU DO WITH THEM?
OH, I ALREADY GAVE THOSE OUT TO PEOPLE IN TOWN.
WHAT?!
THEY'RE PROBABLY STANDING IN LINE AT THE CHECKPOINT THIS VERY MINUTE.
WAIT A... MINUTE!! I NEEDED TO CHECK THEM ONE LAST TIME TO MAKE SURE THERE WEREN'T ANY MISTAKES!!

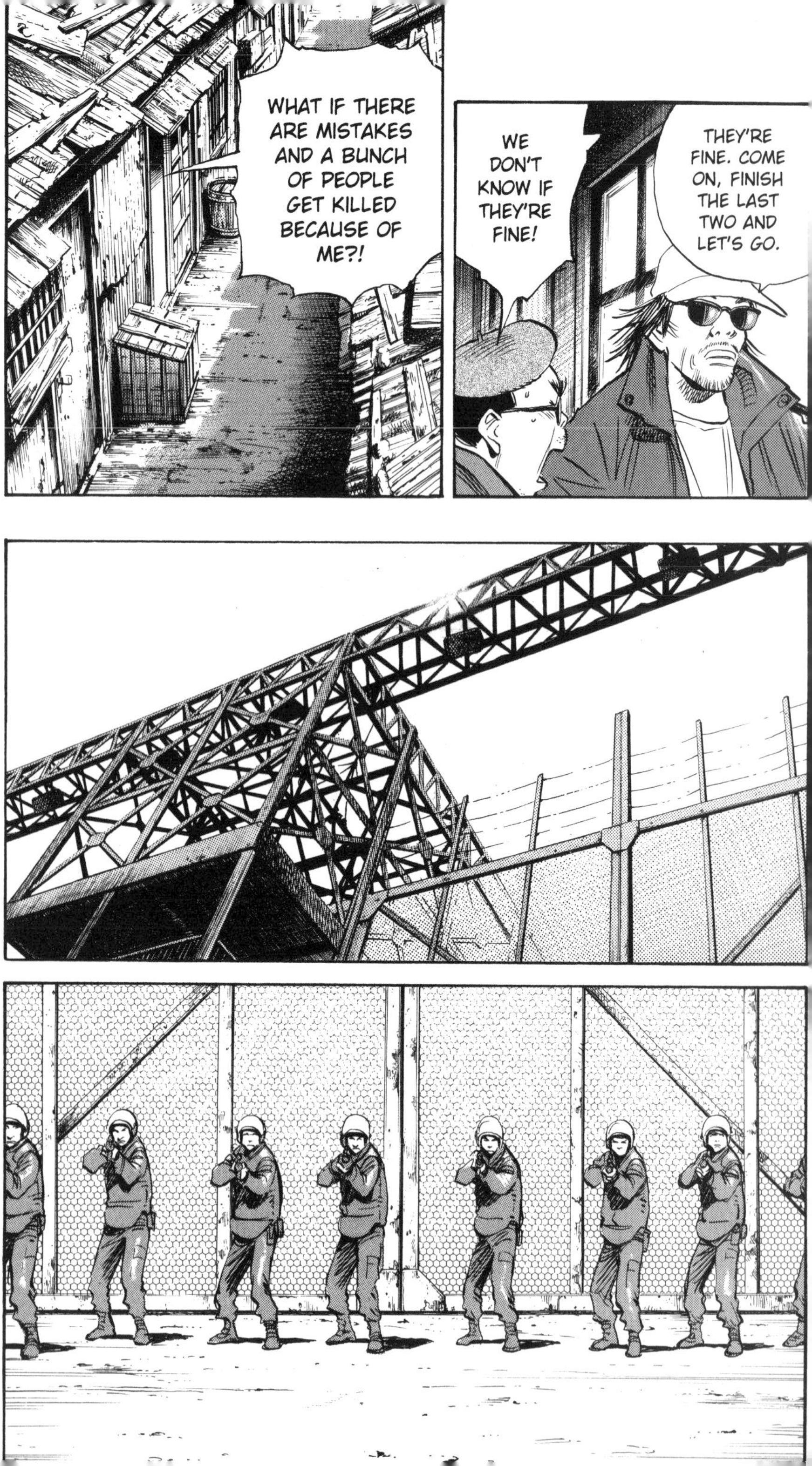
THEY'RE FINE. COME ON, FINISH THE LAST TWO AND LET'S GO.
WE DON'T KNOW IF THEY'RE FINE!
WHAT IF THERE ARE MISTAKES AND A BUNCH OF PEOPLE GET KILLED BECAUSE OF ME?!

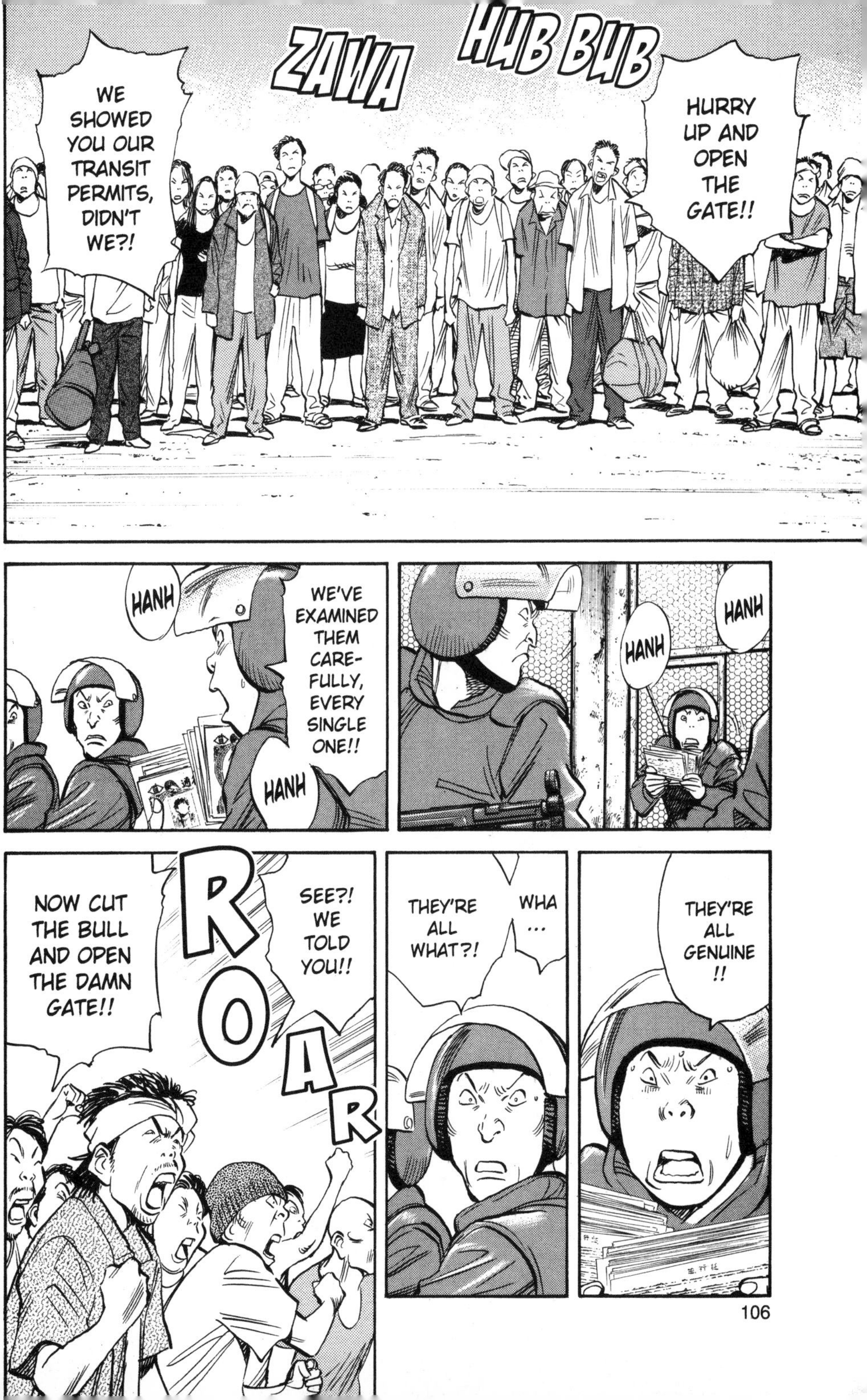
HUB BUB
ZAWA
HURRY UP AND OPEN THE GATE!!
WE SHOWED YOU OUR TRANSIT PERMITS, DIDN'T WE?!
HANH
HANH
WE'VE EXAMINED THEM CARE-FULLY, EVERY SINGLE ONE!!
HANH
HANH
THEY'RE ALL GENUINE !!
WHA ...
THEY'RE ALL WHAT?!
SEE?! WE TOLD YOU!!
ROAR
NOW CUT THE BULL AND OPEN THE DAMN GATE!!

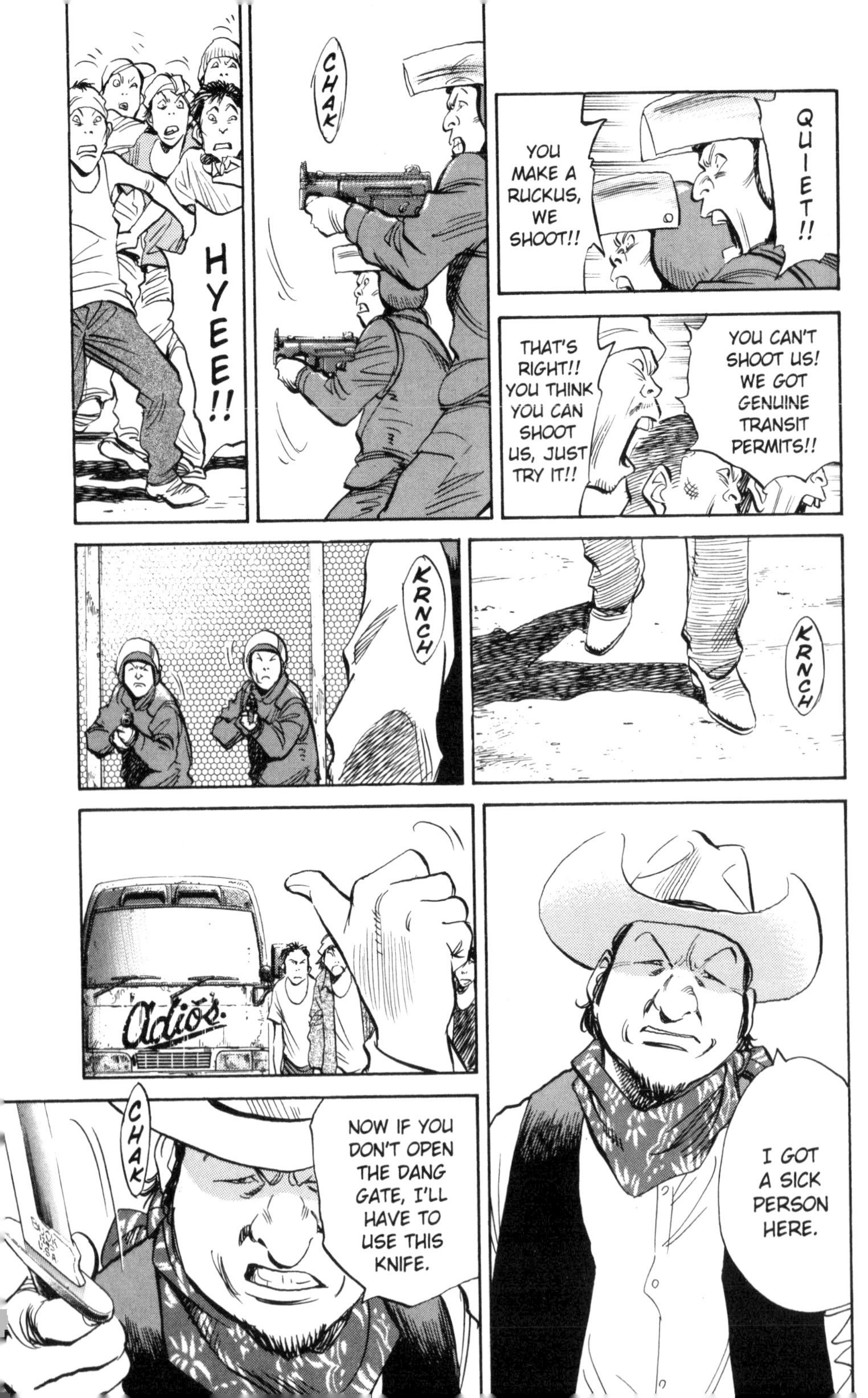
QUIET!!
YOU MAKE A RUCKUS, WE SHOOT!!
YOU CAN'T SHOOT US! WE GOT GENUINE TRANSIT PERMITS!!
THAT'S RIGHT!! YOU THINK YOU CAN SHOOT US, JUST TRY IT!!
CHAK
HYEEE!!
KRNCH
KRNCH
I GOT A SICK PERSON HERE.
Adiós.
CHAK
NOW IF YOU DON'T OPEN THE DANG GATE, I'LL HAVE TO USE THIS KNIFE.

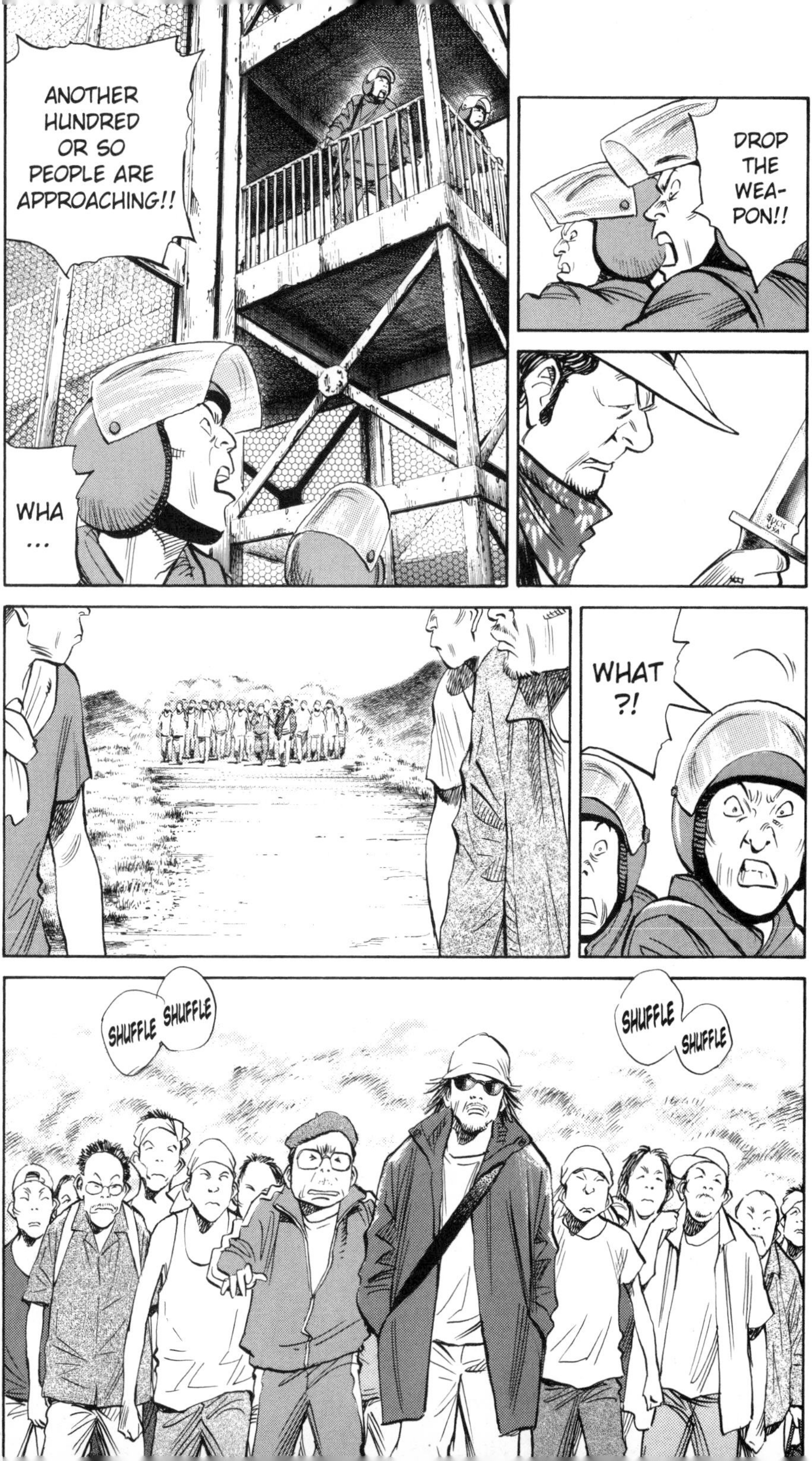
DROP THE WEA-PON!!
ANOTHER HUNDRED OR SO PEOPLE ARE APPROACHING!!
WHA ...
WHAT ?!
SHUFFLE
SHUFFLE
SHUFFLE
SHUFFLE

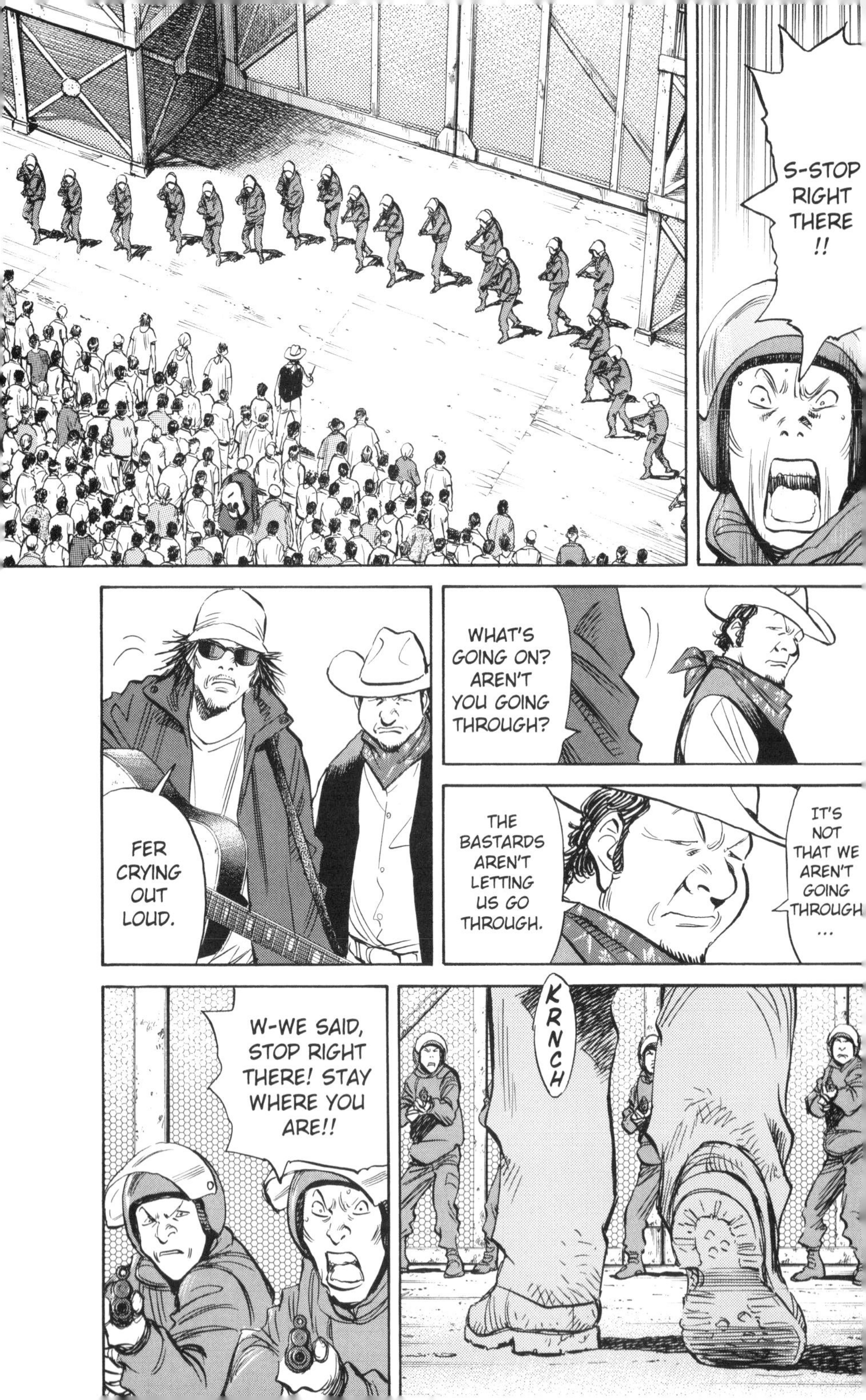
S-STOP RIGHT THERE !!
WHAT'S GOING ON? AREN'T YOU GOING THROUGH?
IT'S NOT THAT WE AREN'T GOING THROUGH...
THE BASTARDS AREN'T LETTING US GO THROUGH.
FER CRYING OUT LOUD.
KRNCH
W-WE SAID, STOP RIGHT THERE! STAY WHERE YOU ARE!!

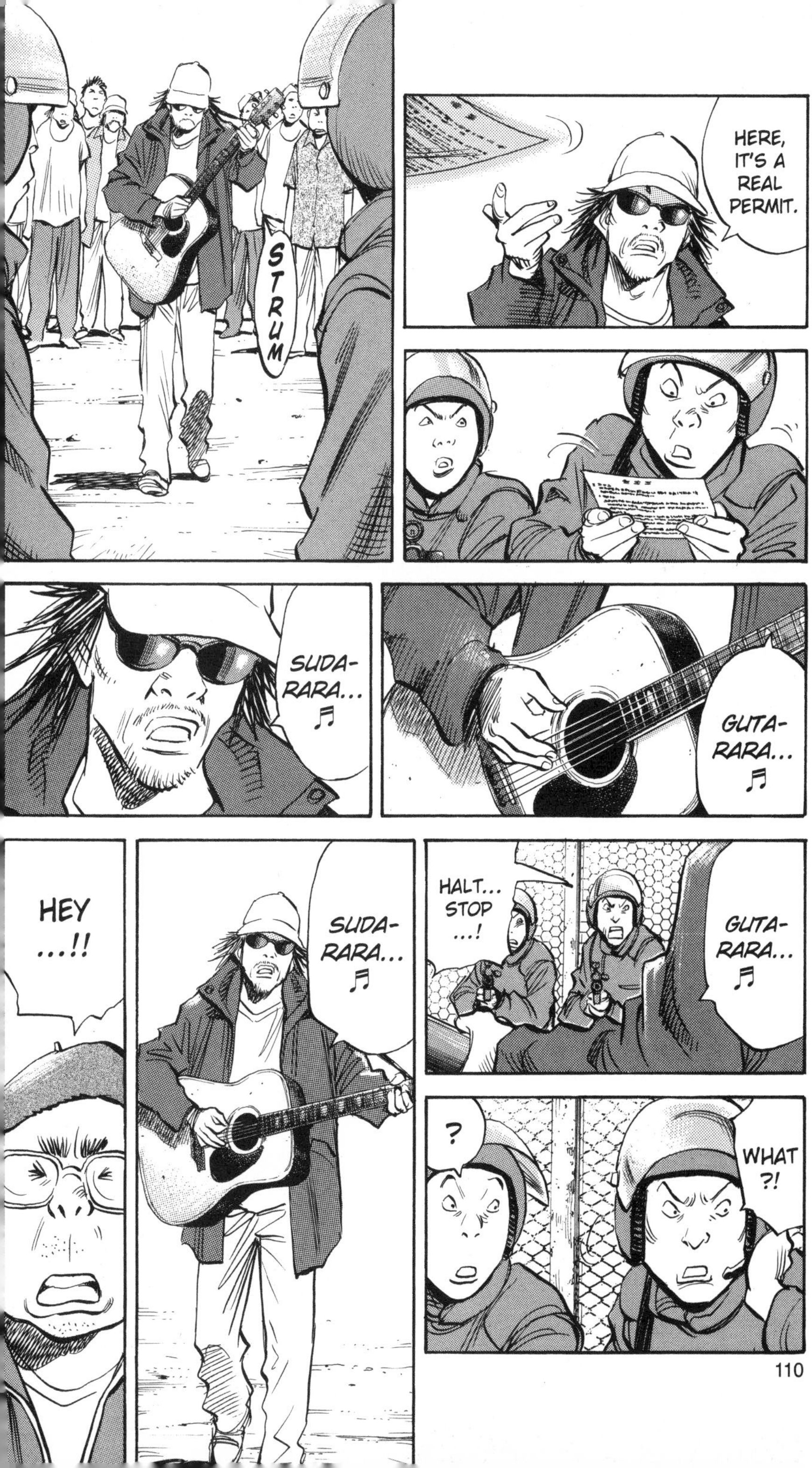
HERE, IT'S A REAL PERMIT.
STRUM
GUTA-RARA... ♬
SUDA-RARA... ♬
GUTA-RARA... ♬
HALT... STOP ...!
WHAT ?!
?
SUDA-RARA... ♬
HEY ...!!

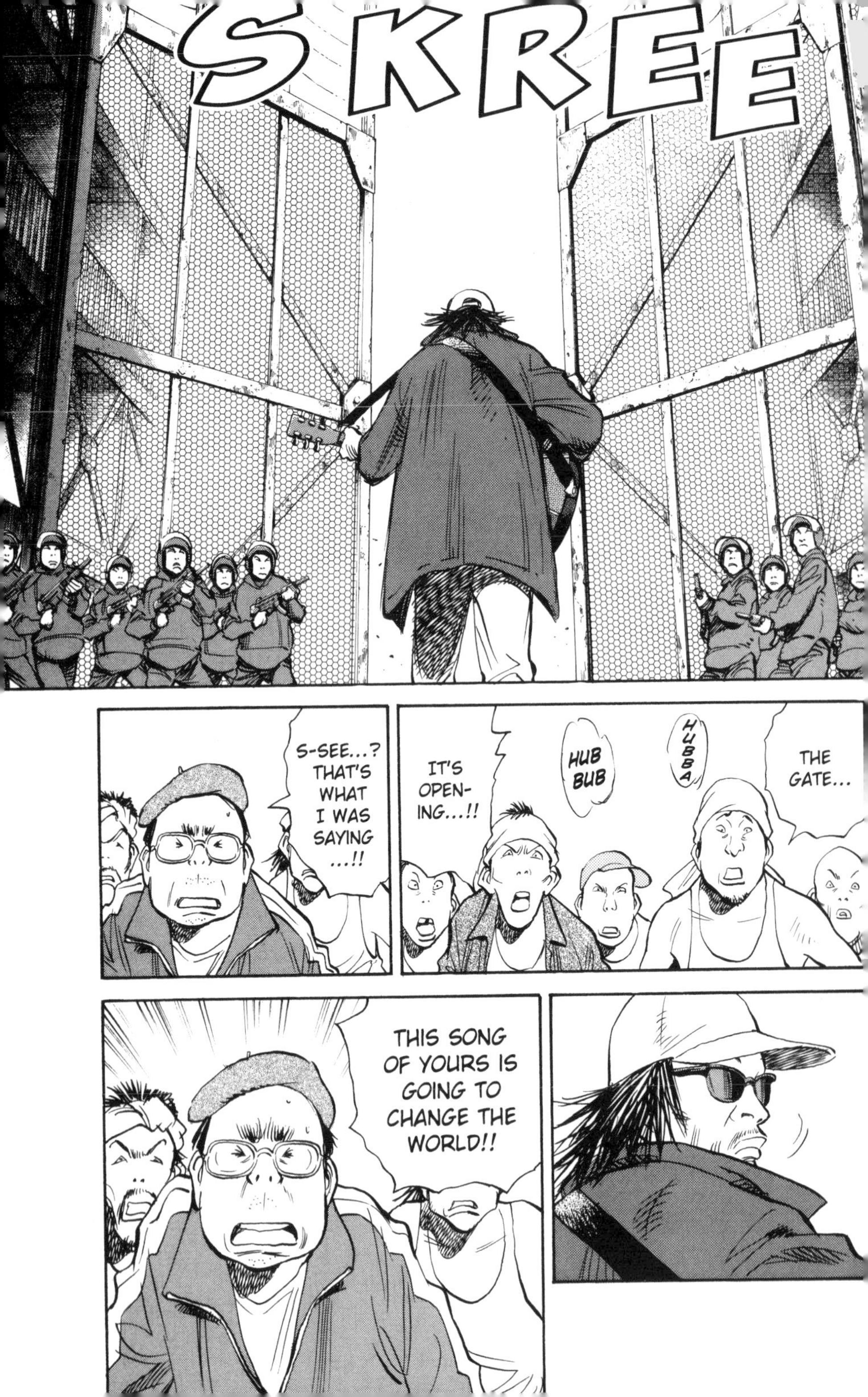
SKREE
THE GATE...
HUBBA
HUB BUB
IT'S OPEN-ING...!!
S-SEE...? THAT'S WHAT I WAS SAYING ...!!
THIS SONG OF YOURS IS GOING TO CHANGE THE WORLD!!

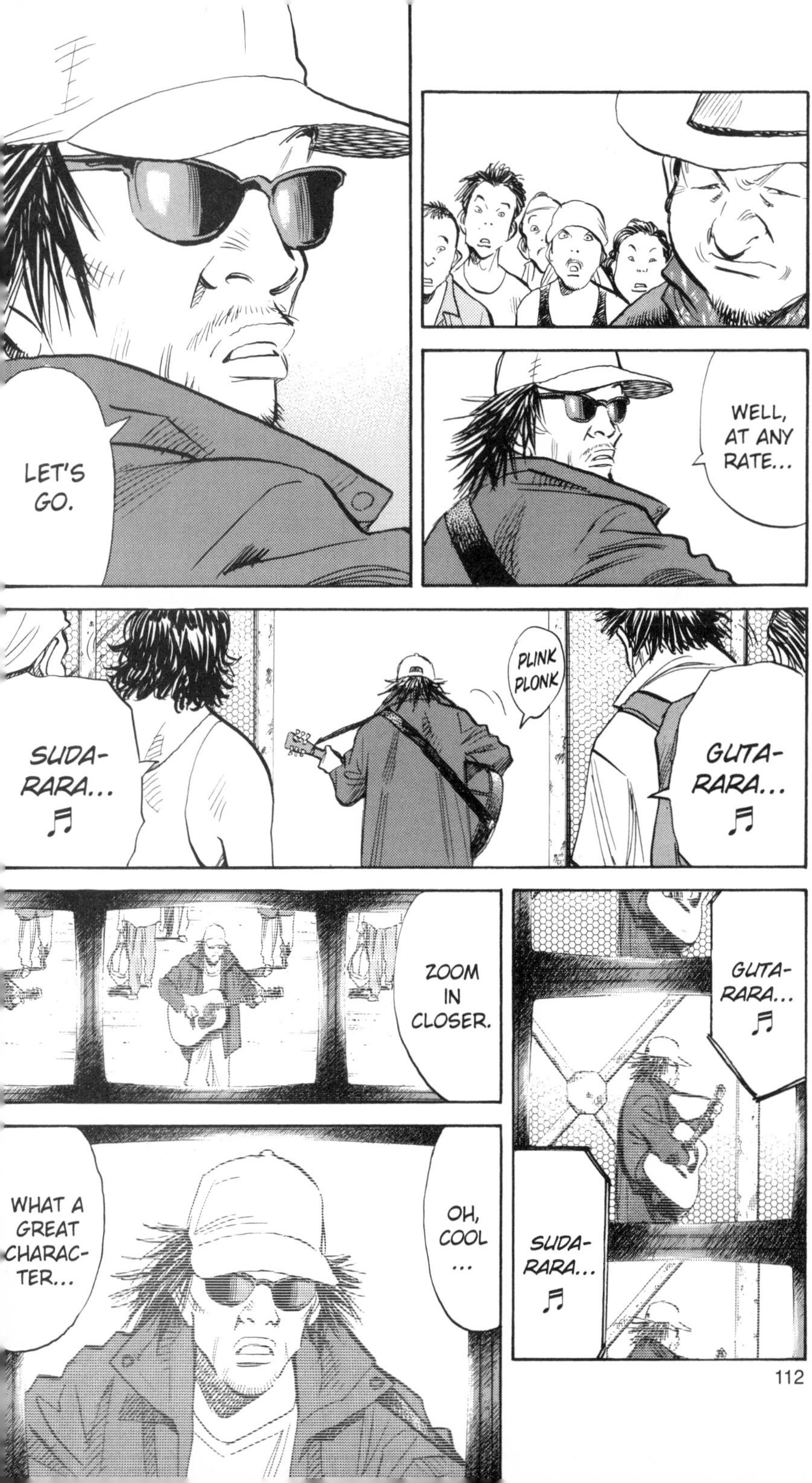
WELL, AT ANY RATE...
LET'S GO.
GUTA-RARA... ♬
PLINK PLONK
SUDA-RARA... ♬
GUTA-RARA... ♬
SUDA-RARA... ♬
ZOOM IN CLOSER.
OH, COOL...
WHAT A GREAT CHARACTER...

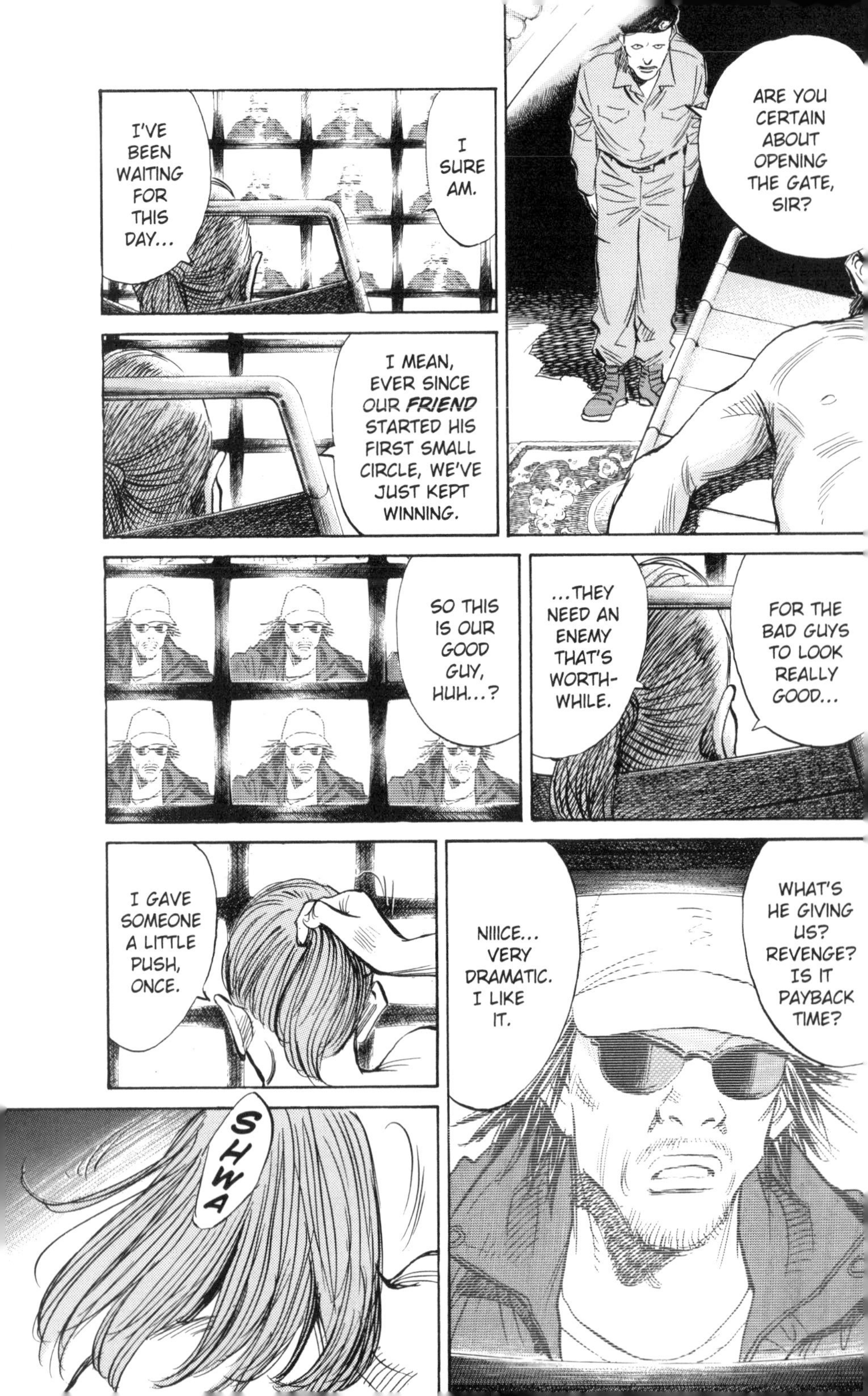
ARE YOU CERTAIN ABOUT OPENING THE GATE, SIR?
I SURE AM.
I'VE BEEN WAITING FOR THIS DAY...
I MEAN, EVER SINCE OUR *FRIEND* STARTED HIS FIRST SMALL CIRCLE, WE'VE JUST KEPT WINNING.
FOR THE BAD GUYS TO LOOK REALLY GOOD...
...THEY NEED AN ENEMY THAT'S WORTH-WHILE.
SO THIS IS OUR GOOD GUY, HUH...?
WHAT'S HE GIVING US? REVENGE? IS IT PAYBACK TIME?
NIIICE... VERY DRAMATIC. I LIKE IT.
I GAVE SOMEONE A LITTLE PUSH, ONCE.
SHWA

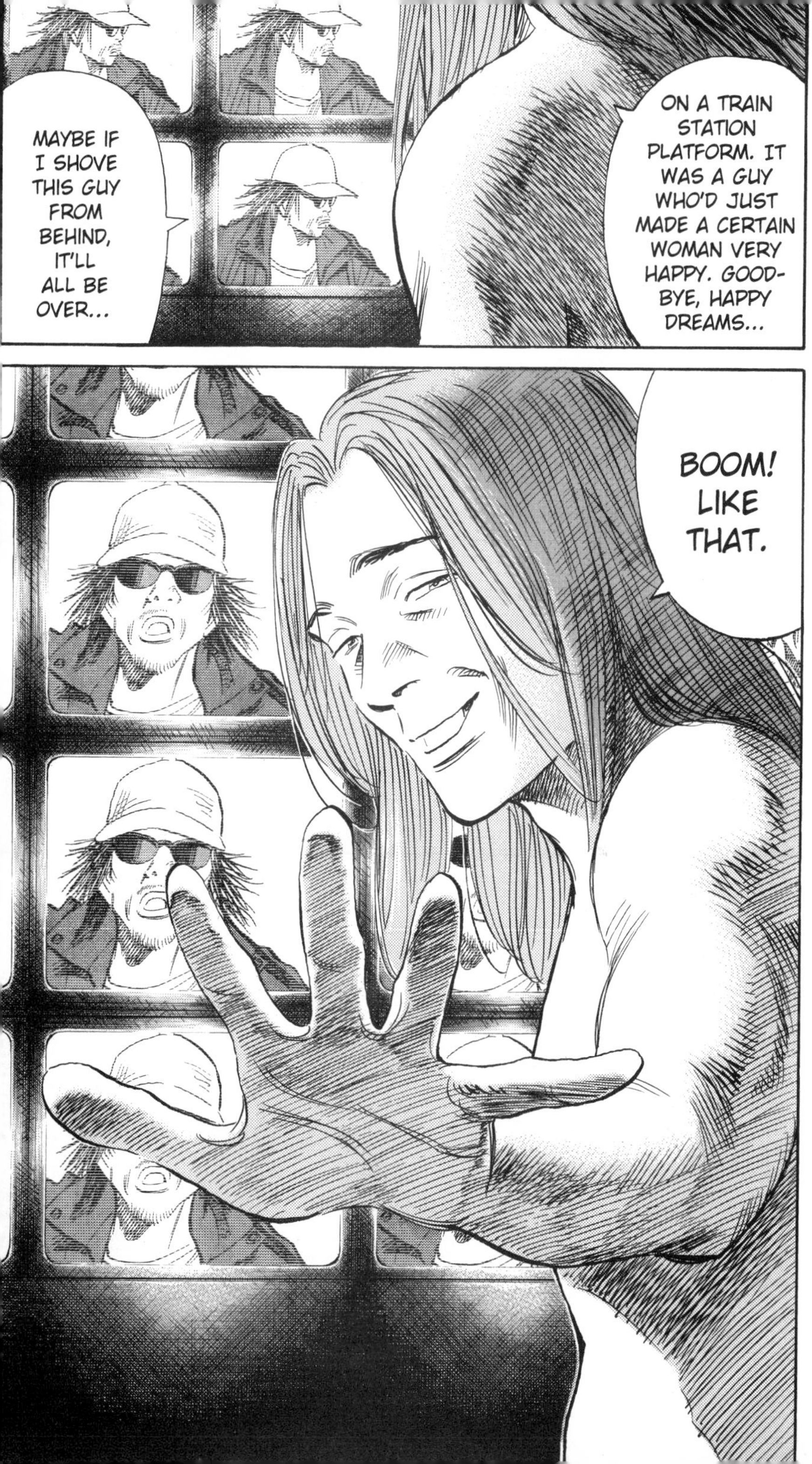
ON A TRAIN STATION PLATFORM. IT WAS A GUY WHO'D JUST MADE A CERTAIN WOMAN VERY HAPPY. GOOD-BYE, HAPPY DREAMS...
MAYBE IF I SHOVE THIS GUY FROM BEHIND, IT'LL ALL BE OVER...
BOOM! LIKE THAT.

Chapter 7 The Seven Samurai of the Badlands

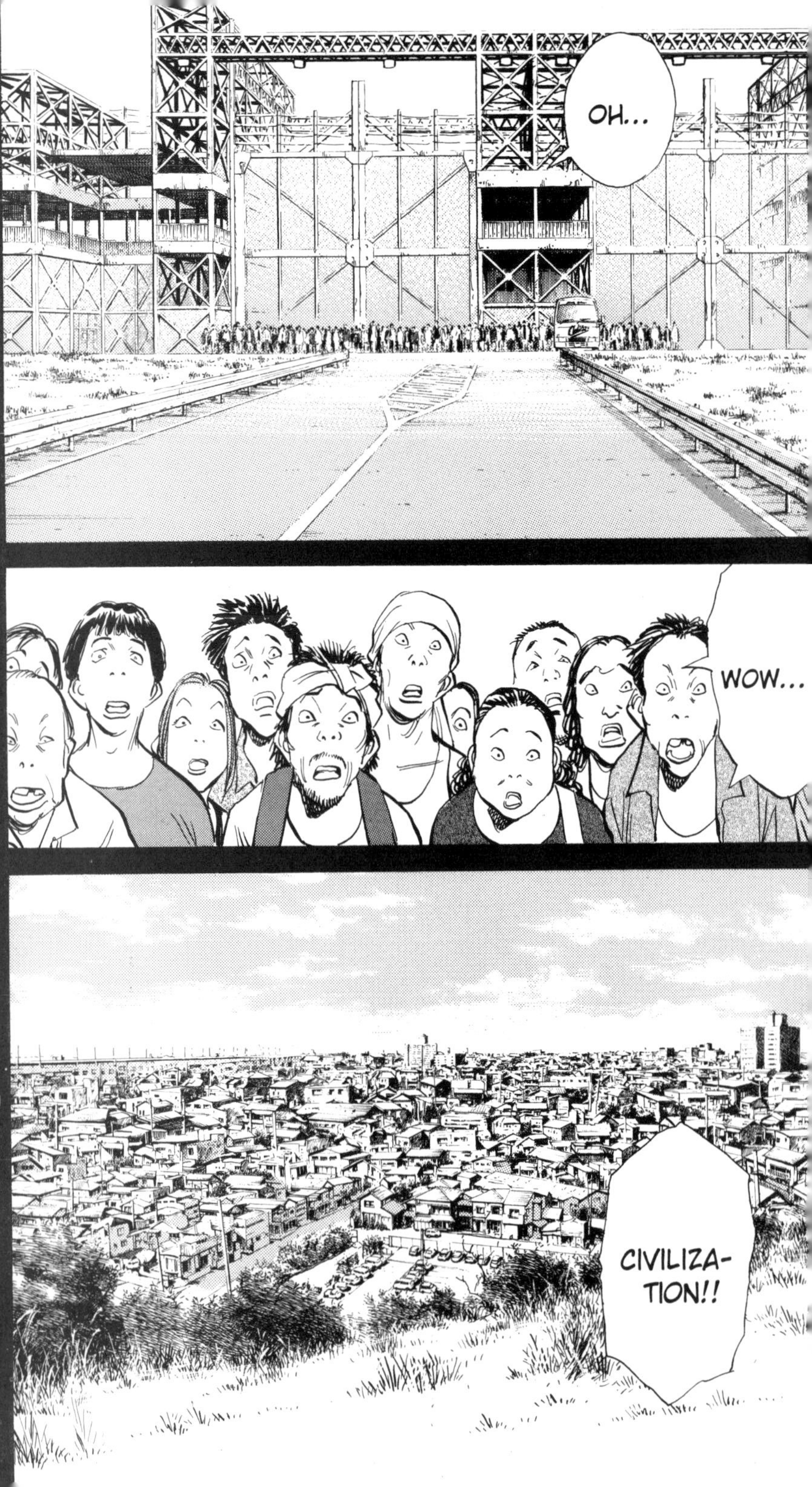

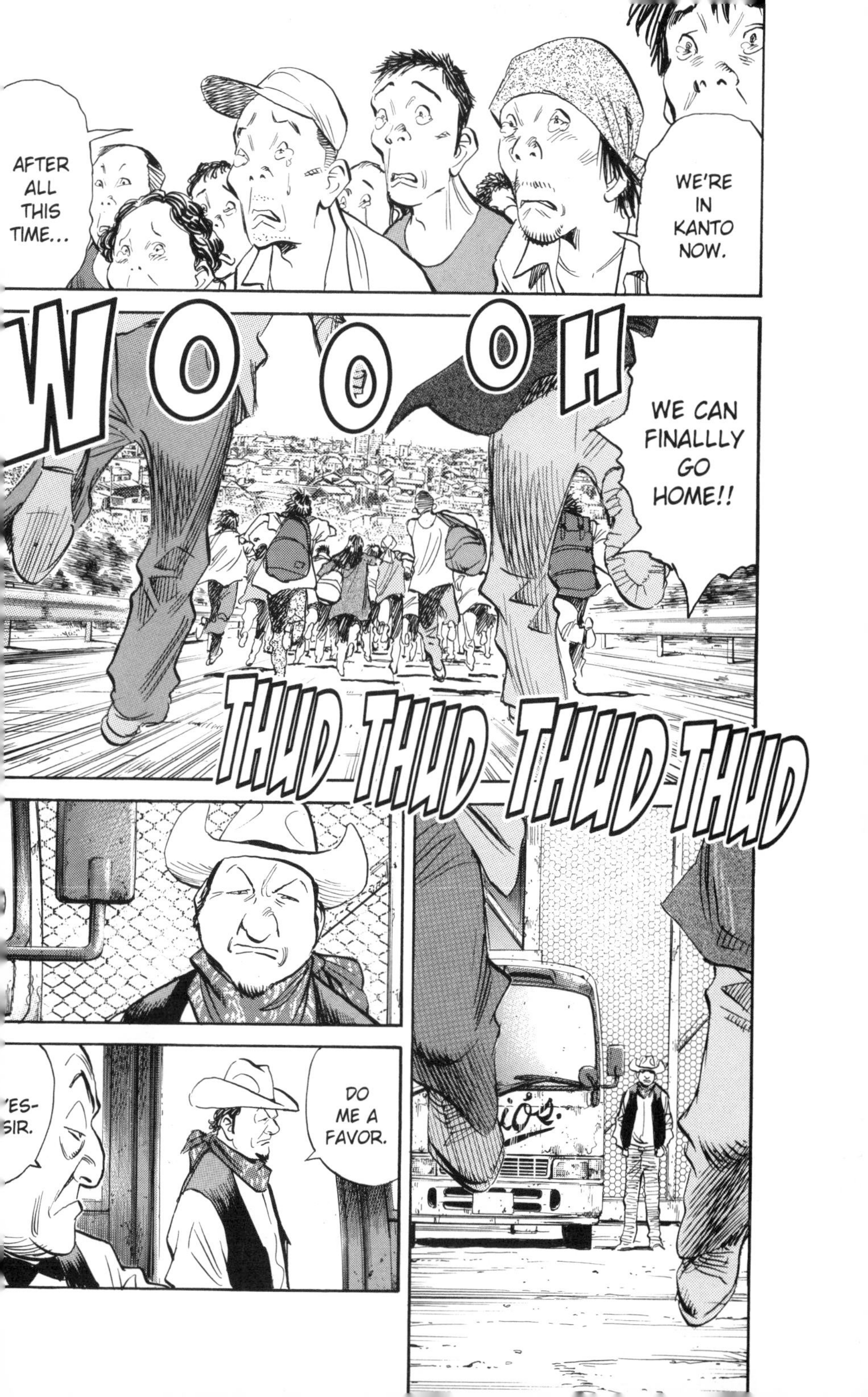
WE'RE IN KANTO NOW.
AFTER ALL THIS TIME...
WOOOH
WE CAN FINALLLY GO HOME!!
THUD THUD THUD THUD
DO ME A FAVOR.
ES- SIR.

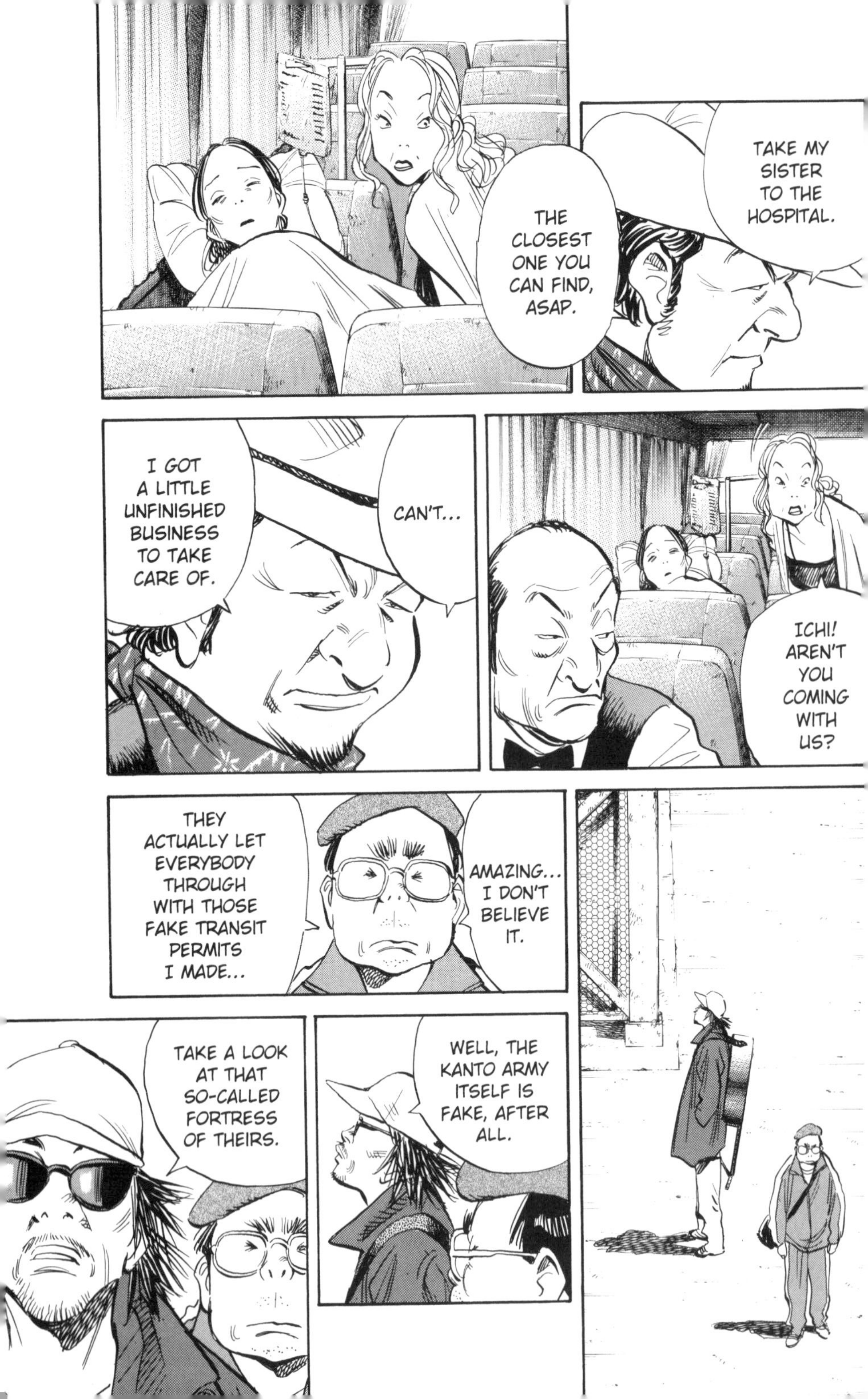
TAKE MY SISTER TO THE HOSPITAL.
THE CLOSEST ONE YOU CAN FIND, ASAP.
ICHI! AREN'T YOU COMING WITH US?
CAN'T...
I GOT A LITTLE UNFINISHED BUSINESS TO TAKE CARE OF.
AMAZING... I DON'T BELIEVE IT.
THEY ACTUALLY LET EVERYBODY THROUGH WITH THOSE FAKE TRANSIT PERMITS I MADE...
WELL, THE KANTO ARMY ITSELF IS FAKE, AFTER ALL.
TAKE A LOOK AT THAT SO-CALLED FORTRESS OF THEIRS.

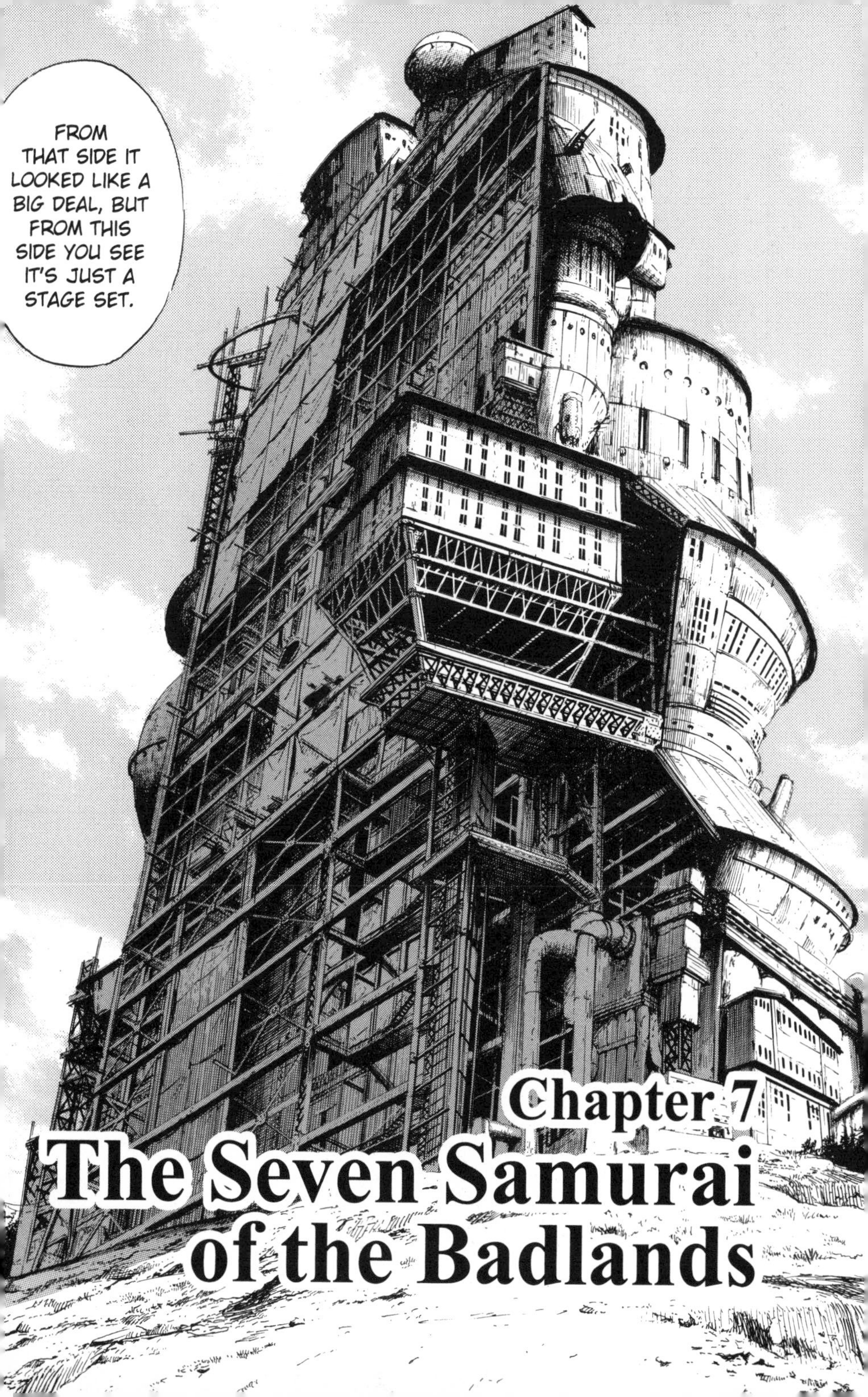
FROM THAT SIDE IT LOOKED LIKE A BIG DEAL, BUT FROM THIS SIDE YOU SEE IT'S JUST A STAGE SET.

Chapter 7
The Seven Samurai of the Badlands

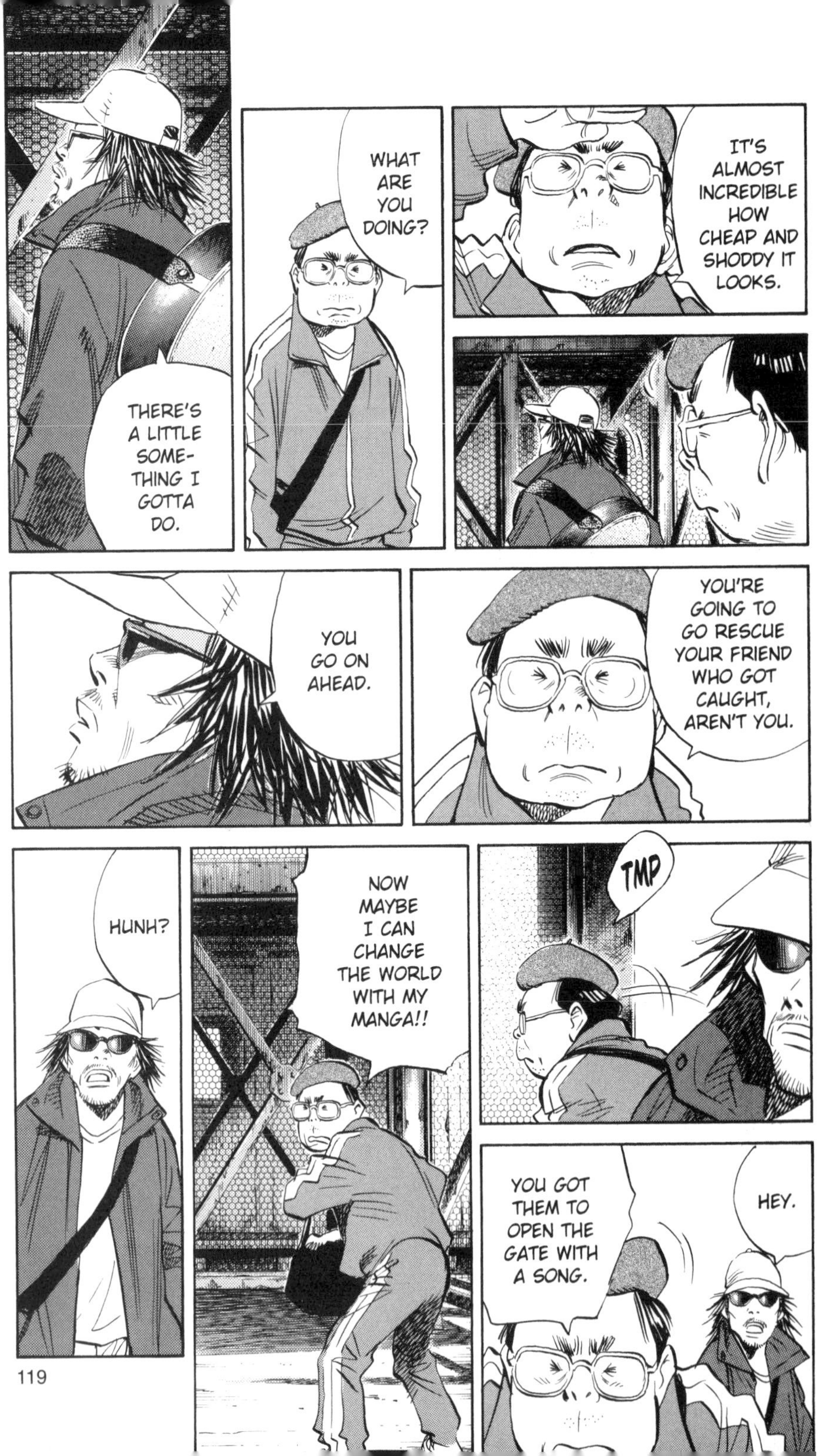
IT'S ALMOST INCREDIBLE HOW CHEAP AND SHODDY IT LOOKS.
WHAT ARE YOU DOING?
THERE'S A LITTLE SOME-THING I GOTTA DO.
YOU'RE GOING TO GO RESCUE YOUR FRIEND WHO GOT CAUGHT, AREN'T YOU.
YOU GO ON AHEAD.
TMP
HEY.
YOU GOT THEM TO OPEN THE GATE WITH A SONG.
NOW MAYBE I CAN CHANGE THE WORLD WITH MY MANGA!!
HUNH?

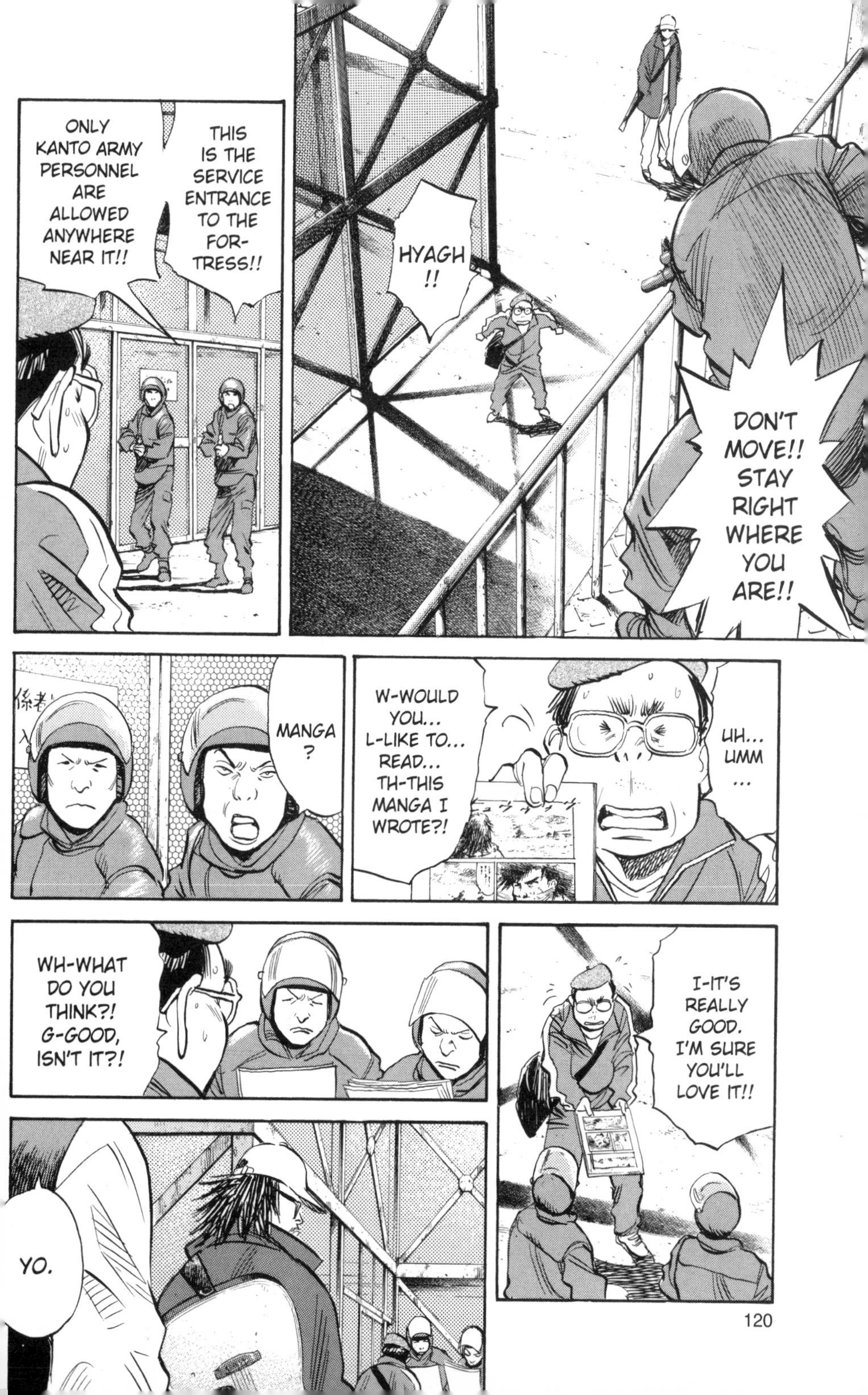

DON'T MOVE!! STAY RIGHT WHERE YOU ARE!!
HYAGH!!
THIS IS THE SERVICE ENTRANCE TO THE FOR-TRESS!!
ONLY KANTO ARMY PERSONNEL ARE ALLOWED ANYWHERE NEAR IT!!
UH... UMM...
W-WOULD YOU... L-LIKE TO... READ... TH-THIS MANGA I WROTE?!
MANGA?
I-IT'S REALLY GOOD. I'M SURE YOU'LL LOVE IT!!
WH-WHAT DO YOU THINK?! G-GOOD, ISN'T IT?!
YO.

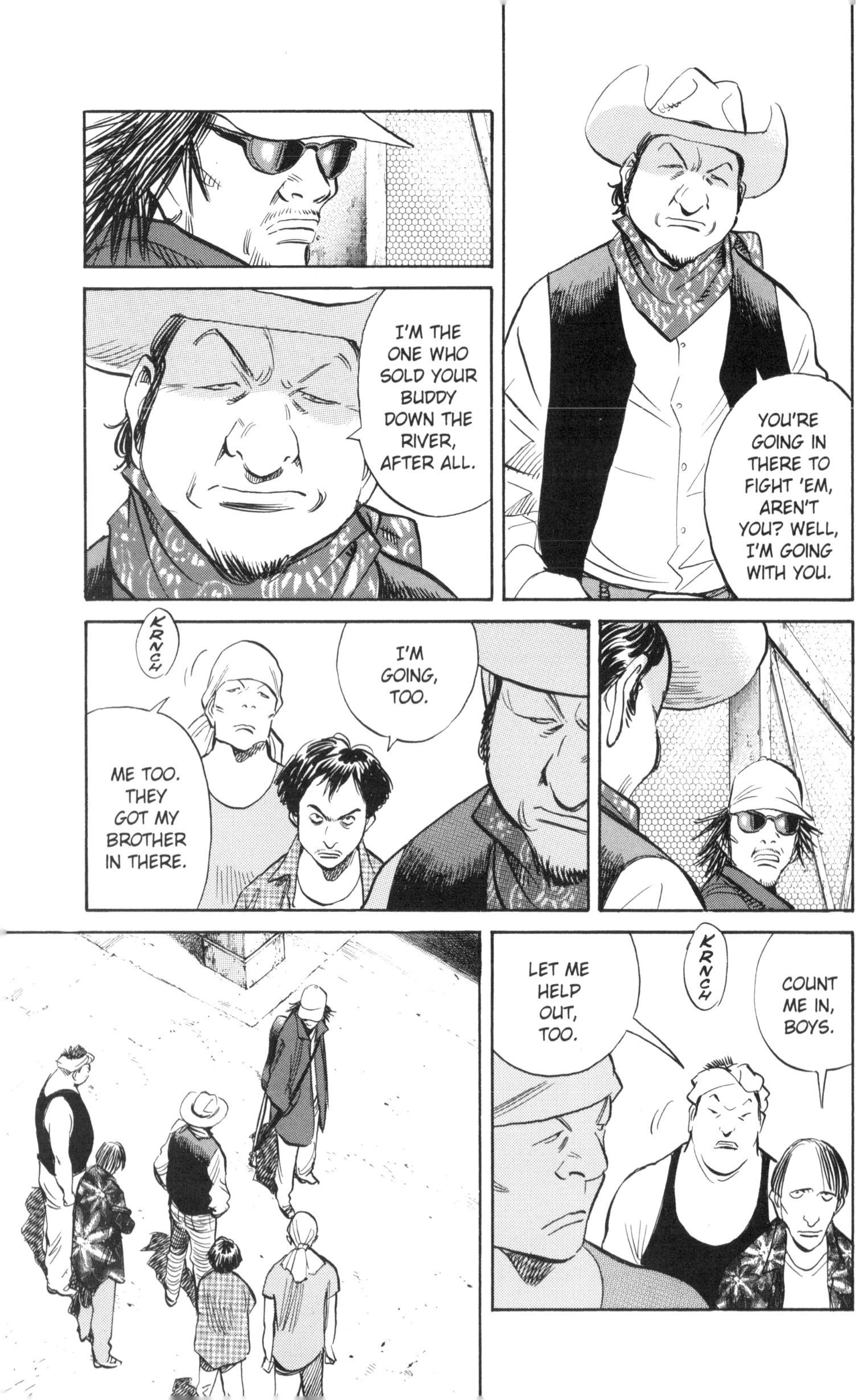
YOU'RE GOING IN THERE TO FIGHT 'EM, AREN'T YOU? WELL, I'M GOING WITH YOU.
I'M THE ONE WHO SOLD YOUR BUDDY DOWN THE RIVER, AFTER ALL.
I'M GOING, TOO.
KRNCH
ME TOO. THEY GOT MY BROTHER IN THERE.
COUNT ME IN, BOYS.
KRNCH
LET ME HELP OUT, TOO.

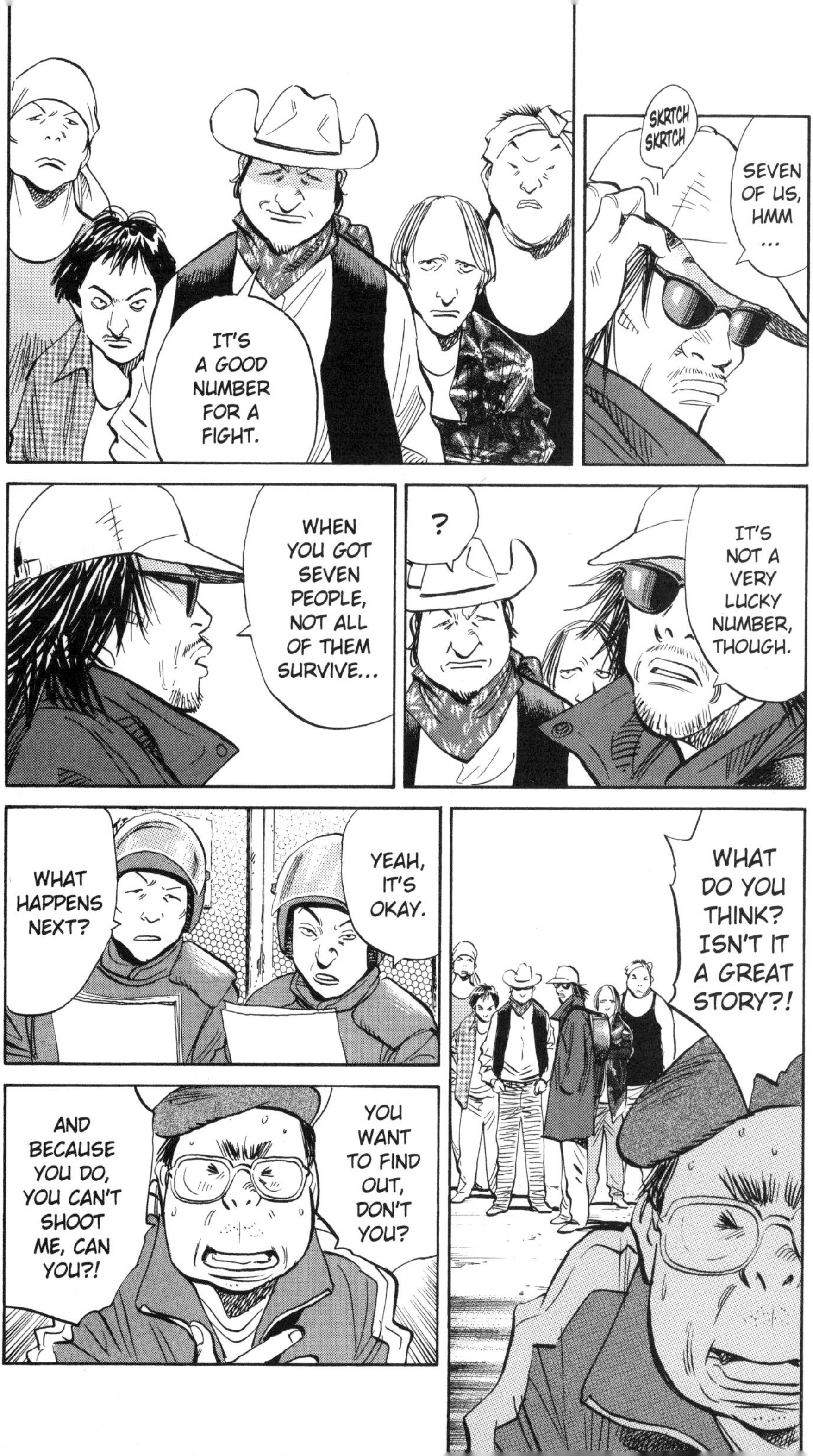
SKRTCH SKRTCH
SEVEN OF US, HMM ...
IT'S A GOOD NUMBER FOR A FIGHT.
?
IT'S NOT A VERY LUCKY NUMBER, THOUGH.
WHEN YOU GOT SEVEN PEOPLE, NOT ALL OF THEM SURVIVE...
WHAT DO YOU THINK? ISN'T IT A GREAT STORY?!
YEAH, IT'S OKAY.
WHAT HAPPENS NEXT?
YOU WANT TO FIND OUT, DON'T YOU?
AND BECAUSE YOU DO, YOU CAN'T SHOOT ME, CAN YOU?!

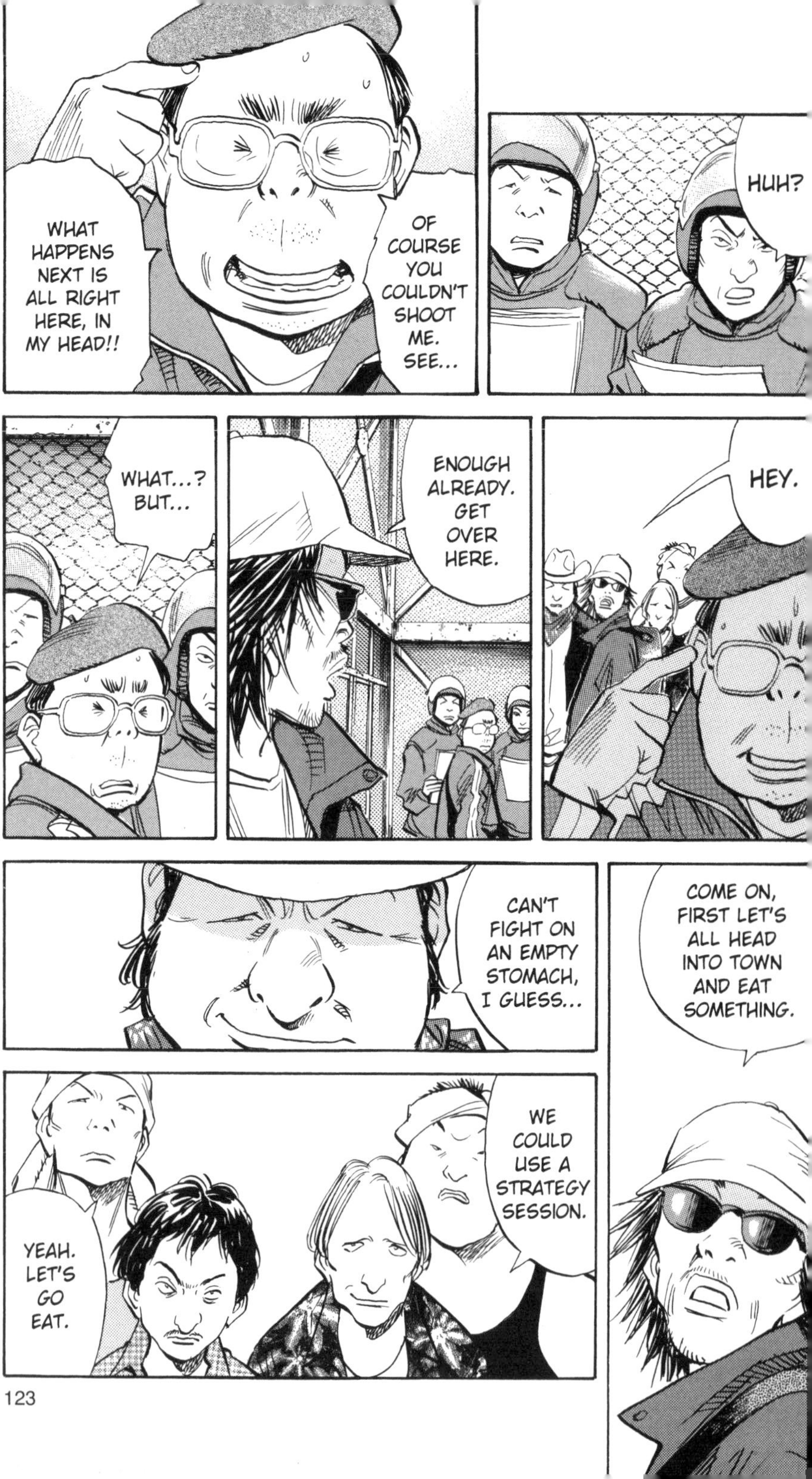
HUH?
OF COURSE YOU COULDN'T SHOOT ME. SEE...
WHAT HAPPENS NEXT IS ALL RIGHT HERE, IN MY HEAD!!
HEY.
ENOUGH ALREADY. GET OVER HERE.
WHAT...? BUT...
COME ON, FIRST LET'S ALL HEAD INTO TOWN AND EAT SOMETHING.
CAN'T FIGHT ON AN EMPTY STOMACH, I GUESS...
WE COULD USE A STRATEGY SESSION.
YEAH. LET'S GO EAT.

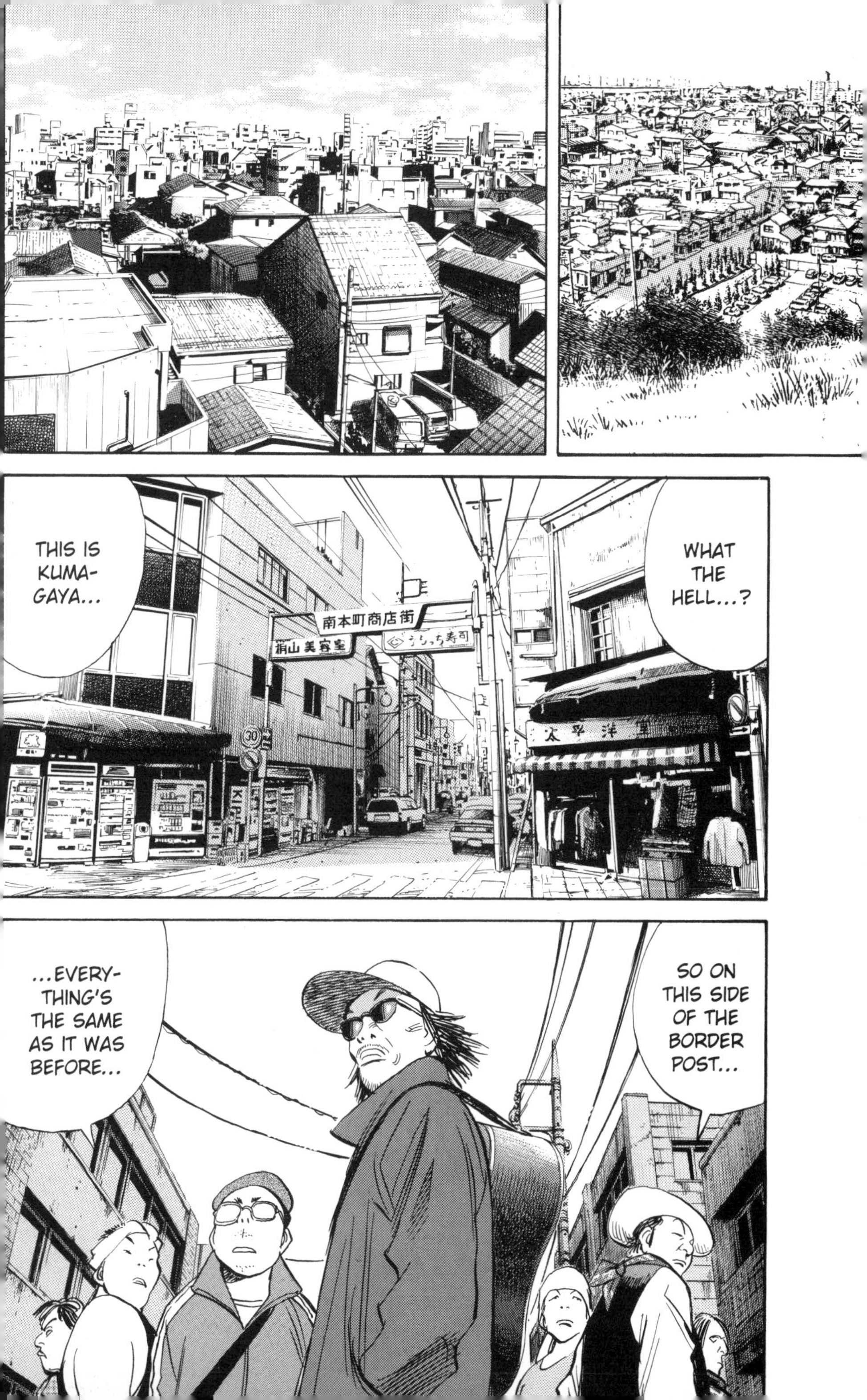
WHAT THE HELL...?
THIS IS KUMA-GAYA...
南本町商店街
SO ON THIS SIDE OF THE BORDER POST...
...EVERY-THING'S THE SAME AS IT WAS BEFORE...

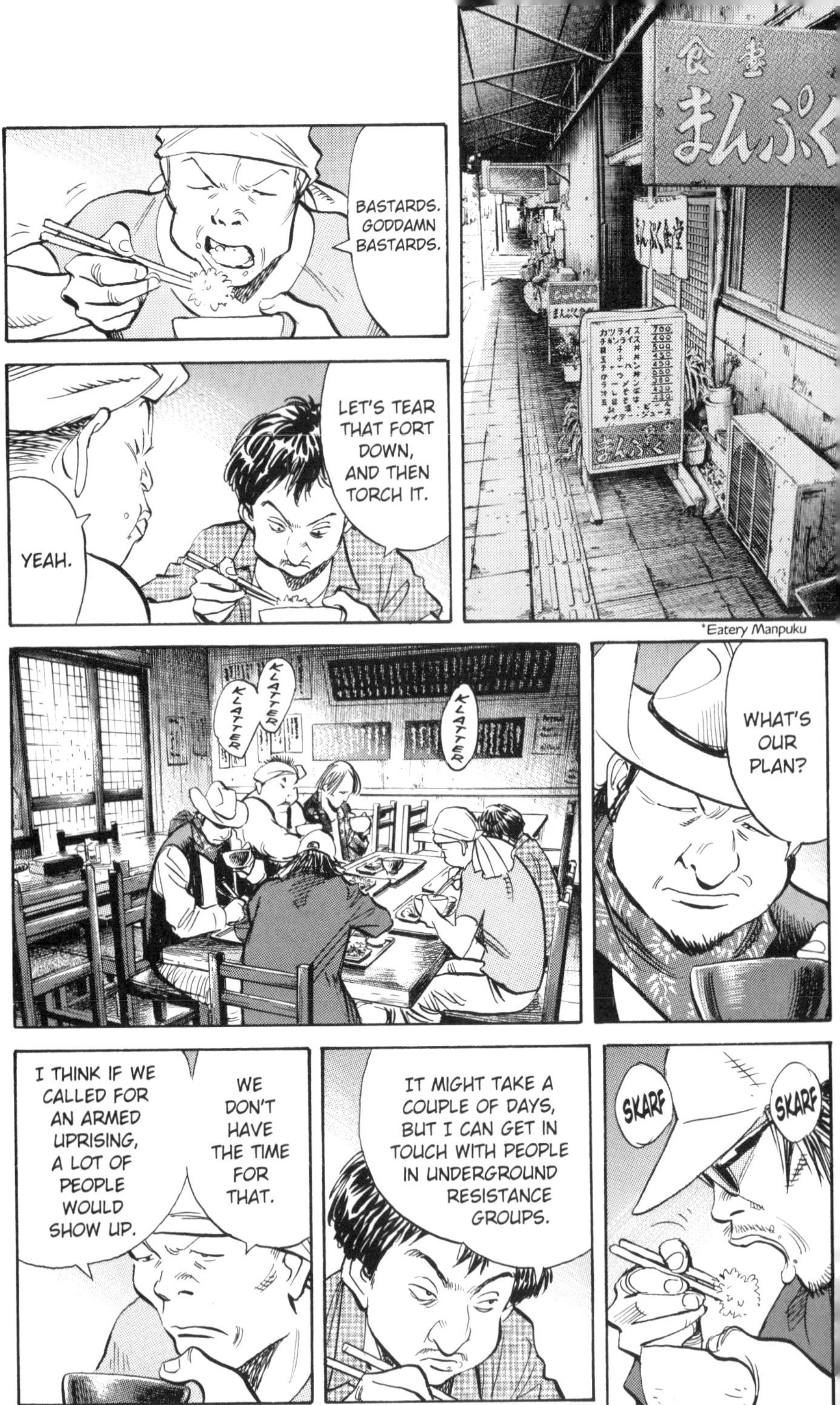
食堂
BASTARDS. GODDAMN BASTARDS.
LET'S TEAR THAT FORT DOWN, AND THEN TORCH IT.
YEAH.
WHAT'S OUR PLAN?
KLATTER
KLATTER
KLATTER
SKARF
SKARF
IT MIGHT TAKE A COUPLE OF DAYS, BUT I CAN GET IN TOUCH WITH PEOPLE IN UNDERGROUND RESISTANCE GROUPS.
I THINK IF WE CALLED FOR AN ARMED UPRISING, A LOT OF PEOPLE WOULD SHOW UP.
WE DON'T HAVE THE TIME FOR THAT.

*Eatery Manpuku

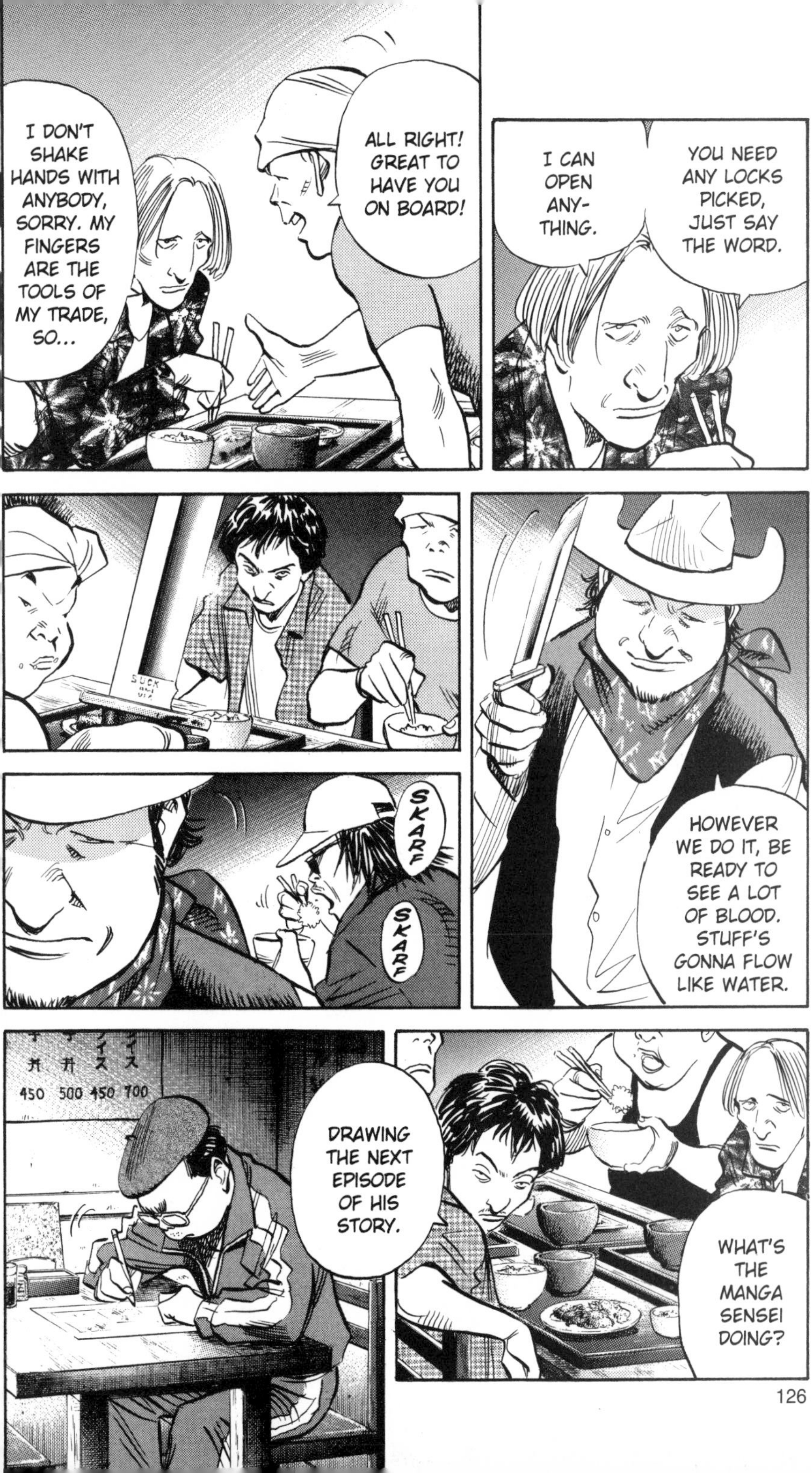

YOU NEED ANY LOCKS PICKED, JUST SAY THE WORD.
I CAN OPEN ANY-THING.
ALL RIGHT! GREAT TO HAVE YOU ON BOARD!
I DON'T SHAKE HANDS WITH ANYBODY, SORRY. MY FINGERS ARE THE TOOLS OF MY TRADE, SO...
HOWEVER WE DO IT, BE READY TO SEE A LOT OF BLOOD. STUFF'S GONNA FLOW LIKE WATER.
SKARF
SKARF
WHAT'S THE MANGA SENSEI DOING?
450 500 450 700
DRAWING THE NEXT EPISODE OF HIS STORY.

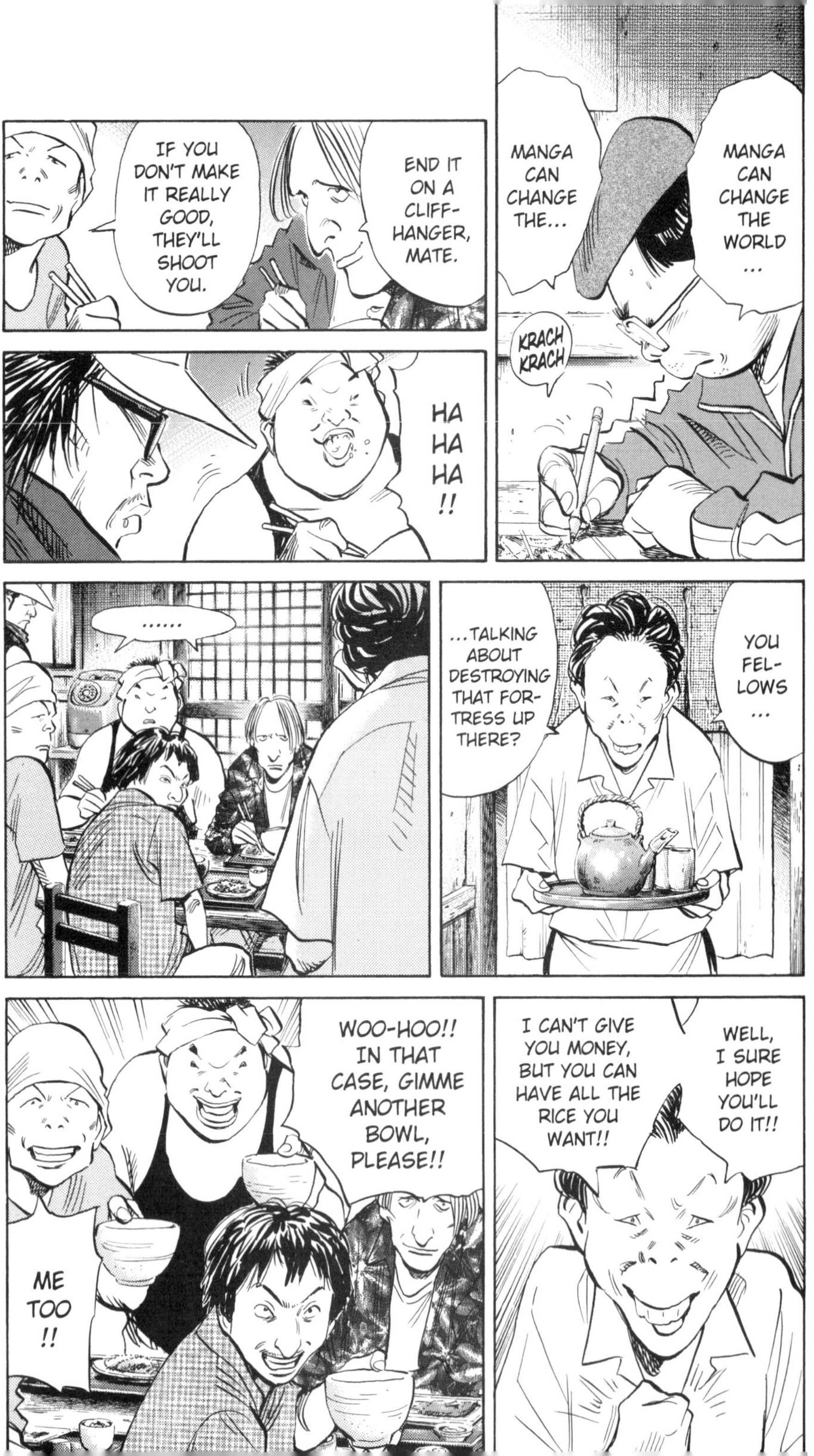
MANGA CAN CHANGE THE WORLD ...
MANGA CAN CHANGE THE...
KRACH KRACH
END IT ON A CLIFF-HANGER, MATE.
IF YOU DON'T MAKE IT REALLY GOOD, THEY'LL SHOOT YOU.
HA HA HA !!
YOU FEL-LOWS ...
...TALKING ABOUT DESTROYING THAT FOR-TRESS UP THERE?
......
WELL, I SURE HOPE YOU'LL DO IT!!
I CAN'T GIVE YOU MONEY, BUT YOU CAN HAVE ALL THE RICE YOU WANT!!
WOO-HOO!! IN THAT CASE, GIMME ANOTHER BOWL, PLEASE!!
ME TOO !!

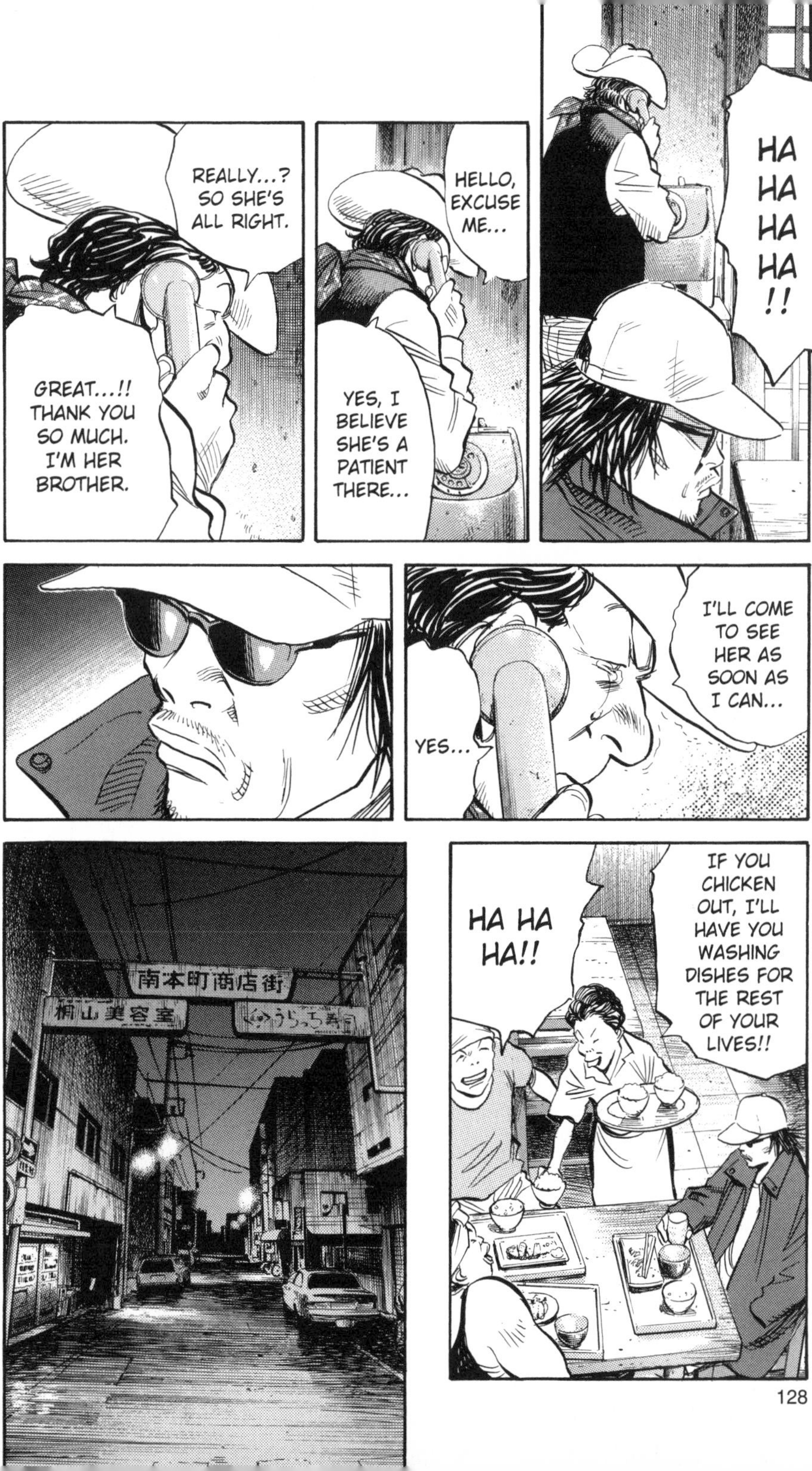
HA HA HA HA !!
HELLO, EXCUSE ME...
YES, I BELIEVE SHE'S A PATIENT THERE...
REALLY...? SO SHE'S ALL RIGHT.
GREAT...!! THANK YOU SO MUCH. I'M HER BROTHER.
I'LL COME TO SEE HER AS SOON AS I CAN...
YES...
IF YOU CHICKEN OUT, I'LL HAVE YOU WASHING DISHES FOR THE REST OF YOUR LIVES!!
HA HA HA!!
南本町商店街
桐山美容室

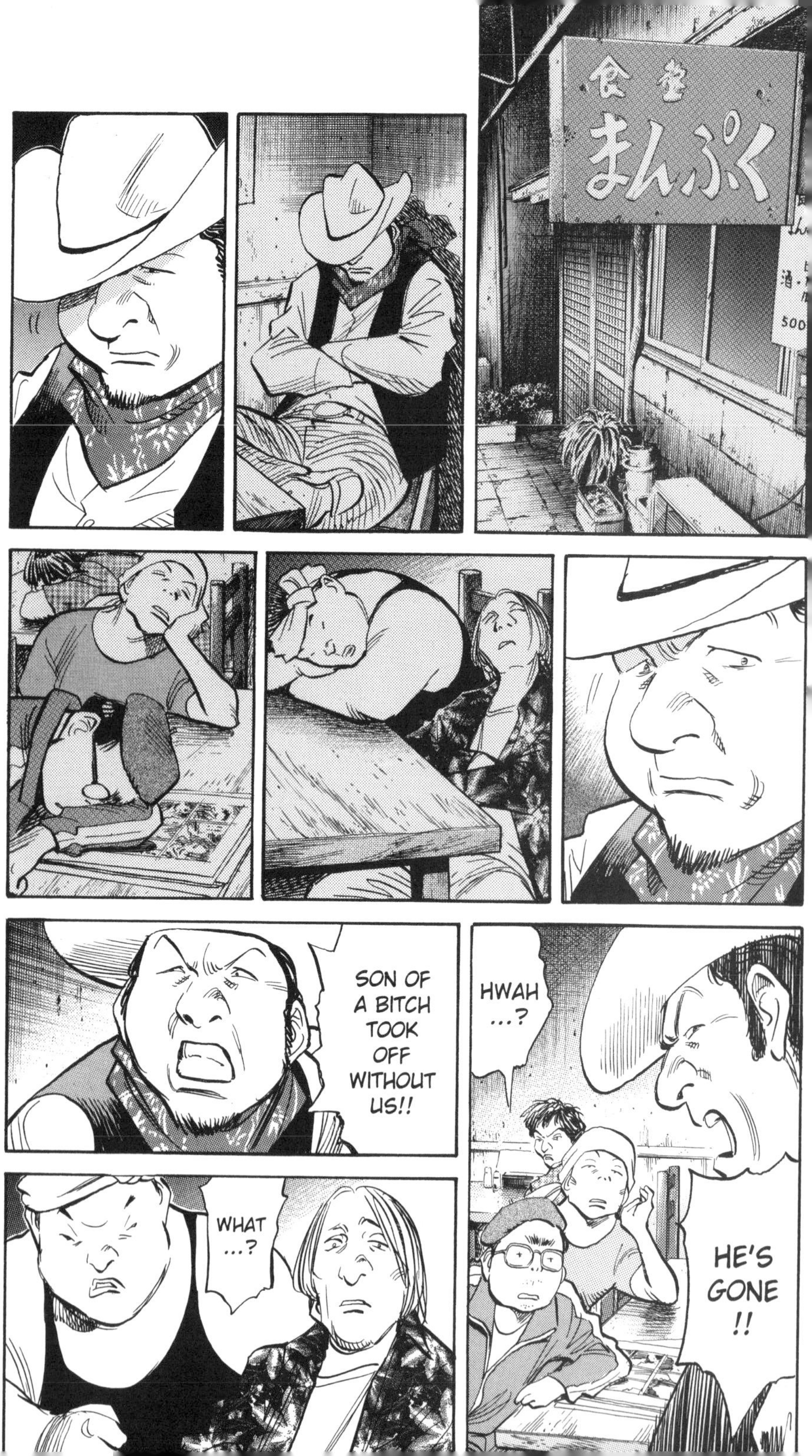
食堂
まんぷく
HWAH ...?
HE'S GONE !!
SON OF A BITCH TOOK OFF WITHOUT US!!
WHAT ...?

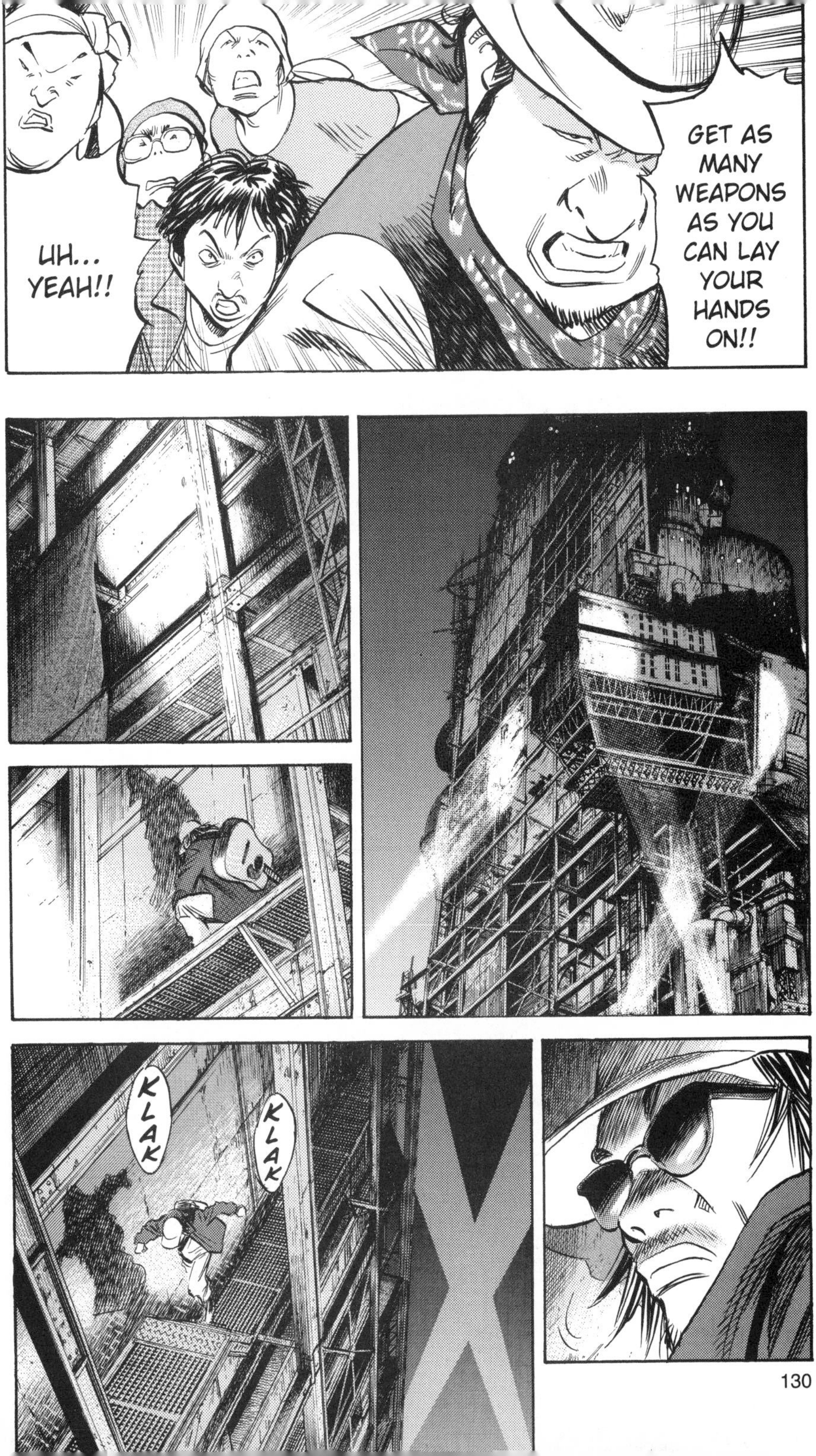
GET AS MANY WEAPONS AS YOU CAN LAY YOUR HANDS ON!!
UH... YEAH!!
KLAK
KLAK

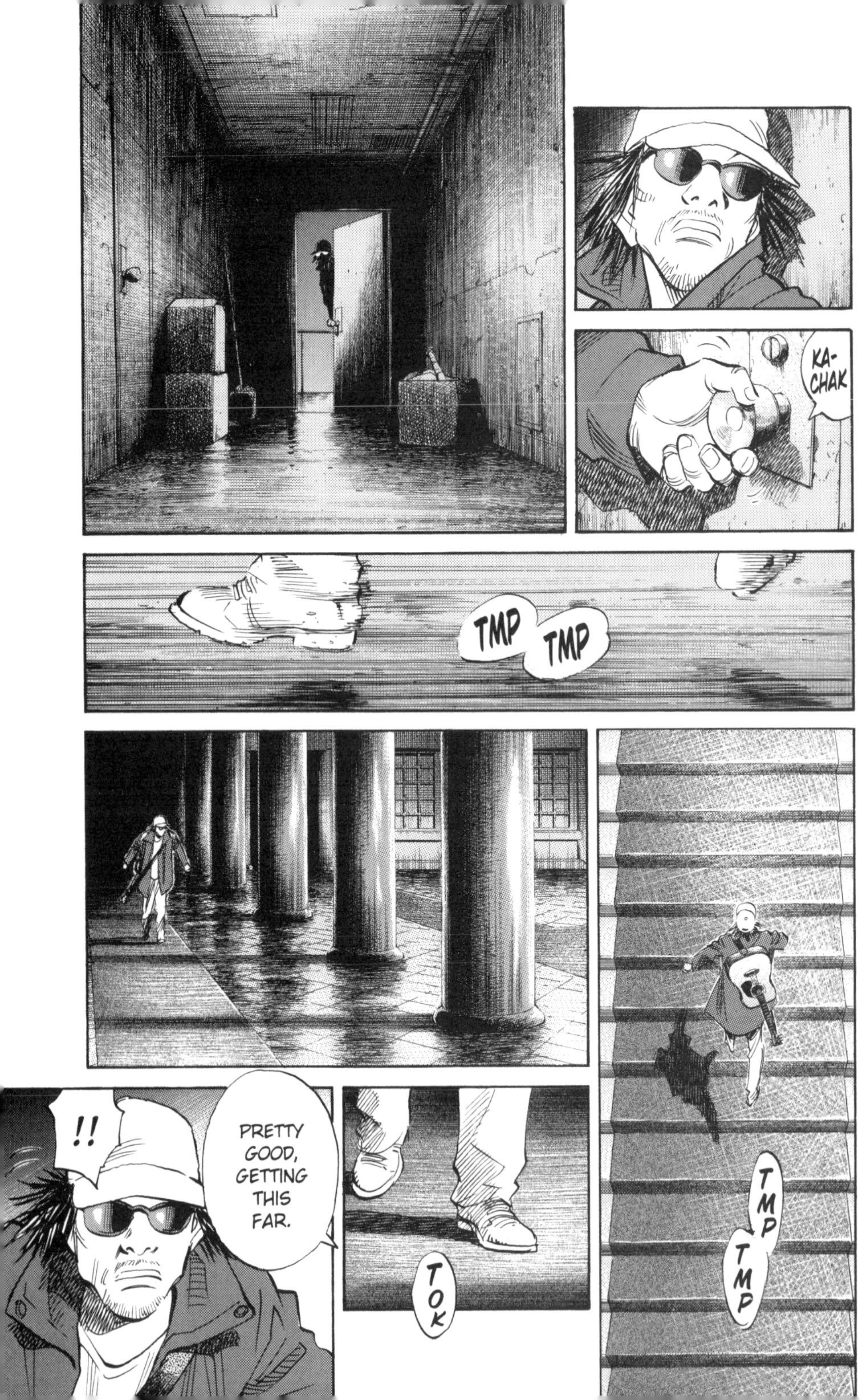
KA-CHAK
TMP TMP
TMP TMP
TOK
!!
PRETTY GOOD, GETTING THIS FAR.

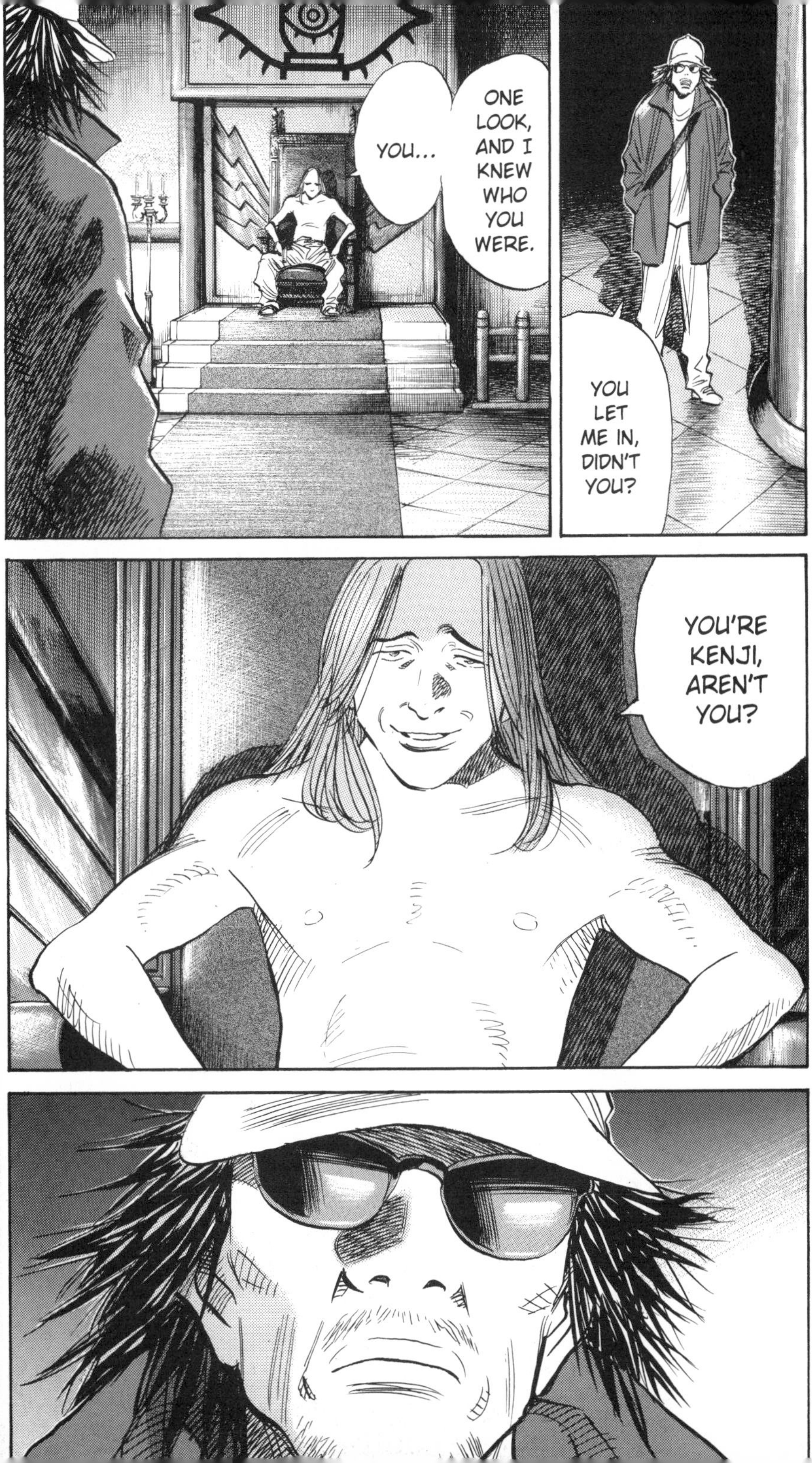
YOU LET ME IN, DIDN'T YOU?
YOU... ONE LOOK, AND I KNEW WHO YOU WERE.
YOU'RE KENJI, AREN'T YOU?

Chapter 8 Gotcha

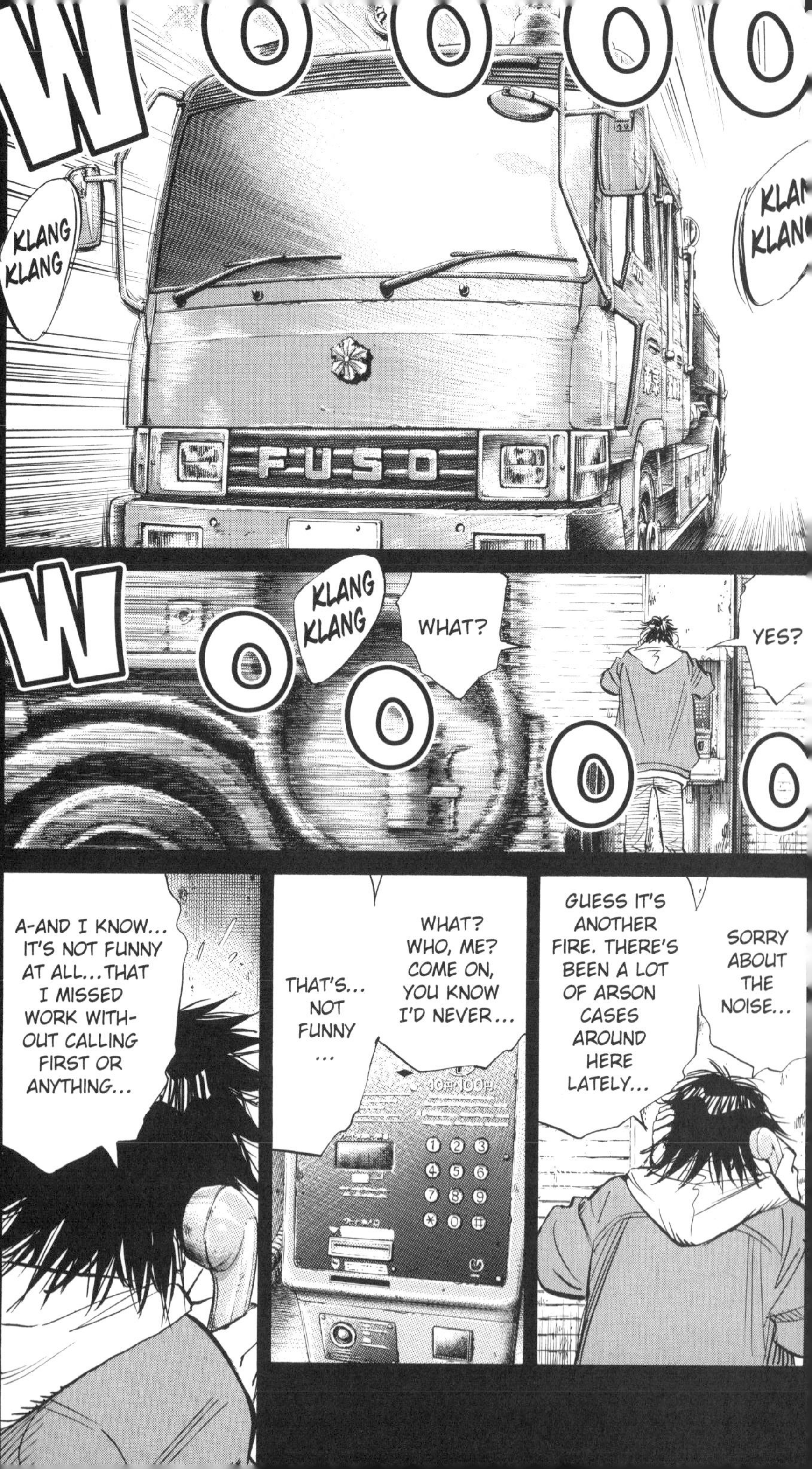
WOOOOO
KLANG KLANG
KLANG KLANG
YES?
WOOOO
WHAT?
KLANG KLANG
W
SORRY ABOUT THE NOISE...
GUESS IT'S ANOTHER FIRE. THERE'S BEEN A LOT OF ARSON CASES AROUND HERE LATELY...
WHAT? WHO, ME? COME ON, YOU KNOW I'D NEVER...
THAT'S... NOT FUNNY...
A-AND I KNOW... IT'S NOT FUNNY AT ALL...THAT I MISSED WORK WITHOUT CALLING FIRST OR ANYTHING...

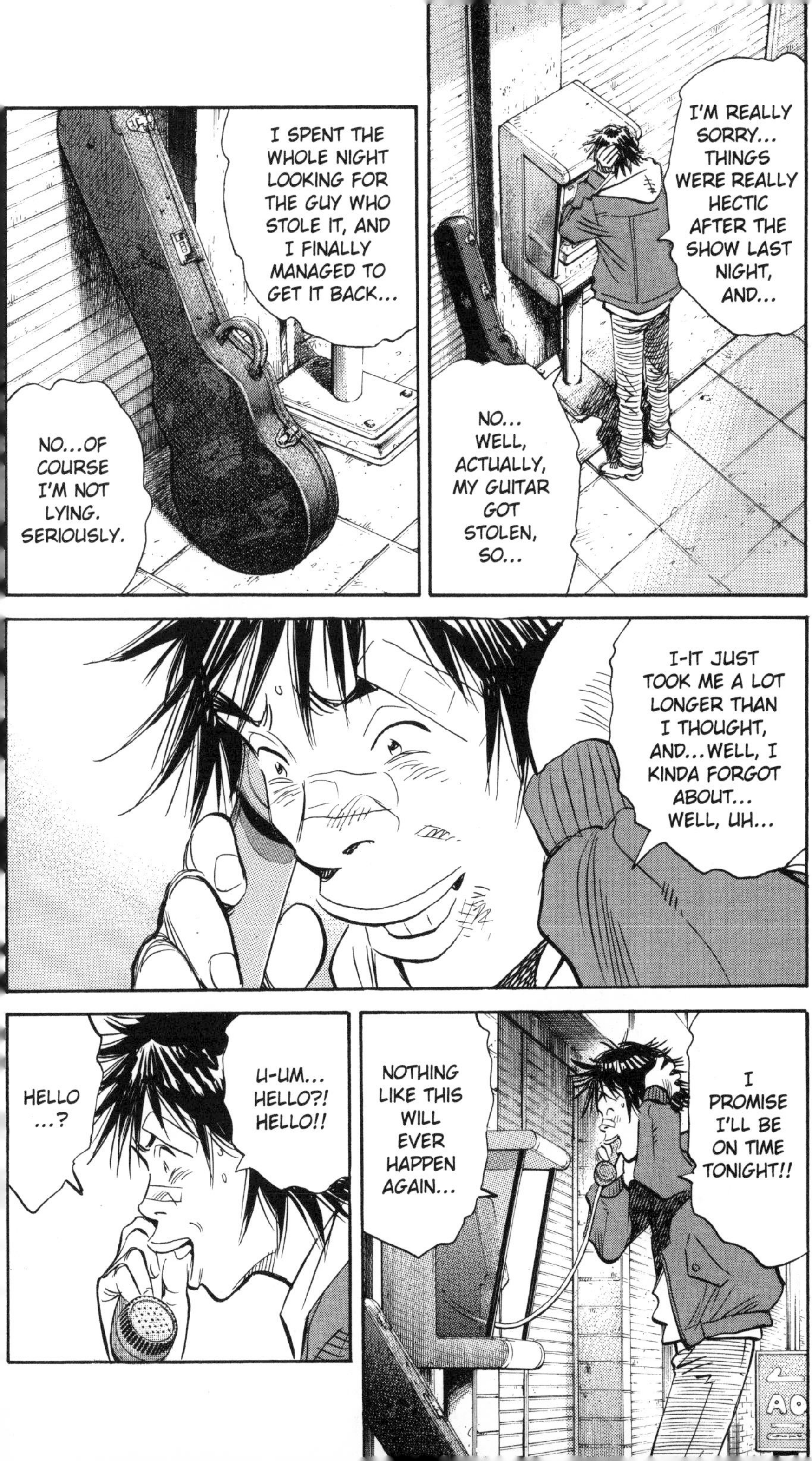
I'M REALLY SORRY... THINGS WERE REALLY HECTIC AFTER THE SHOW LAST NIGHT, AND...
NO... WELL, ACTUALLY, MY GUITAR GOT STOLEN, SO...
I SPENT THE WHOLE NIGHT LOOKING FOR THE GUY WHO STOLE IT, AND I FINALLY MANAGED TO GET IT BACK...
NO...OF COURSE I'M NOT LYING. SERIOUSLY.
I-IT JUST TOOK ME A LOT LONGER THAN I THOUGHT, AND...WELL, I KINDA FORGOT ABOUT... WELL, UH...
I PROMISE I'LL BE ON TIME TONIGHT!!
NOTHING LIKE THIS WILL EVER HAPPEN AGAIN...
U-UM... HELLO?! HELLO!!
HELLO ...?

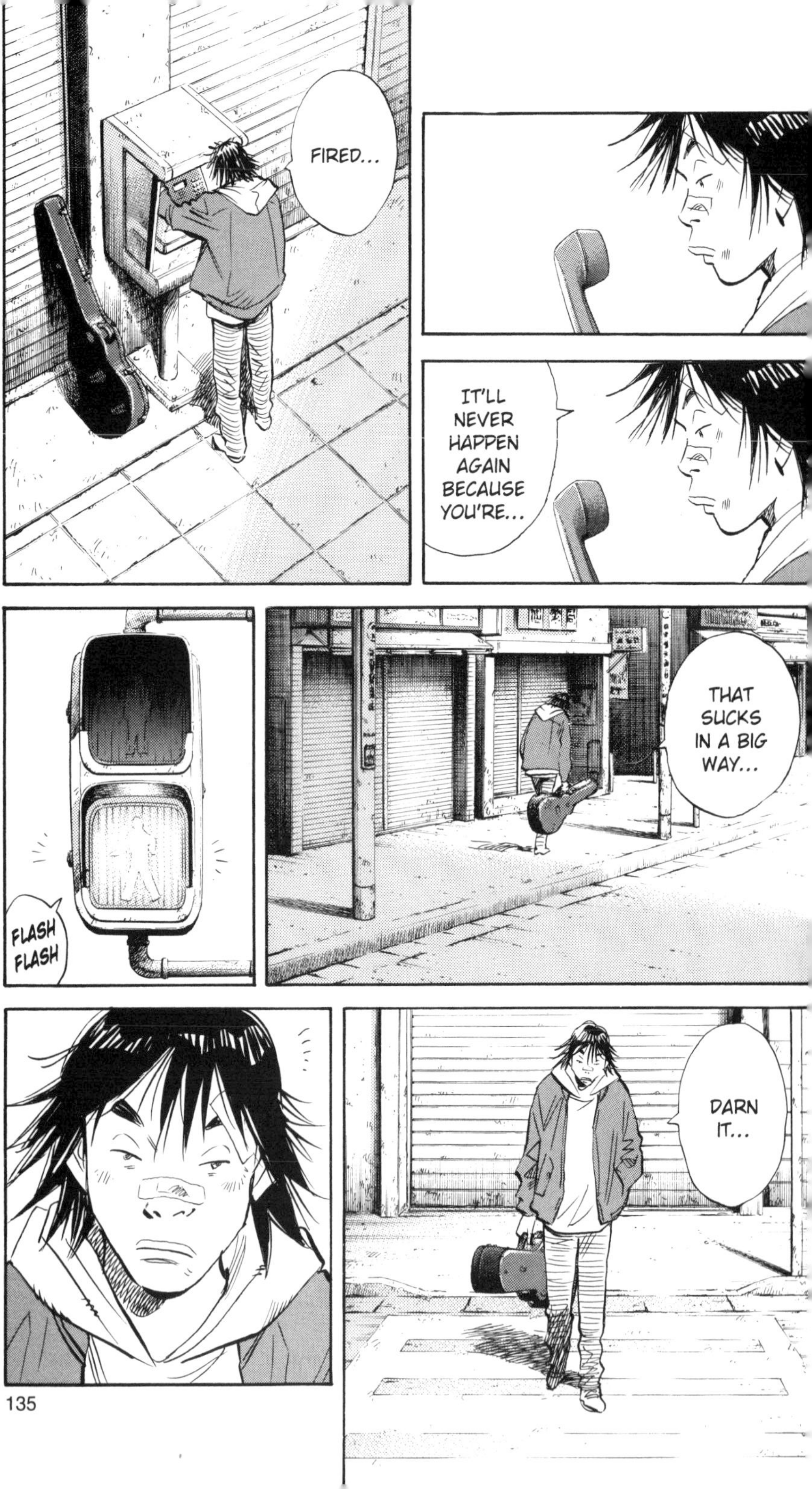
IT'LL NEVER HAPPEN AGAIN BECAUSE YOU'RE...
FIRED...
THAT SUCKS IN A BIG WAY...
FLASH FLASH
DARN IT...

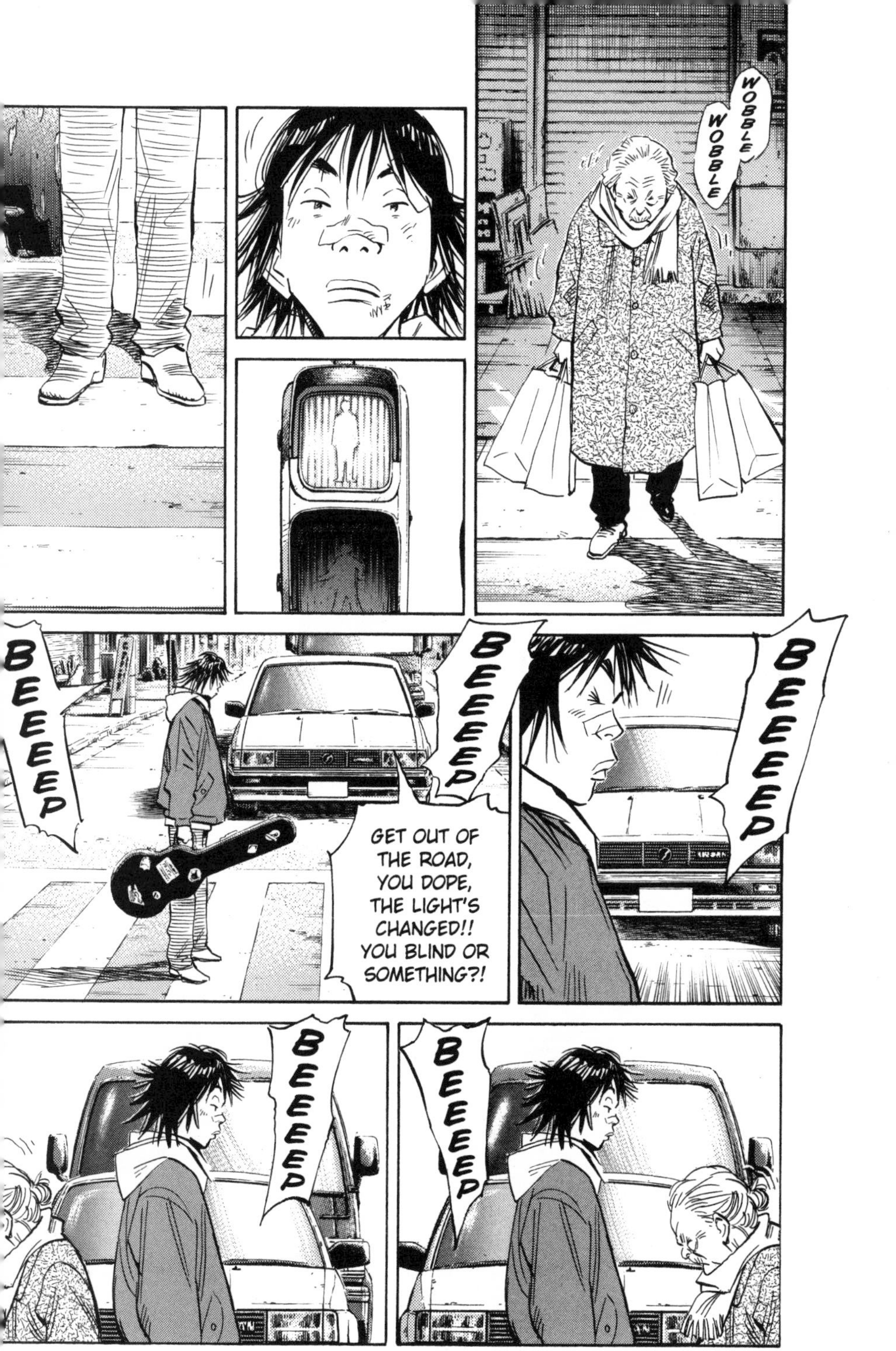
WOBBLE
WOBBLE
BEEEEEEP
BEEEEEP
GET OUT OF THE ROAD, YOU DOPE, THE LIGHT'S CHANGED!! YOU BLIND OR SOMETHING?!
BEEEEEEP
BEEEEEP
BEEEEEP

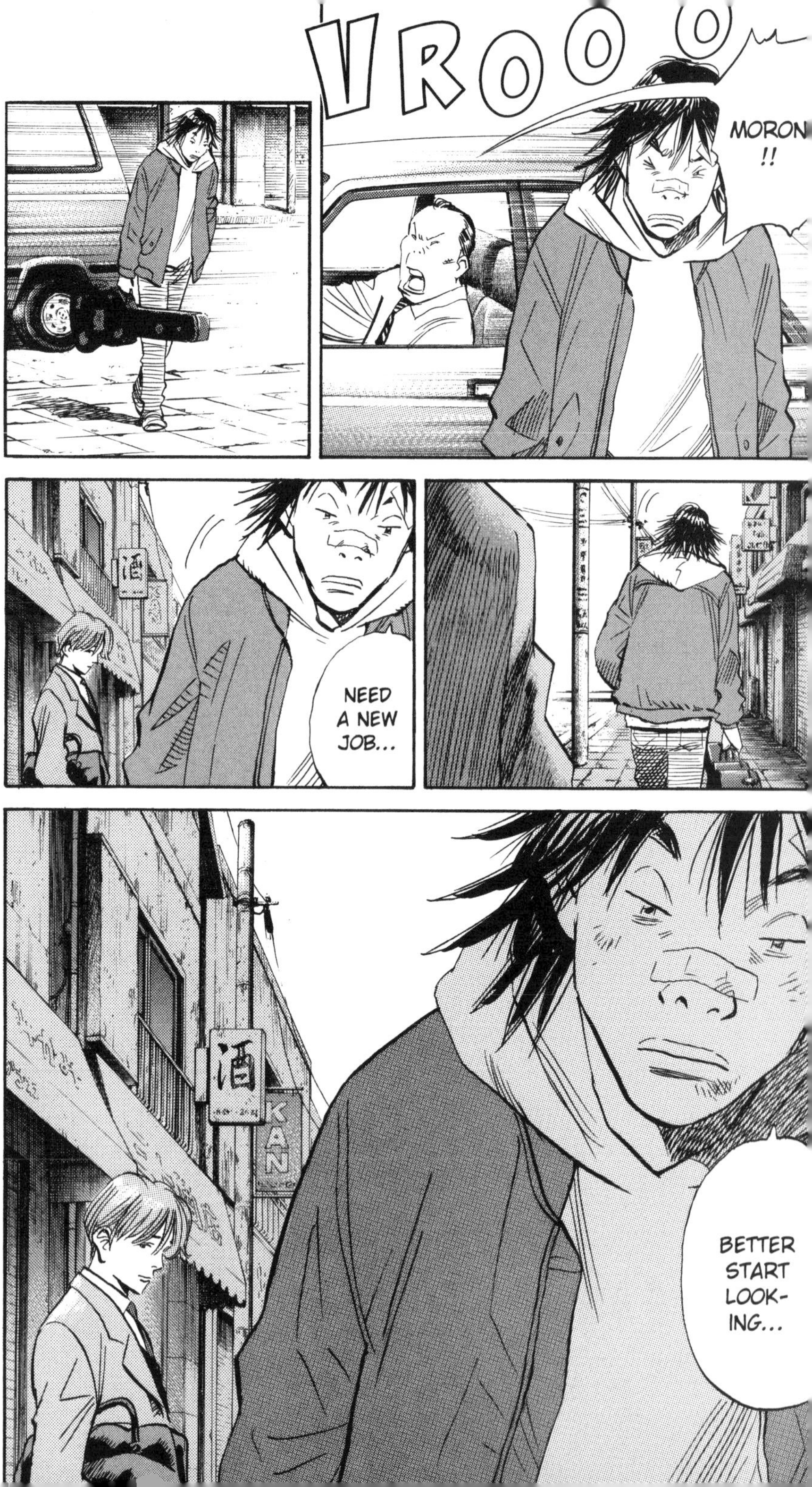
VROOO
MORON !!
NEED A NEW JOB...
酒
KAN
BETTER START LOOK-ING...

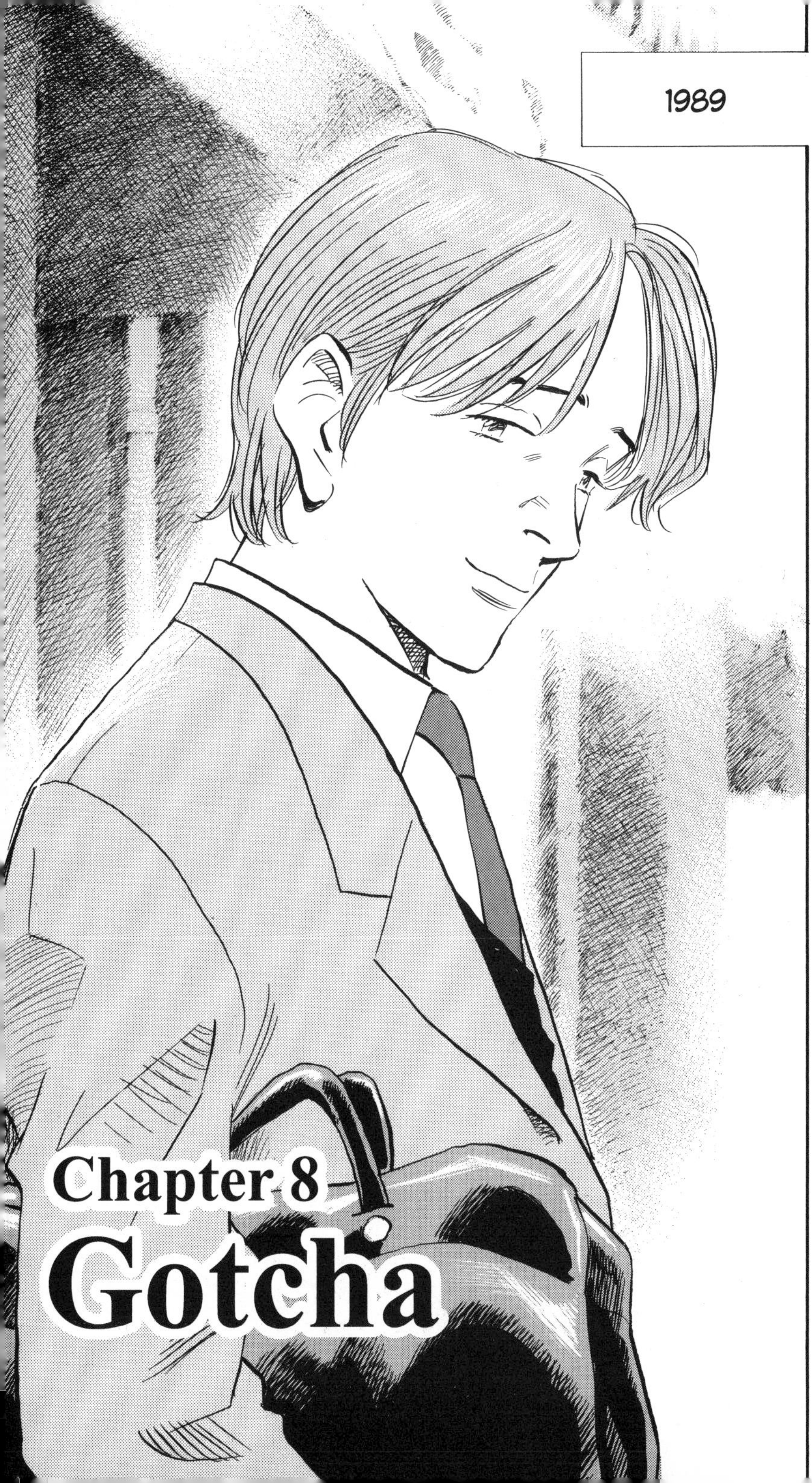
1989
Chapter 8
Gotcha

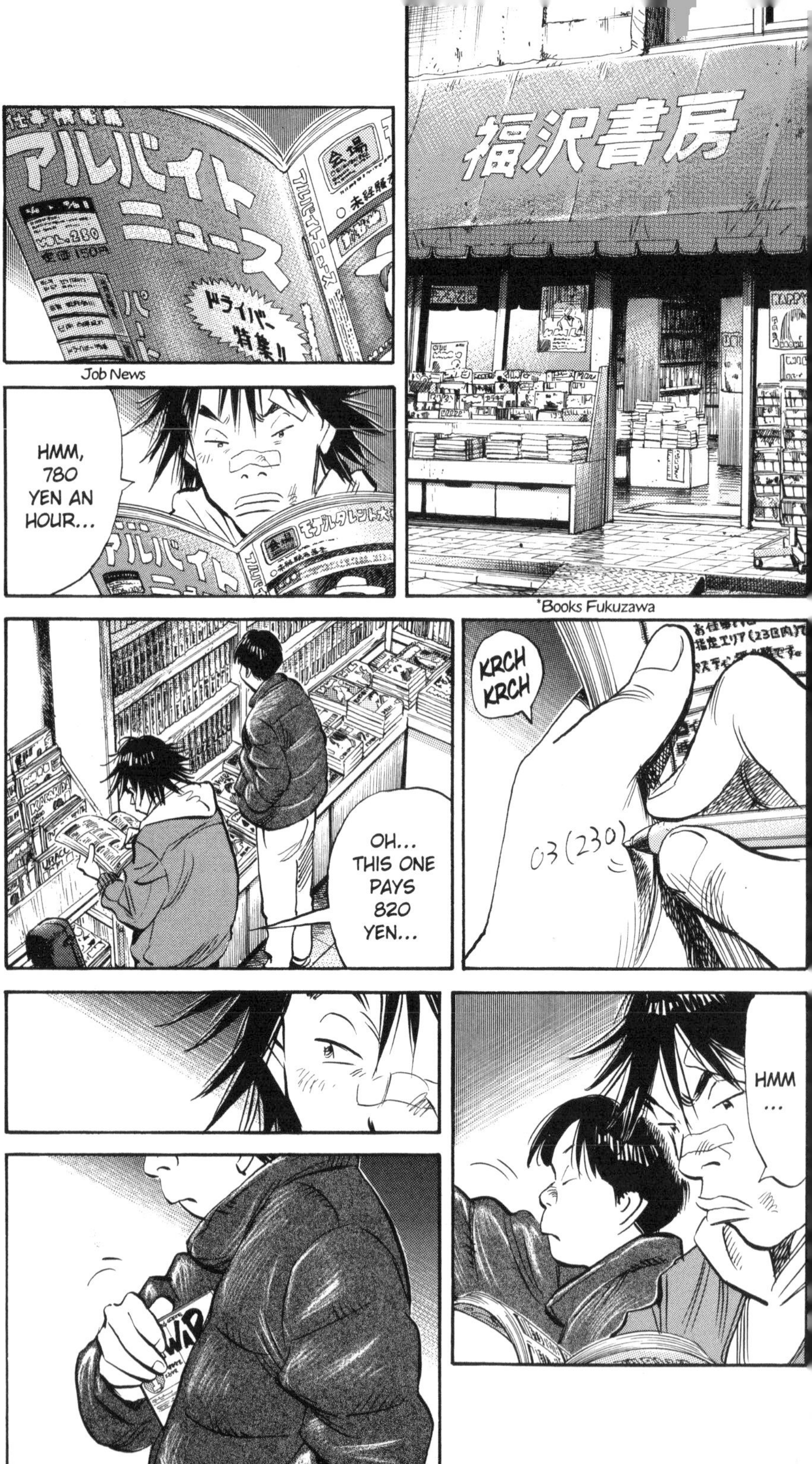
福沢書房
*Books Fukuzawa
アルバイトニュース
ドライバー特集!!
Job News
HMM, 780 YEN AN HOUR...
KRCH KRCH
03(230)
OH... THIS ONE PAYS 820 YEN...
HMM...

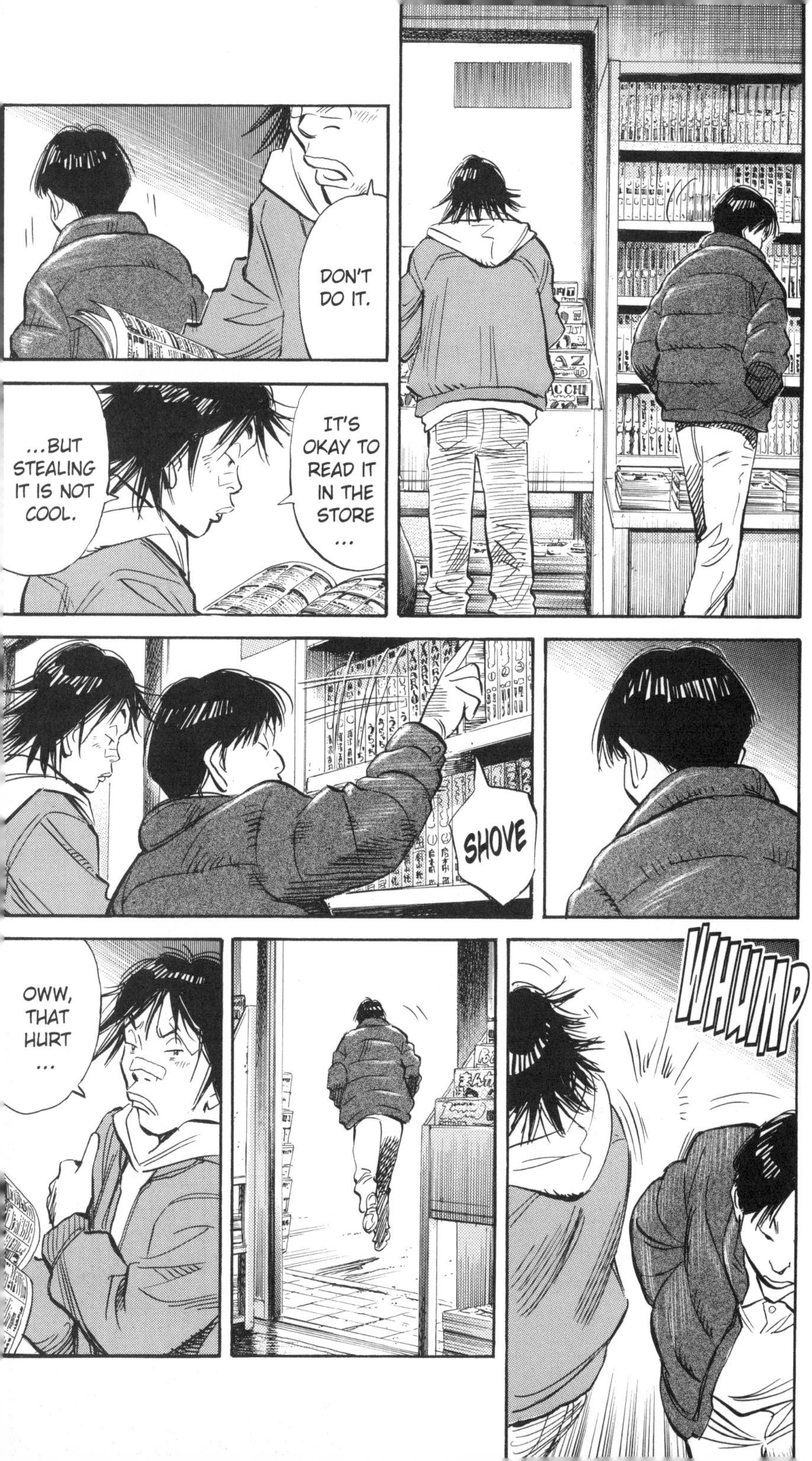
DON'T DO IT.
IT'S OKAY TO READ IT IN THE STORE ...
...BUT STEALING IT IS NOT COOL.
SHOVE
WHUMP
OWW, THAT HURT ...

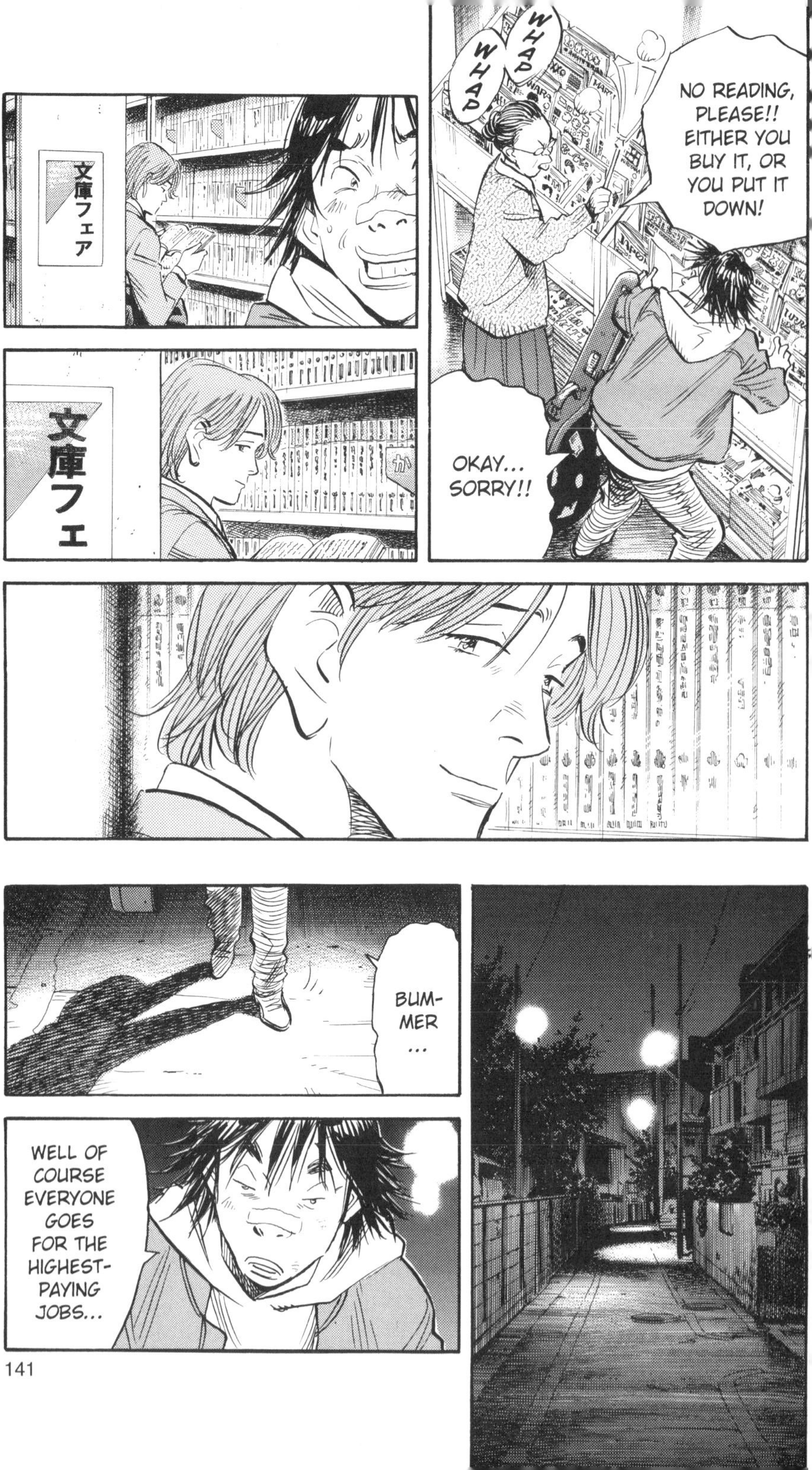
WHAP WHAP
NO READING, PLEASE!! EITHER YOU BUY IT, OR YOU PUT IT DOWN!
OKAY... SORRY!!
文庫フェア
文庫フェ
BUM-MER...
WELL OF COURSE EVERYONE GOES FOR THE HIGHEST-PAYING JOBS...

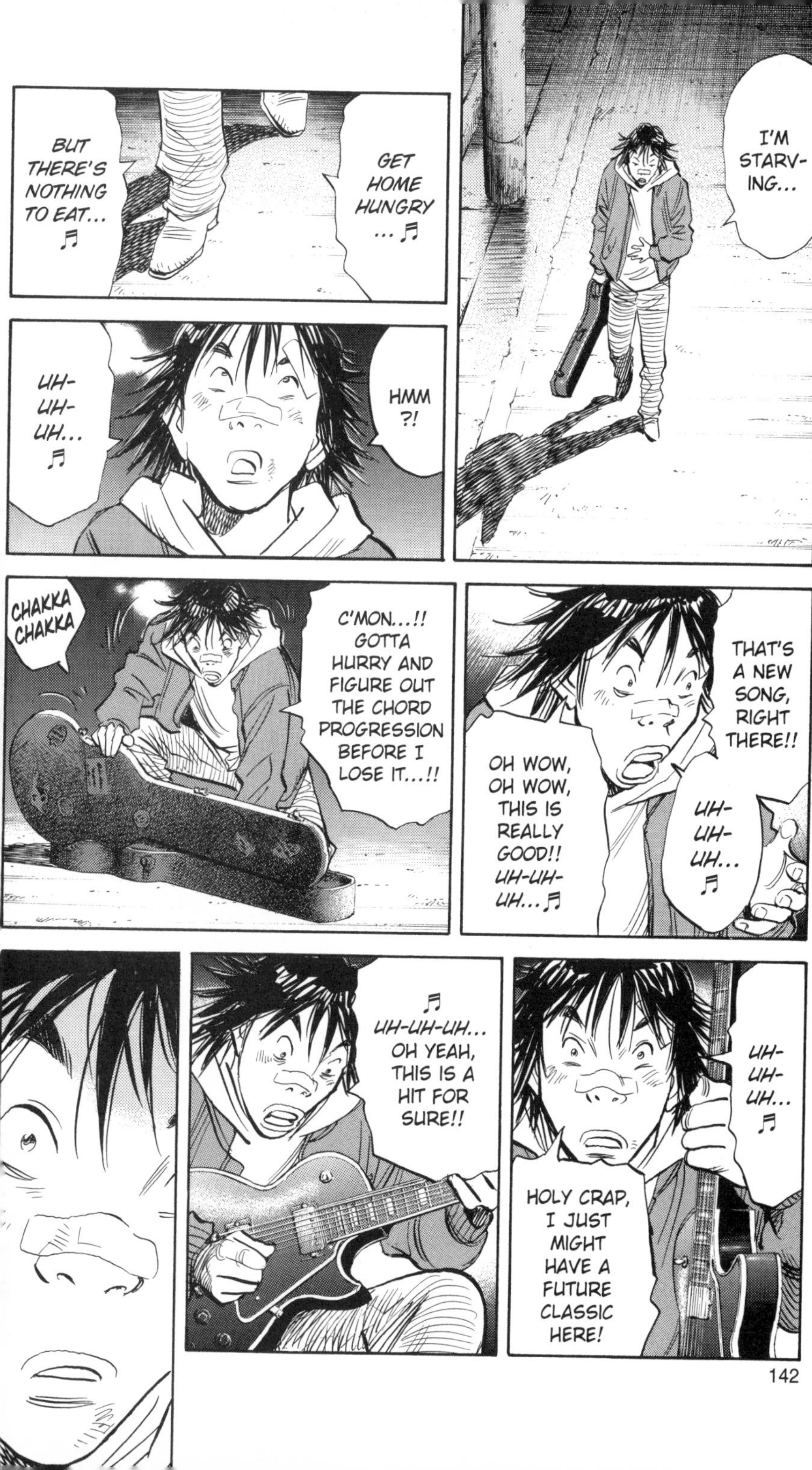
I'M STARVING...
GET HOME HUNGRY ...♬
BUT THERE'S NOTHING TO EAT... ♬
HMM ?!
UH-UH-UH... ♬
THAT'S A NEW SONG, RIGHT THERE!!
UH-UH-UH... ♬
OH WOW, OH WOW, THIS IS REALLY GOOD!! UH-UH-UH...♬
C'MON...!! GOTTA HURRY AND FIGURE OUT THE CHORD PROGRESSION BEFORE I LOSE IT...!!
CHAKKA CHAKKA
UH-UH-UH... ♬
HOLY CRAP, I JUST MIGHT HAVE A FUTURE CLASSIC HERE!
♬ UH-UH-UH... OH YEAH, THIS IS A HIT FOR SURE!!

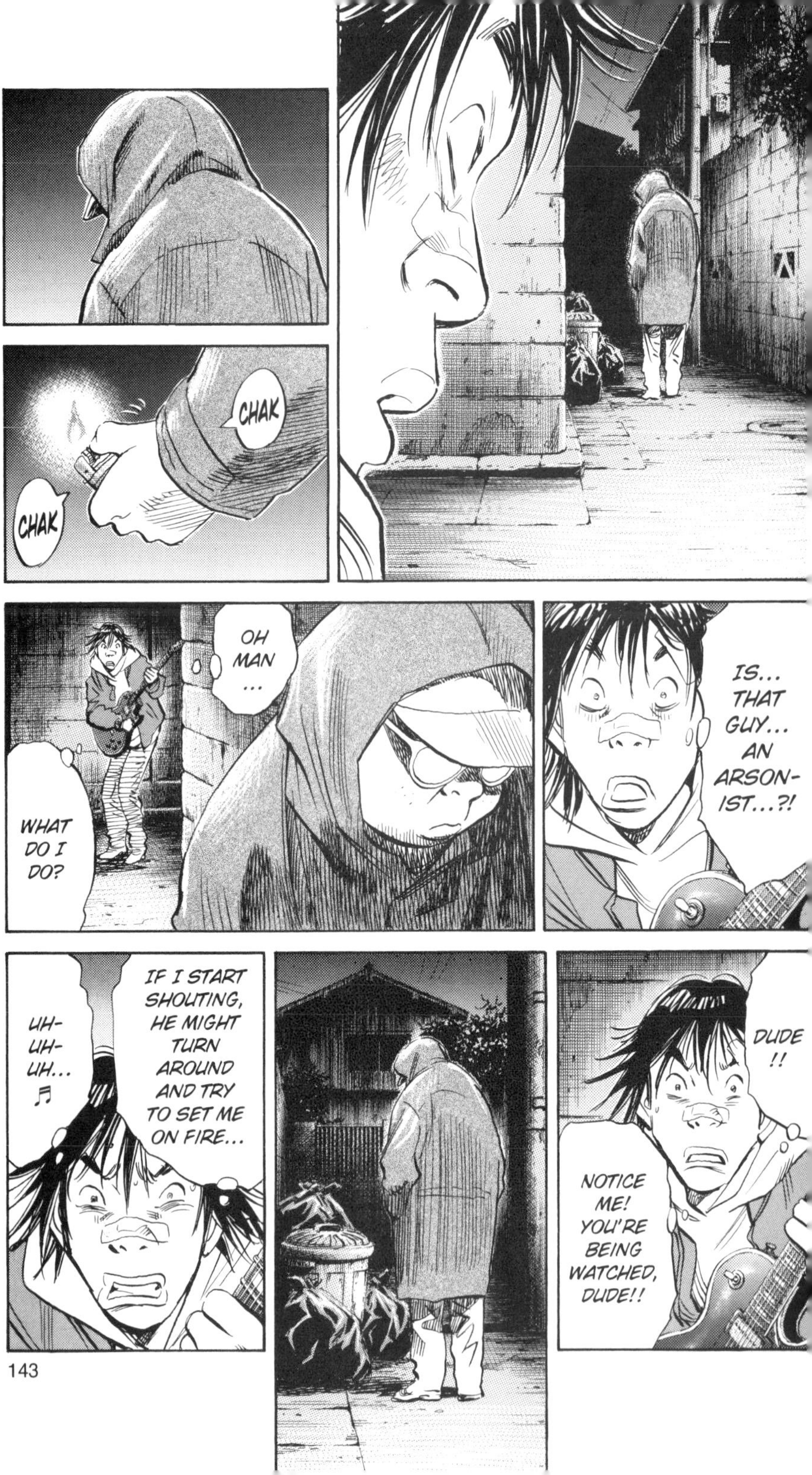
CHAK
CHAK
IS... THAT GUY... AN ARSON-IST...?!
OH MAN ...
WHAT DO I DO?
DUDE!!
NOTICE ME! YOU'RE BEING WATCHED, DUDE!!
IF I START SHOUTING, HE MIGHT TURN AROUND AND TRY TO SET ME ON FIRE...
UH-UH-UH... ♬

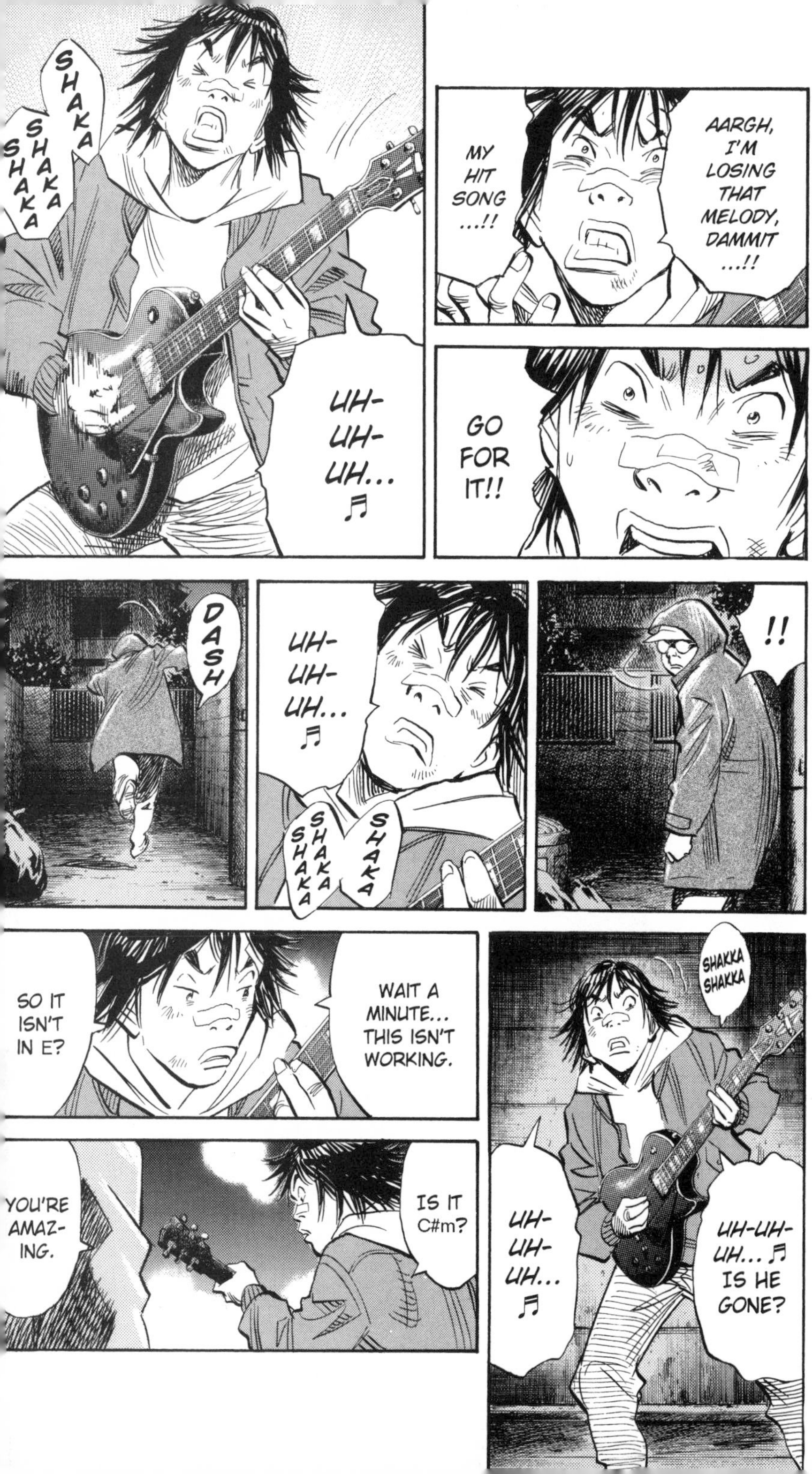
AARGH, I'M LOSING THAT MELODY, DAMMIT...!!
MY HIT SONG...!!
GO FOR IT!!
UH-UH-UH...♬
SHAKA SHAKA SHAKA
!!
UH-UH-UH...♬
SHAKA SHAKA SHAKA
DASH
SHAKKA SHAKKA
UH-UH-UH...♬ IS HE GONE?
UH-UH-UH...♬
WAIT A MINUTE... THIS ISN'T WORKING.
SO IT ISN'T IN E?
IS IT C#m?
YOU'RE AMAZ-ING.

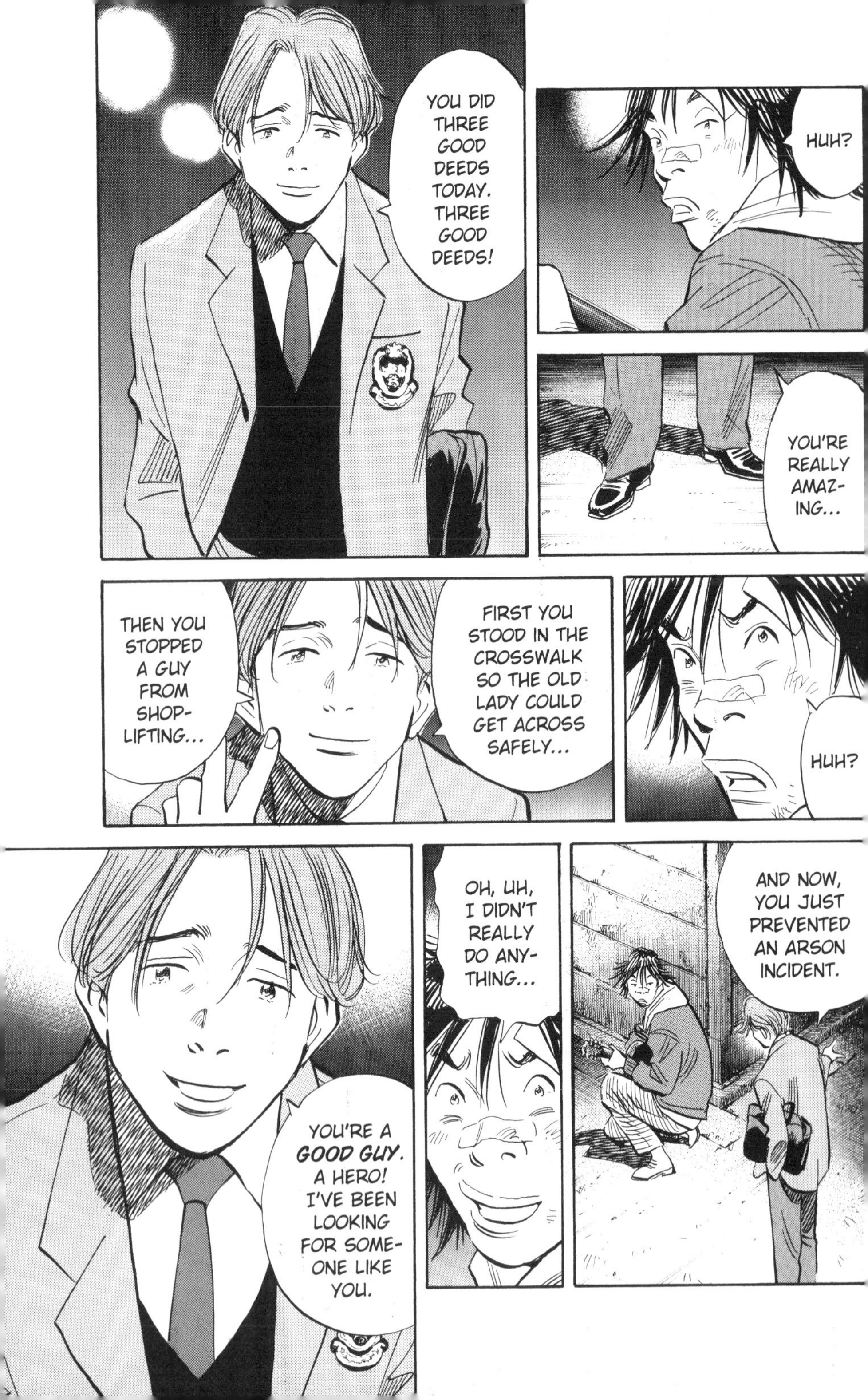
HUH?
YOU'RE REALLY AMAZ-ING...
YOU DID THREE GOOD DEEDS TODAY. THREE GOOD DEEDS!
HUH?
FIRST YOU STOOD IN THE CROSSWALK SO THE OLD LADY COULD GET ACROSS SAFELY...
THEN YOU STOPPED A GUY FROM SHOP-LIFTING...
AND NOW, YOU JUST PREVENTED AN ARSON INCIDENT.
OH, UH, I DIDN'T REALLY DO ANY-THING...
YOU'RE A GOOD GUY. A HERO! I'VE BEEN LOOKING FOR SOME-ONE LIKE YOU.

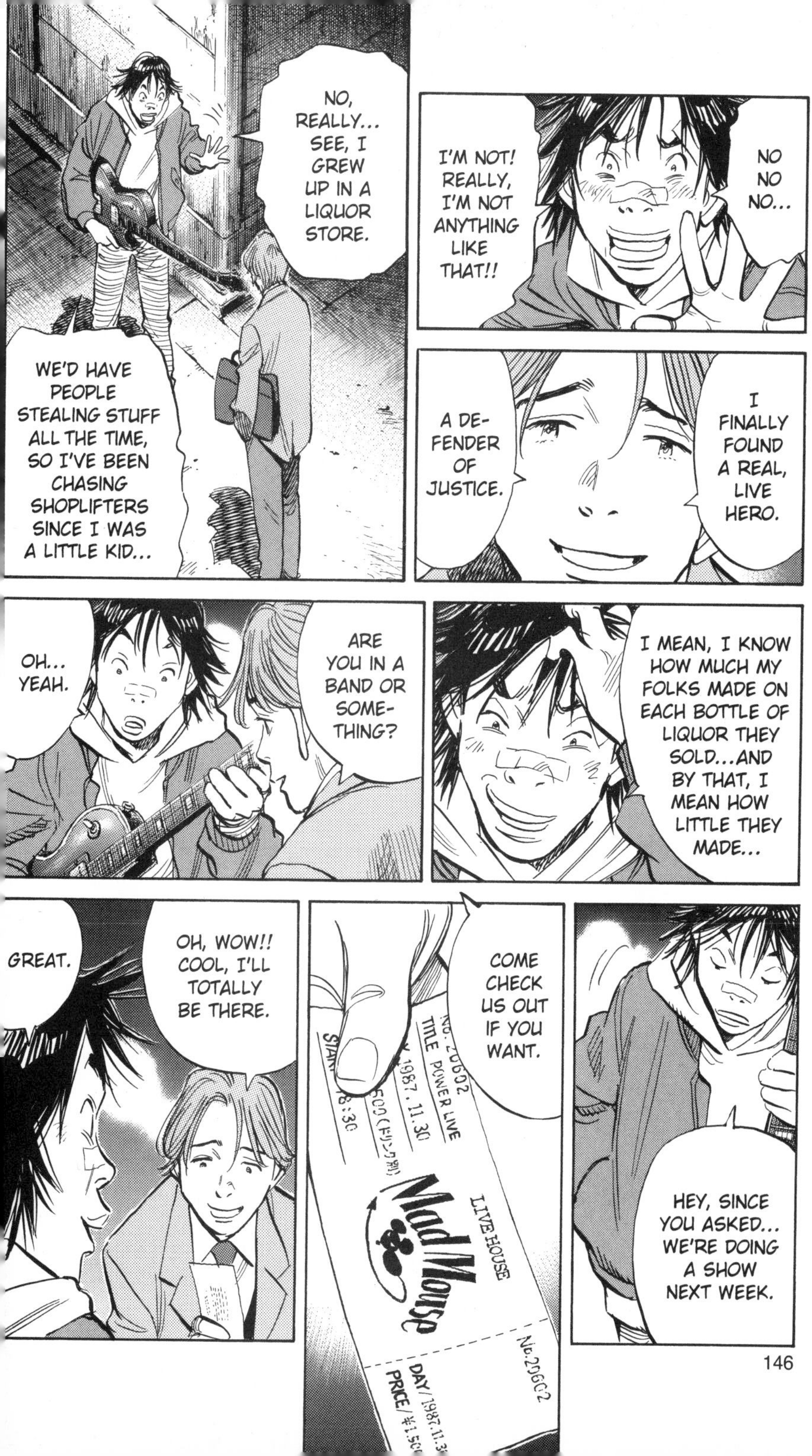
NO NO NO...
I'M NOT! REALLY, I'M NOT ANYTHING LIKE THAT!!
I FINALLY FOUND A REAL, LIVE HERO.
A DEFENDER OF JUSTICE.
NO, REALLY... SEE, I GREW UP IN A LIQUOR STORE.
WE'D HAVE PEOPLE STEALING STUFF ALL THE TIME, SO I'VE BEEN CHASING SHOPLIFTERS SINCE I WAS A LITTLE KID...
I MEAN, I KNOW HOW MUCH MY FOLKS MADE ON EACH BOTTLE OF LIQUOR THEY SOLD...AND BY THAT, I MEAN HOW LITTLE THEY MADE...
ARE YOU IN A BAND OR SOME-THING?
OH... YEAH.
HEY, SINCE YOU ASKED... WE'RE DOING A SHOW NEXT WEEK.
COME CHECK US OUT IF YOU WANT.
TITLE POWER LIVE
LIVE HOUSE
Mad Mouse
No.20602
OH, WOW!! COOL, I'LL TOTALLY BE THERE.
GREAT.

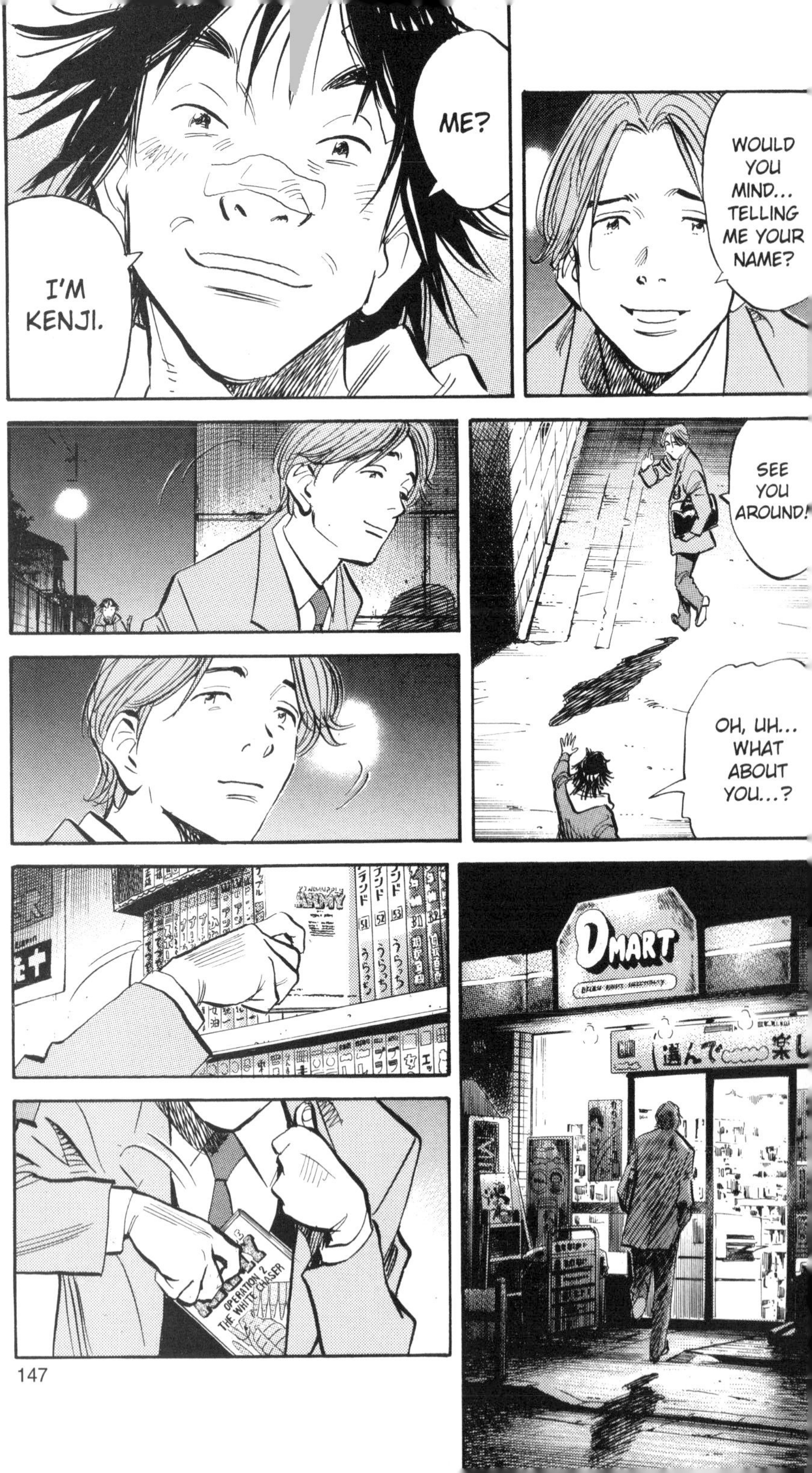

WOULD YOU MIND... TELLING ME YOUR NAME?
ME?
I'M KENJI.
SEE YOU AROUND!
OH, UH... WHAT ABOUT YOU...?
DMART
OPERATION 2 THE WHITE CHASER

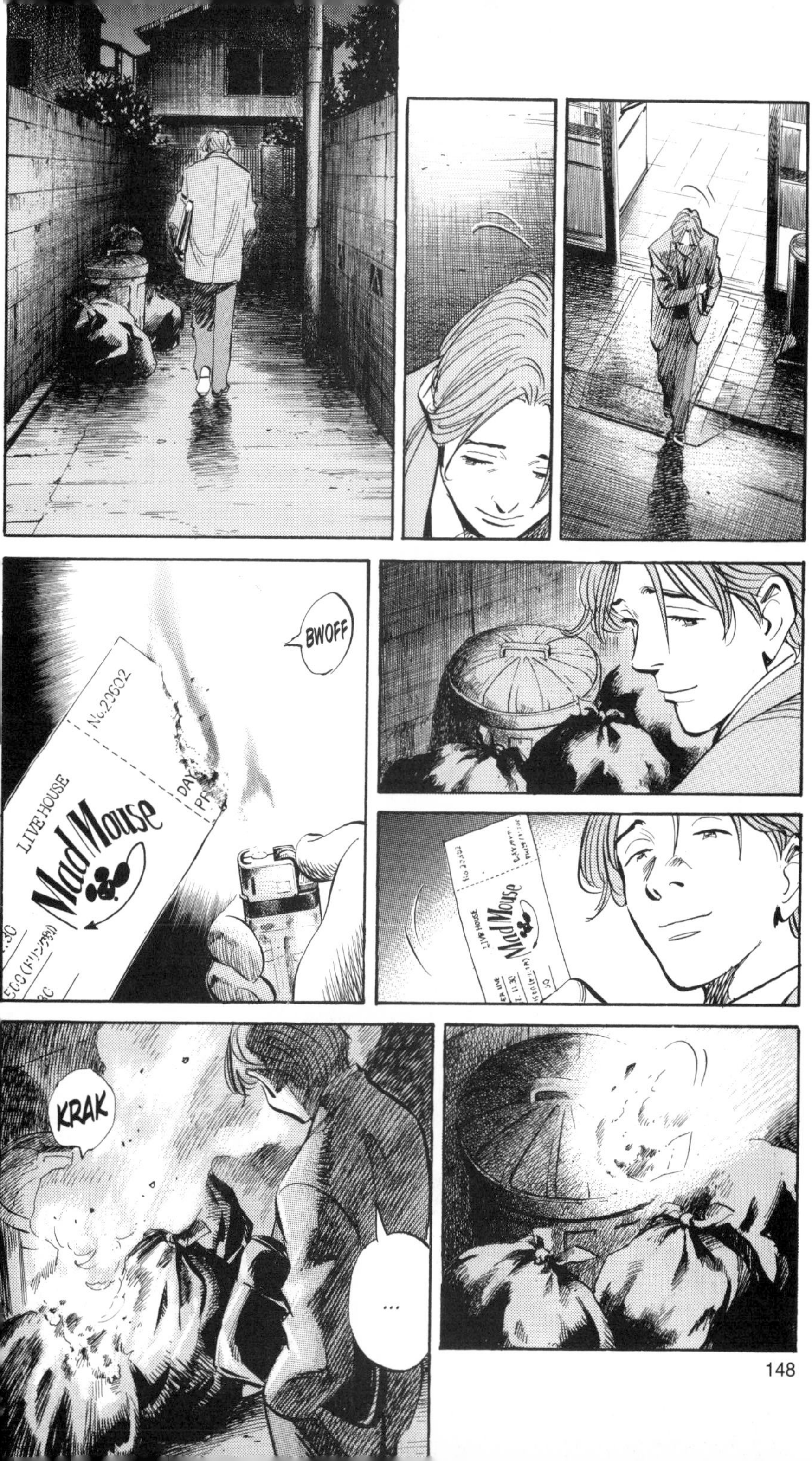
BWOFF
No.22602
LIVE HOUSE
Mad Mouse
KRAK
...

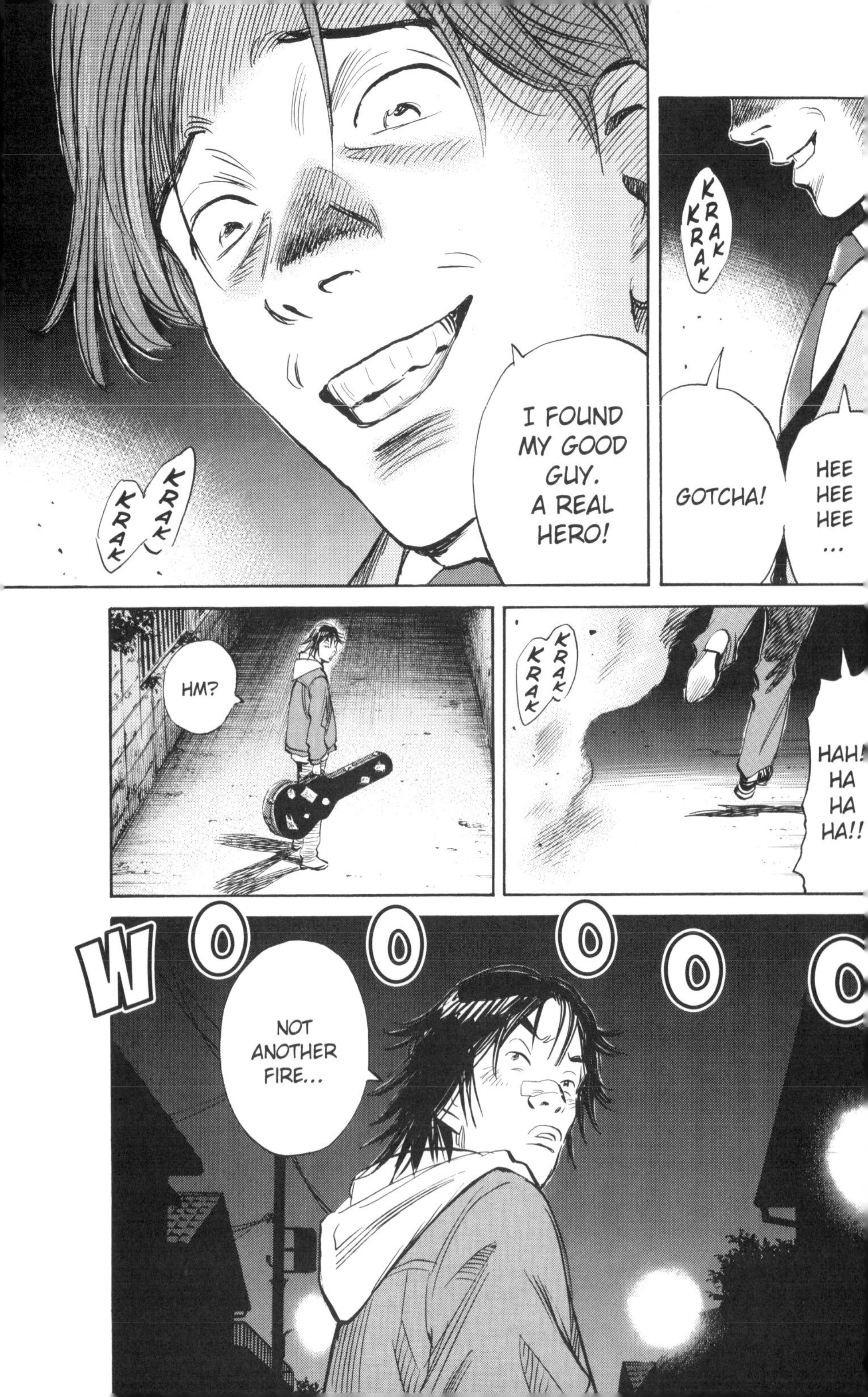
KRAK KRAK
HEE HEE HEE...
GOTCHA!
I FOUND MY GOOD GUY. A REAL HERO!
KRAK KRAK
KRAK KRAK
HAH! HA HA HA!!
HM?
WOOOOO
NOT ANOTHER FIRE...

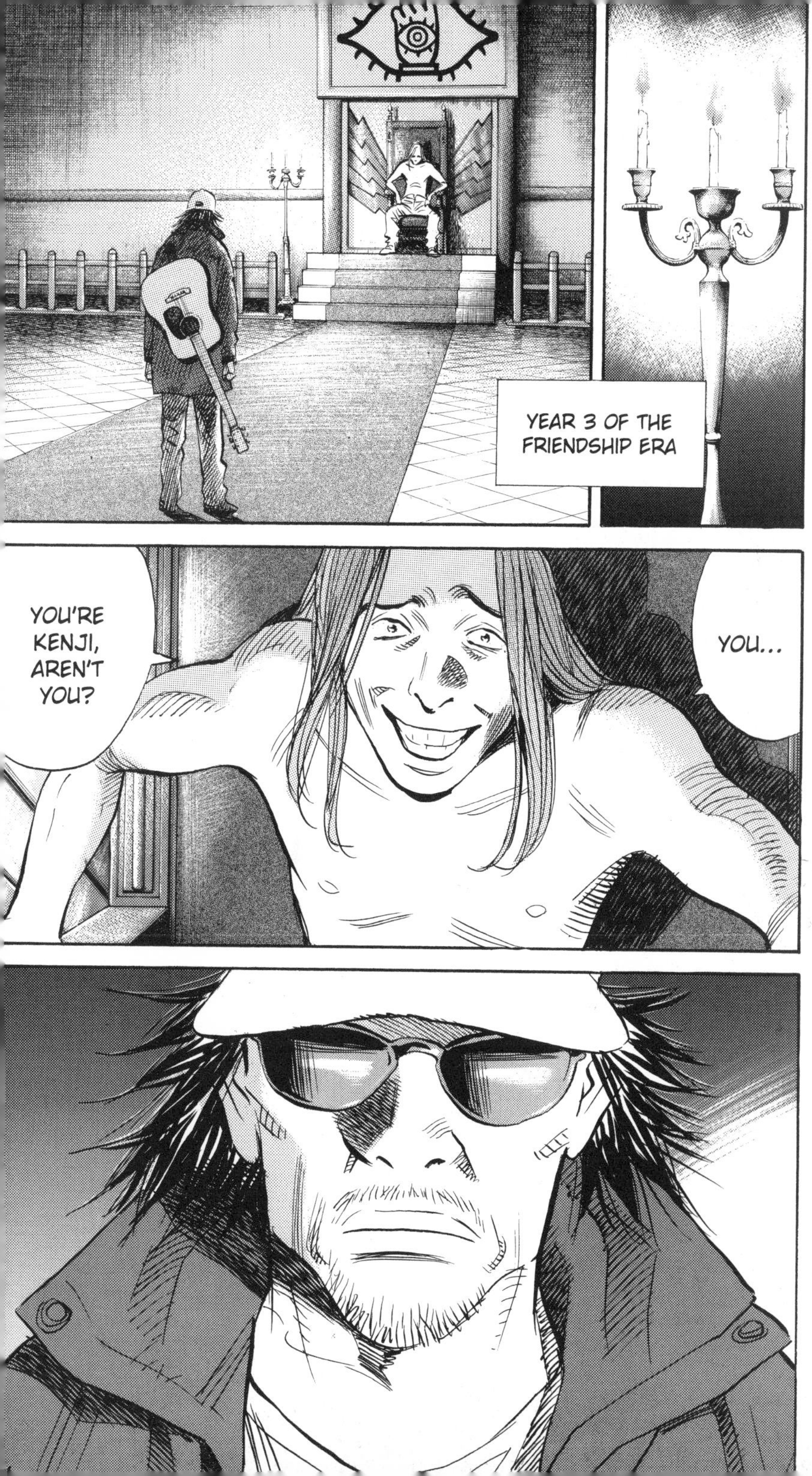
YEAR 3 OF THE FRIENDSHIP ERA
YOU...
YOU'RE KENJI, AREN'T YOU?

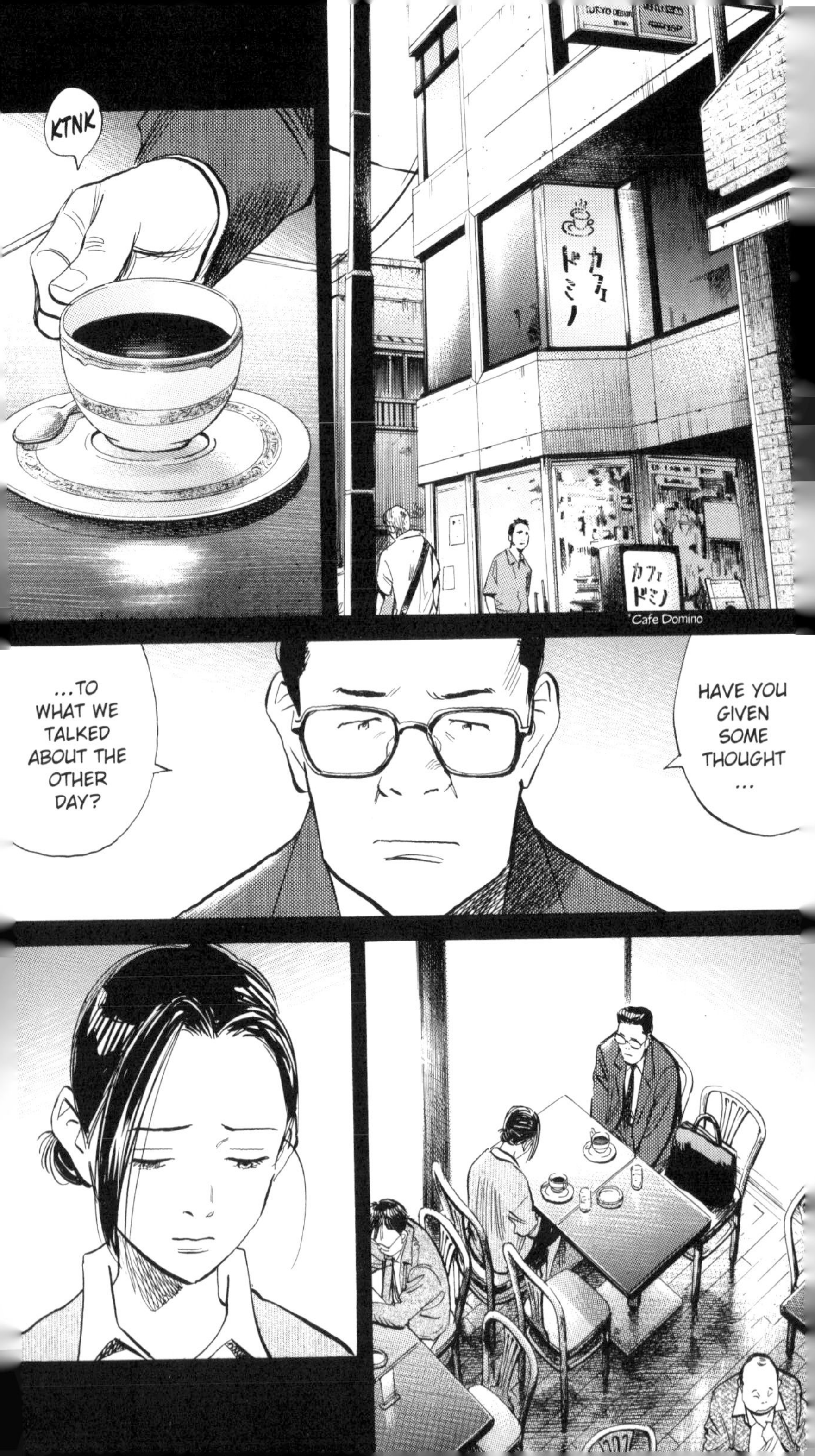
カフェ ドミノ
カフェ ドミノ
Cafe Domino
KTNK
HAVE YOU GIVEN SOME THOUGHT ...
...TO WHAT WE TALKED ABOUT THE OTHER DAY?

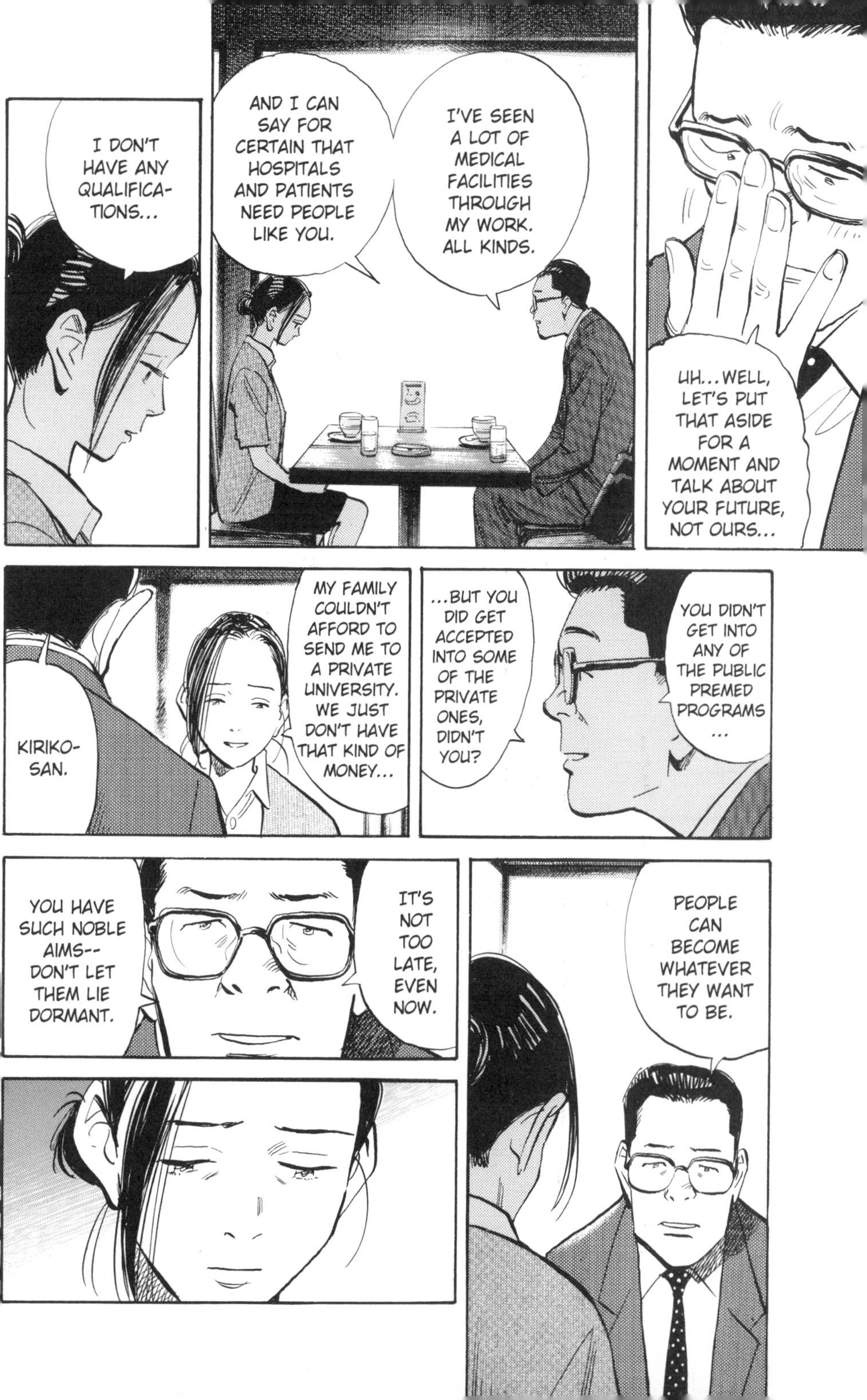
UH...WELL, LET'S PUT THAT ASIDE FOR A MOMENT AND TALK ABOUT YOUR FUTURE, NOT OURS...
I'VE SEEN A LOT OF MEDICAL FACILITIES THROUGH MY WORK. ALL KINDS.
AND I CAN SAY FOR CERTAIN THAT HOSPITALS AND PATIENTS NEED PEOPLE LIKE YOU.
I DON'T HAVE ANY QUALIFICATIONS...
YOU DIDN'T GET INTO ANY OF THE PUBLIC PREMED PROGRAMS...
...BUT YOU DID GET ACCEPTED INTO SOME OF THE PRIVATE ONES, DIDN'T YOU?
MY FAMILY COULDN'T AFFORD TO SEND ME TO A PRIVATE UNIVERSITY. WE JUST DON'T HAVE THAT KIND OF MONEY...
KIRIKO-SAN.
PEOPLE CAN BECOME WHATEVER THEY WANT TO BE.
IT'S NOT TOO LATE, EVEN NOW.
YOU HAVE SUCH NOBLE AIMS-- DON'T LET THEM LIE DORMANT.

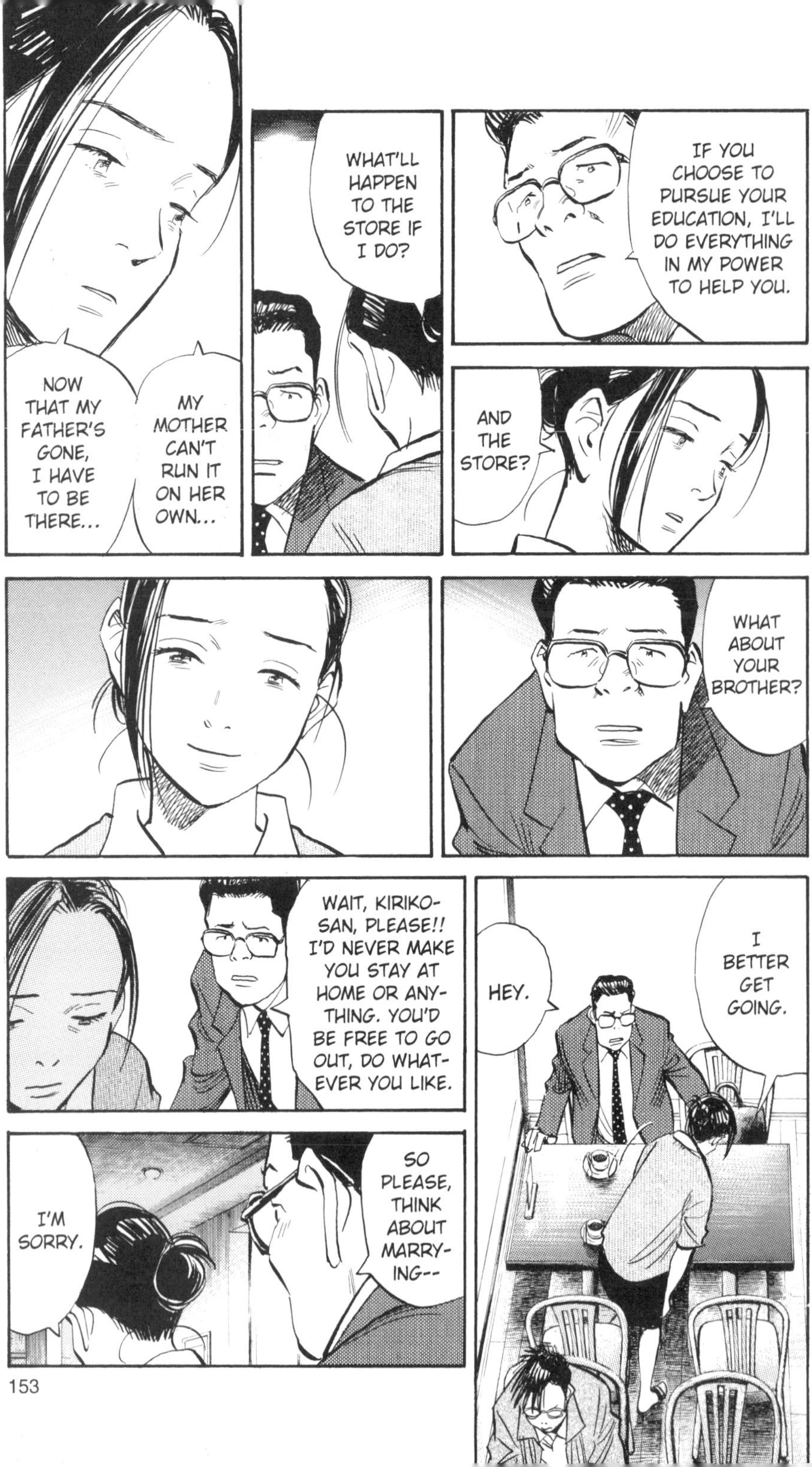
IF YOU CHOOSE TO PURSUE YOUR EDUCATION, I'LL DO EVERYTHING IN MY POWER TO HELP YOU.
AND THE STORE?
WHAT'LL HAPPEN TO THE STORE IF I DO?
MY MOTHER CAN'T RUN IT ON HER OWN...
NOW THAT MY FATHER'S GONE, I HAVE TO BE THERE...
WHAT ABOUT YOUR BROTHER?
I BETTER GET GOING.
HEY.
WAIT, KIRIKO-SAN, PLEASE!! I'D NEVER MAKE YOU STAY AT HOME OR ANYTHING. YOU'D BE FREE TO GO OUT, DO WHATEVER YOU LIKE.
SO PLEASE, THINK ABOUT MARRYING--
I'M SORRY.

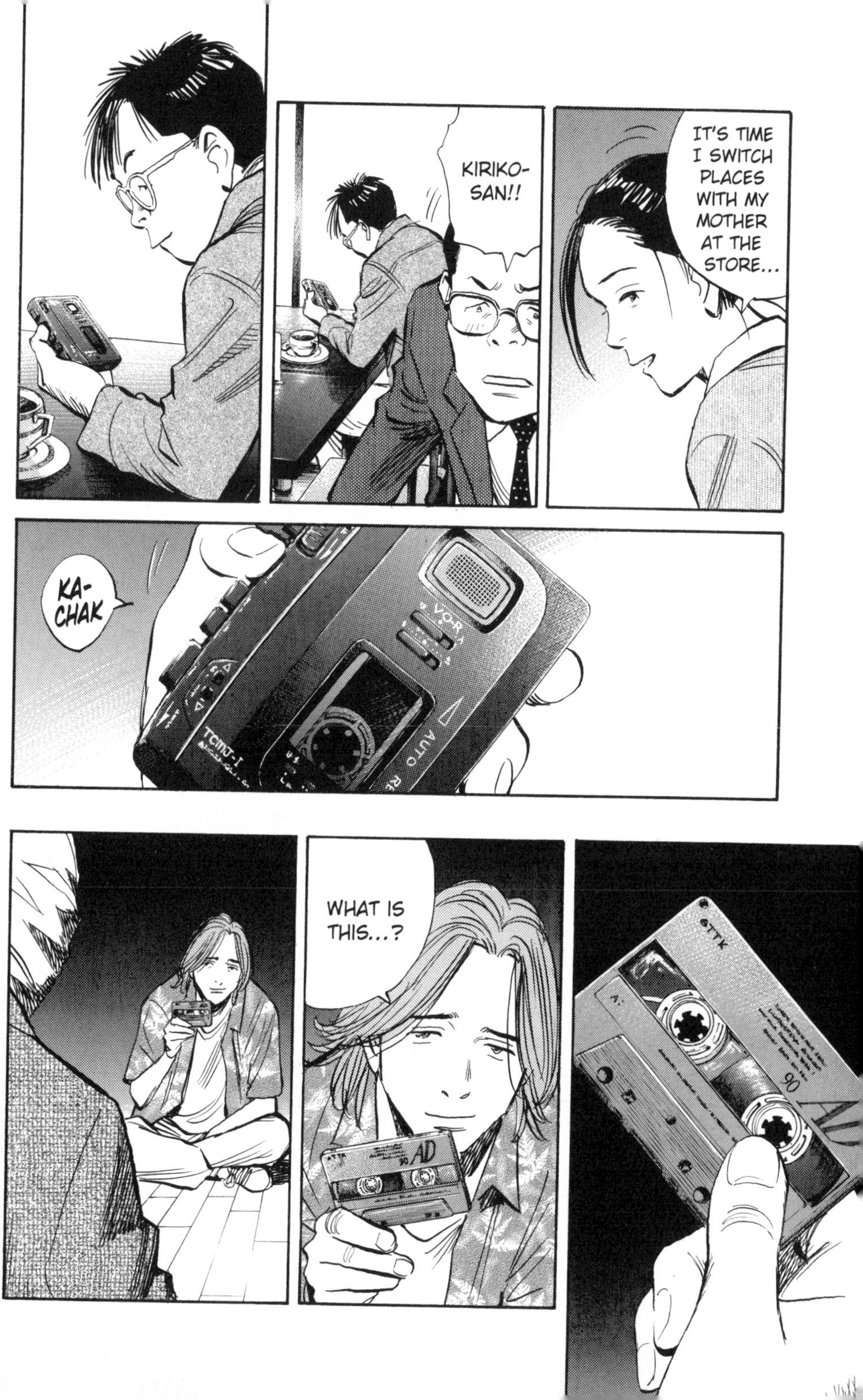
IT'S TIME I SWITCH PLACES WITH MY MOTHER AT THE STORE...
KIRIKO-SAN!!
KA-CHAK
WHAT IS THIS...?

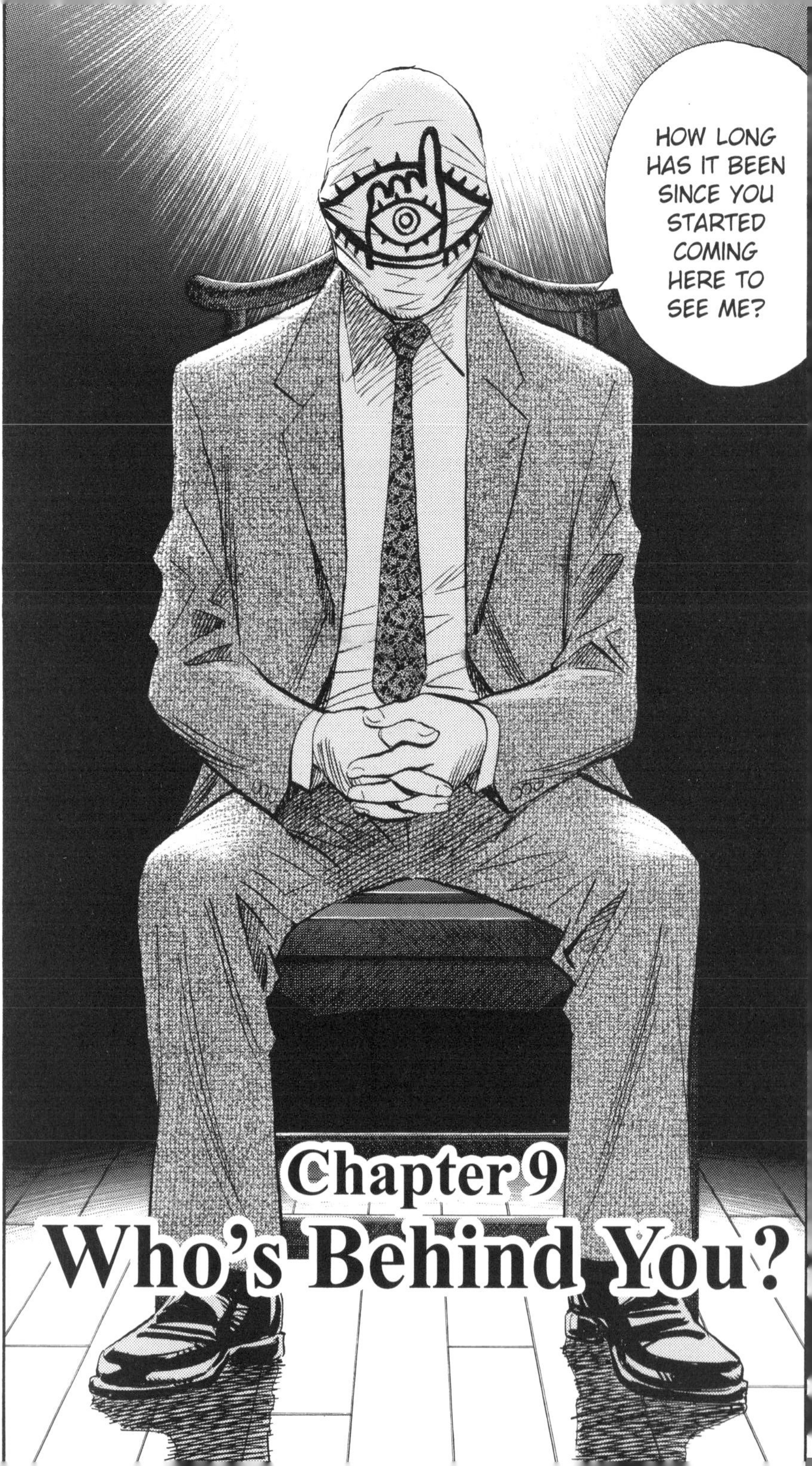
HOW LONG HAS IT BEEN SINCE YOU STARTED COMING HERE TO SEE ME?
Chapter 9
Who's Behind You?

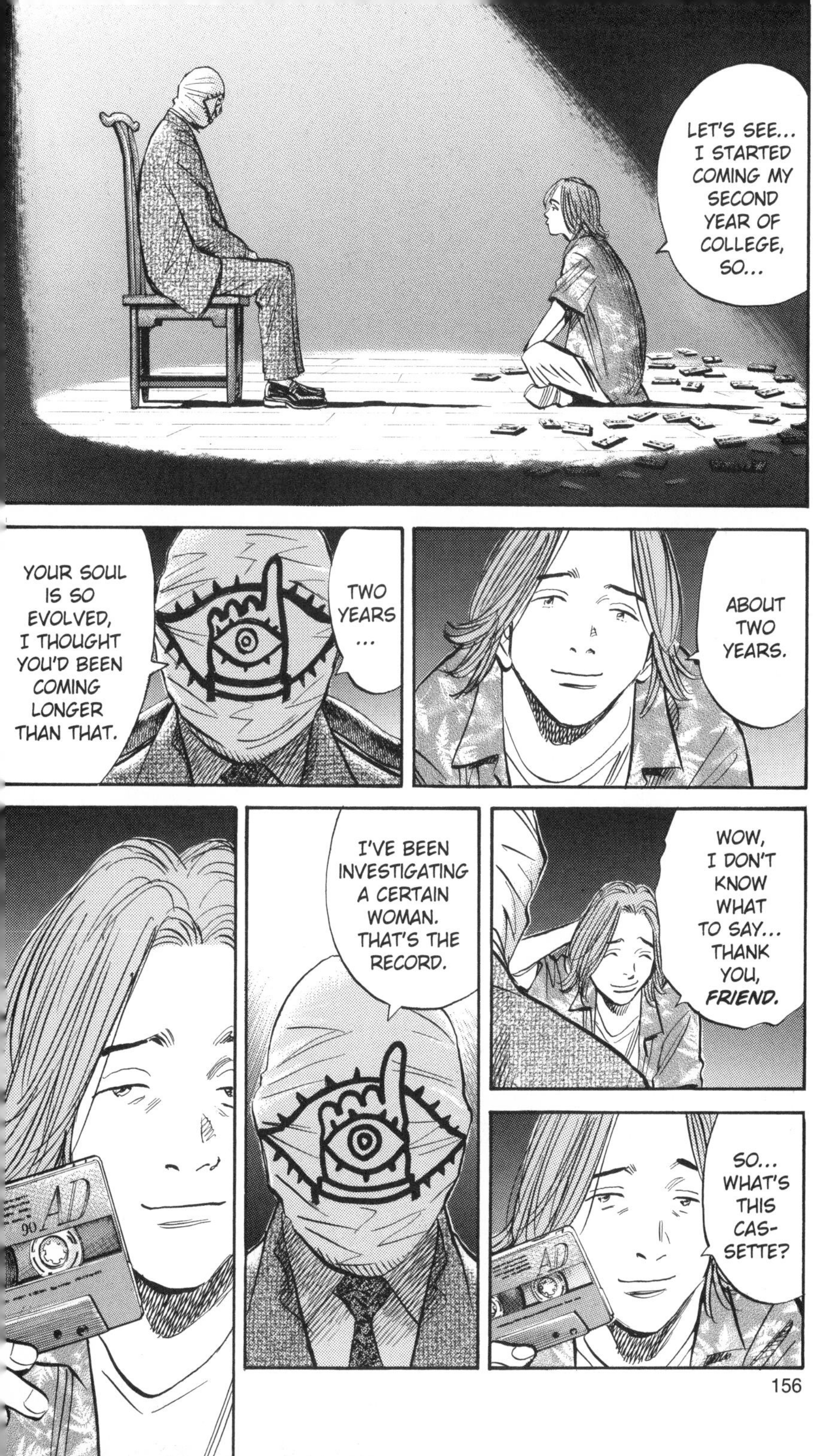
LET'S SEE... I STARTED COMING MY SECOND YEAR OF COLLEGE, SO...
ABOUT TWO YEARS.
TWO YEARS...
YOUR SOUL IS SO EVOLVED, I THOUGHT YOU'D BEEN COMING LONGER THAN THAT.
WOW, I DON'T KNOW WHAT TO SAY... THANK YOU, ***FRIEND.***
SO... WHAT'S THIS CAS-SETTE?
I'VE BEEN INVESTIGATING A CERTAIN WOMAN. THAT'S THE RECORD.

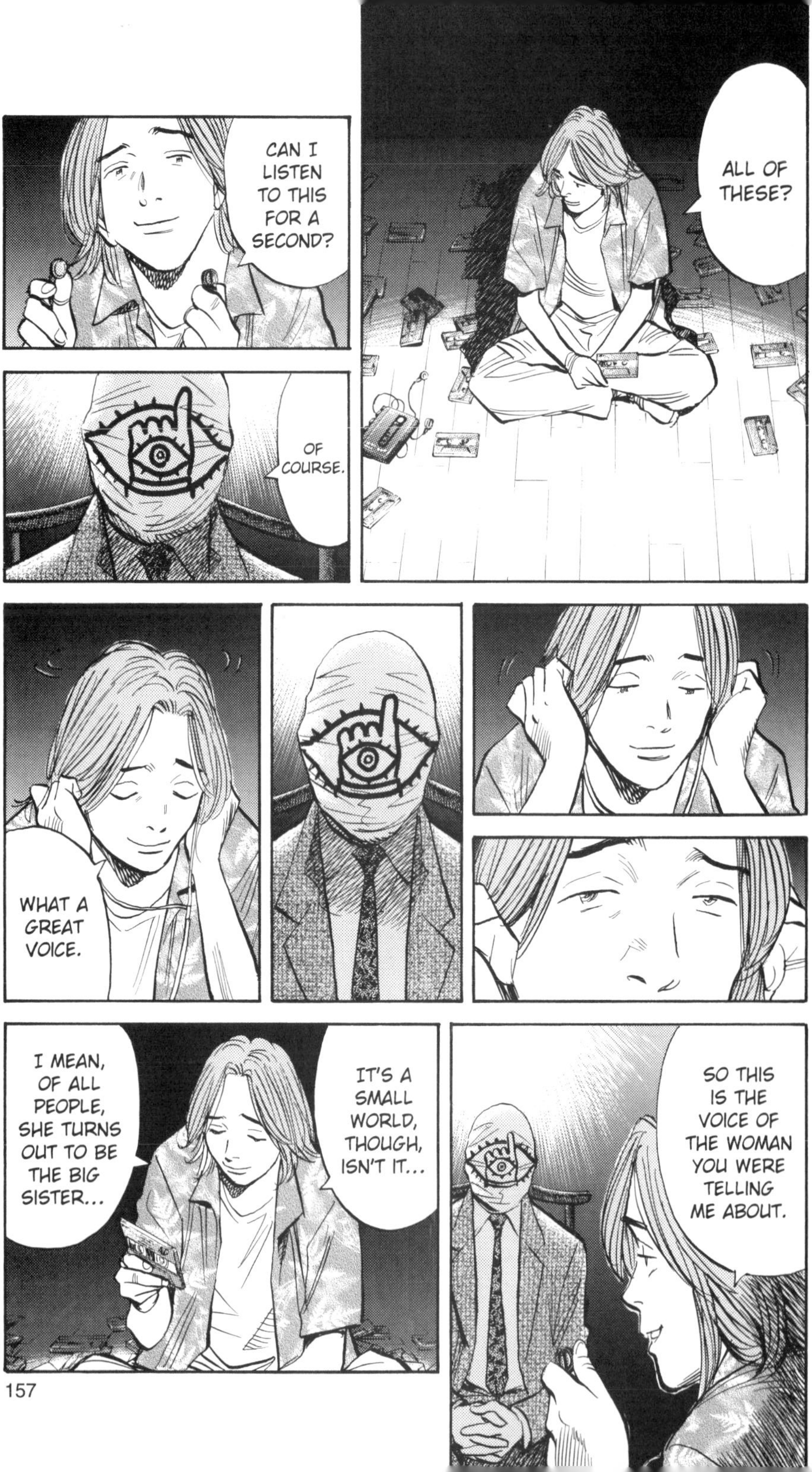
ALL OF THESE?
CAN I LISTEN TO THIS FOR A SECOND?
OF COURSE.
WHAT A GREAT VOICE.
SO THIS IS THE VOICE OF THE WOMAN YOU WERE TELLING ME ABOUT.
IT'S A SMALL WORLD, THOUGH, ISN'T IT...
I MEAN, OF ALL PEOPLE, SHE TURNS OUT TO BE THE BIG SISTER...

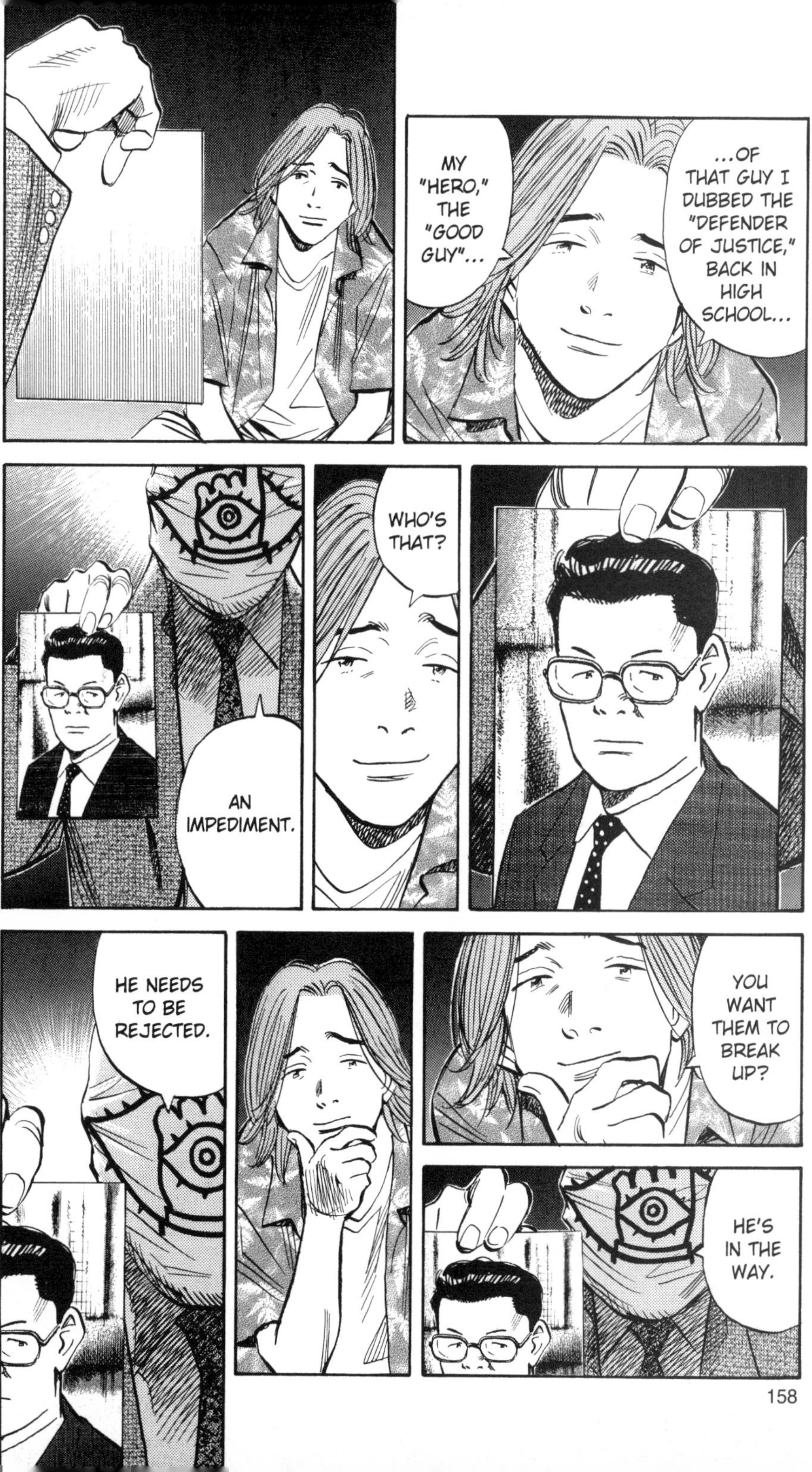
...OF THAT GUY I DUBBED THE "DEFENDER OF JUSTICE," BACK IN HIGH SCHOOL...
MY "HERO," THE "GOOD GUY"...
WHO'S THAT?
AN IMPEDIMENT.
YOU WANT THEM TO BREAK UP?
HE'S IN THE WAY.
HE NEEDS TO BE REJECTED.

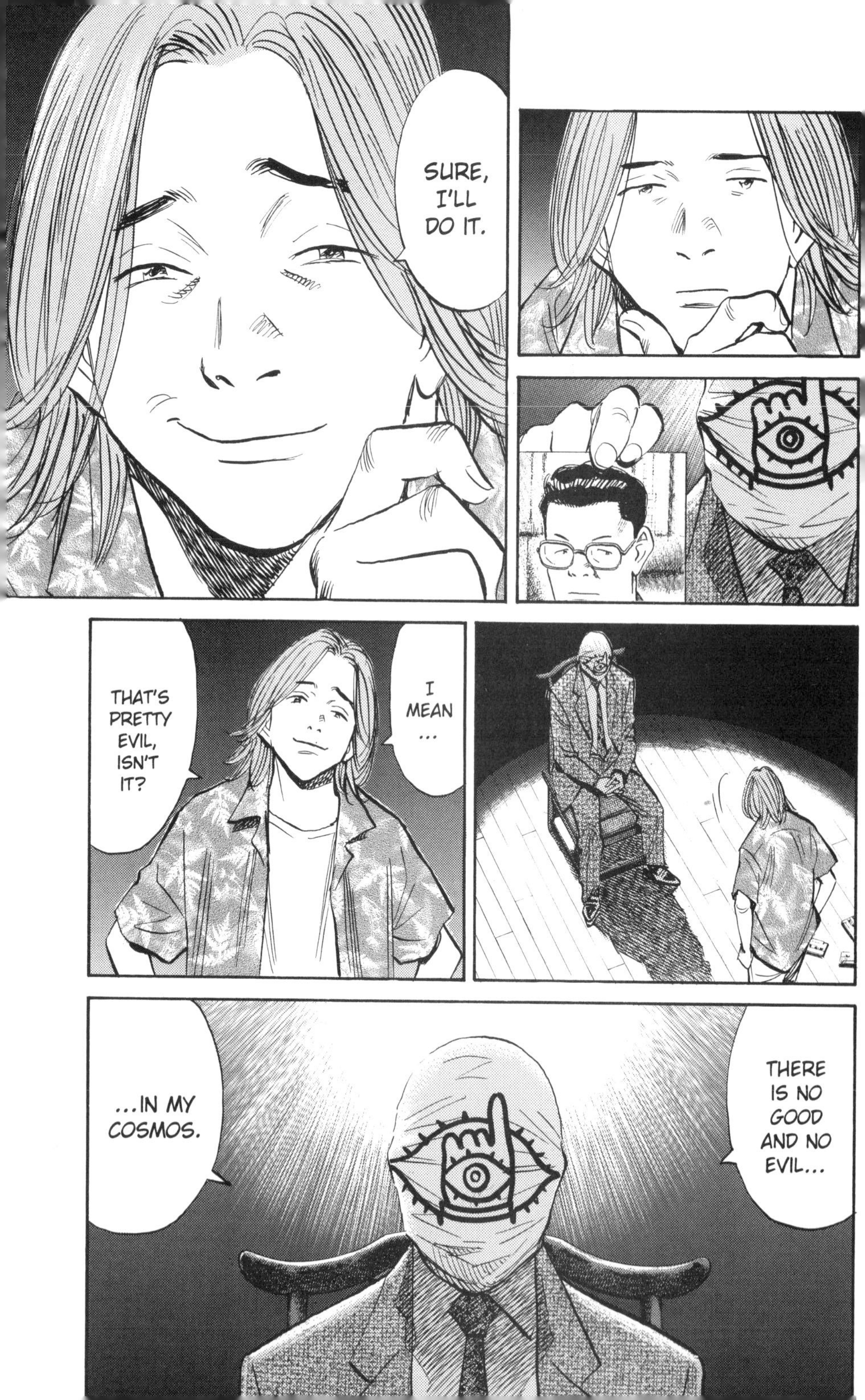
SURE, I'LL DO IT.
I MEAN...
THAT'S PRETTY EVIL, ISN'T IT?
THERE IS NO GOOD AND NO EVIL...
...IN MY COSMOS.

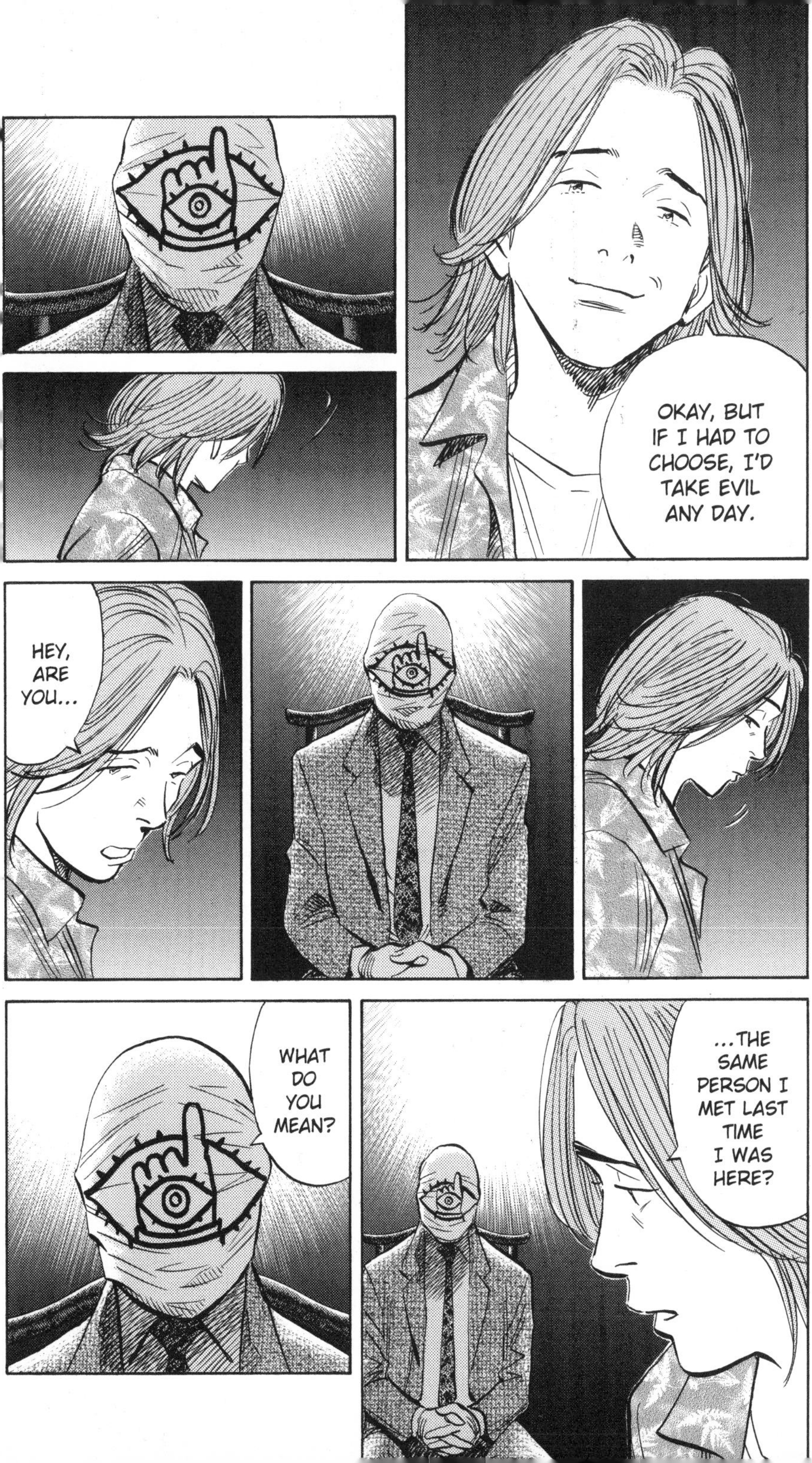
OKAY, BUT IF I HAD TO CHOOSE, I'D TAKE EVIL ANY DAY.
HEY, ARE YOU...
...THE SAME PERSON I MET LAST TIME I WAS HERE?
WHAT DO YOU MEAN?

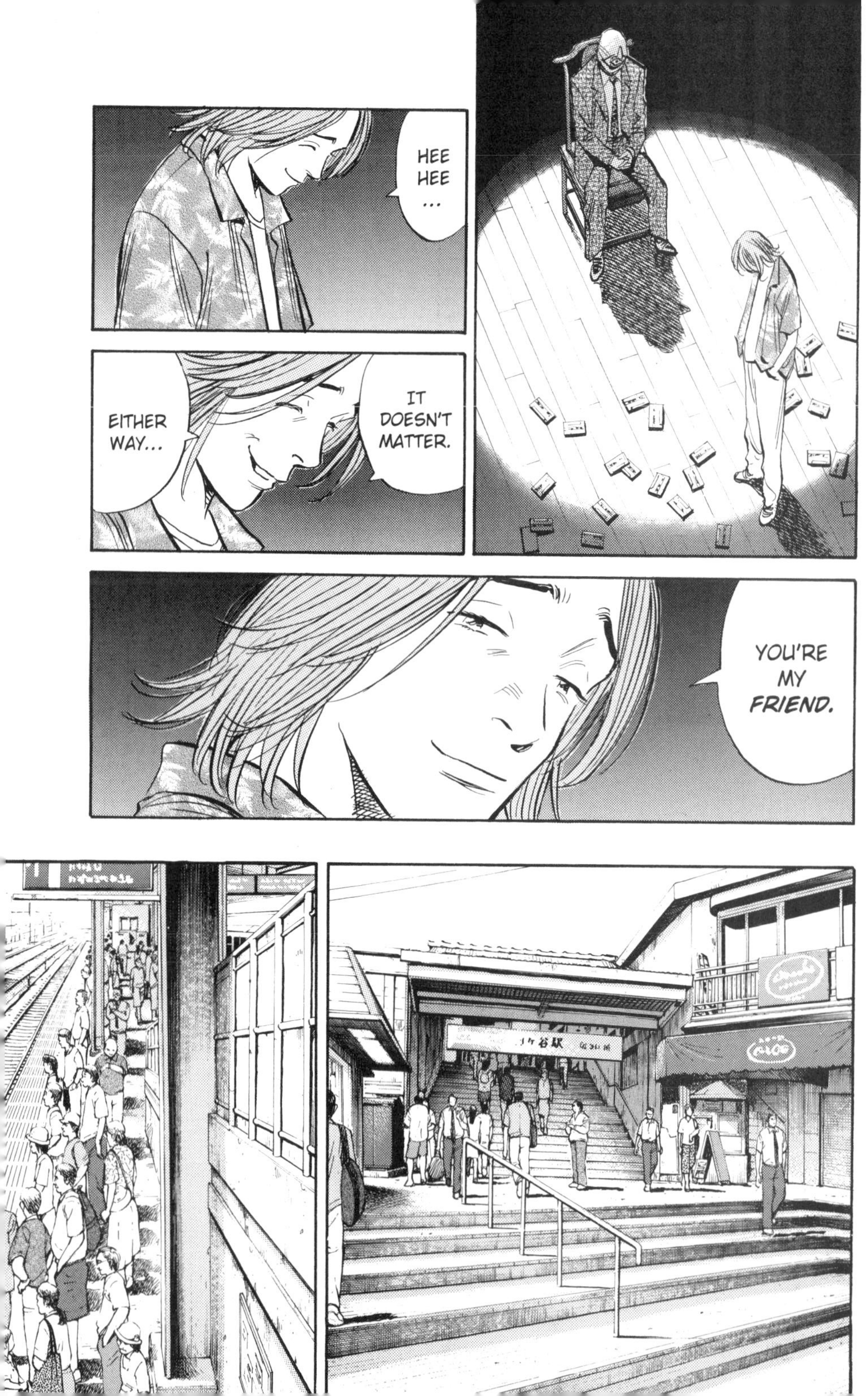
HEE HEE ...
IT DOESN'T MATTER.
EITHER WAY...
YOU'RE MY *FRIEND.*

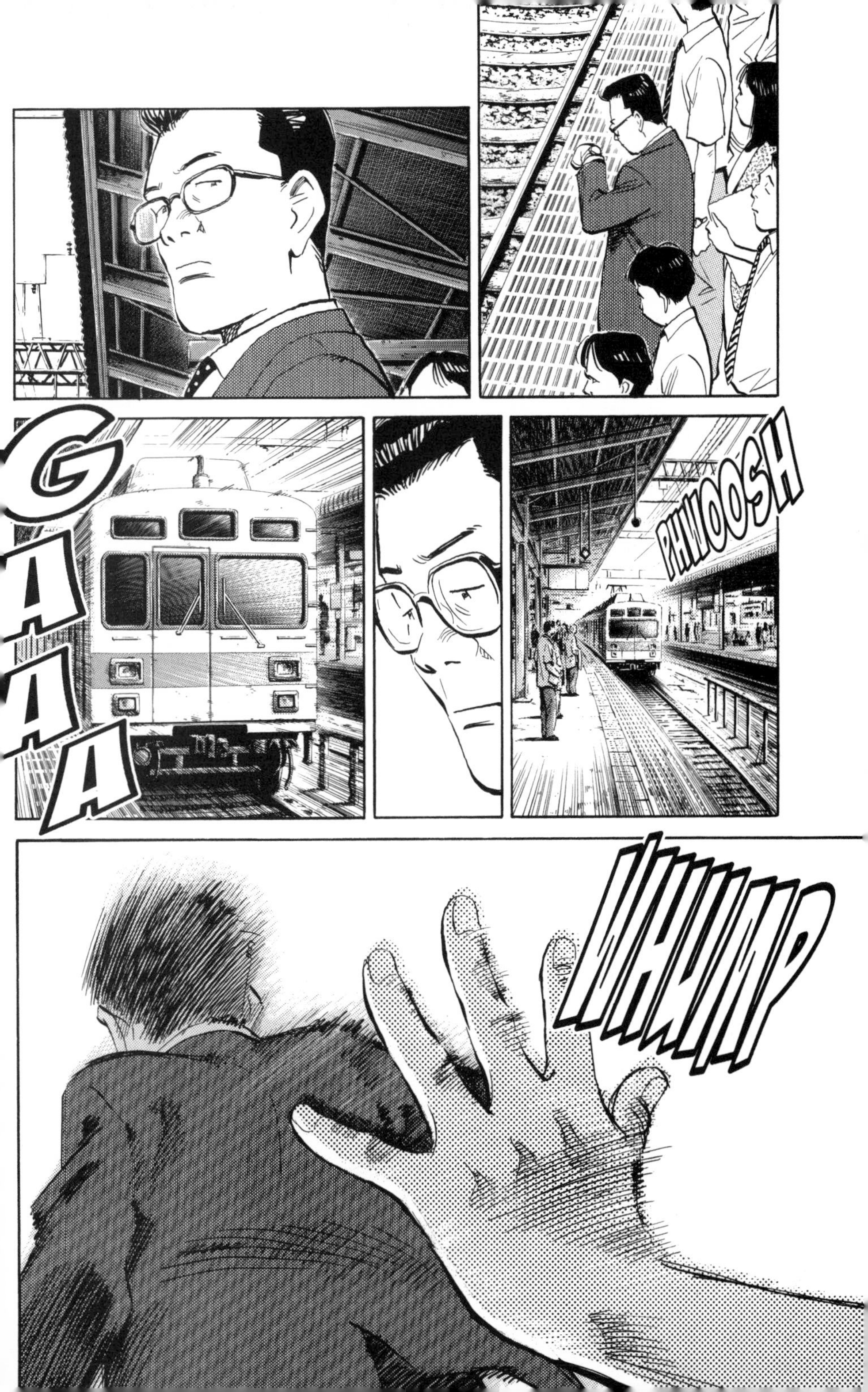
PHWOOSH
GAAAA
WHUMP

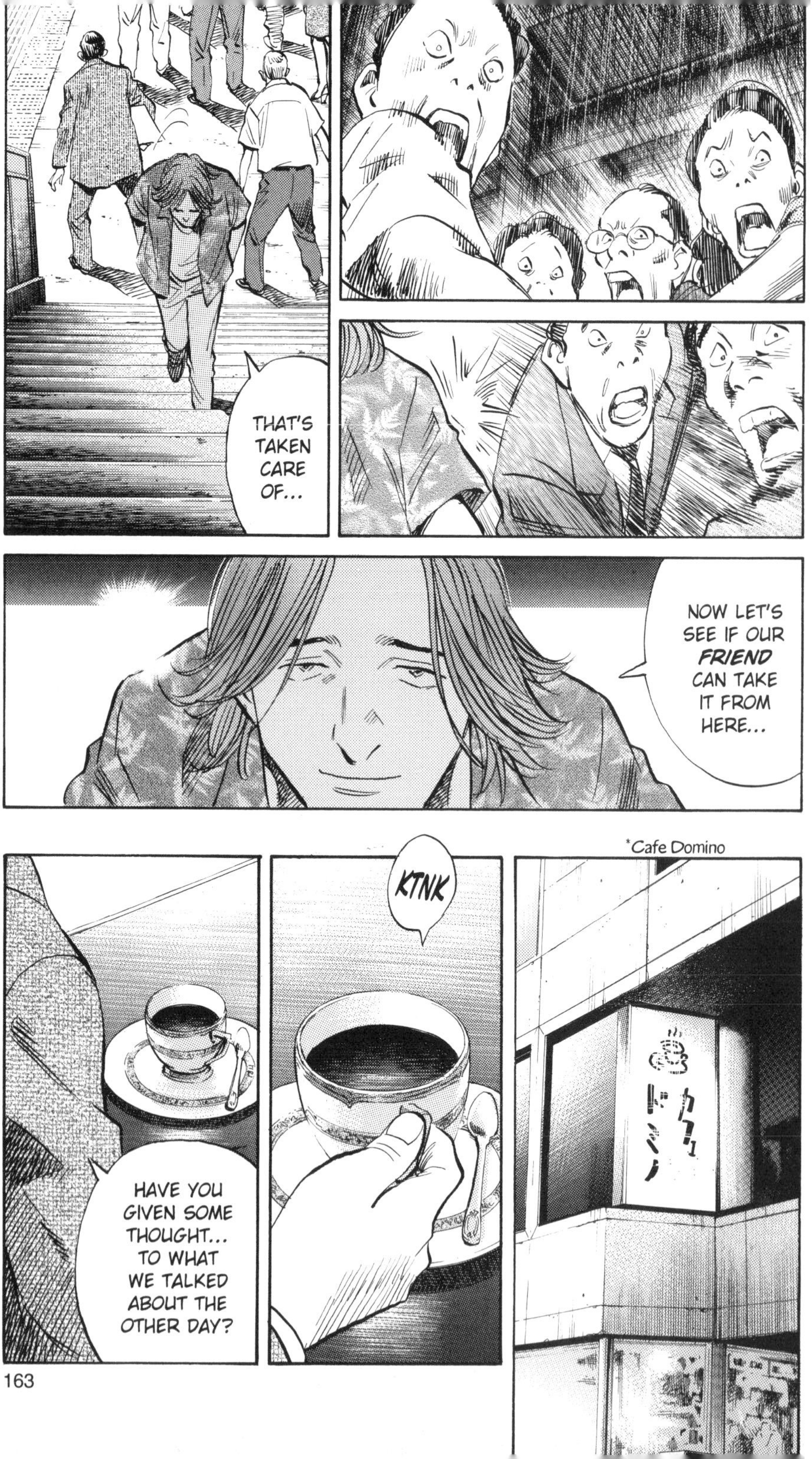
THAT'S TAKEN CARE OF...
NOW LET'S SEE IF OUR *FRIEND* CAN TAKE IT FROM HERE...
*Cafe Domino
カフェ ドミノ
KTNK
HAVE YOU GIVEN SOME THOUGHT... TO WHAT WE TALKED ABOUT THE OTHER DAY?

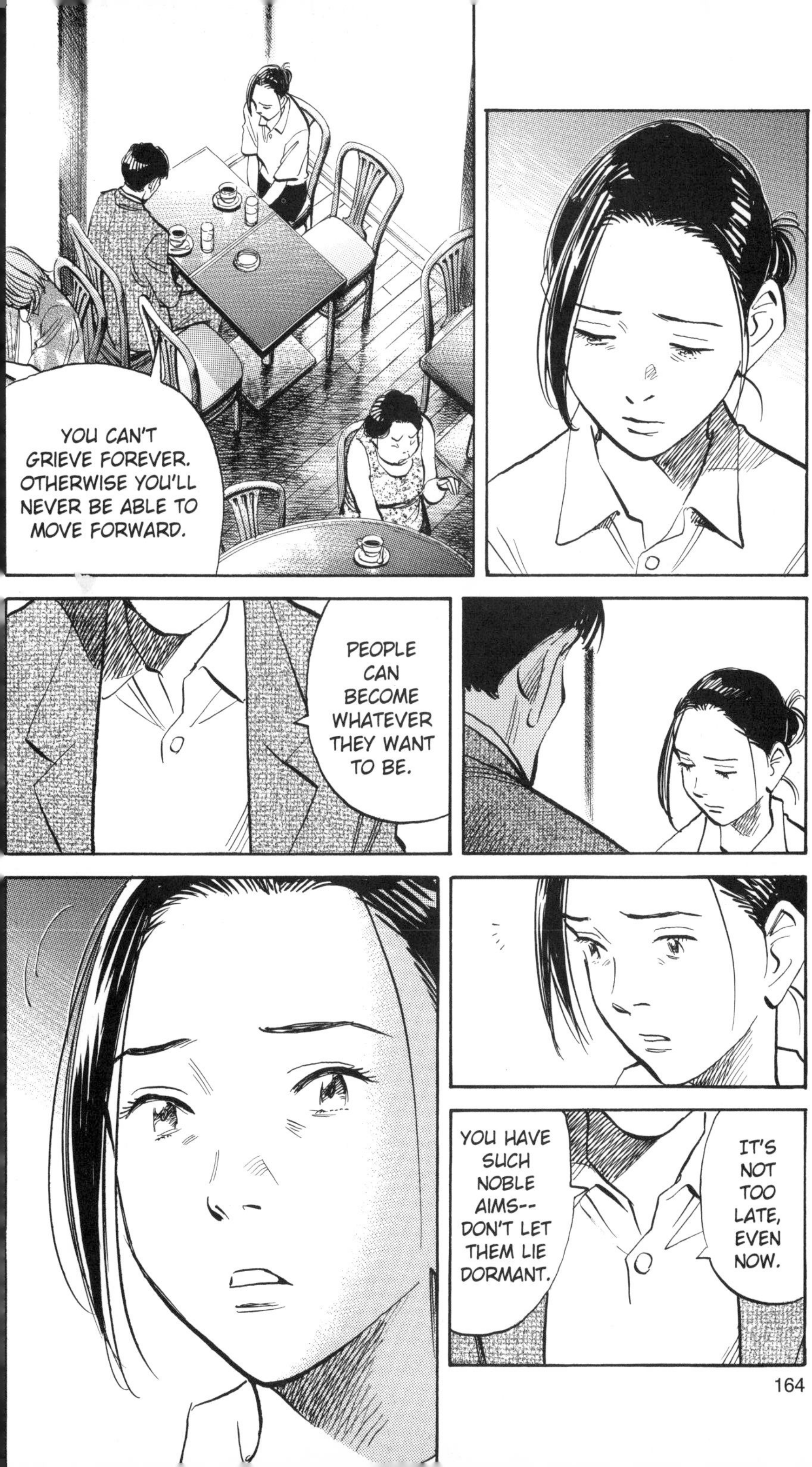
YOU CAN'T GRIEVE FOREVER. OTHERWISE YOU'LL NEVER BE ABLE TO MOVE FORWARD.
PEOPLE CAN BECOME WHATEVER THEY WANT TO BE.
IT'S NOT TOO LATE, EVEN NOW.
YOU HAVE SUCH NOBLE AIMS-- DON'T LET THEM LIE DORMANT.

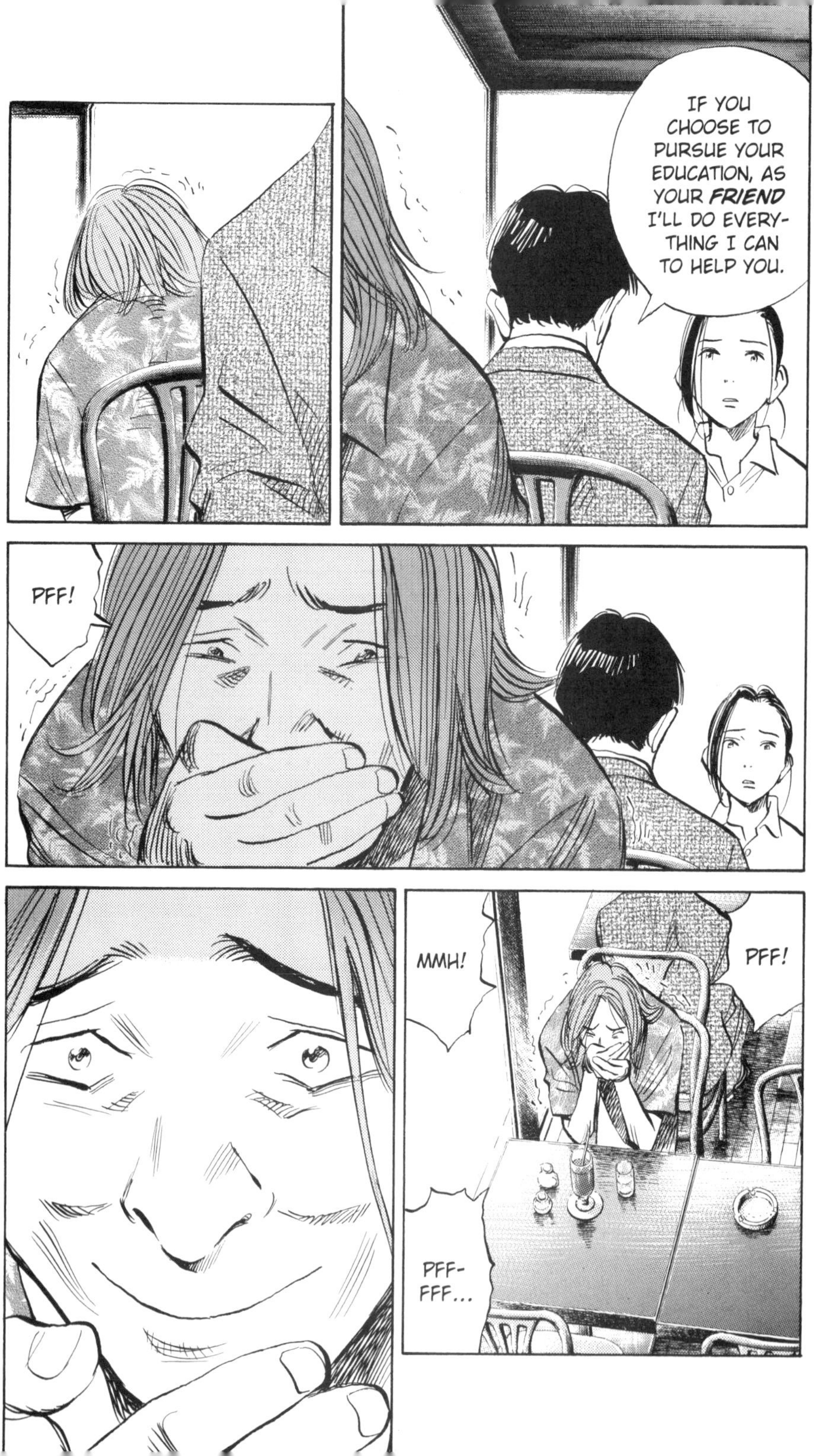
IF YOU CHOOSE TO PURSUE YOUR EDUCATION, AS YOUR ***FRIEND*** I'LL DO EVERY-THING I CAN TO HELP YOU.
PFF!
PFF!
MMH!
PFF-FFF...

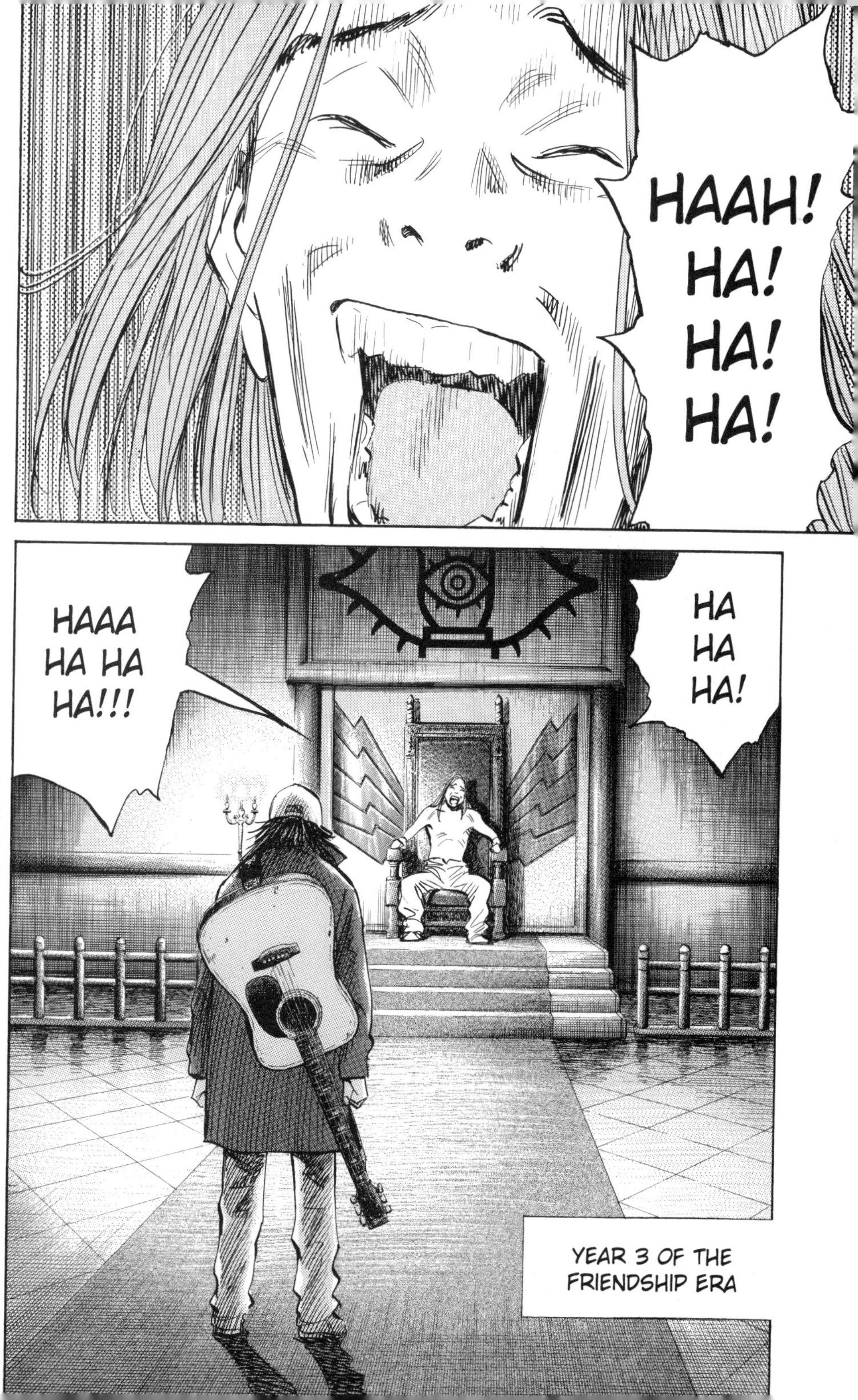
HAAH! HA! HA! HA!
HA HA HA!
HAAA HA HA HA!!!
YEAR 3 OF THE FRIENDSHIP ERA

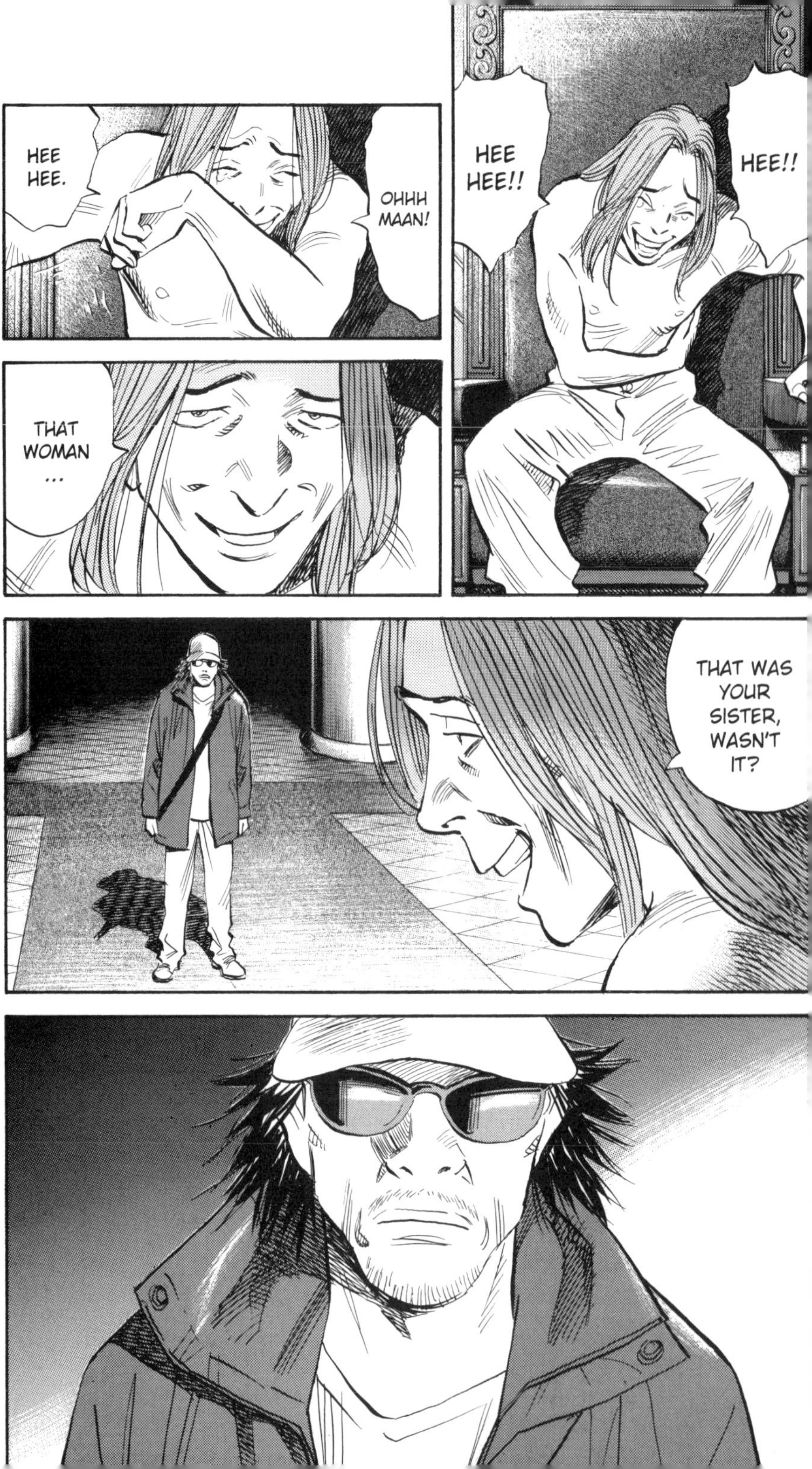
HEE!!
HEE HEE!!
OHHH MAAN!
HEE HEE.
THAT WOMAN ...
THAT WAS YOUR SISTER, WASN'T IT?

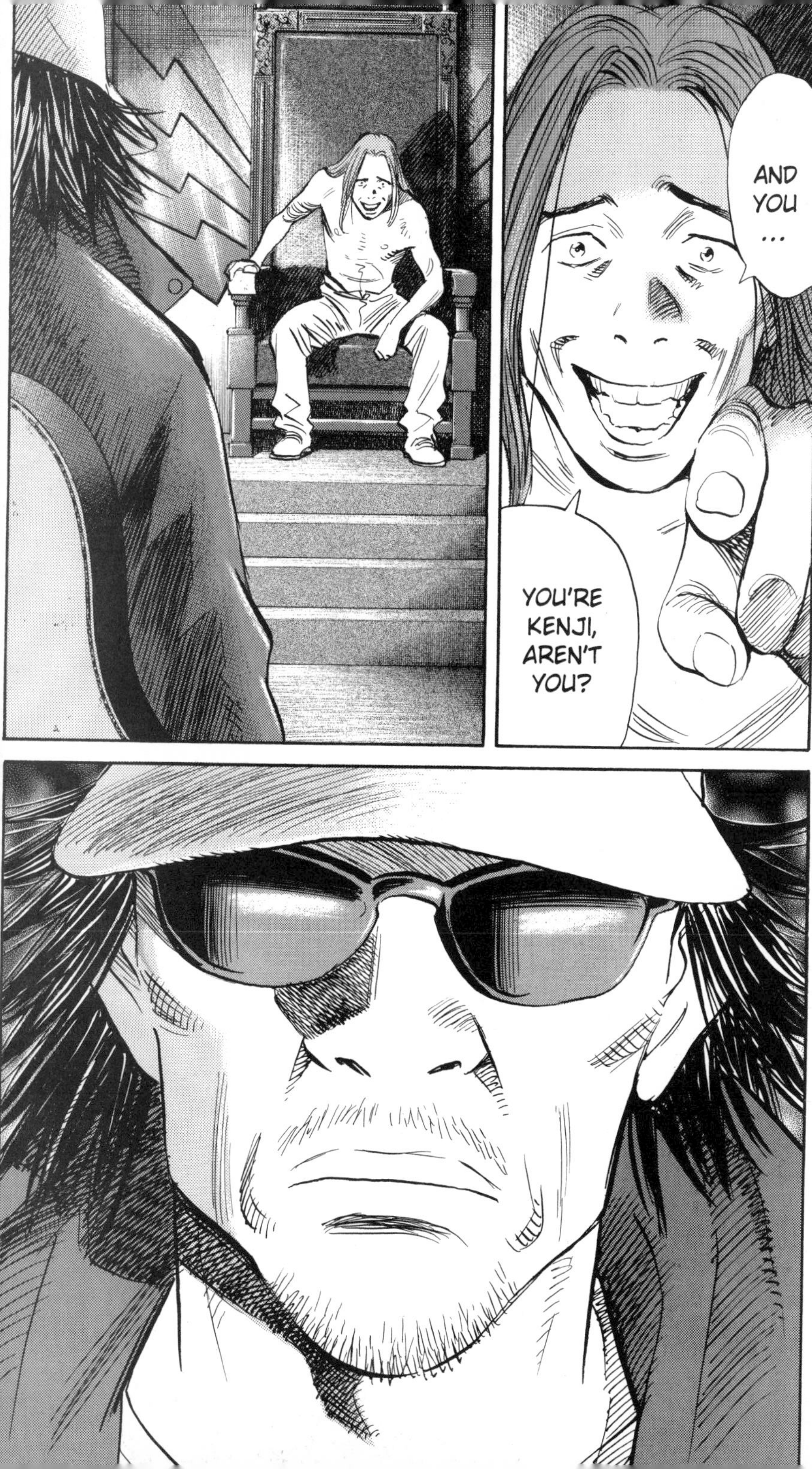
AND YOU ...
YOU'RE KENJI, AREN'T YOU?

Chapter 10 Ultimate Evil

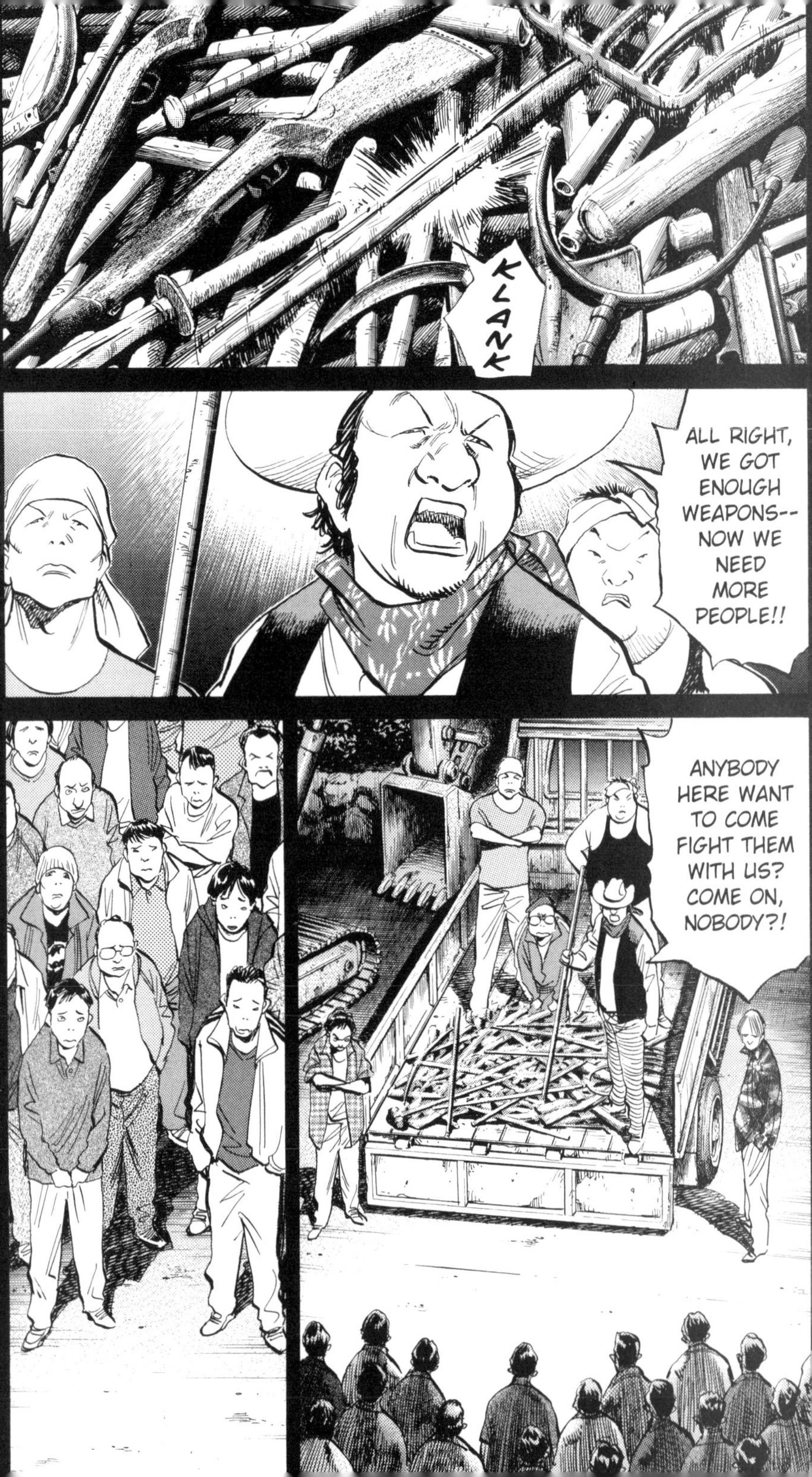
KLANK
ALL RIGHT, WE GOT ENOUGH WEAPONS-- NOW WE NEED MORE PEOPLE!!
ANYBODY HERE WANT TO COME FIGHT THEM WITH US? COME ON, NOBODY?!

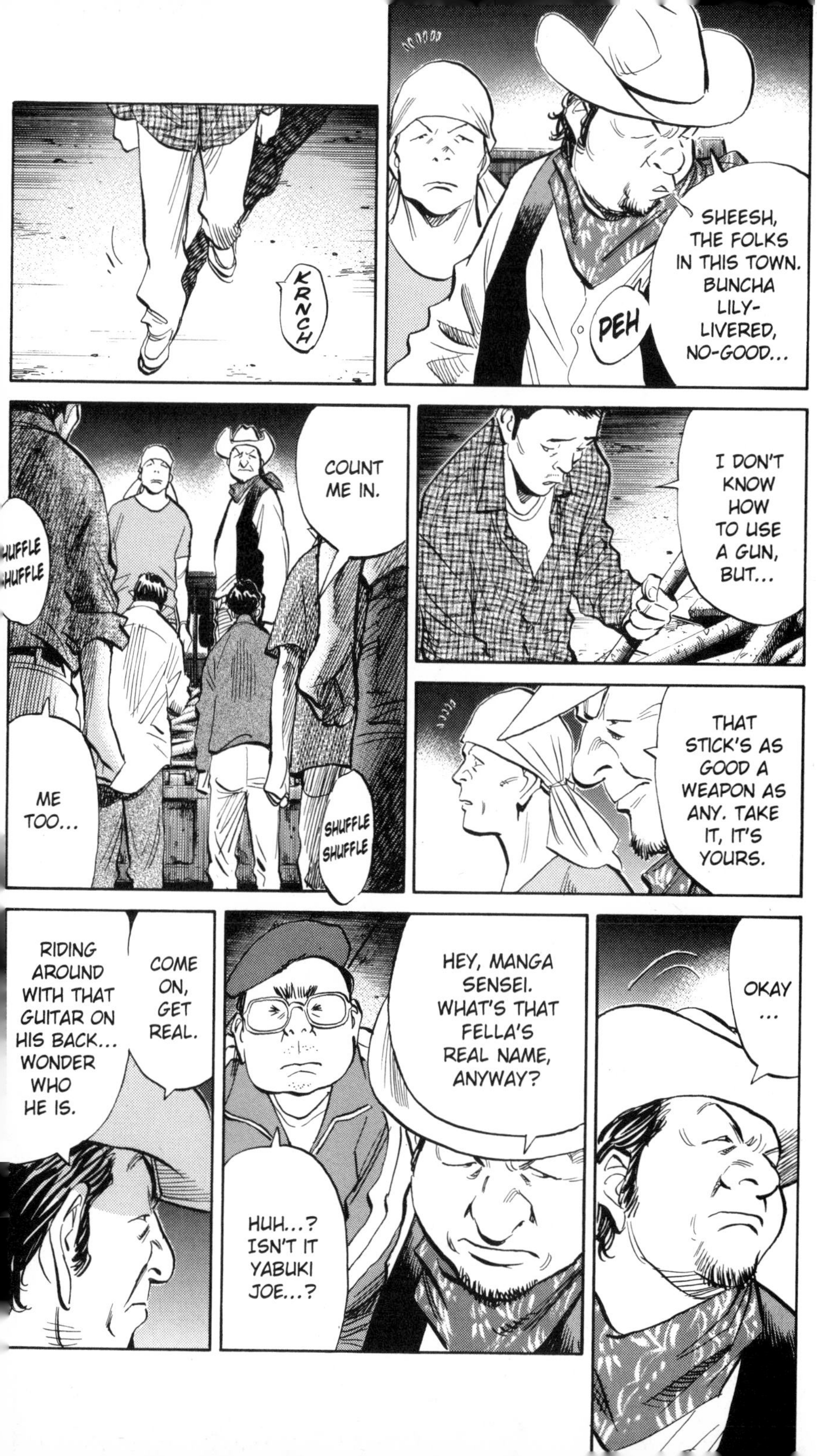
SHEESH, THE FOLKS IN THIS TOWN. BUNCHA LILY-LIVERED, NO-GOOD...
PEH
KRNCH
I DON'T KNOW HOW TO USE A GUN, BUT...
THAT STICK'S AS GOOD A WEAPON AS ANY. TAKE IT, IT'S YOURS.
COUNT ME IN.
SHUFFLE SHUFFLE
ME TOO...
SHUFFLE SHUFFLE
OKAY...
HEY, MANGA SENSEI. WHAT'S THAT FELLA'S REAL NAME, ANYWAY?
HUH...? ISN'T IT YABUKI JOE...?
COME ON, GET REAL.
RIDING AROUND WITH THAT GUITAR ON HIS BACK... WONDER WHO HE IS.

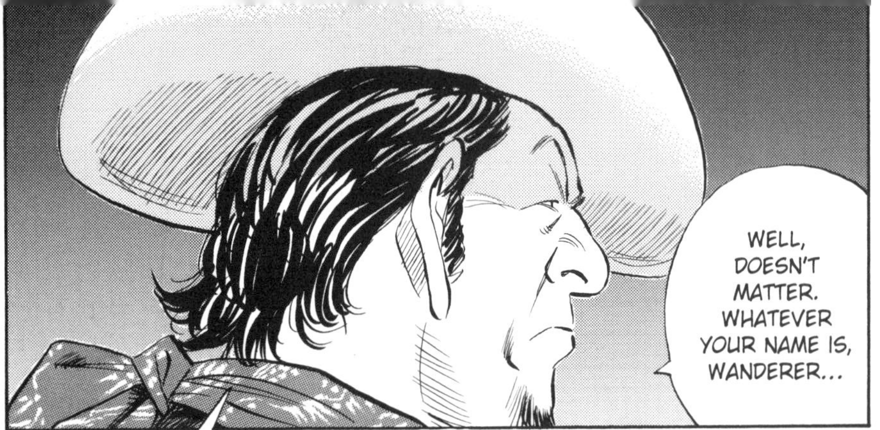
WELL, DOESN'T MATTER. WHATEVER YOUR NAME IS, WANDERER...
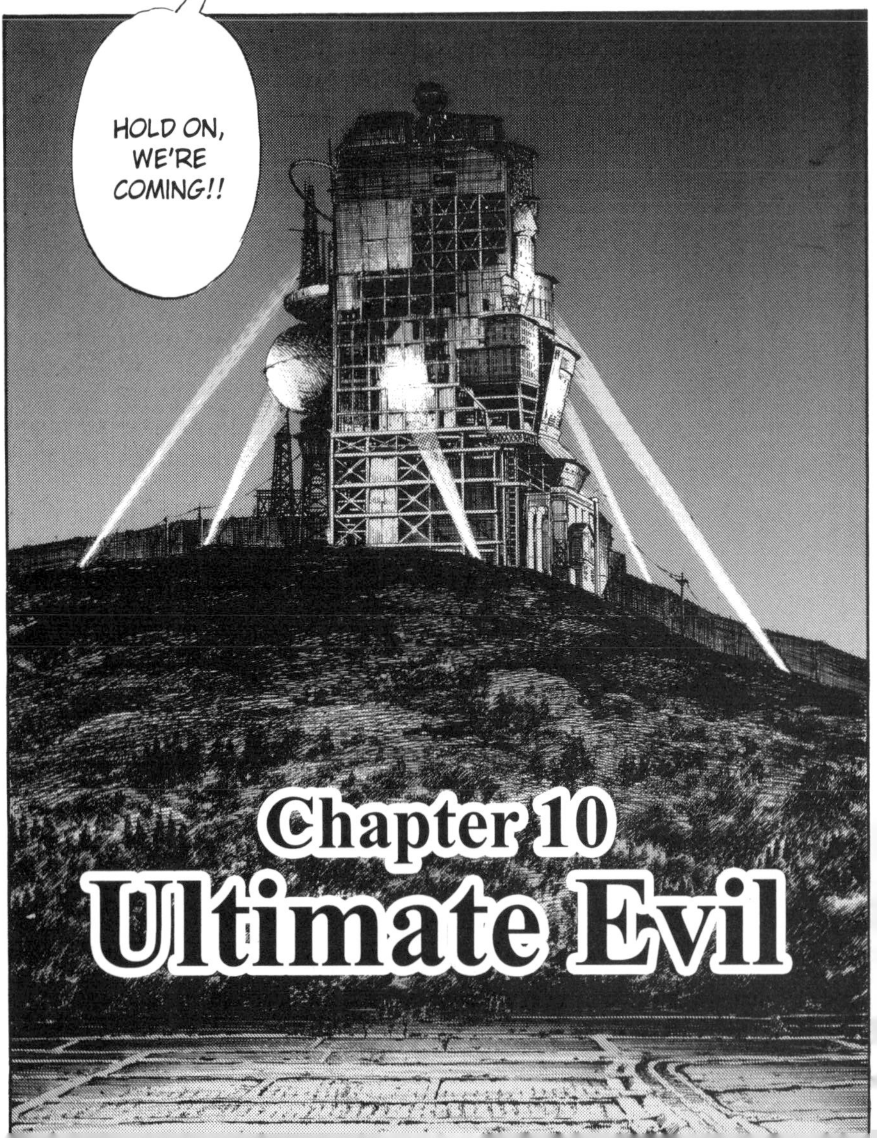
HOLD ON, WE'RE COMING!!

Chapter 10
Ultimate Evil

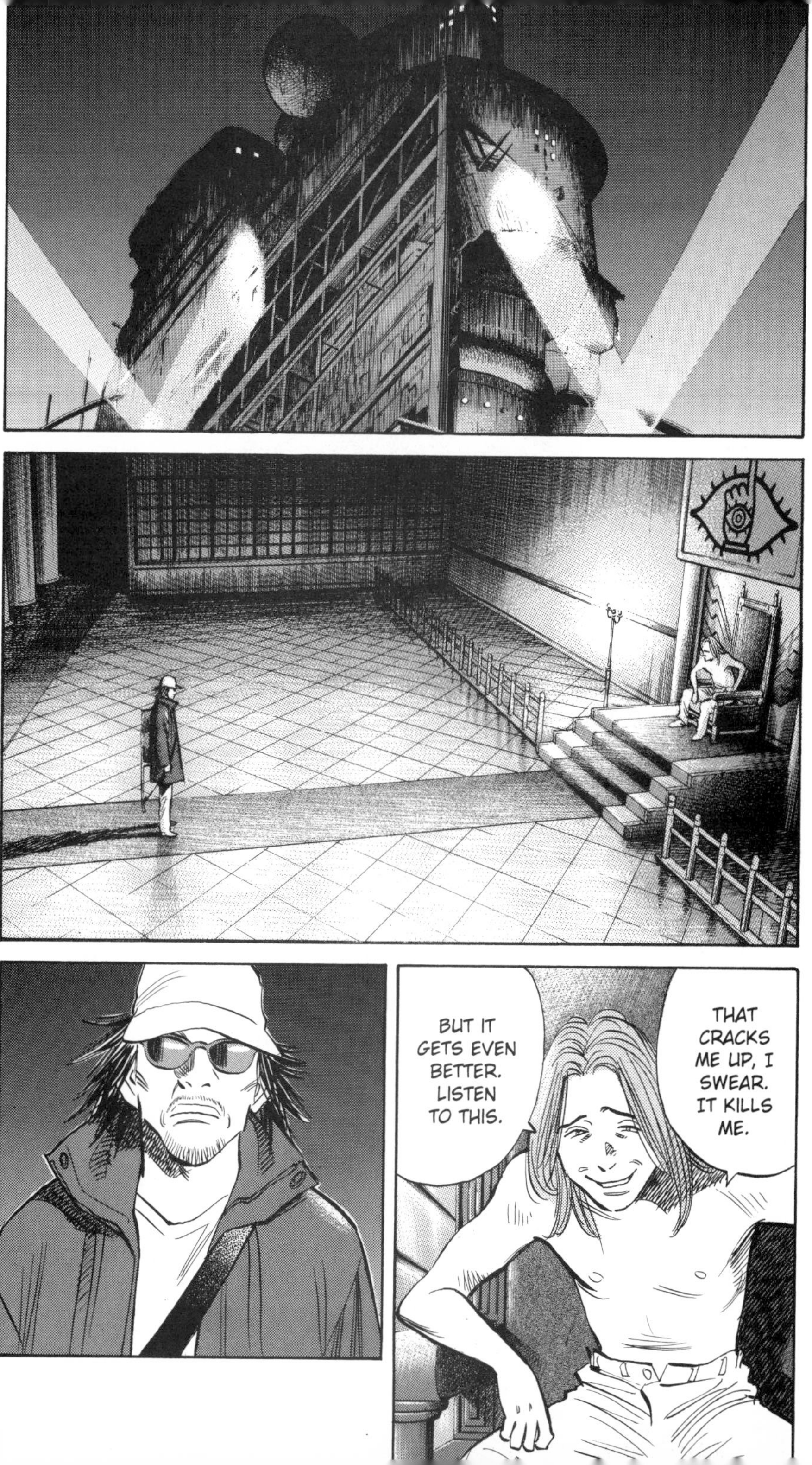
THAT CRACKS ME UP, I SWEAR. IT KILLS ME.
BUT IT GETS EVEN BETTER. LISTEN TO THIS.

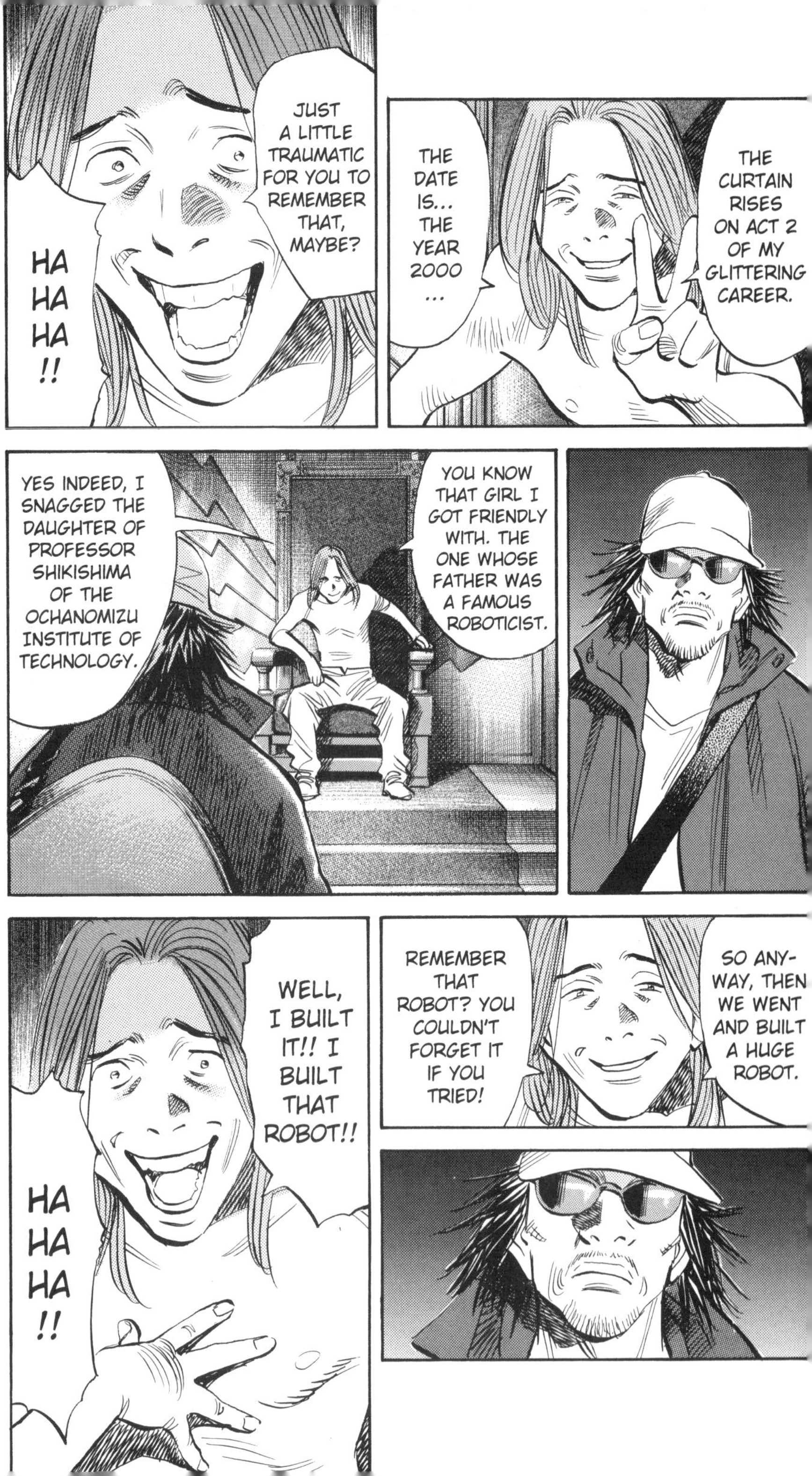
THE CURTAIN RISES ON ACT 2 OF MY GLITTERING CAREER.
THE DATE IS... THE YEAR 2000 ...
JUST A LITTLE TRAUMATIC FOR YOU TO REMEMBER THAT, MAYBE?
HA HA HA !!
YOU KNOW THAT GIRL I GOT FRIENDLY WITH. THE ONE WHOSE FATHER WAS A FAMOUS ROBOTICIST.
YES INDEED, I SNAGGED THE DAUGHTER OF PROFESSOR SHIKISHIMA OF THE OCHANOMIZU INSTITUTE OF TECHNOLOGY.
SO ANY-WAY, THEN WE WENT AND BUILT A HUGE ROBOT.
REMEMBER THAT ROBOT? YOU COULDN'T FORGET IT IF YOU TRIED!
WELL, I BUILT IT!! I BUILT THAT ROBOT!!
HA HA HA !!

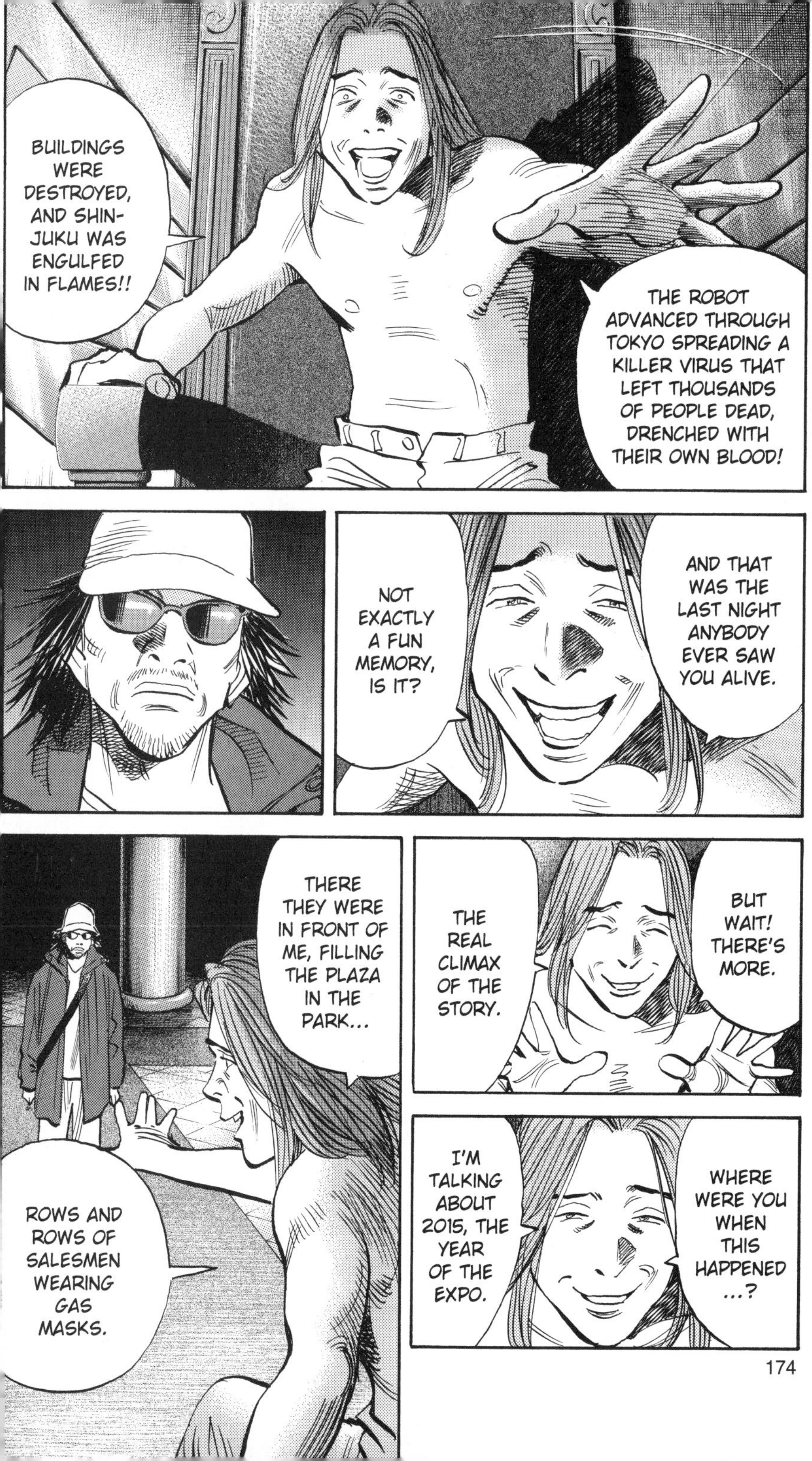
THE ROBOT ADVANCED THROUGH TOKYO SPREADING A KILLER VIRUS THAT LEFT THOUSANDS OF PEOPLE DEAD, DRENCHED WITH THEIR OWN BLOOD!
BUILDINGS WERE DESTROYED, AND SHIN-JUKU WAS ENGULFED IN FLAMES!!
AND THAT WAS THE LAST NIGHT ANYBODY EVER SAW YOU ALIVE.
NOT EXACTLY A FUN MEMORY, IS IT?
BUT WAIT! THERE'S MORE.
THE REAL CLIMAX OF THE STORY.
WHERE WERE YOU WHEN THIS HAPPENED ...?
I'M TALKING ABOUT 2015, THE YEAR OF THE EXPO.
THERE THEY WERE IN FRONT OF ME, FILLING THE PLAZA IN THE PARK...
ROWS AND ROWS OF SALESMEN WEARING GAS MASKS.

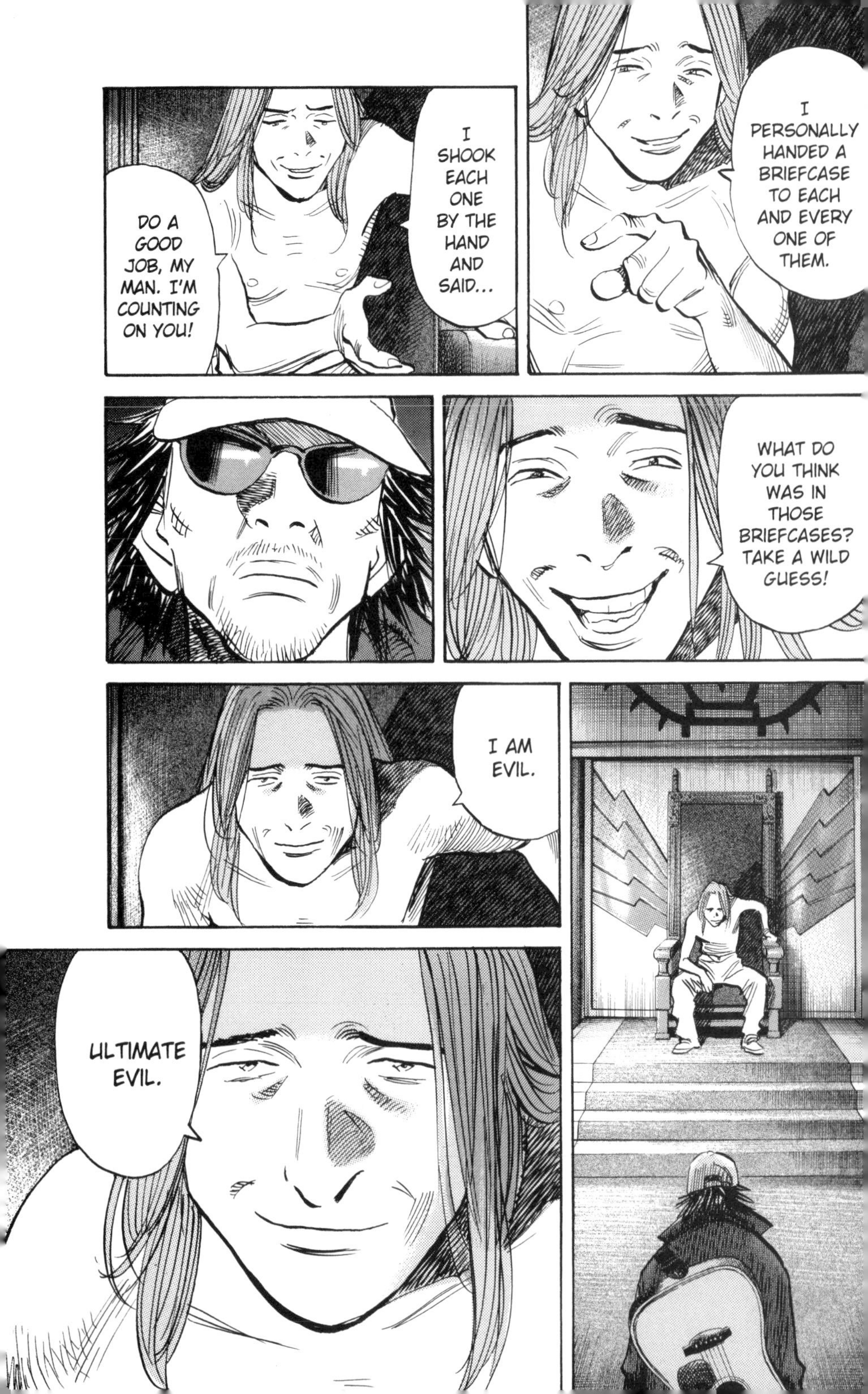
I PERSONALLY HANDED A BRIEFCASE TO EACH AND EVERY ONE OF THEM.
I SHOOK EACH ONE BY THE HAND AND SAID...
DO A GOOD JOB, MY MAN. I'M COUNTING ON YOU!
WHAT DO YOU THINK WAS IN THOSE BRIEFCASES? TAKE A WILD GUESS!
I AM EVIL.
ULTIMATE EVIL.

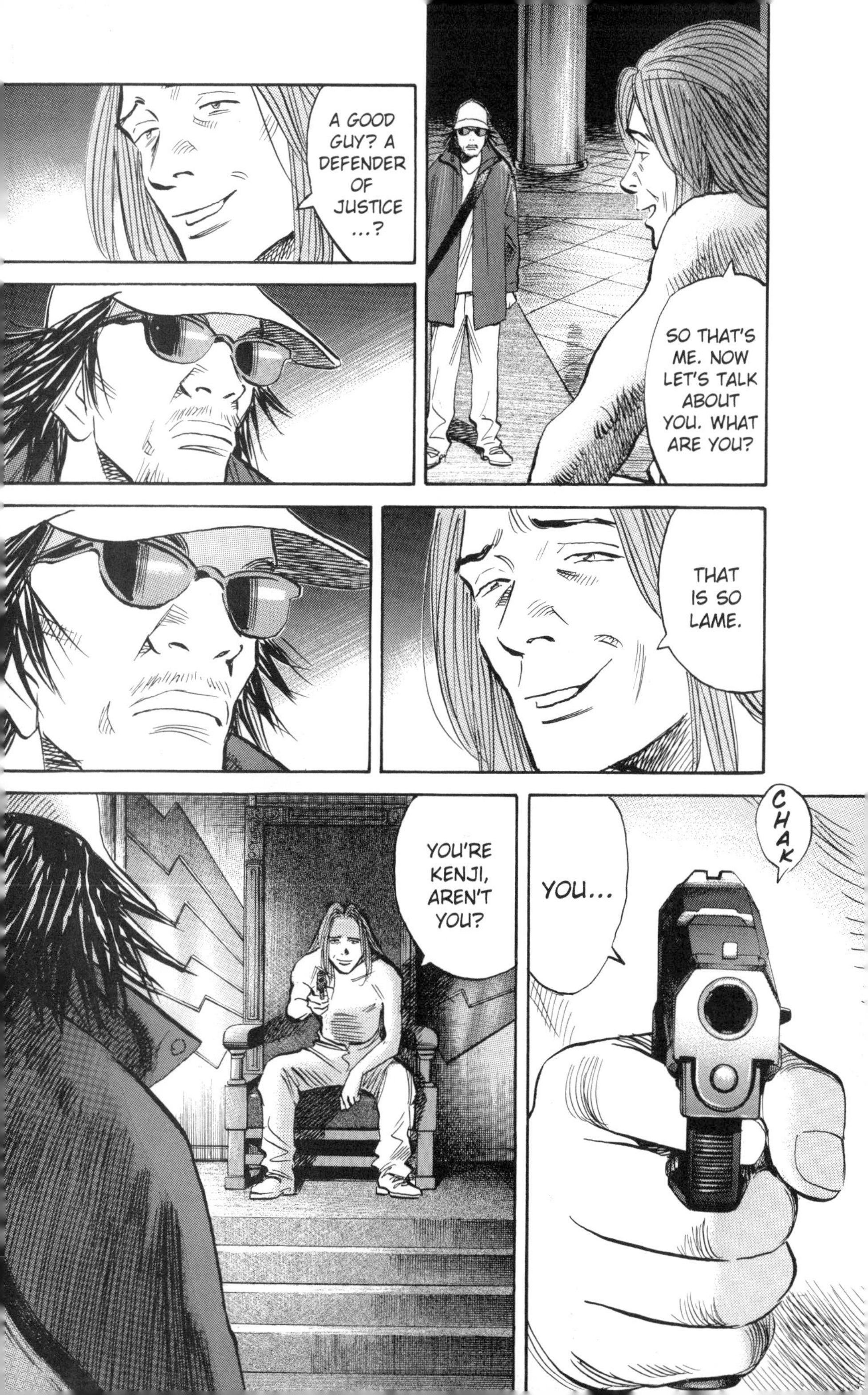
SO THAT'S ME. NOW LET'S TALK ABOUT YOU. WHAT ARE YOU?
A GOOD GUY? A DEFENDER OF JUSTICE ...?
THAT IS SO LAME.
CHAK
YOU...
YOU'RE KENJI, AREN'T YOU?

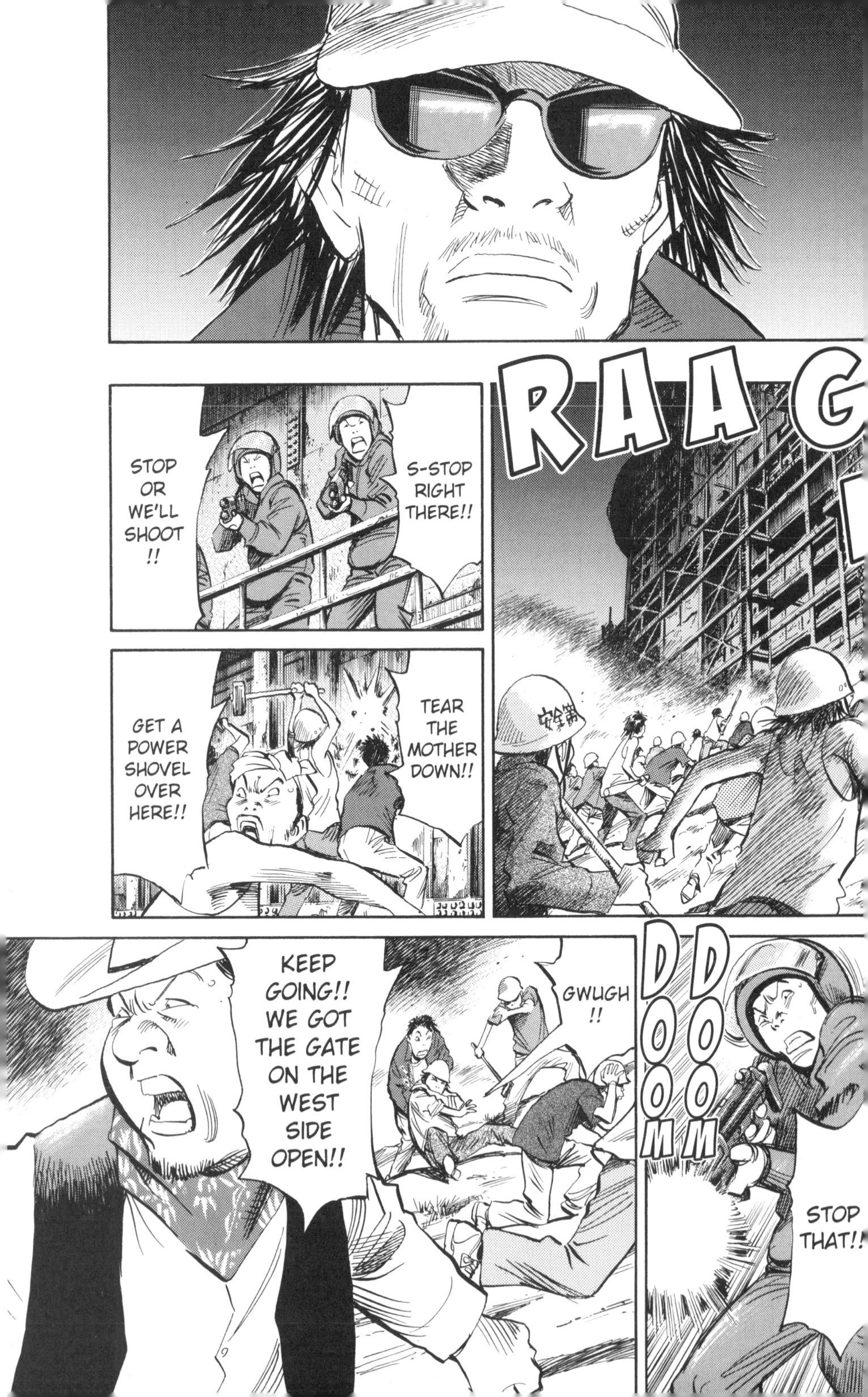
RAAG
S-STOP RIGHT THERE!!
STOP OR WE'LL SHOOT !!
TEAR THE MOTHER DOWN!!
GET A POWER SHOVEL OVER HERE!!
DOOOM
DOOOM
STOP THAT!!
GWUGH !!
KEEP GOING!! WE GOT THE GATE ON THE WEST SIDE OPEN!!

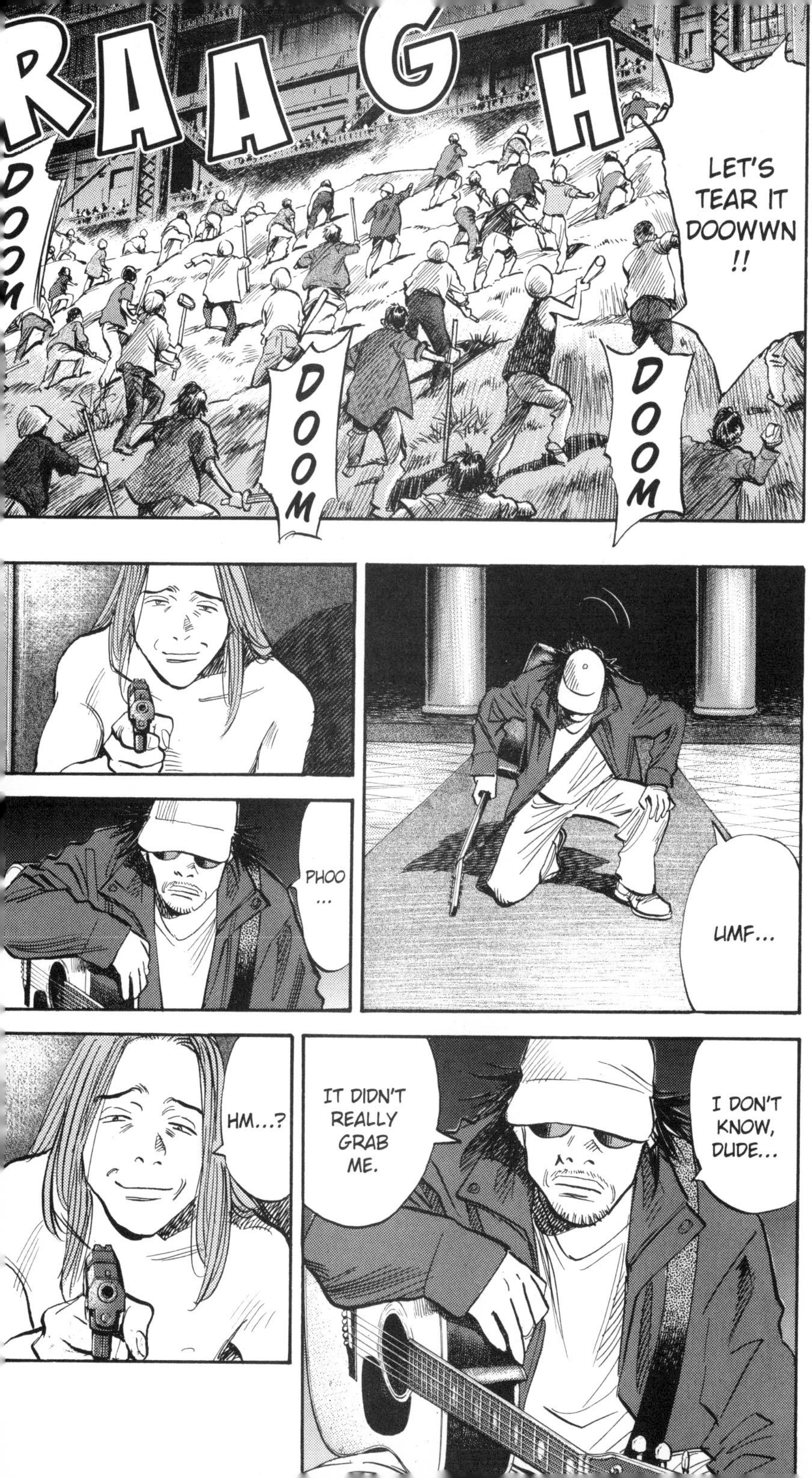
LET'S TEAR IT DOOWWN!!
RAAGH
DOOOM
DOOOM
DOOOM
UMF...
PHOO...
I DON'T KNOW, DUDE...
IT DIDN'T REALLY GRAB ME.
HM...?

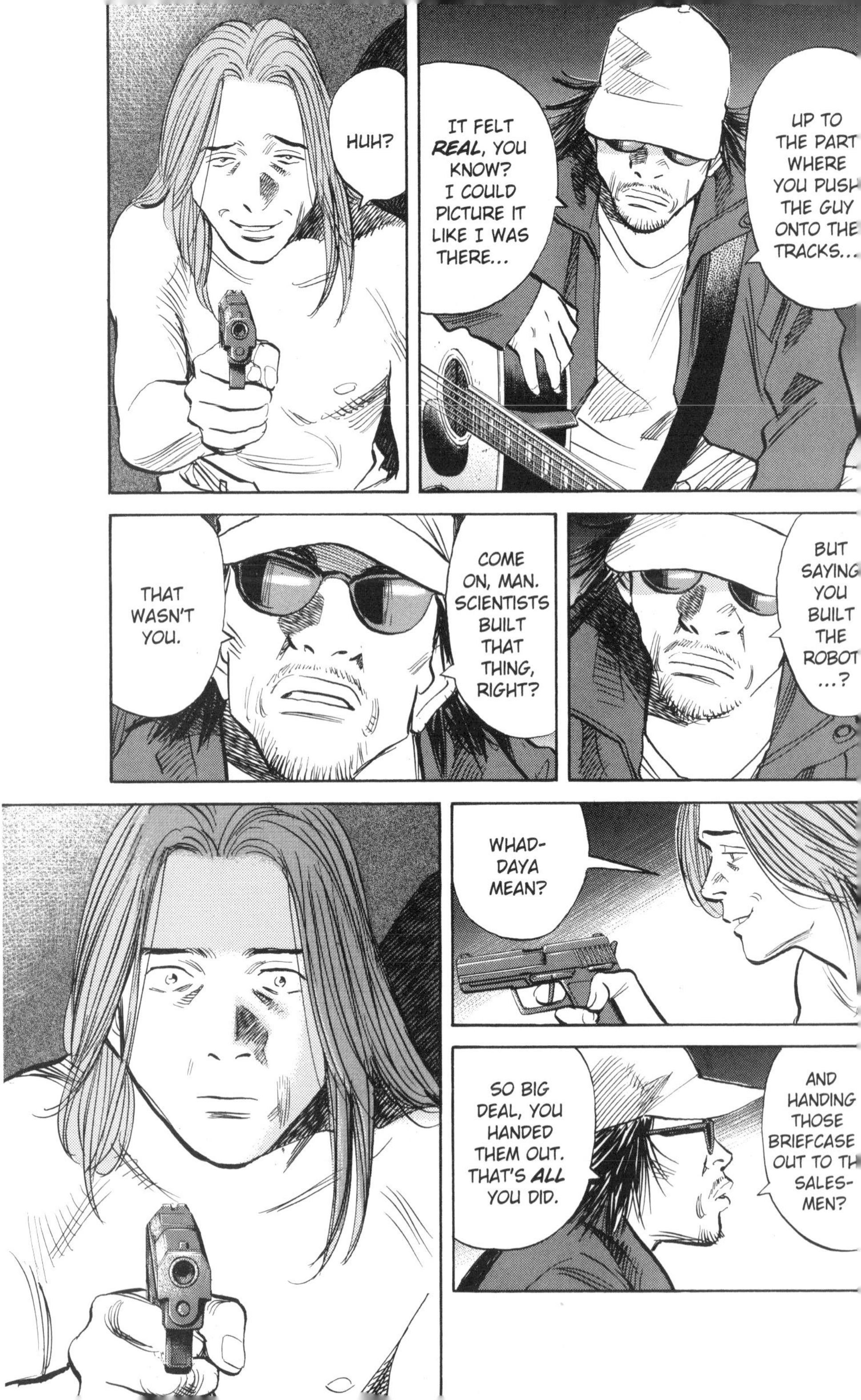
UP TO THE PART WHERE YOU PUSH THE GUY ONTO THE TRACKS...
IT FELT ***REAL***, YOU KNOW? I COULD PICTURE IT LIKE I WAS THERE...
HUH?
BUT SAYING YOU BUILT THE ROBOT ...?
COME ON, MAN. SCIENTISTS BUILT THAT THING, RIGHT?
THAT WASN'T YOU.
WHADDAYA MEAN?
AND HANDING THOSE BRIEFCASE OUT TO TH SALES-MEN?
SO BIG DEAL, YOU HANDED THEM OUT. THAT'S ***ALL*** YOU DID.

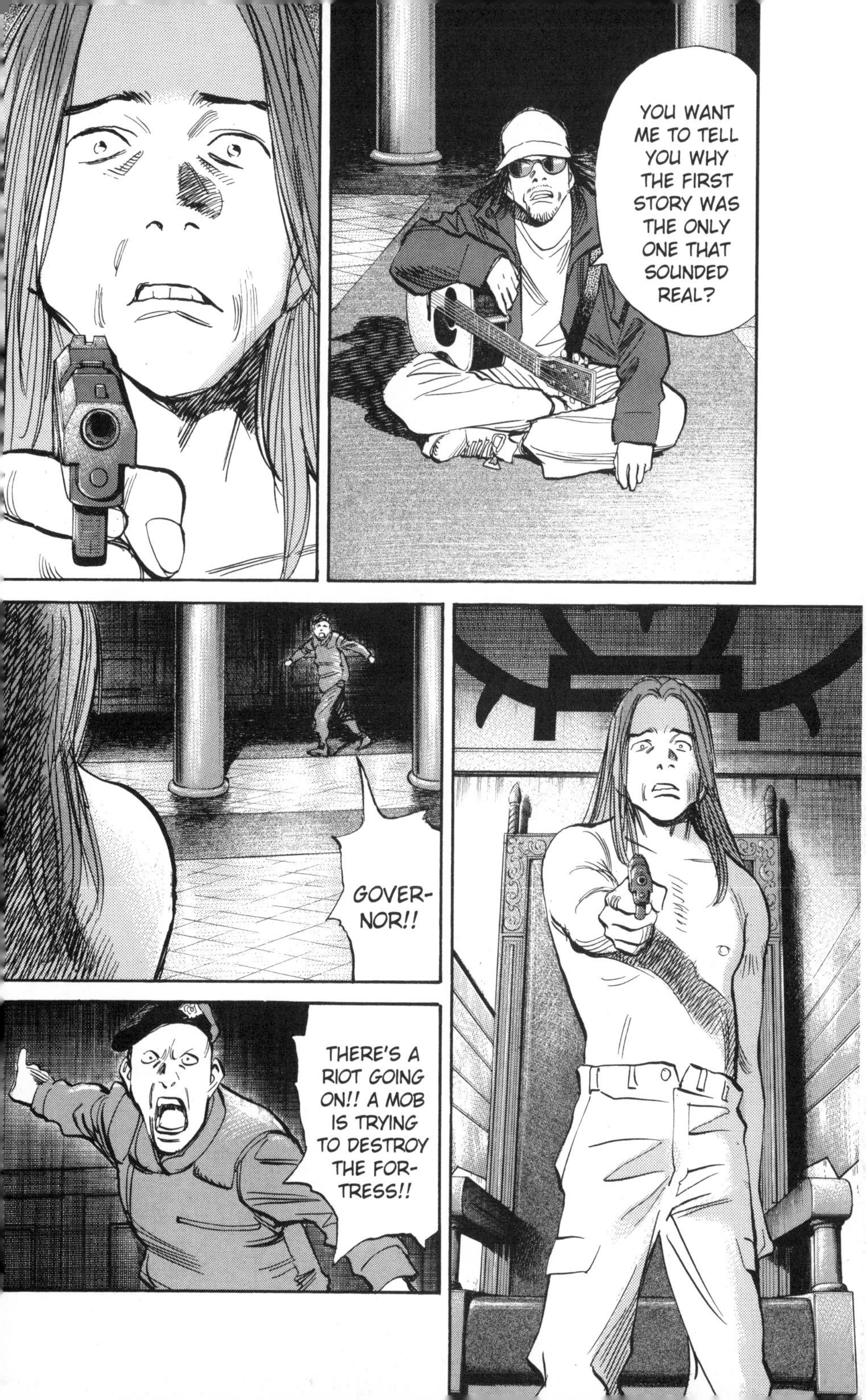
YOU WANT ME TO TELL YOU WHY THE FIRST STORY WAS THE ONLY ONE THAT SOUNDED REAL?
GOVER-NOR!!
THERE'S A RIOT GOING ON!! A MOB IS TRYING TO DESTROY THE FOR-TRESS!!

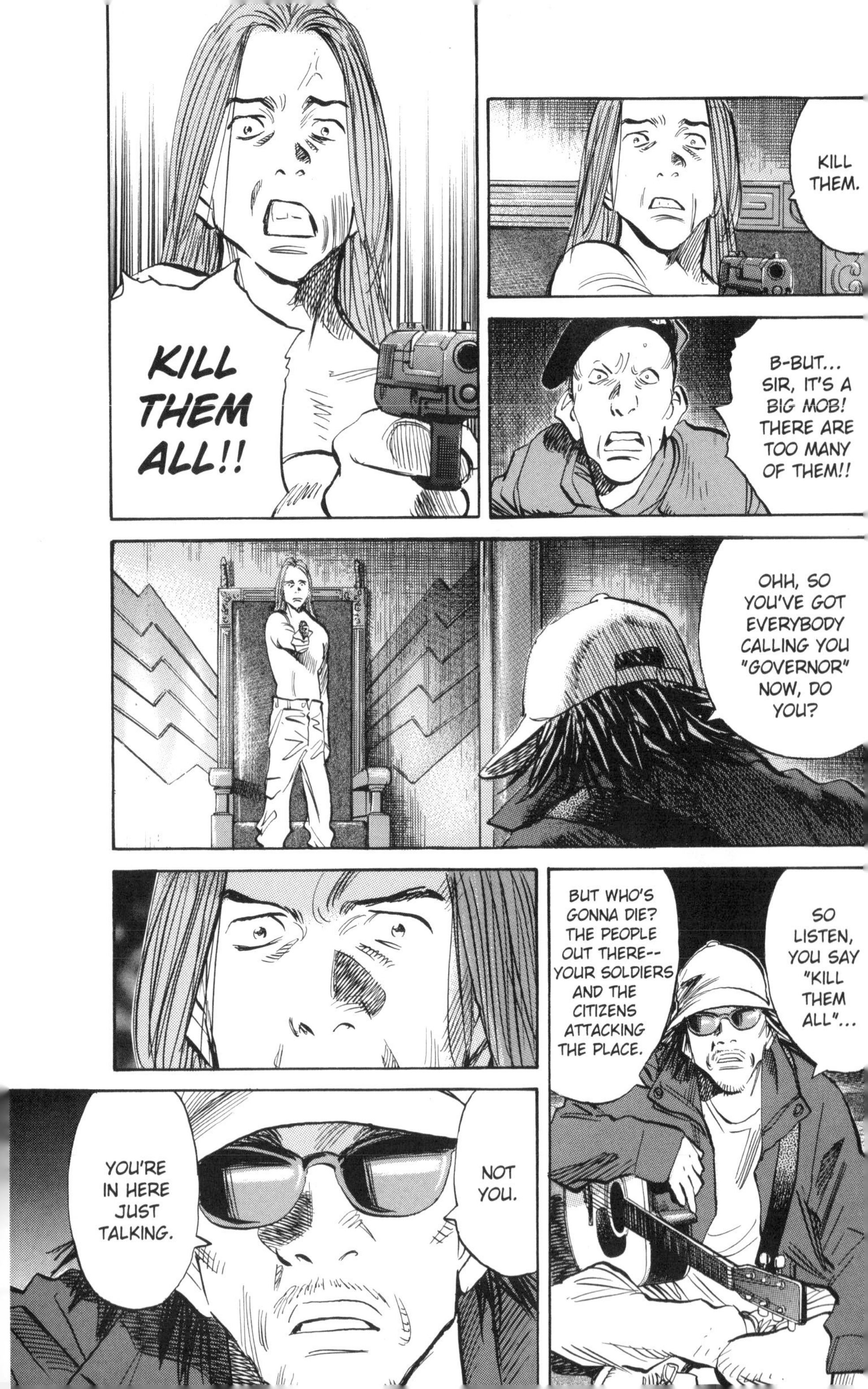
KILL THEM.
B-BUT... SIR, IT'S A BIG MOB! THERE ARE TOO MANY OF THEM!!
KILL THEM ALL!!
OHH, SO YOU'VE GOT EVERYBODY CALLING YOU "GOVERNOR" NOW, DO YOU?
SO LISTEN, YOU SAY "KILL THEM ALL"...
BUT WHO'S GONNA DIE? THE PEOPLE OUT THERE-- YOUR SOLDIERS AND THE CITIZENS ATTACKING THE PLACE.
NOT YOU.
YOU'RE IN HERE JUST TALKING.

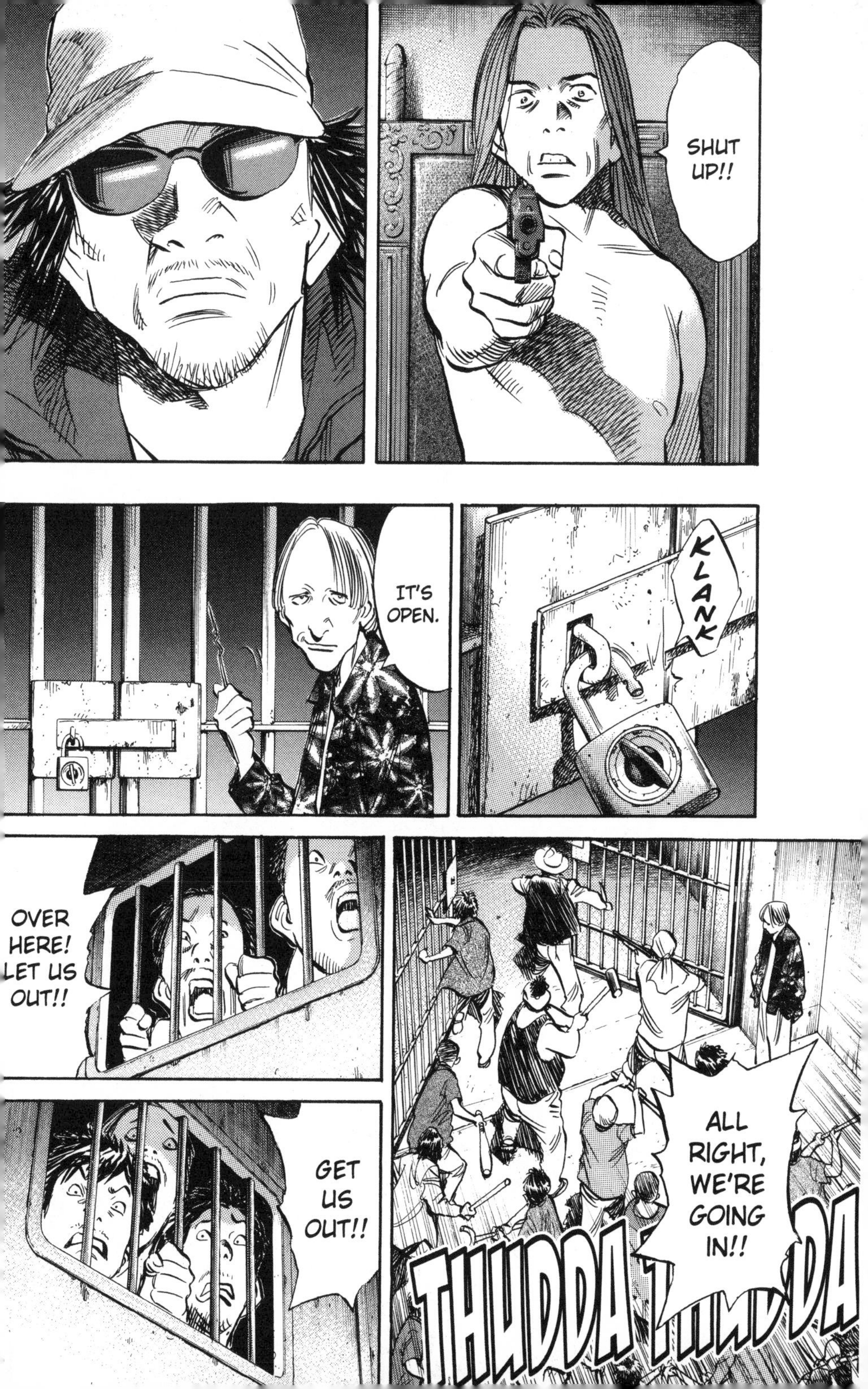
SHUT UP!!
KLANK
IT'S OPEN.
ALL RIGHT, WE'RE GOING IN!!
THUDDA
OVER HERE! LET US OUT!!
GET US OUT!!

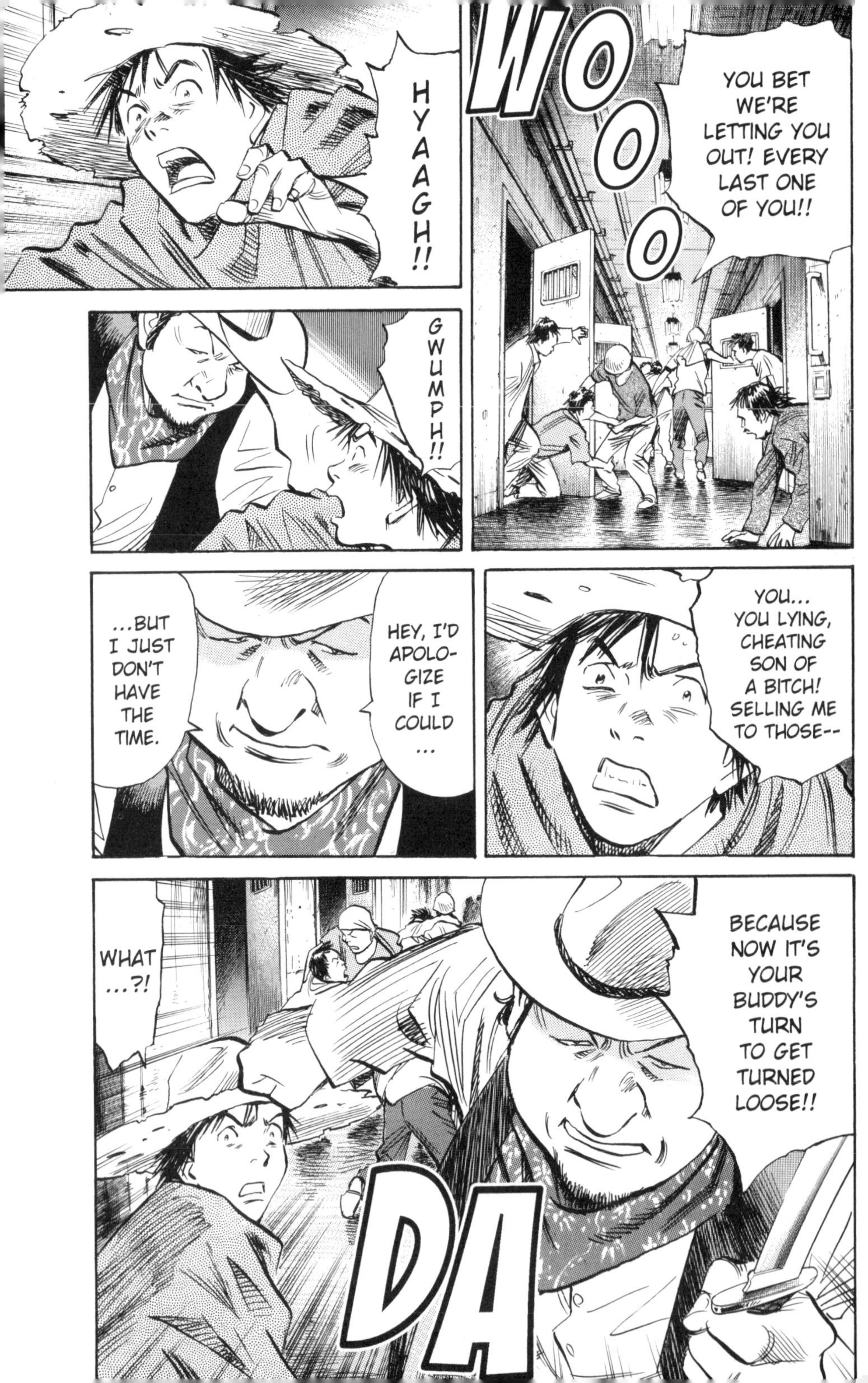
WOOO
YOU BET WE'RE LETTING YOU OUT! EVERY LAST ONE OF YOU!!
HYAAAGH!!
GWUMPH!!
YOU... YOU LYING, CHEATING SON OF A BITCH! SELLING ME TO THOSE--
HEY, I'D APOLOGIZE IF I COULD...
...BUT I JUST DON'T HAVE THE TIME.
BECAUSE NOW IT'S YOUR BUDDY'S TURN TO GET TURNED LOOSE!!
WHAT...?!
DA

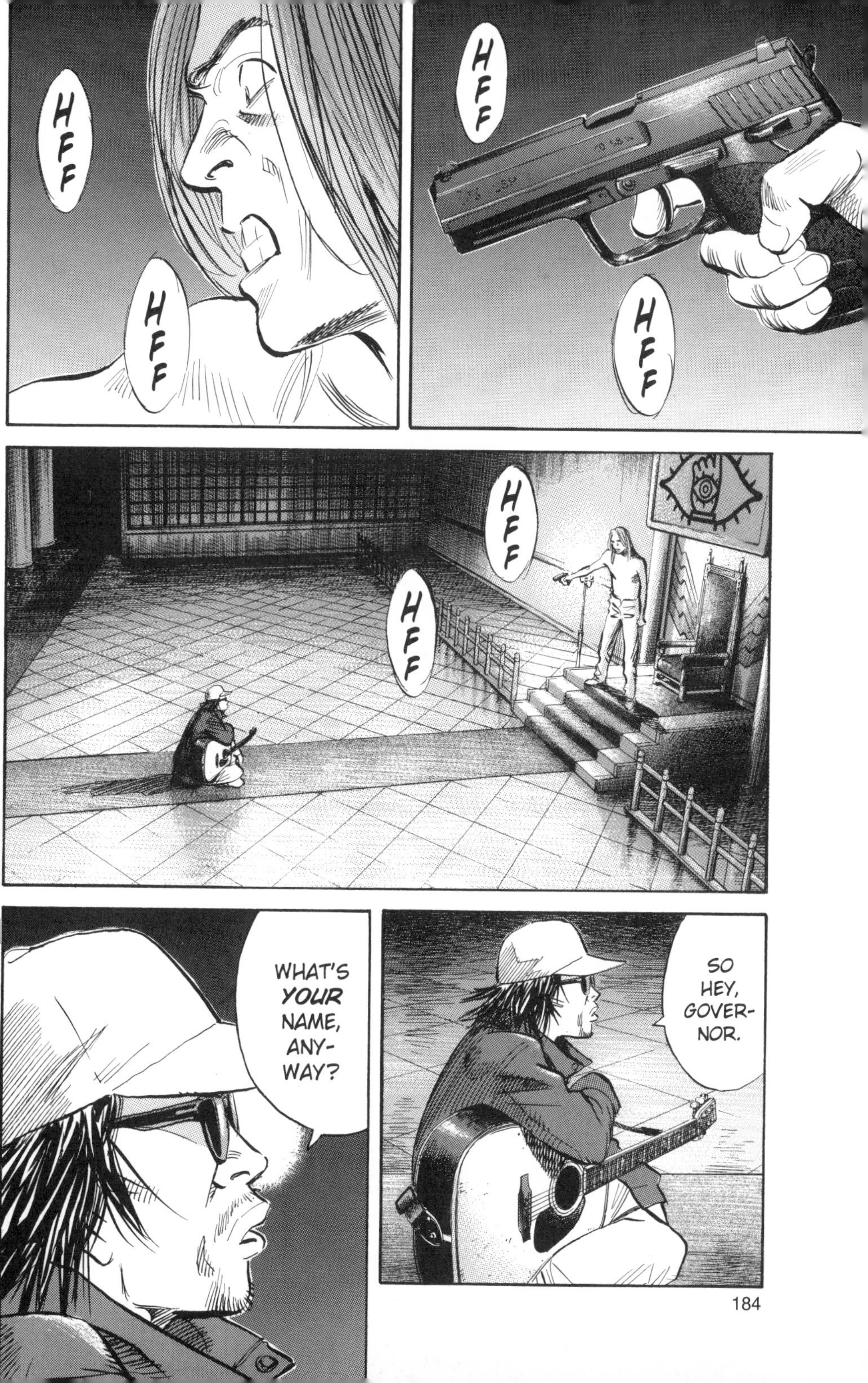
HFF
HFF
HFF
HFF
HFF
HFF
SO HEY, GOVERNOR.
WHAT'S *YOUR* NAME, ANYWAY?

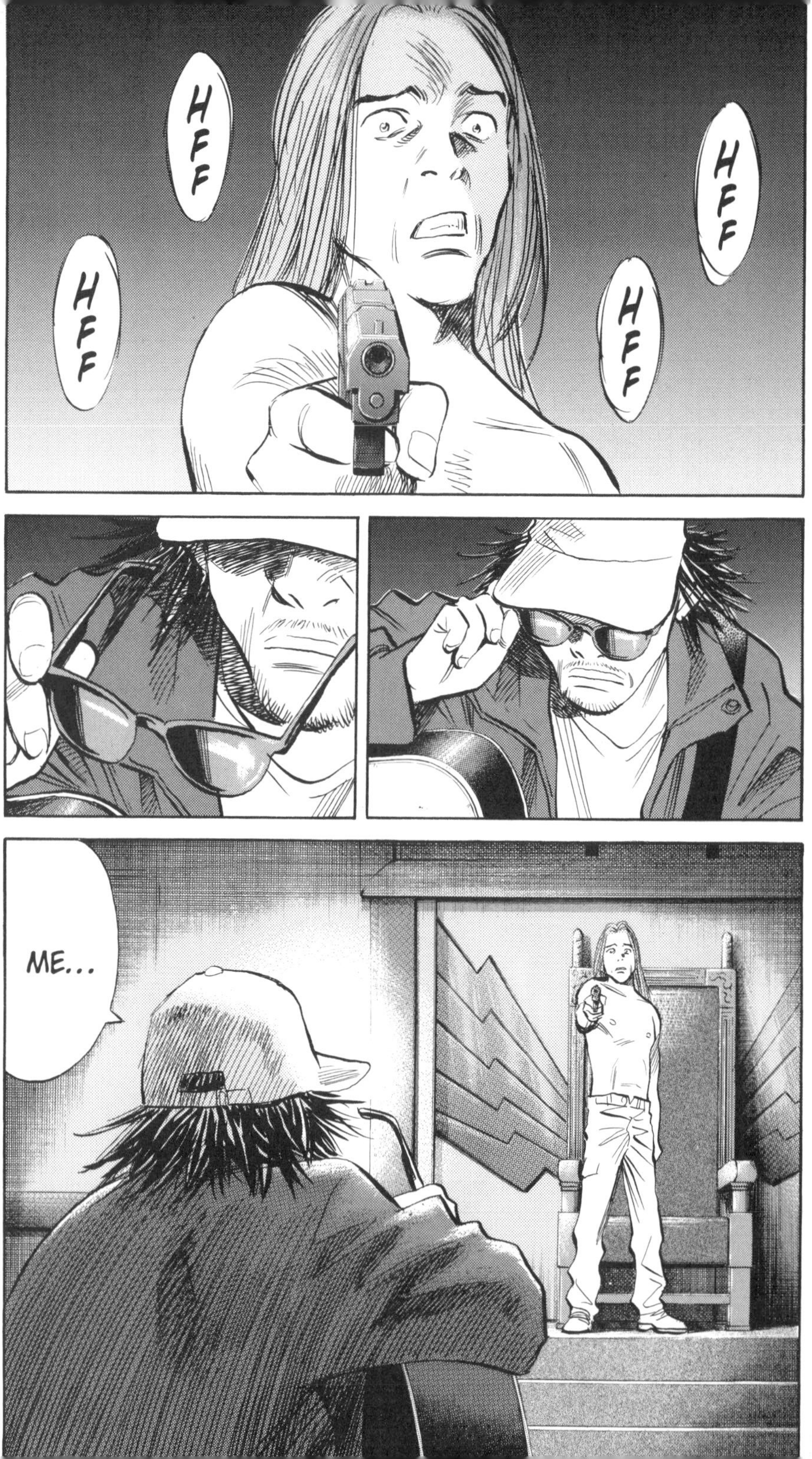
HFF
HFF
HFF
HFF
ME...

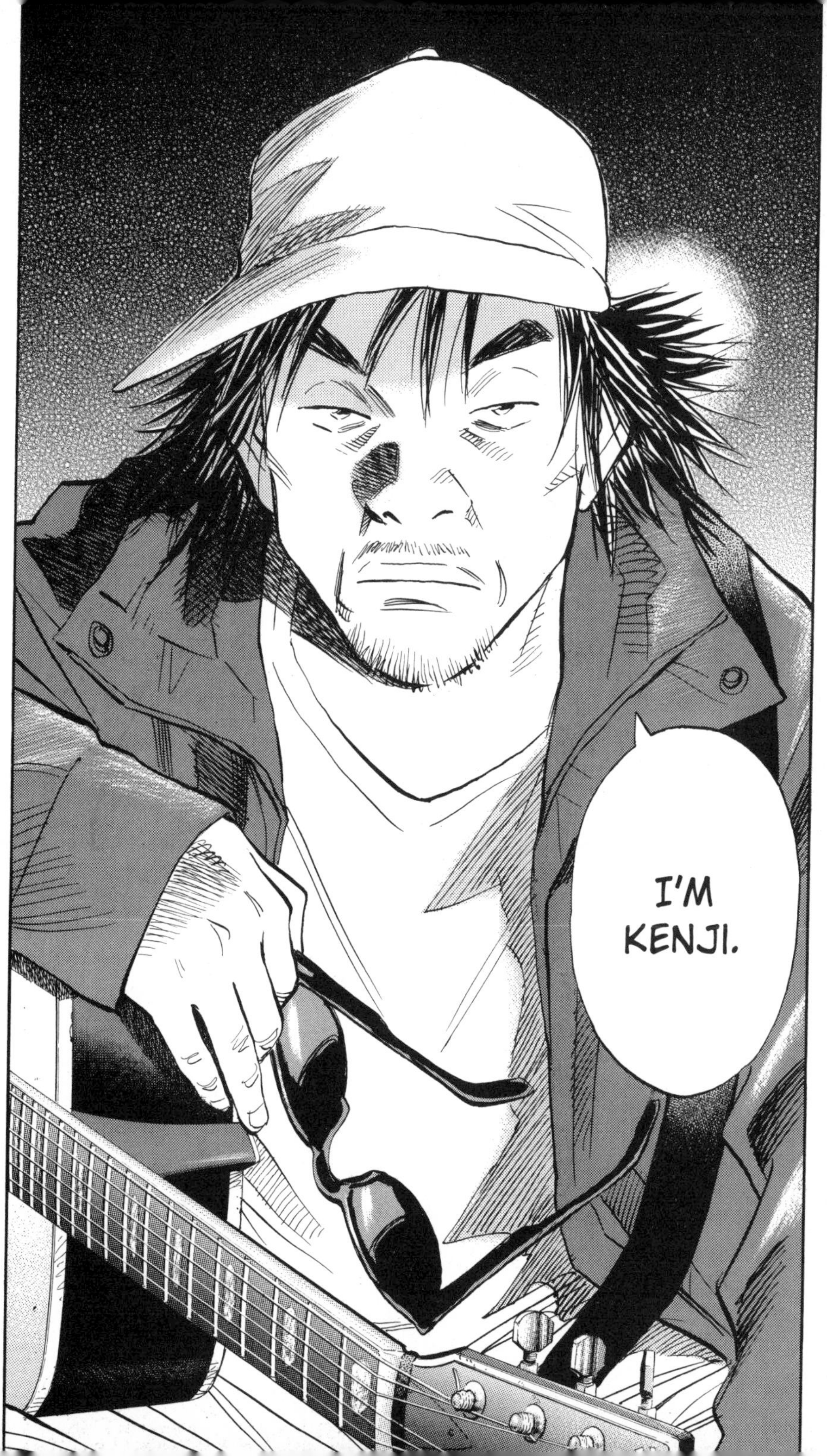
I'M KENJI.

Chapter 11 The Man Who Came Back

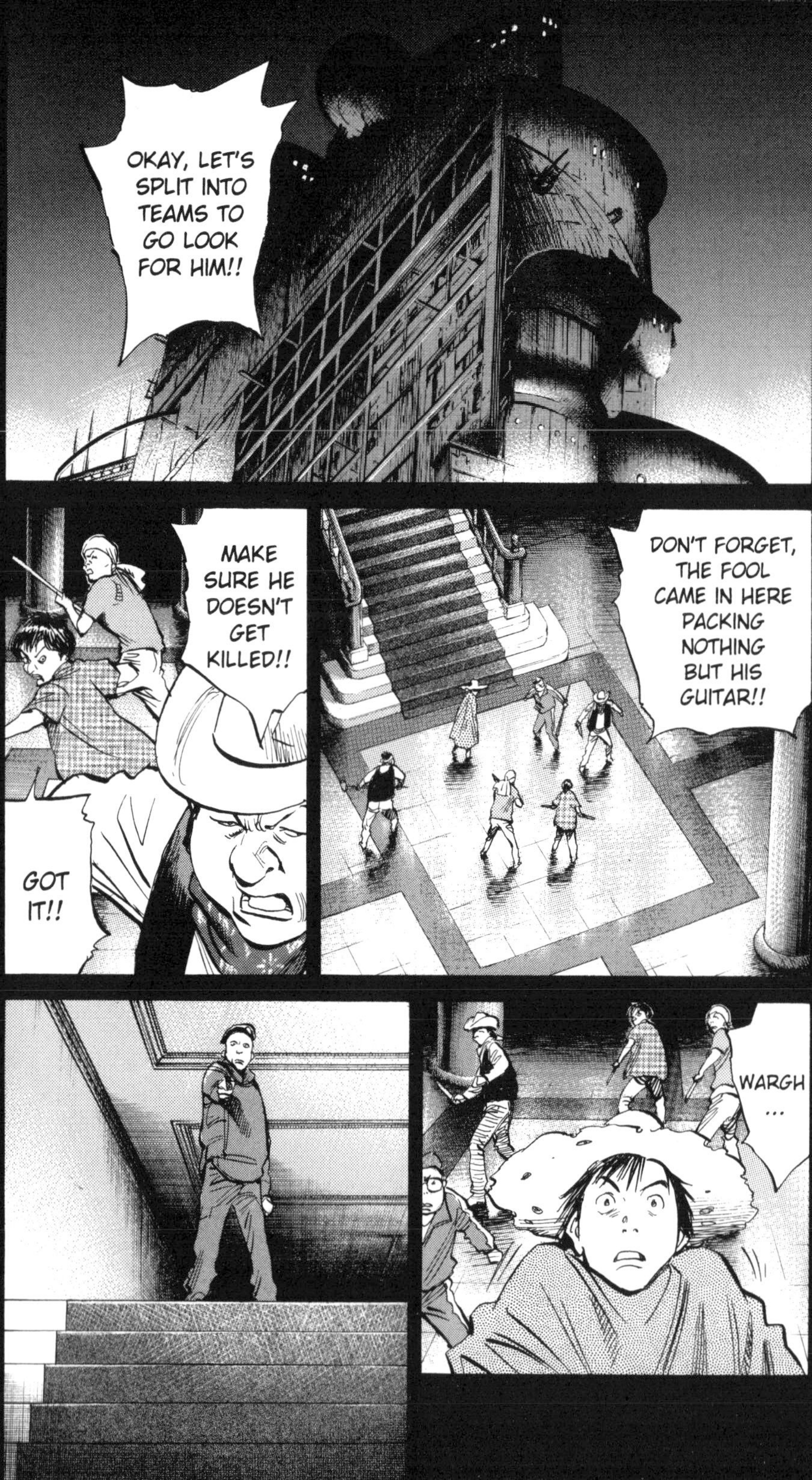
OKAY, LET'S SPLIT INTO TEAMS TO GO LOOK FOR HIM!!
DON'T FORGET, THE FOOL CAME IN HERE PACKING NOTHING BUT HIS GUITAR!!
MAKE SURE HE DOESN'T GET KILLED!!
GOT IT!!
WARGH ...

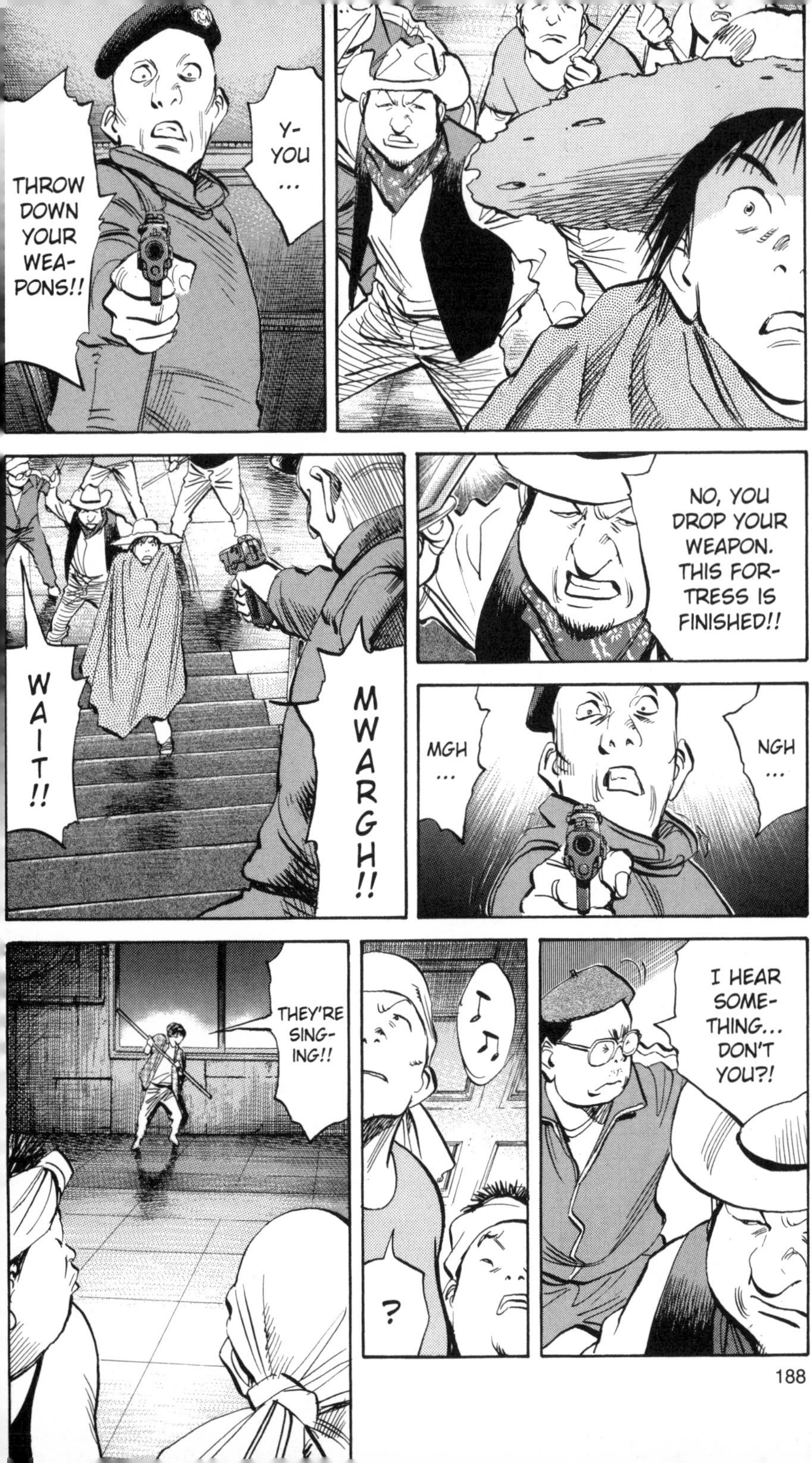
Y-YOU...
THROW DOWN YOUR WEAPONS!!
NO, YOU DROP YOUR WEAPON. THIS FORTRESS IS FINISHED!!
NGH...
MGH...
MWARGH!!
WAIT!!
I HEAR SOMETHING... DON'T YOU?!
♪♪
?
THEY'RE SINGING!!

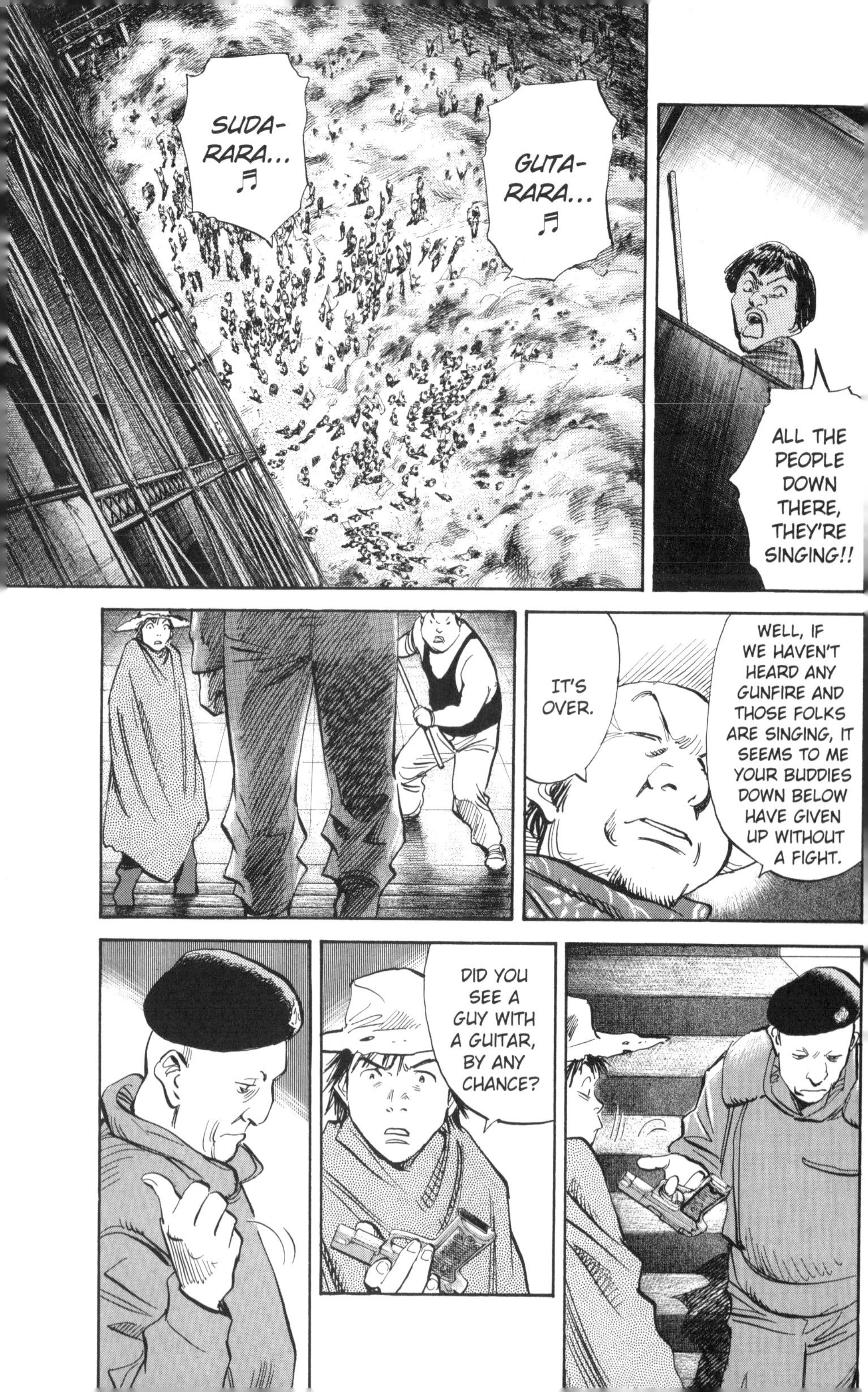
ALL THE PEOPLE DOWN THERE, THEY'RE SINGING!!
GUTA-RARA... ♬
SUDA-RARA... ♬
WELL, IF WE HAVEN'T HEARD ANY GUNFIRE AND THOSE FOLKS ARE SINGING, IT SEEMS TO ME YOUR BUDDIES DOWN BELOW HAVE GIVEN UP WITHOUT A FIGHT.
IT'S OVER.
DID YOU SEE A GUY WITH A GUITAR, BY ANY CHANCE?

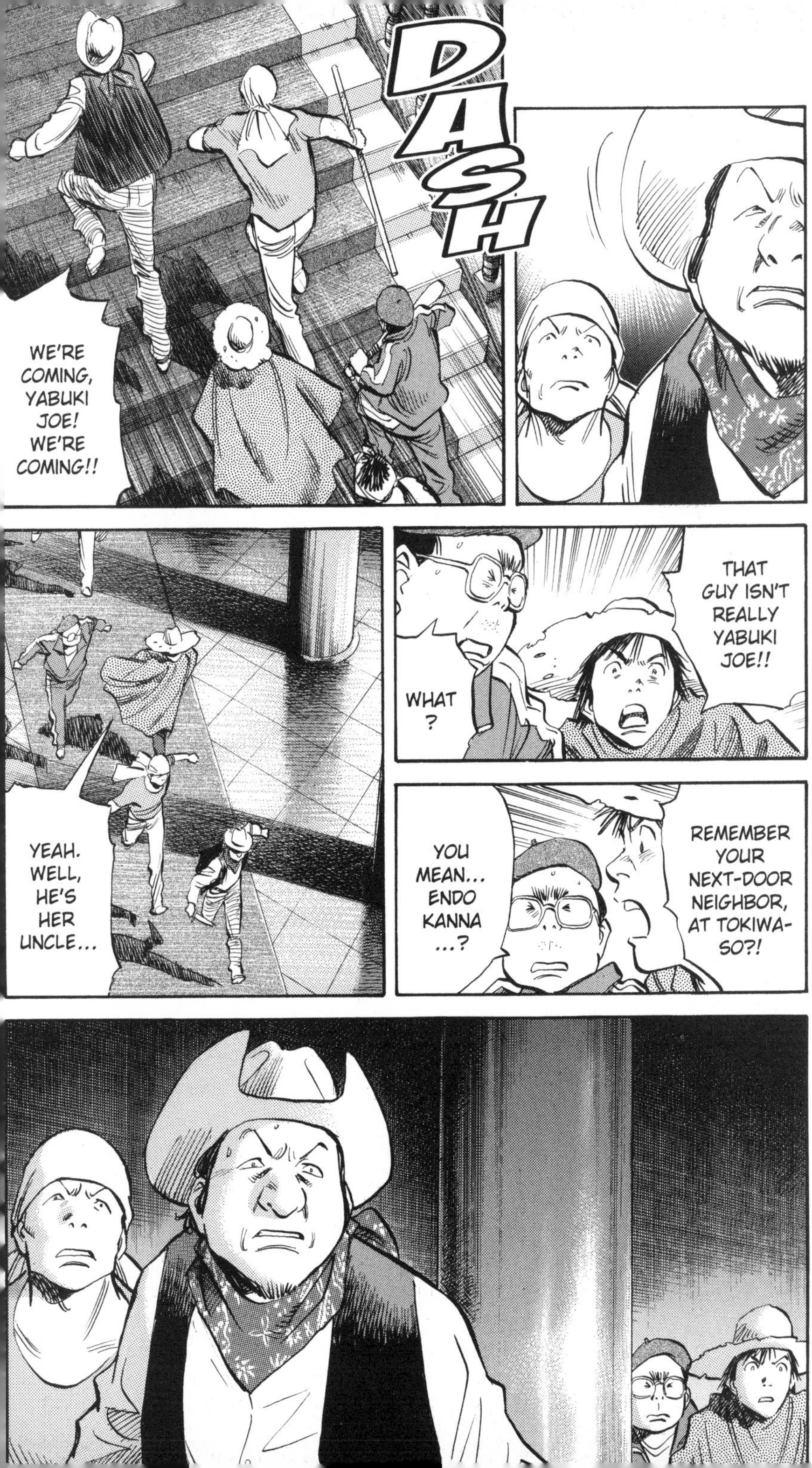
DASH
WE'RE COMING, YABUKI JOE! WE'RE COMING!!
THAT GUY ISN'T REALLY YABUKI JOE!!
WHAT?
REMEMBER YOUR NEXT-DOOR NEIGHBOR, AT TOKIWA-SO?!
YOU MEAN... ENDO KANNA...?
YEAH. WELL, HE'S HER UNCLE...

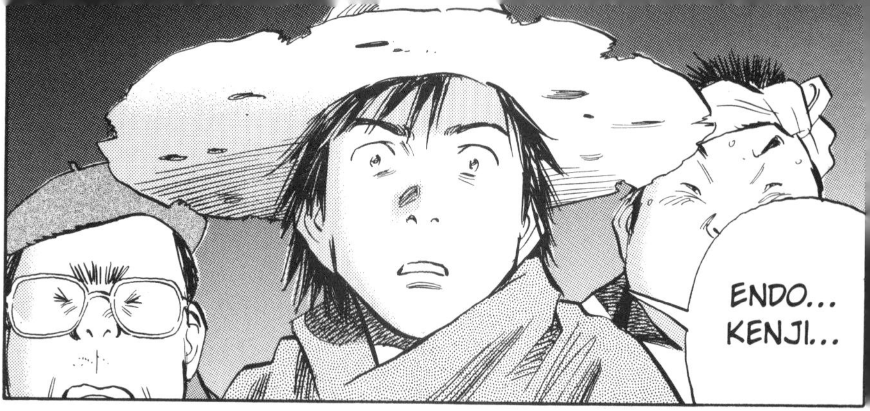
ENDO... KENJI...

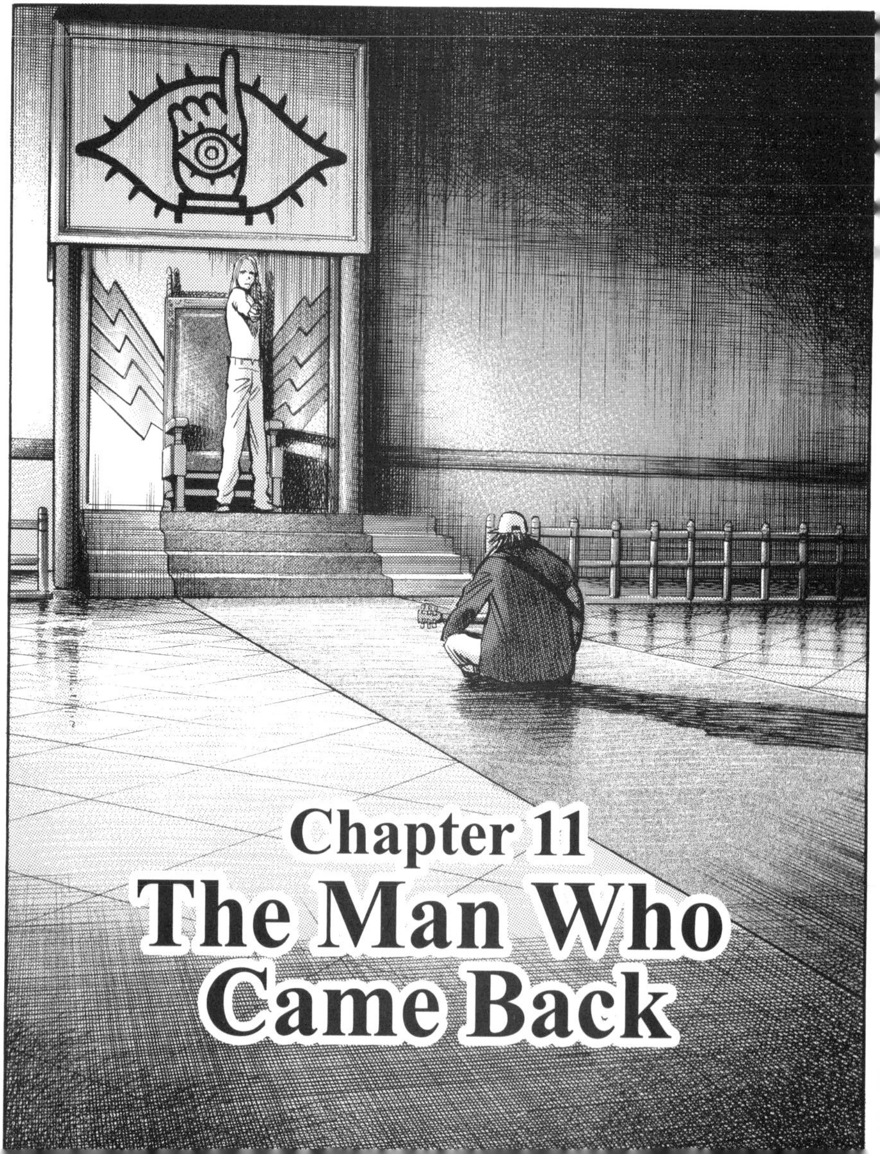
Chapter 11
The Man Who Came Back

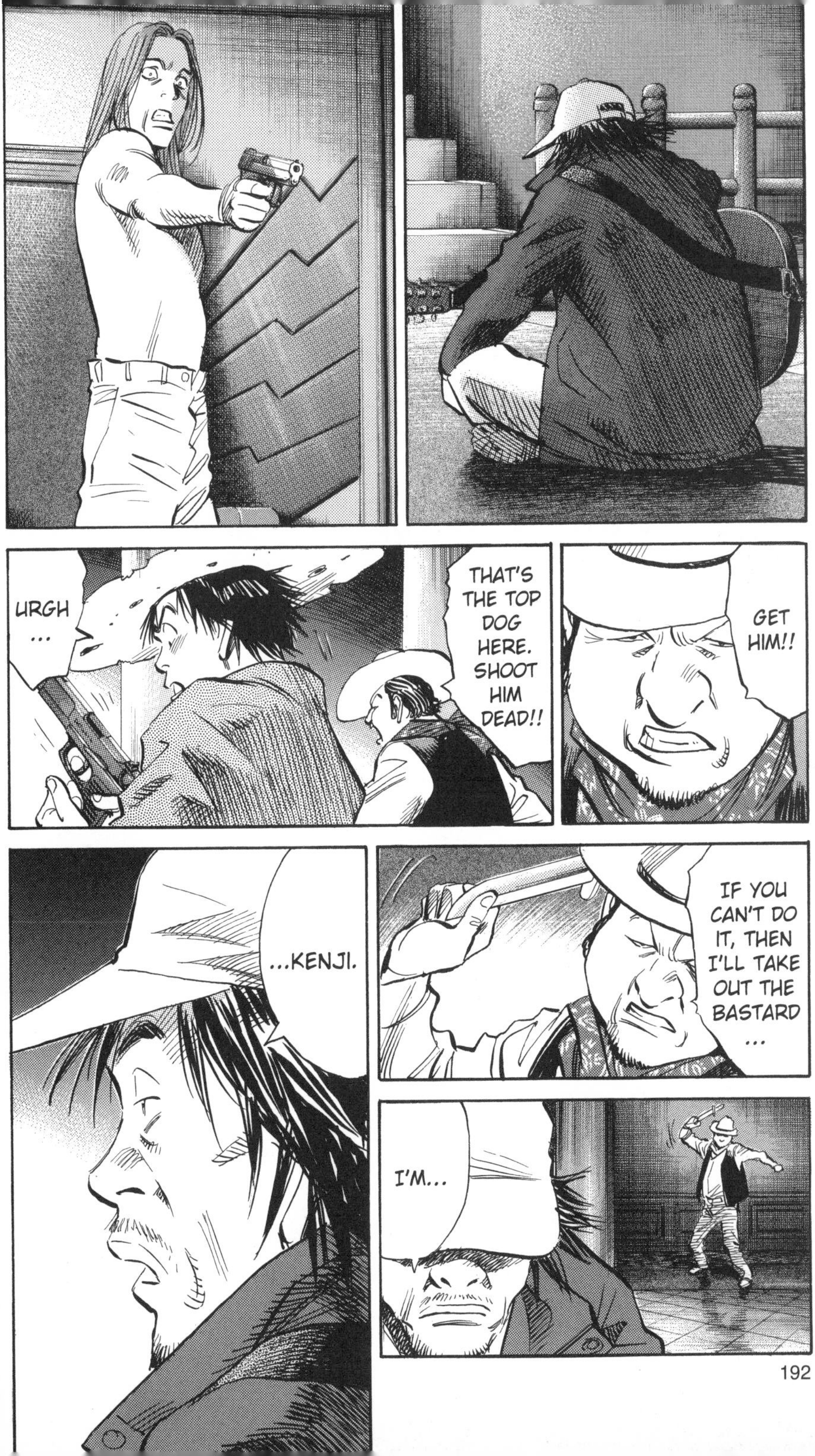

GET HIM!!
THAT'S THE TOP DOG HERE. SHOOT HIM DEAD!!
URGH ...
IF YOU CAN'T DO IT, THEN I'LL TAKE OUT THE BASTARD ...
I'M...
...KENJI.

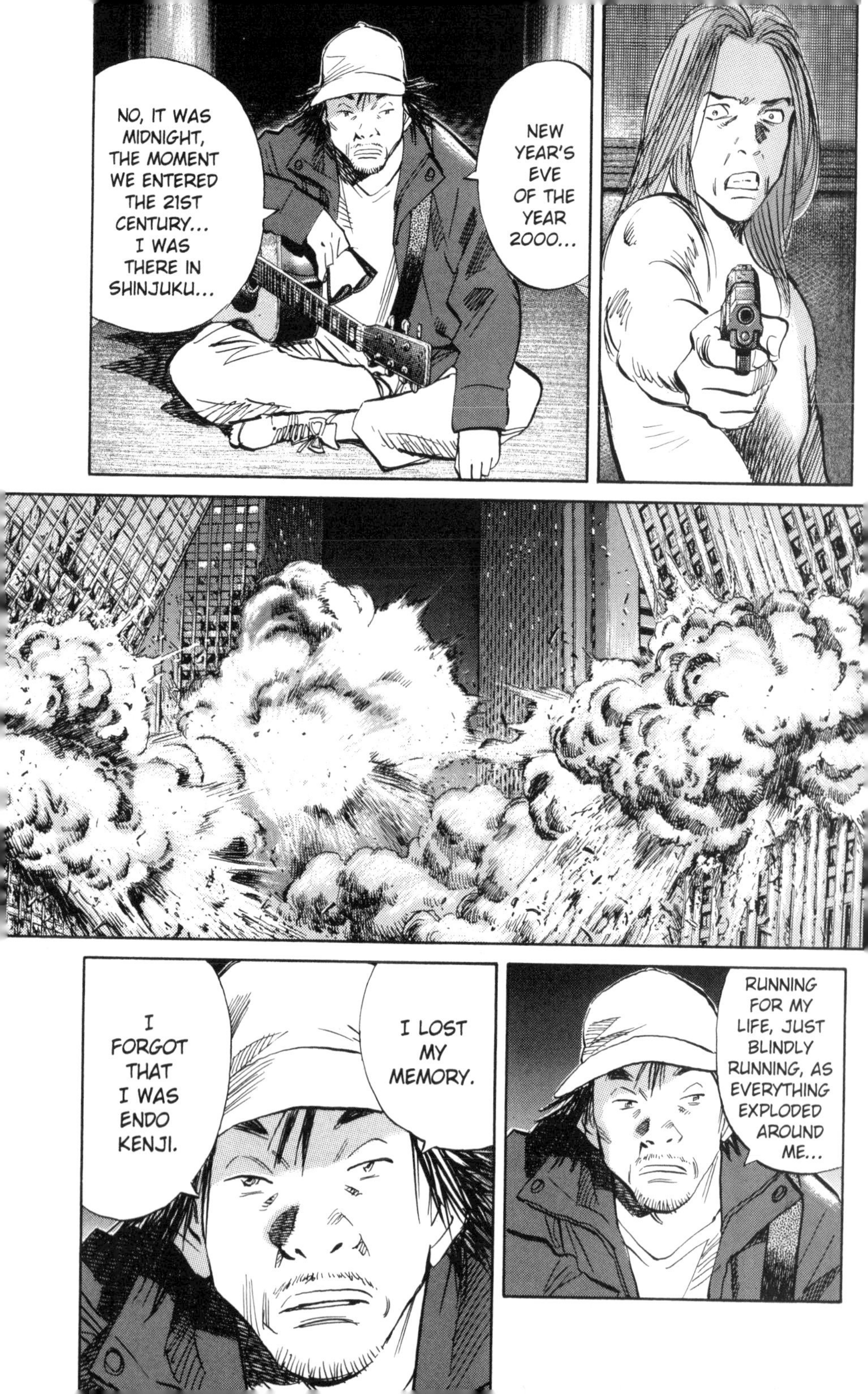
NEW YEAR'S EVE OF THE YEAR 2000...
NO, IT WAS MIDNIGHT, THE MOMENT WE ENTERED THE 21ST CENTURY... I WAS THERE IN SHINJUKU...
RUNNING FOR MY LIFE, JUST BLINDLY RUNNING, AS EVERYTHING EXPLODED AROUND ME...
I LOST MY MEMORY.
I FORGOT THAT I WAS ENDO KENJI.

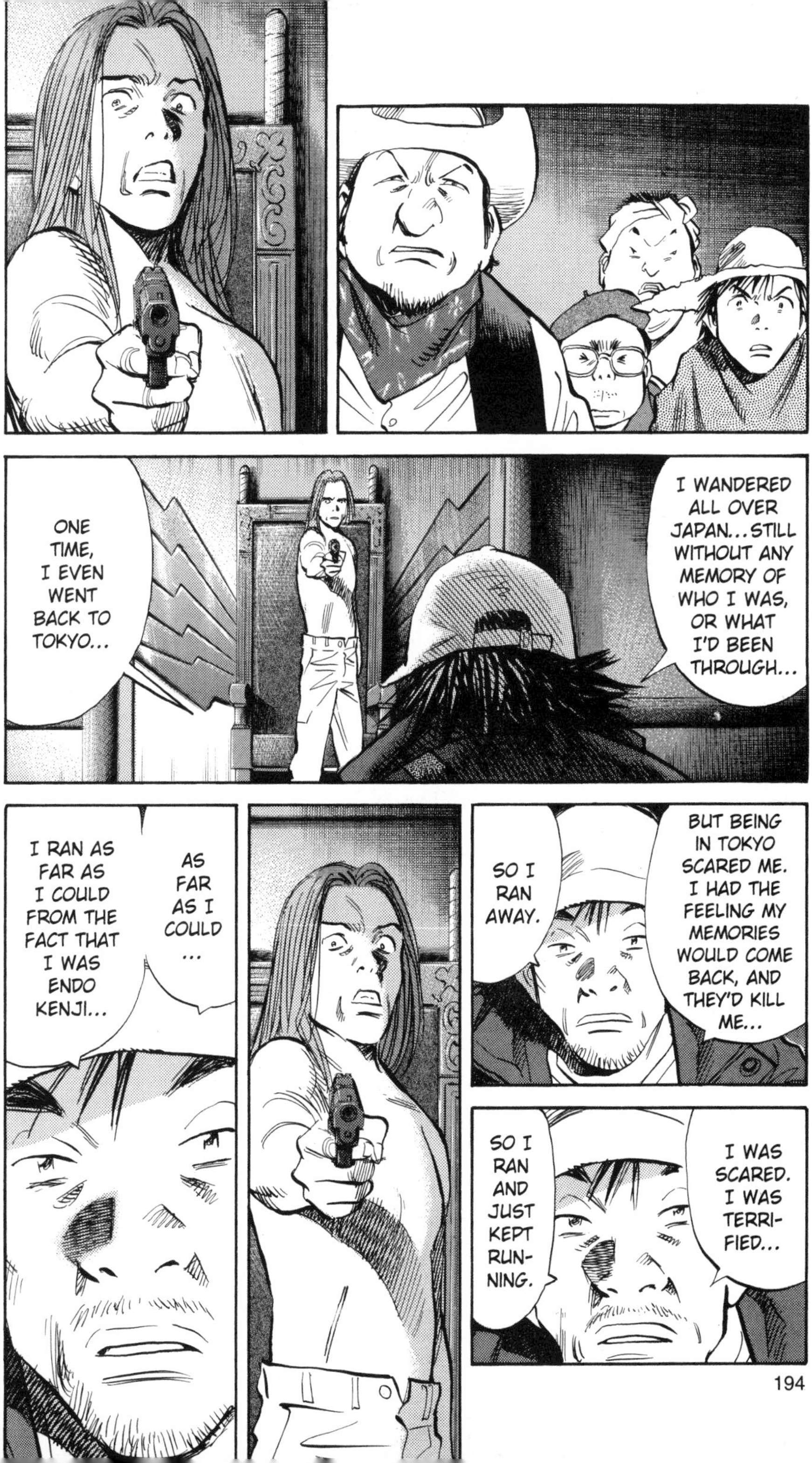
I WANDERED ALL OVER JAPAN...STILL WITHOUT ANY MEMORY OF WHO I WAS, OR WHAT I'D BEEN THROUGH...
ONE TIME, I EVEN WENT BACK TO TOKYO...
BUT BEING IN TOKYO SCARED ME. I HAD THE FEELING MY MEMORIES WOULD COME BACK, AND THEY'D KILL ME...
SO I RAN AWAY.
I WAS SCARED. I WAS TERRI-FIED...
SO I RAN AND JUST KEPT RUN-NING.
AS FAR AS I COULD...
I RAN AS FAR AS I COULD FROM THE FACT THAT I WAS ENDO KENJI...

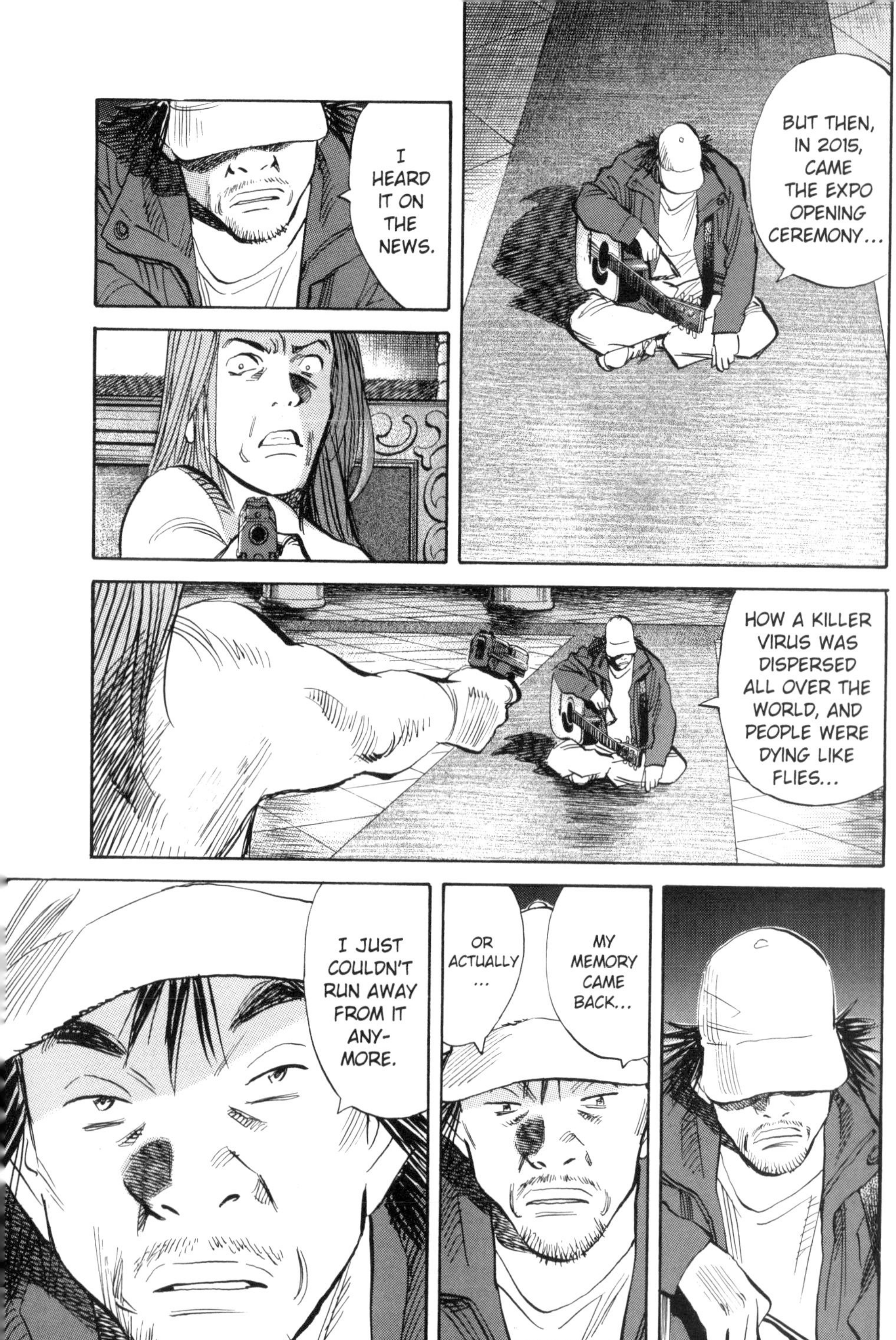
BUT THEN, IN 2015, CAME THE EXPO OPENING CEREMONY...
I HEARD IT ON THE NEWS.
HOW A KILLER VIRUS WAS DISPERSED ALL OVER THE WORLD, AND PEOPLE WERE DYING LIKE FLIES...
MY MEMORY CAME BACK...
OR ACTUALLY...
I JUST COULDN'T RUN AWAY FROM IT ANY-MORE.

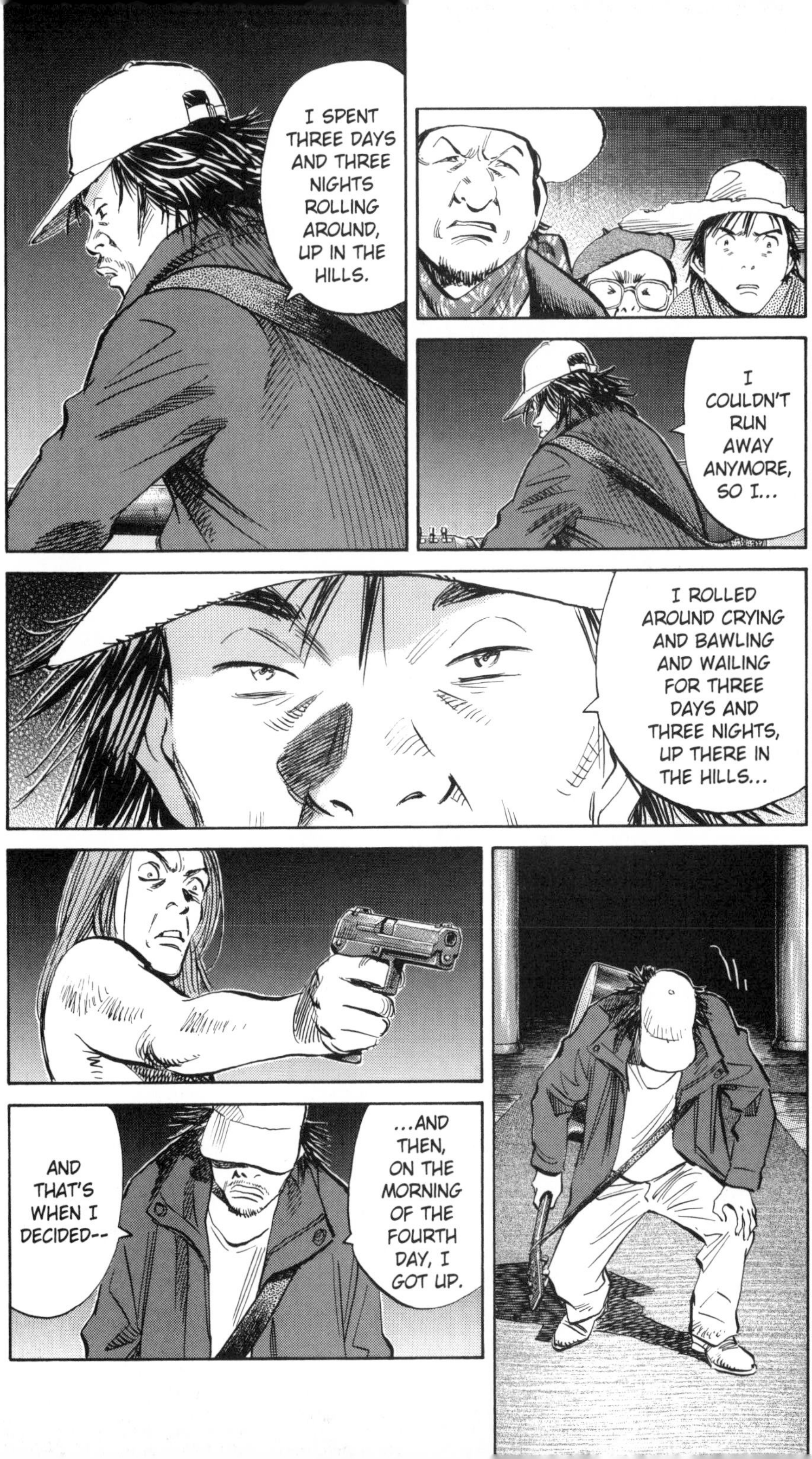
I COULDN'T RUN AWAY ANYMORE, SO I...
I SPENT THREE DAYS AND THREE NIGHTS ROLLING AROUND, UP IN THE HILLS.
I ROLLED AROUND CRYING AND BAWLING AND WAILING FOR THREE DAYS AND THREE NIGHTS, UP THERE IN THE HILLS...
...AND THEN, ON THE MORNING OF THE FOURTH DAY, I GOT UP.
AND THAT'S WHEN I DECIDED--

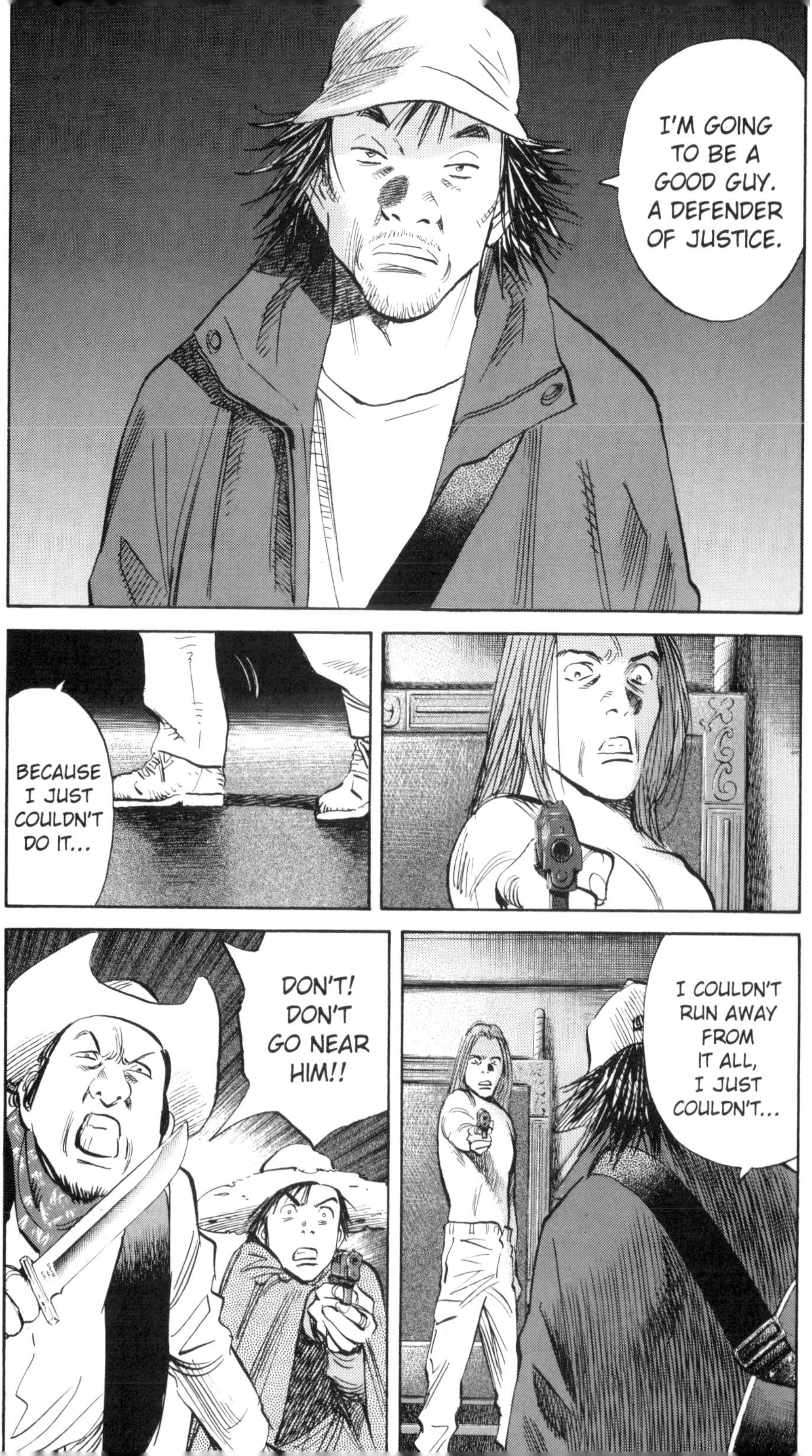
I'M GOING TO BE A GOOD GUY. A DEFENDER OF JUSTICE.
BECAUSE I JUST COULDN'T DO IT...
I COULDN'T RUN AWAY FROM IT ALL, I JUST COULDN'T...
DON'T! DON'T GO NEAR HIM!!

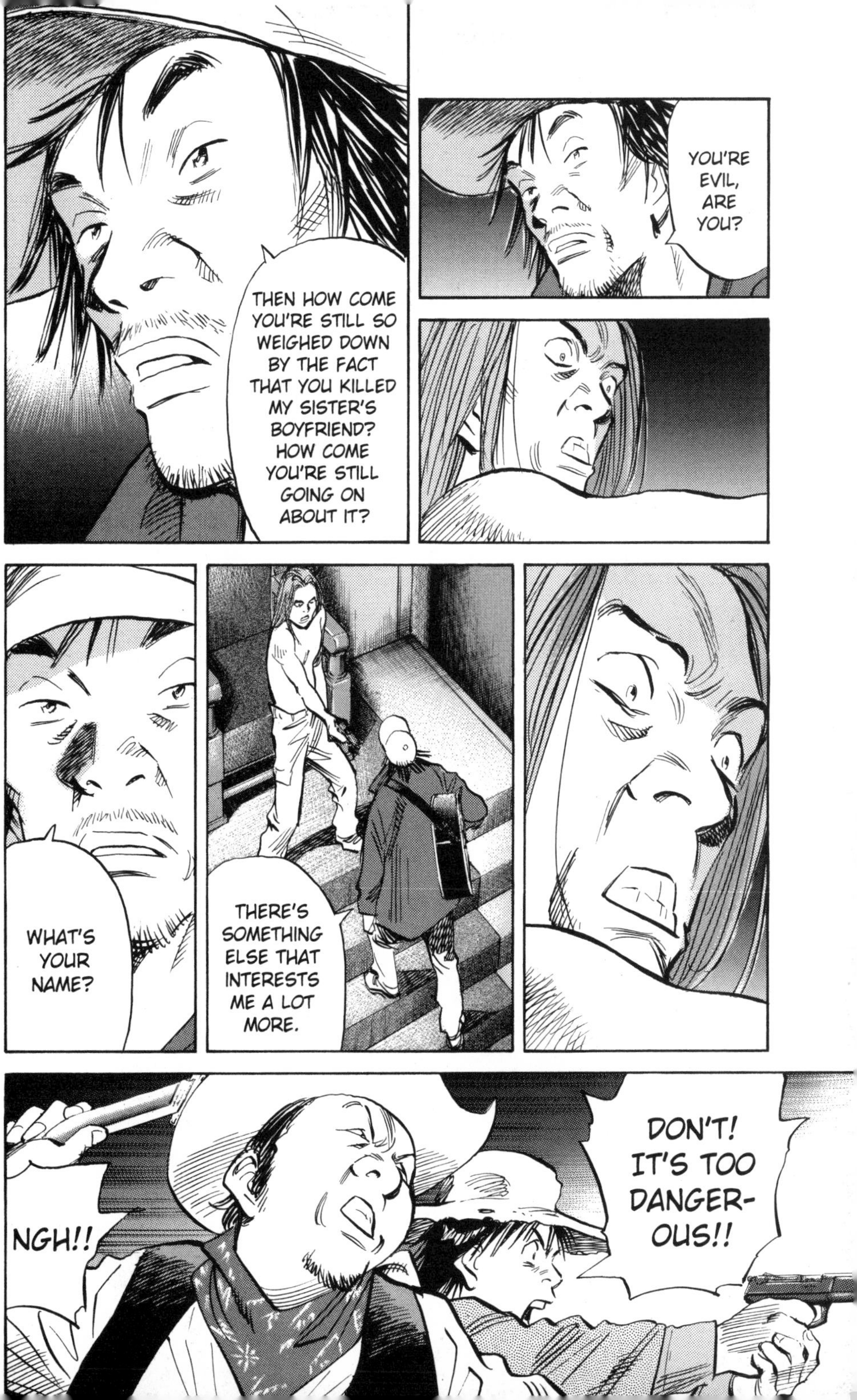
YOU'RE EVIL, ARE YOU?
THEN HOW COME YOU'RE STILL SO WEIGHED DOWN BY THE FACT THAT YOU KILLED MY SISTER'S BOYFRIEND? HOW COME YOU'RE STILL GOING ON ABOUT IT?
THERE'S SOMETHING ELSE THAT INTERESTS ME A LOT MORE.
WHAT'S YOUR NAME?
DON'T! IT'S TOO DANGER-OUS!!
NGH!!

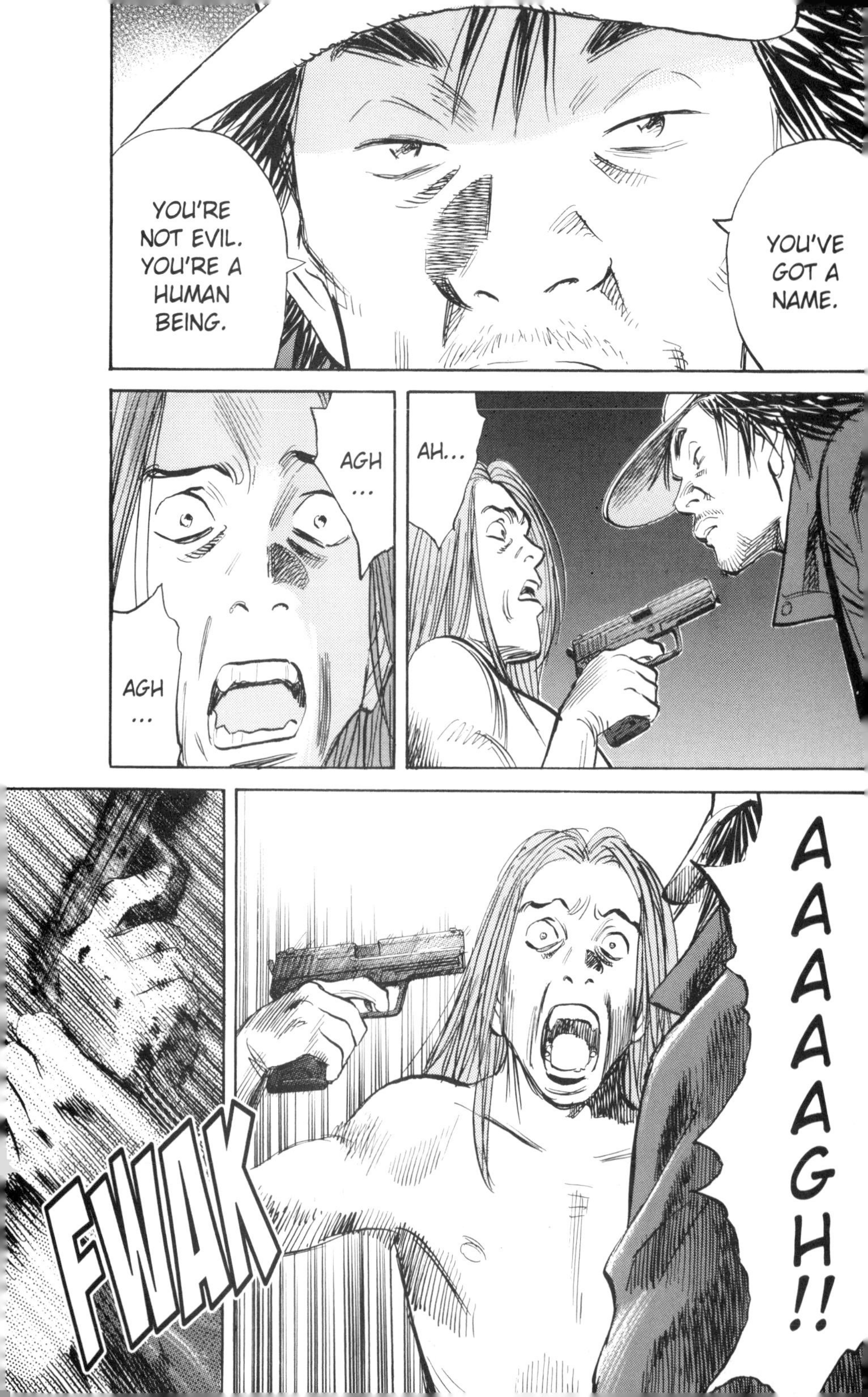
YOU'VE GOT A NAME.
YOU'RE NOT EVIL. YOU'RE A HUMAN BEING.
AH...
AGH ...
AGH ...
AAAAAAGH!!
FWAK

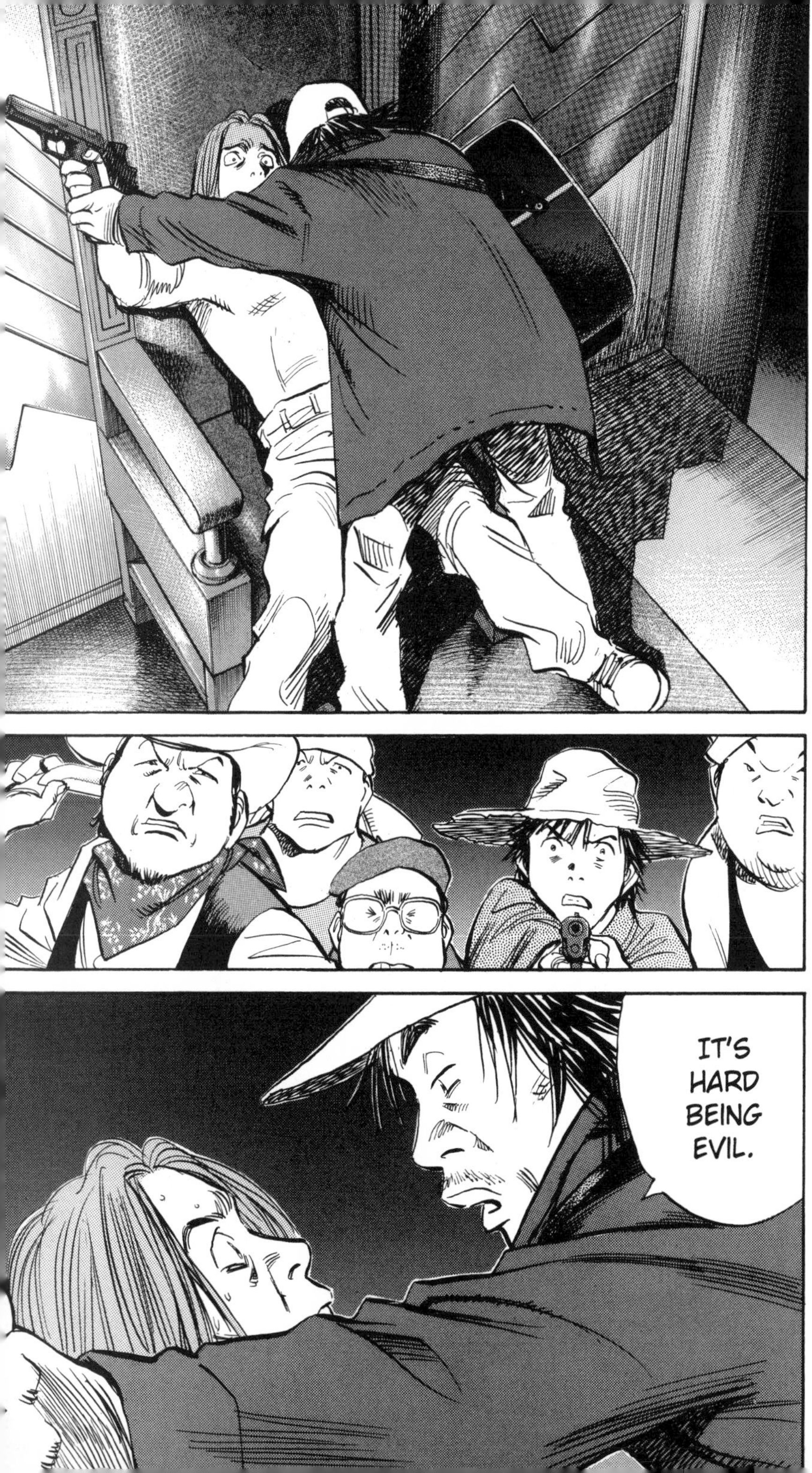
IT'S HARD BEING EVIL.

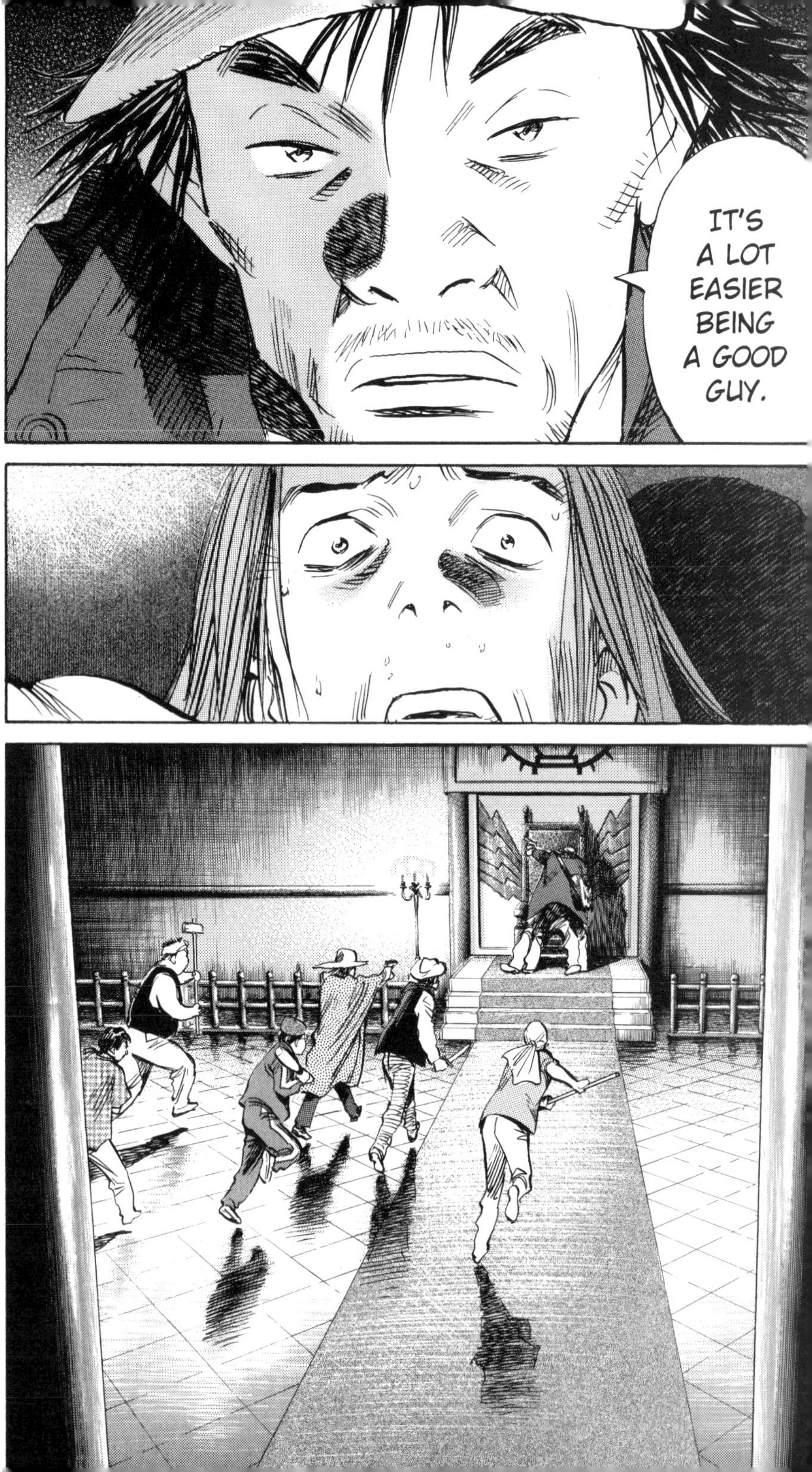
IT'S A LOT EASIER BEING A GOOD GUY.

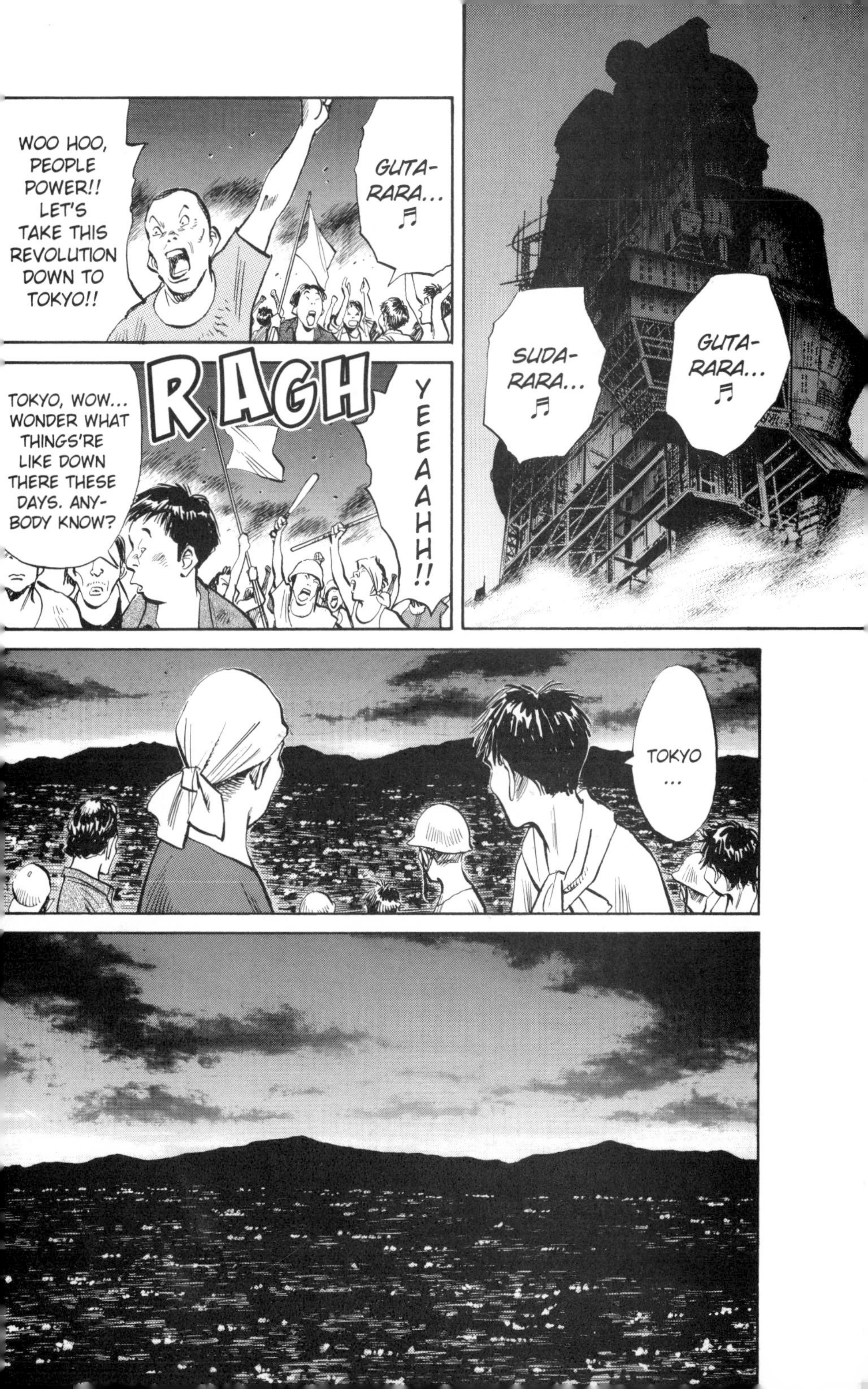
GUTA-RARA... ♬
SUDA-RARA... ♬
GUTA-RARA... ♬
WOO HOO, PEOPLE POWER!! LET'S TAKE THIS REVOLUTION DOWN TO TOKYO!!
YEEAAHH!!
RAGH
TOKYO, WOW... WONDER WHAT THINGS'RE LIKE DOWN THERE THESE DAYS. ANYBODY KNOW?
TOKYO...

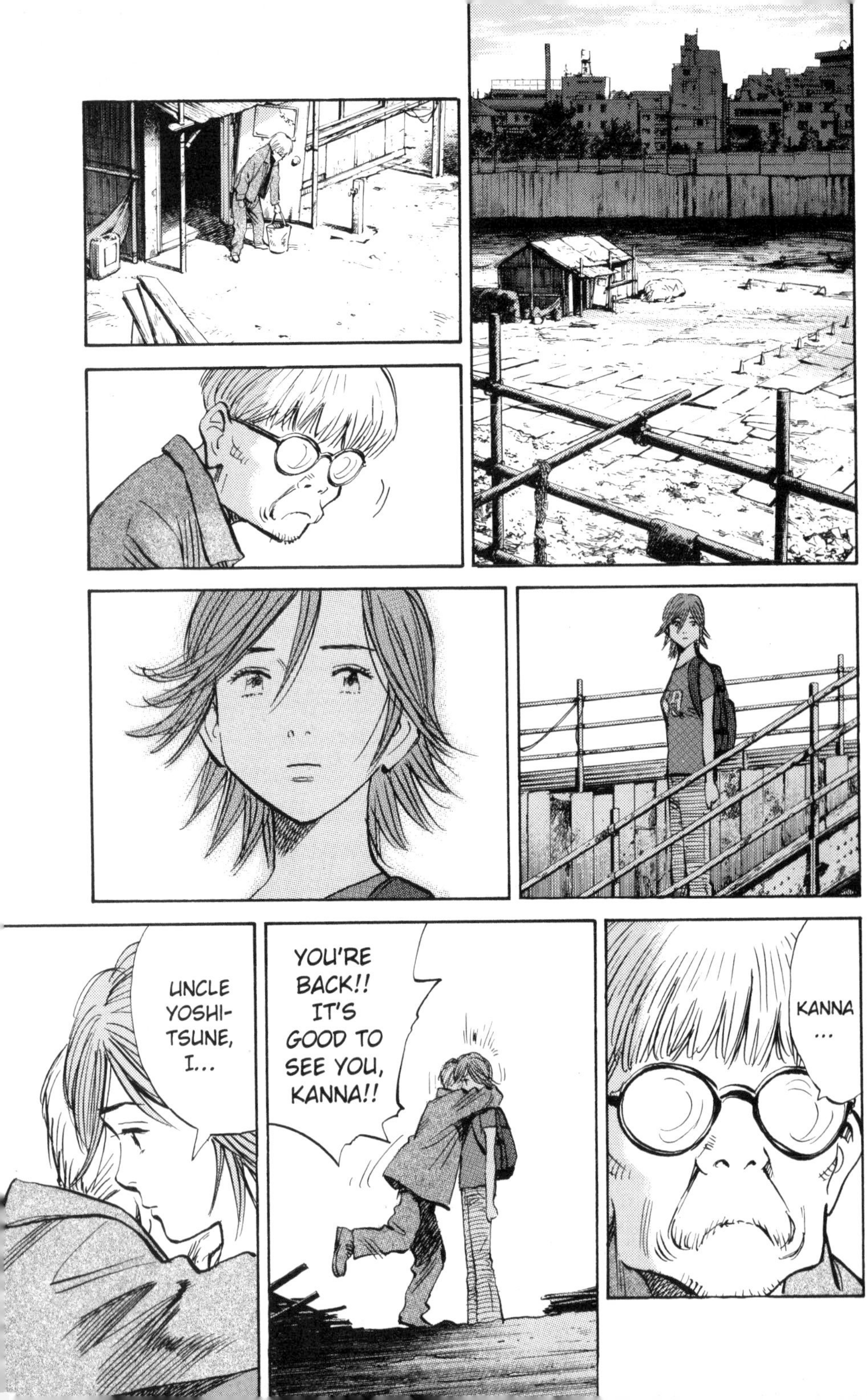
KANNA ...
YOU'RE BACK!! IT'S GOOD TO SEE YOU, KANNA!!
UNCLE YOSHI-TSUNE, I...

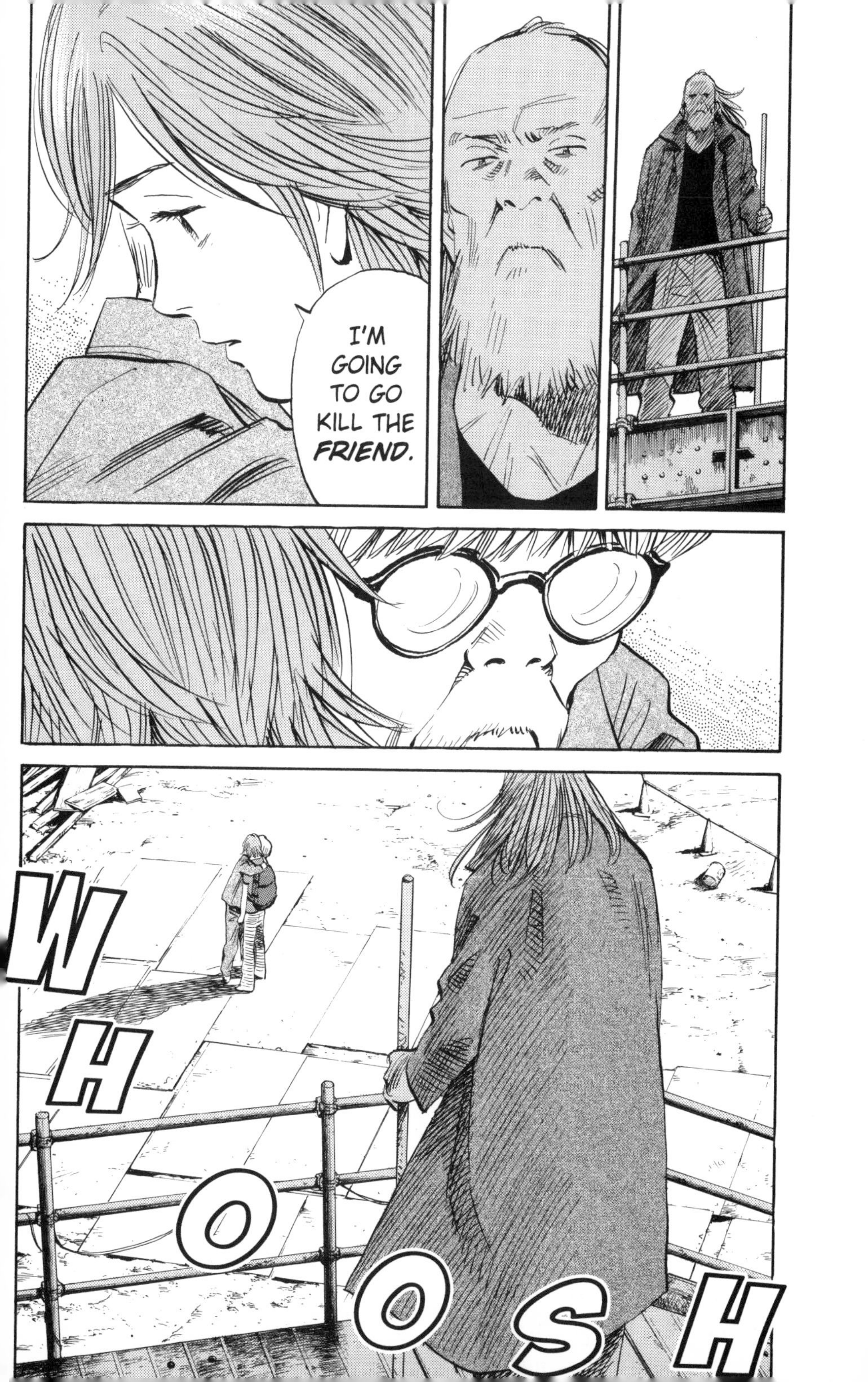
I'M GOING TO GO KILL THE *FRIEND*.
WHOOOSH

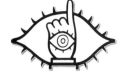

NOTES FROM THE TRANSLATOR

This series follows the Japanese naming convention, with a character's family name followed by their given name. Honorifics such as *-san* and *-kun* are also preserved.

Page 97: Goa is the villian from Osamu Tezuka's *Magma Taishi.*

Page 97: "Yamato no shokun" (People of Yamato) is an iconic line from *Space Battleship Yamato* (also known as *Star Blazers* in the U.S.).

Page 97: Piccolo is a character from Akira Toriyama's *Dragon Ball.*

Page 97: Raoh is a character from Buronson and Tetsuo Hara's *Fist of the North Star.*

Page 97: Black Ghost is the evil organization from Shotaro Ishinomori's *Cyborg 009.*

Page 97: Tiger Jeet Singh is a pro wrestler active in Japan begining in the 1970s.